ACCA

PAPER P2

CORPORATE REPORTING
(UNITED KINGDOM)

In this June 2007 new edition

- We discuss the **best strategies** for revising and taking your ACCA exams

- We show you how to be well prepared for the **December 2007 exam**

- We give you **lots of great guidance** on tackling questions

- We show you how you can **build your own exams**

- We provide you with **three** mock exams including the **Pilot paper**

- We provide the **ACCA examiner's answers** as well as our own to key exam questions and the Pilot Paper as an additional revision aid

Our **i-Pass** product also supports this paper.

FOR EXAMS IN DECEMBER 2007

BPP
LEARNING MEDIA

First edition June 2007

ISBN 9780 7571 3369 3

British Library Cataloguing-in-Publication Data
A catalogue record for this book
is available from the British Library

Published by

BPP Learning Media Ltd
BPP House, Aldine Place
London W12 8AA

www.bpp.com/learningmedia

Printed in Great Britain by
Page Bros
Mile Cross Lane
Norwich
NR6 6SA

We are grateful to the Association of Chartered Certified
Accountants for permission to reproduce past
examination questions. The answers to past examination
questions have been prepared by BPP Learning Media
Ltd.

Your learning materials, published by BPP Learning
Media Ltd, are printed on paper sourced from
sustainable, managed forests.

Contents

Question index

The headings in this checklist/index indicate the main topics of questions, but questions often cover several different topics.

Questions set under the old syllabus *Advanced Corporate Reporting* paper are included because their style and content are similar to those which appear in the P2 exam. The questions have been amended to reflect the current exam format.

Mock exam 1

Questions G1 to G4

Mock exam 2

Questions G5 to G8

Mock exam 3 (Pilot paper)

Questions G9 to G12

Planning your question practice

Our guidance from page 27 shows you how to organise your question practice, either by attempting questions from each syllabus area or **by building your own exams** – tackling questions as a series of practice exams.

Topic index

Listed below are the key Paper P2 syllabus topics and the numbers of the questions in this Kit covering those topics.

If you need to concentrate your practice and revision on certain topics or if you want to attempt all available questions that refer to a particular subject, you will find this index useful.

Using your BPP Practice and Revision Kit

Tackling revision and the exam

You can significantly improve your chances of passing by tackling revision and the exam in the right ways. Our advice is based on feedback from ACCA examiners.

- We look at the dos and don'ts of revising for, and taking, ACCA exams
- We focus on Paper P2; we discuss revising the syllabus, what to do (and what not to do) in the exam, how to approach different types of question and ways of obtaining easy marks

Selecting questions

We provide signposts to help you plan your revision.

- A full **question index**
- A **topic index** listing all the questions that cover key topics, so that you can locate the questions that provide practice on these topics, and see the different ways in which they might be examined
- **BPP's question plan** highlighting the most important questions and explaining why you should attempt them
- **Build your own exams**, showing how you can practise questions in a series of exams

Making the most of question practice

At BPP we realise that you need more than just questions and model answers to get the most from your question practice.

- Our **Top tips** provide essential advice on tackling questions, presenting answers and the key points that answers need to include
- We show you how you can pick up **Easy marks** on questions, as we know that picking up all readily available marks often can make the difference between passing and failing
- We summarise **Examiner's comments**
- We include **marking guides** to show you what the examiner rewards
- A number of questions include **Analysis** and **Helping hands** attached to show you how to approach them if you are struggling
- In a bank at the end of this Kit we include the **examiner's answers** to the Pilot paper and other questions. Used in conjunction with our answers they provide an indication of all possible points that could be made, issues that could be covered and approaches to adopt.

Attempting mock exams

There are three mock exams that provide practice at coping with the pressures of the exam day. We strongly recommend that you attempt them under exam conditions. **Mock exams 1 and 2** reflect the question styles and syllabus coverage of the exam; **Mock exam 3** is the Pilot paper. To help you get the most out of doing these exams, we not only provide help with each answer, but also guidance on how you should have approached the whole exam.

BPP
LEARNING MEDIA

Passing ACCA exams

Revising and taking ACCA exams

To maximise your chances of passing your ACCA exams, you must make best use of your time, both before the exam during your revision, and when you are actually doing the exam.

- Making the most of your revision time can make a big, big difference to how well-prepared you are for the exam

- Time management is a core skill in the exam hall; all the work you've done can be wasted if you don't make the most of the three hours you have to attempt the exam

In this section we simply show you what to do and what not to do during your revision, and how to increase and decrease your prospects of passing your exams when you take them. Our advice is grounded in feedback we've had from ACCA examiners. You may be surprised to know that much examiner advice is the same whatever the exam, and the reasons why many students fail don't vary much between subjects and exam levels. So if you follow the advice we give you over the next few pages, you will **significantly** enhance your chances of passing **all** your ACCA exams.

How to revise

☑ Plan your revision

At the start of your revision period, you should draw up a **timetable** to plan how long you will spend on each subject and how you will revise each area. You need to consider the total time you have available and also the time that will be required to revise for other exams you're taking.

☑ Practise Practise Practise

The **more exam-standard questions** you do, the **more likely you are to pass** the exam. Practising full questions will mean that you'll get used to the time pressure of the exam. When the time is up, you should note where you've got to and then try to complete the question, giving yourself practice at everything the question tests.

☑ Revise enough

Make sure that your revision covers the breadth of the syllabus, as all topics could be examined in a compulsory question. However it is true that some topics are **key** – they are likely to appear often or are a particular interest of the examiner – and you need to spend sufficient time revising these. Make sure you also know the **basics** – the fundamental calculations, proformas and report layouts.

☑ Deal with your difficulties

Difficult areas are topics you find dull and pointless, or subjects that you found problematic when you were studying them. You mustn't become negative about these topics; instead you should build up your knowledge by reading the **Passcards** and using the **Quick Quiz** questions in the Study Text to test yourself. When practising questions in the Kit, go back to the Text if you're struggling.

☑ Learn from your mistakes

Having completed a question you must try to look at your answer critically. Always read the **Top tips guidance** in the answers; it's there to help you. Look at **Easy marks** to see how you could have quickly gained credit on the questions that you've done. As you go through the Kit, it's worth noting any traps you've fallen into, and key points in the **Top tips** or **Examiner's comments** sections, and referring to these notes in the days before the exam. Aim to learn at least one new point from each question you attempt, a technical point perhaps or a point on style or approach.

☑ Read the examiners' guidance

We refer throughout this Kit to **Examiner's comments**. As well as highlighting weaknesses, Examiner's comments often provide clues to future questions, as many examiners will test areas that are likely to cause students problems. ACCA's website also contains articles by examiners which you **must** read, as they may form the basis of questions on any paper after they've been published.

Read through the examiner's answers to key exam questions and the Pilot paper included at the back of the Kit. In general these are far longer and more comprehensive than any answer you could hope to produce in the exam, but used in conjunction with our more realistic solutions, they provide a useful revision tool, covering all possible points and approaches.

☑ Complete all three mock exams

You should attempt the **Mock exams** at the end of the Kit under **strict exam conditions**, to gain experience of selecting questions, managing your time and producing answers.

How NOT to revise

☒ Revise selectively

Examiners are well aware that some students try to forecast the contents of exams, and only revise those areas that they think will be examined. Examiners try to prevent this by doing the unexpected, for example setting the same topic in successive sittings.

☒ Spend all the revision period reading

You cannot pass the exam just by learning the contents of Passcards, Course Notes or Study Texts. You have to develop your **application skills** by practising questions.

☒ Audit the answers

This means reading the answers and guidance without having attempted the questions. Auditing the answers gives you **false reassurance** that you would have tackled the questions in the best way and made the points that our answers do. The feedback we give in our answers will mean more to you if you've attempted the questions and thought through the issues.

☒ Practise some types of question, but not others

Although you may find the numerical parts of certain papers challenging, you shouldn't just practise calculations. These papers will also contain written elements, and you therefore need to spend time practising written question parts.

☒ Get bogged down

Don't spend a lot of time worrying about all the minute detail of certain topic areas, and leave yourself insufficient time to cover the rest of the syllabus. Remember that a key skill in the exam is the ability to **concentrate on what's important** and this applies to your revision as well.

☒ Overdo studying

Studying for too long without interruption will mean your studying becomes less effective. A five minute break each hour will help. You should also make sure that you are leading a **healthy lifestyle** (proper meals, good sleep and some times when you're not studying).

How to PASS your exams

☑ Prepare for the day

Make sure you set at least one alarm (or get an alarm call), and allow plenty of time to get to the exam hall. You should have your route planned in advance and should listen on the radio for potential travel problems. You should check the night before to see that you have pens, pencils, erasers, watch, calculator with spare batteries, also exam documentation and evidence of identity.

☑ Select the right questions

You should select the optional questions you feel you can answer **best**, basing your selection on the topics covered, the requirements of the question, how easy it will be to apply the requirements and the availability of easy marks.

☑ Plan your three hours

You need to make sure that you will be answering the correct number of questions, and that you spend the right length of time on each question – this will be determined by the number of marks available. Each mark carries with it a **time allocation** of **1.8 minutes**. A 25 mark question therefore should be selected, completed and checked in 45 minutes. With some papers, it's better to do certain types of question first or last.

☑ Read the questions carefully

To score well, you must follow the requirements of the question, understanding what aspects of the subject area are being covered, and the tasks you will have to carry out. The requirements will also determine what information and examples you should provide. Reading the question scenarios carefully will help you decide what **issues** to discuss, **techniques** to use, **information** and **examples** to include and how to **organise** your answer.

☑ Plan your answers

Five minutes of planning plus twenty-five minutes of writing is certain to earn you more marks than thirty minutes of writing. Consider when you're planning how your answer should be **structured,** what the **format** should be and **how long** each part should take.

Confirm before you start writing that your plan makes **sense,** covers **all relevant points** and does not include **irrelevant material.**

☑ Show evidence of judgement

Remember that examiners aren't just looking for a display of knowledge; they want to see how well you can **apply** the knowledge you have. Evidence of application and judgement will include writing answers that only contain **relevant** material, using the material in scenarios to **support** what you say, **criticising** the **limitations** and **assumptions** of the techniques you use and making **reasonable recommendations** that follow from your discussion.

☑ Stay until the end of the exam

Use any spare time to **check and recheck** your script. This includes checking you have filled out the candidate details correctly, you have labelled question parts and workings clearly, you have used headers and underlining effectively and spelling, grammar and arithmetic are correct.

How to FAIL your exams

☒ Don't do enough questions

If you don't attempt sufficient questions on the paper, you are making it harder for yourself to pass the questions that you do attempt. If for example you don't do a 20 mark question, then you will have to score 50 marks out of 80 marks on the rest of the paper, and therefore have to obtain 63% of the marks on the questions you do attempt. Failing to attempt all of the paper is symptomatic of poor time management or poor question selection.

☒ Include irrelevant material

Markers are given detailed mark guides and will not give credit for irrelevant content. Therefore you should **NOT** braindump all you know about a broad subject area; the markers will only give credit for what is **relevant**, and you will also be showing that you lack the ability to **judge what's important**. Similarly forcing irrelevant theory into every answer won't gain you marks, nor will providing uncalled for features such as situation analyses, executive summaries and background information.

☒ Fail to use the details in the scenario

General answers or reproductions of Kit answers that don't refer to what is in the scenario in **this** question won't score enough marks to pass.

☒ Copy out the scenario details

Examiners see **selective** use of the right information as a key skill. If you copy out chunks of the scenario which aren't relevant to the question, or don't use the information to support your own judgements, you won't achieve good marks.

☒ Don't do what the question asks

Failing to provide all the examiner asks for will limit the marks you score. You will also decrease your chances by not providing an answer with enough **depth** – producing a single line bullet point list when the examiner asks for a discussion.

☒ Present your work poorly

Markers will only be able to give you credit if they can read your writing. There are also plenty of other things that will make it more difficult for markers to reward you. Examples include:

- Not using black or blue ink
- Not showing clearly which question you're attempting
- Scattering question parts from the same question throughout your answer booklet
- Not showing clearly workings or the results of your calculations

Paragraphs that are too long or which lack headers also won't help markers and hence won't help you.

Using your BPP products

This Kit gives you the question practice and guidance you need in the exam. Our other products can also help you pass:

- **Learning to Learn Accountancy** gives further valuable advice on revision

- **Passcards** provide you with clear topic summaries and exam tips

- **Success CDs** help you revise on the move

- **i-Pass CDs** offer tests of knowledge against the clock

- **Learn Online** is an e-learning resource delivered via the Internet, offering comprehensive tutor support and featuring areas such as study, practice, email service, revision and useful resources

You can purchase these products by visiting www.bpp.com/mybpp.

Visit our website www.bpp.com/acca/learnonline to sample aspects of Learn Online free of charge. Learn Online is hosted by BPP Professional Education.

Passing P2

Revising P2

P2 – or its old syllabus equivalent - has the reputation of being a difficult paper. However its pass rate is usually quite high. Although the examiner, Graham Holt, sets challenging questions, the styles of question he uses are now familiar because he has been the examiner for many years. He has also provided a great deal of feedback in his examiner's reports and in the very detailed published marking schemes, many of which are included in this Kit.

Graham Holt has warned very strongly against question-spotting and trying to predict the topics that will be included in the exam. He has on occasions examined the same topic in two successive sittings. He regards few areas as off-limits for questions, and nearly all of the major areas of the syllabus can and have been tested.

Topics to revise

That said, exams over the years have shown that the following areas of the syllabus are very important, and your revision therefore needs to cover them particularly well.

- **Group accounts.** You should not omit any aspect of group accounts, as they come up every sitting. We would advise against question spotting, but if a cash flow statement, say, has not come up for a few sittings, it might be a good bet. Group accounts will always be examined as part of the 50 mark case study question, in which you may also expect a question on some aspect of **ethics**

- **Emerging issues.** The impact of a change in accounting standards on the financial statements is often examined.

- **Share based payment** usually comes up as part of a question.

- **Financial instruments** was the subject of a *Student Accountant* article, so is ripe for examination.

- **Developments in financial reporting**, for example, the Operating and Financial Review or the proposals on business combinations.

Question practice

Question practice under timed conditions is essential, so that you can get used to the pressures of answering exam questions in **limited time** and practise not only the key techniques but allocating your time between different requirements in each question. Our list of recommended questions includes compulsory Section A and optional Section B questions; it's particularly important to do all the Section A case-study-style questions in full as a case study involving group accounts will always come up.

Passing the P2 exam

What to expect on the paper

Of course you cannot know in advance what questions are going to come up, but you can have a fair idea of what kind of questions.

Question 1

This will always be a case study, with half or a little more than half on group accounts. It will often involve high speed number crunching. Easy marks, it cannot be said too often, will always be available for basic consolidation techniques. You cannot pass the groups part on these alone, but it can give you a foothold. Question 1 usually has a bit of a twist, for example financial instruments or pensions. This question will also contain an element of written explanation and a question on ethics or corporate social accounting. For example, the Pilot Paper had a consolidated cash flow statement; then you were asked to explain whether an investment should be consolidated and the ethics of not consolidating it.

Question 4

This question is generally on developments in financial reporting. It is usually general in nature, rather than linked to a specific accounting standard. It may cover an aspect of reporting financial performance – for example the Operating and Financial Review. It may also cover performance measures, small company reporting, EBITDA or the environment. On the Pilot Paper, Question 4 asked for implementation issues relating to the move to IFRS, and also for a discussion of the implication of the proposals on business combinations.

While you certainly cannot bluff your way through Question 4, if you know your material it is a good way of earning marks without high speed number crunching.

Questions 2 and 3

These are very often – although not always - multi-standard, mini-case-studies, involving you in giving advice to the directors on accounting treatment, possibly where the directors have followed the wrong treatment. Being multi-standard, you may be able to answer parts, but not all of a question, so it makes sense to look through the paper to select a question where you can answer most of it. If Part (a) is on an area you are not confident about, do not dismiss the question out of hand.

The examiner is testing whether you can identify the issues. Even if you don't get the accounting treatment exactly right, you will still gain some credit for showing that you have seen what the problem is about. So do not be afraid to have a stab at something, even if you are not sure of the details.

Exam technique for P2

Do not be needlessly intimidated

There is no shortcut to passing this exam. It looks very difficult indeed, and many students wonder if they will ever pass. But most students generally do. Why is this?

Easy marks

All the questions are demanding, but there are many easy marks to be gained. Suppose, for example, you had a consolidated cash flow statement with a disposal, some foreign exchange complications and an impairment calculation. There will be easy marks available simply for the basic cash flow aspects, setting out the proforma, setting up your workings, presenting your work neatly. If you recognise, as you should, that the disposal needs to be taken into account, of course you will get marks for that, even if you make a mistake in the arithmetic. If you get the foreign exchange right, so much the better, but you could pass the question comfortably while omitting this altogether. If you're short of time, this is what you should do.

Be ruthless in ignoring the complications

Look at the question. Within reason, if there are complications – often only worth a few marks – that you know you will not have time or knowledge to do, cross them out. It will make you feel better. Than tackle the bits you can do. This is how people pass a seemingly impossible paper.

Be ruthless in allocating your time

At BPP, we have seen how very intelligent students do two almost perfect questions, one averagely good and one sketchy. The first eight to ten marks are the easiest to get. Then you have to push it up to what you think is fifteen (thirty for the case study question), to get yourself a pass.

Do your best question either first or second, and the compulsory question either first or second. The compulsory question, being on groups, will always have some easy marks available for consolidation techniques.

Exam information

The paper will comprise two sections.

		Number of marks
Section A:	1 compulsory case study	50
Section B:	Choice of 2 from 3 questions (25 marks each)	50
		100

Section A will consist of one scenario based question worth 50 marks. It will deal with the preparation of consolidated financial statements including group cash flow statements and with issues in financial reporting.

Students will be required to answer two out of three questions in Section B, which will normally comprise two questions which will be scenario or case-study based and one question which will be an essay. Section B could deal with any aspects of the syllabus.

Additional information

The Study Guide provides more detailed guidance on the syllabus.

Pilot paper

Section A

1   Cash flow statement; criteria for consolidation; ethical behaviour

Section B

2   Environmental provision; leasing; EABSD; share-based payment
3   Deferred tax with pension scheme and financial instruments
4   Adoption of IFRS; proposals on business combinations

Useful websites

The websites below provide additional sources of information of relevance to your studies for *Advanced Corporate Reporting*.

- ACCA   www.accaglobal.com
- BPP   www.bpp.com
- Financial Times   www.ft.com
- Accounting Standards Board   www.asb.org.uk
- International Accounting Standards Board   www.iasb.org.uk

Planning your question practice

Planning your question practice

We have already stressed that question practice should be right at the centre of your revision. Whilst you will spend some time looking at your notes and Paper P2 Passcards, you should spend the majority of your revision time practising questions.

We recommend two ways in which you can practise questions.

- Use **BPP's question plan** to work systematically through the syllabus and attempt key and other questions on a section-by-section basis

- **Build your own exams** – attempt questions as a series of practice exams

These ways are suggestions and simply following them is no guarantee of success. You or your college may prefer an alternative but equally valid approach.

BPP's question plan

The BPP plan below requires you to devote a **minimum of 50 hours** to revision of Paper P2. Any time you can spend over and above this should only increase your chances of success.

Step 1   **Review your notes** and the chapter summaries in the Paper P2 **Passcards** for each section of the syllabus.

Step 2   **Answer the key questions** for that section. These questions have boxes round the question number in the table below and you should answer them in full. Even if you are short of time you must attempt these questions if you want to pass the exam. You should complete your answers without referring to our solutions.

Step 3   **Attempt the other questions** in that section. For some questions we have suggested that you prepare **answer plans or do the calculations** rather than full solutions. Planning an answer means that you should spend about 40% of the time allowance for the questions brainstorming the question and drawing up a list of points to be included in the answer.

Step 4   Attempt **Mock exams 1, 2 and 3** under strict exam conditions.

Syllabus section	2007 Passcards chapters	Questions in this Kit	Comments	Done ☑
Ethical framework	2	A1	Learn our answer. Not a typical exam question but covers many areas that will come up as part of one.	☐
Environmental, social and cultural issues	3	A2	Comes up regularly. This question covers most topics you're likely to need.	☐
Fixed assets	4	B1	Prochain. A recent old syllabus question that requires you to think clearly about the issues. Do in full.	☐
Taxation	7	B5	Cohort. Answer in full.	☐
Retirement benefits	6	B9	Accounting for retirement benefits. Do in full. Make sure that you understand how the calculation 'works'.	☐
Leasing contracts	10	B13	AB. Leasing is always topical and practical. Make sure you can iron out the wrinkles under exam conditions.	☐
Financial instruments	8	B15	Ambush. Do in full. Very topical.	☐

Syllabus section	2007 Passcards chapters	Questions in this Kit	Comments	Done ☑
Off balance sheet finance	11	B16	Timber products. A very practical area. Do in full and sharpen your skills for the exams.	☐
Measurement of performance	12	C1	Mineral. Useful question. Answer plan.	☐
Reporting financial performance	14	C4	Rockby and Bye. Redo if necessary to make sure you have this topic well sorted for the exam.	☐
Share-based payment	15	C5	Vident. A full question on a favourite topic.	☐
Related party disclosures	13	C8	Egin Group. Useful question. Prepare an answer plan and make sure you remember the key learning points for exam purposes.	☐
Associates and joint ventures	17	D3	Status of investment. An excellent introduction to this topic.	☐
		D5	Baden. Will put you through your paces on FRS 9. Prepare a full answer.	☐
Complex groups	18	D8	Largo. A high priority question. Make sure you review your answer thoroughly. Identify areas where you require remedial action.	☐
		D9		☐
		D10	Multi-company case study questions. Do in full.	☐
Changes in group structures	19	D13	Ejoy. Good, recent question.	☐
		D14	Base group – case study questions testing changes in group structure. Do in full.	☐
Foreign currency transactions	20	D17	Memo. A useful question. Have a good stab at it.	☐
Cash flow statements	21	D21	Andash : a cash study question with a group cash flow statement. Do in full.	☐
		D22	Squire. Cash flow statements can yield sure marks. Do and redo till you can complete one quickly and accurately in an exam.	☐
			This case is a study question. Do in full.	
Current events	24	F1	Useful coverage of range of issues. Do in full.	☐

Build your own exams

Having revised your notes and the BPP Passcards, you can attempt the questions in the Kit as a series of practice exams.

	Practice exams				
	1	2	3	4	5
Section A					
1	D9	D10	D14	D21	D22
Section B					
2	B5	B6	B8	B9	B3
3	B13	B11	C5	C6	C1
4	C7	E1	F1	F2	E2

Whichever practice exams you use, you must attempt **Mock exams 1, 2 and 3** at the end of your revision.

Questions

REGULATORY AND ETHICAL FRAMEWORK

Questions A1 and A2 cover the Regulatory and Ethical Framework, the subject of Part A of the BPP Study Text for Paper P2.

A1 Barriers to ethical standards   45 mins

(a)   Identify some common barriers to the successful adoption of ethical standards in business practice.

(11 marks)

(b)   Explain the practical steps that organisations can take towards creating an ethical framework for corporate governance.   **(14 marks)**

(Total = 25 marks)

A2 Question with answer plan: Glowball   45 mins

ACR, Pilot paper

The directors of Glowball, a public limited company, had discussed the study by the Institute of Environmental Management which indicated that over 35% of the world's 250 largest corporations are voluntarily releasing green reports to the public to promote corporate environmental performance and to attract customers and investors. They have heard that their main competitors are applying the *Global Reporting Initiative* (GRI) in an effort to develop a worldwide format for corporate environmental reporting. However, the directors are unsure as to what this initiative actually means. Additionally they require advice as to the nature of any legislation or standards relating to environmental reporting as they are worried that any environmental report produced by the company may not be of sufficient quality and may detract from and not enhance their image if the report does not comply with recognised standards. Glowball has a reputation for ensuring the preservation of the environment in its business activities.

Further the directors have collected information in respect of a series of events which they consider to be important and worthy of note in the environmental report but are not sure as to how they would be incorporated in the environmental report or whether they should be included in the financial statements.

The events are as follows.

(a)   Glowball is a company that pipes gas from offshore gas installations to major consumers. The company purchased its main competitor during the year and found that there were environmental liabilities arising out of the restoration of many miles of farmland that had been affected by the laying of a pipeline. There was no legal obligation to carry out the work, but the company felt that there would be a cost of around £150 million if the farmland was to be restored.

(b)   Most of the offshore gas installations are governed by operating licences which specify limits to the substances which can be discharged to the air and water. These limits vary according to local legislation and tests are carried out by the regulatory authorities. During the year the company was prosecuted for infringements of an environmental law in the USA when toxic gas escaped into the atmosphere. In 20X9 the company was prosecuted five times and in 20X8 eleven times for infringement of the law. The final amount of the fine/costs to be imposed by the courts has not been determined but is expected to be around £5 million. The escape occurred over the sea and it was considered that there was little threat to human life.

(c)   The company produced statistics which measure their improvement in the handling of emissions of gases which may have an impact on the environment. The statistics deal with:

   (i)   Measurement of the release of gases with the potential to form acid rain. The emissions have been reduced by 84% over five years due to the closure of old plants.

      (ii)   Measurement of emissions of substances potentially hazardous to human health. The emissions are down by 51% on 20X5 levels.

      (iii)   Measurement of emissions to water which removes dissolved oxygen and substances that may have an adverse effect on aquatic life. Accurate measurement of these emissions is not possible but the company is planning to spend £70 million on research in this area.

(d)   The company tries to reduce the environmental impacts associated with the siting and construction of its gas installations. This is done in a way that minimises the impact on wildlife and human beings. Additionally when the installations are at the end of their life, they are dismantled and are not sunk into the sea. The current provision for the decommissioning of these installations is £215 million and there are still decommissioning costs of £407 million to be provided as the company's policy is to build up the required provision over the life of the installation.

Required

Prepare a report suitable for presentation to the directors of Glowball in which you discuss the following elements.

(a)   Current reporting requirements and guidelines relating to environmental reporting.   **(10 marks)**

(b)   The nature of any disclosure which would be required in an environmental report and/or the financial statements for the events (a) – (d) above.   **(15 marks)**

                                                  (Total = 25 marks)

ACCOUNTING STANDARDS

Questions B1 to B16 cover Accounting Standards, the subject of Part B of the BPP Study Text for Paper P2.

B1 Prochain

45 mins

`ACR, 6/06`

Prochain, a public limited company, operates in the fashion industry and has a financial year end of 31 May 20X6. The company sells its products in department stores throughout the world. Prochain insists on creating its own selling areas within department stores which are called 'model areas'. Prochain is allocated space in the department store where it can display and market its fashion goods. The company feels that this helps to promote its merchandise. Prochain pays for all the costs of the 'model areas' including design, decoration and construction costs. The areas are used for approximately two years after which the company has to dismantle the 'model areas'. The costs of dismantling the 'model areas' are normally 20% of the original construction cost and the elements of the area are worthless when dismantled. The current accounting practice followed by Prochain is to charge the full cost of the 'model areas' against profit or loss in the year when the area is dismantled. The accumulated cost of the 'model areas' shown in the balance sheet at 31 May 20X6 is £20 million. The company has estimated that the average age of the 'model areas' is eight months at 31 May 20X6. **(7 marks)**

Prochain acquired 100% of a sports goods and clothing manufacturer, Badex, a private limited company on 1 June 20X5. Prochain intends to develop its own brand of sports clothing which it will sell in the department stores. The shareholders of Badex valued the company at £125 million based on profit forecasts which assumed significant growth in the demand for the 'Badex' brand name. Prochain had taken a more conservative view of the value of the company and estimated the fair value to be in the region of £108 million to £112 million of which £20 million relates to the brand name 'Badex'. Prochain is only prepared to pay the full purchase price if profits from the sale of 'Badex' clothing and sports goods reach the forecast levels. The agreed purchase price was £100 million plus a further payment of £25 million in two years on 31 May 20X7. This further payment will comprise of a guaranteed payment of £10 million with no performance conditions and a further payment of £15 million if the actual profits during this two year period from the sale of Badex clothing and goods exceed the forecast profit. The forecast profit on Badex goods and clothing over the two year period is £16 million and the actual profits in the year to 31 May 20X6 were £4 million. Prochain did not feel at any time since acquisition that the actual profits would meet the forecast profit levels. **(8 marks)**

After the acquisition of Badex, Prochain started developing its own sports clothing brand 'Pro'. The expenditure in the period to 31 May 20X6 was as follows.

Period from		Expenditure type	£m
1 June 20X5	– 31 August 20X5	Research as to the extent of the market	3
1 September 20X5	– 30 November 20X5	Prototype clothing and goods design	4
1 December 20X5	– 31 January 20X6	Employee costs in refinement of products	2
1 February 20X6	– 30 April 20X6	Development work undertaken to finalise design of product	5
1 May 20X6	– 31 May 20X6	Production and launch of products	6
			20

The costs of the production and launch of the products include the cost of upgrading the existing machinery (£3 million), market research costs (£2 million) and legal costs (£1 million) in registering the brand name 'Pro'. Currently an intangible asset of £20 million is shown in the financial statements for the year ended 31 May 20X6. **(6 marks)**

Prochain owns a number of prestigious apartments which it leases to famous persons who are under a contract of employment to promote its fashion clothing. The apartments are let at below the market rate. The lease terms are short and are normally for six months. The leases terminate when the contract for promoting the clothing terminate.

Prochain wishes to account for the apartments as investment properties with the difference between the market rate and actual rental charge to be recognised as an employee benefit expense. **(4 marks)**

Assume a discount rate of 5.5% where necessary.

Required

Discuss how the above items should be dealt with in the financial statements of Prochain for the year ended 31 May 20X6 under UK accounting standards.

(Total = 25 marks)

B2 Question with helping hands: Impairment of assets 45 mins

Under FRS 11 *Impairment of fixed assets and goodwill*, impairment is measured by comparing the value of a fixed asset with its recoverable amount. The issues of how one identifies an impaired asset, the measurement of an asset where impairment has occurred and the recognition of impairment losses are also dealt with in the standard.

Required

(a) (i) Describe the circumstances which indicate that an impairment loss relating to a fixed asset may have occurred. **(7 marks)**

(ii) Explain how FRS 11 deals with the recognition and measurement of the impairment of fixed assets and the implications of this for future accounting periods. **(7 marks)**

(b) AB, a public limited company, complies with FRS 11 as regards the impairment of its fixed assets. The following information is relevant to the impairment review.

(i) Certain items of machinery appeared to have suffered a fall in value. The product produced by the machines was being sold below its cost and this occurrence had affected the value of the productive machinery. The carrying value at historical cost of these machines is £290,000 and their net realisable value was estimated at £120,000. The anticipated net cash inflows from the machines were £100,000 per annum for the next three years. A market discount rate of 10% per annum is to be used in any present value computations. **(4 marks)**

(ii) AB acquired a car taxi business on 1 January 20X8 for £230,000. The values of the assets of the business at that date based on net realisable values were as follows.

	£'000
Vehicles	120
Intangible assets (taxi licence)	30
Debtors	10
Cash	50
Creditors	(20)
	190

On 1 February 20X8, the taxi company had three of its vehicles stolen. The net realisable value of these vehicles was £30,000 and because of non-disclosure of certain risks to the insurance company, the vehicles were uninsured. As a result of this event, AB wishes to recognise an impairment loss of £45,000 (inclusive of the loss of the stolen vehicles) due to the decline in the value in use of the income generating unit, that is the taxi business. On 1 March 20X8 a rival taxi company commenced business in the same area. It is anticipated that the business revenue will be reduced by 25% and that a further impairment loss has occurred due to a decline in the present value in use of the business which is calculated at £150,000. The NRV of the taxi licence has fallen to £25,000 as a result of the rival taxi operator. The net realisable values of the other assets have remained the same as at 1 January 20X8 throughout the period. **(7 marks)**

Required

Describe how AB should treat the above impairments of assets in its financial statements. (In part (b)(ii) candidates should show the treatment of the impairment loss at 1 February 20X8 and 1 March 20X8).

Please note that the mark allocation is shown after paragraph (b)(i) and (b)(ii) above.

(Total = 25 marks)

Helping hands

1   Part (a) is easy, memory work. Make sure you make the right number of points to get the easy marks.

2   Compares carrying value, fair value less costs to sell and value in use. Remember that if fair value less costs to sell is lower than the others, you would not sell it.

3   Recognise a loss against the stolen vehicles, and the balance against goodwill.

4   For the loss at 1 March 20X8, recognise against intangible assets and the balance against goodwill.

B3 Ryder

45 mins

ACR, 12/05

Ryder, a public limited company, is reviewing certain events which have occurred since its year end of 31 October 20X5. The company wishes to ascertain the impact of adopting FRS 21 *Events after the balance sheet date* in its financial statements for the year ended 31 October 20X5. The financial statements were authorised on 12 December 20X5. The following events are relevant to the financial statements for the year ended 31 October 20X5.

(a)   Ryder has disposed of a wholly owned subsidiary, Krup, a public limited company, on 10 December 20X5 and made a loss of £9 million on the transaction in the group financial statements. As at 31 October 20X5, Ryder had no intention of selling the subsidiary which was material to the group. The directors of Ryder have stated that there were no significant events which have occurred since 31 October 20X5 which could have resulted in a reduction in the value of Krup. The carrying value of the net assets and purchased goodwill of Krup at 31 October 20X5 were £20 million and £12 million respectively. Krup had made a loss of £2 million in the period 1 November 20X5 to 10 December 20X5.   **(6 marks)**

(b)   Ryder acquired a wholly owned subsidiary, Metalic, a public limited company, on 21 January 20X4. The consideration payable in respect of the acquisition of Metalic was 2 million ordinary shares of £1 of Ryder plus a further 300,000 ordinary shares if the profit of Metalic exceeded £6 million for the year ended 31 October 20X5. The profit for the year of Metalic was £7 million and the ordinary shares were issued on 12 November 20X5. The annual profits of Metalic had averaged £7 million over the last few years and therefore, Ryder had included an estimate of the contingent consideration in the cost of the acquisition at 21 January 20X4. The fair value used for the ordinary shares of Ryder at this date including the contingent consideration was £10 per share. The fair value of the ordinary shares on 12 November 20X5 was £11 per share. Ryder also made a one for four bonus issue on 13 November 20X5 which was applicable to the contingent shares issued. The directors are unsure of the impact of the above on the calculation of earnings per share under FRS 22 *Earnings per share* and the accounting for the acquisition.   **(8 marks)**

(c)   The company acquired a property on 1 November 20X4 which it intended to sell. The property was obtained as a result of a default on a loan agreement by a third party and was valued at £20 million on that date for accounting purposes which exactly offset the defaulted loan. The property is in a state of disrepair and Ryder intends to complete the repairs before it sells the property. The repairs were completed on 30 November 2005. The property was sold after costs for £27 million on 9 December 20X5. The property was classified as 'held for sale' at the year end but shown at the net sale proceeds of £27 million. Property is depreciated at 5% per annum on the straight line basis and no depreciation has been charged in the year. The company wishes to adopt FRED 32 *Disposal of non-current assets and presentation of discontinued operations* in its financial statements where possible. **(6 marks)**

(d) The company granted share appreciation rights (SARs) to its employees on 1 November 20X3 based on ten million shares. The SARs provide employees at the date the rights are exercised with the right to receive cash equal to the appreciation in the company's share price since the grant date. The rights vested on 31 October 20X5 and payment was made on schedule on 1 December 20X5. The fair value of the SARs per share at 31 October 20X4 was £6, at 31 October 20X5 was £8 and at 1 December 20X5 was £9. The company has recognised a liability for the SARs as at 31 October 20X4 based upon FRS 20 *Share-based payment* but the liability was stated at the same amount at 31 October 20X5. **(5 marks)**

Required

Discuss the accounting treatment of the above events in the financial statements of the Ryder Group for the year ended 31 October 20X5, taking into account the implications of events occurring after the balance sheet date.

(The mark allocations are set out after each paragraph above.) **(Total = 25 marks)**

B4 Finaleyes   45 mins

The following questions relate to Finaleyes plc, a car seat manufacturer. The company is pursuing a policy of growth by acquisition and it has targeted a number of specific companies for takeover during the next three years.

For the year ended 30 April 20X6 its turnover was £100m; post tax profits £13m applying a tax rate of 30%; net assets £80m and issued share capital £10m in 25p shares. At 30 April 20X6 its share price was £6 per share and at 31 May 20X6 its share price was £7 per share.

The financial director is reviewing the accounting treatment of various items prior to the signing of the 20X6 accounts which is planned for July 20X6.

The items are as follows.

(a) *A share issue*

On 31 January 20X6 it was announced that the company was raising £14m before expenses by the issue of shares for cash. The issue took place on 31 May 20X6 at market share price.

(b) *Acquisition of a plant*

On 1 May 20X5 the company acquired a factory in Norway for £4m. On 30 April 20X6 they obtained professional advice that the building had an expected life of 40 years with no residual value but that the heating systems would require replacing every 15 years at an expected cost of £450,000.

Depreciation on the buildings has been charged following the company's normal accounting policy of using the straight line method.

A charge of £30,000 has been made to the profit and loss account to create a provision for the replacement of the heating system assuming a 15 year life. The initial reasoning for making the charge for the heating system replacement was that it complied with the ASB definition of a liability, ie 'liabilities are an entity's obligations to transfer economic benefits as a result of past transactions or events.'

(c) *Sale and lease back*

At 30 April 20X6 the balance sheet included the main offices of the company at a figure of £10m. On 15 May 20X6 the company exchanged contracts with the Helpful Friendly Society Ltd for the sale of the main offices for £12m with lease back for an initial period of 20 years at market rentals. The company intended to use the proceeds to invest in office property in Kuala Lumpur. The contract provided that the cash consideration would be paid to Finaleyes plc on 14 June 20X6.

(d)   *Stock valuation errors*

The company's policy on stock valuation was to value stock in accordance with SSAP 9 at the lower of cost and net realisable value. The company discovered in May 20X6 that there had been an omission for three years to apply this policy to stock held in a warehouse in Cyprus; the provisions required to bring the stock down to net realisable value were £63,000 for 20X3, £70,000 for 20X4, £105,000 for 20X5 and £115,000 for 20X6.

The adjustment has been treated as a prior period adjustment and reduced the profit and loss account balance brought forward at 1 May 20X5 and the stock by £238,000 being the total of the provisions required for the years ended 30 April 20X3 to 20X5.

Required

For each of the items (a) to (d) above:

(i)   State your view on the appropriate treatment in the financial statements as at 30 April 20X6 giving your reasons.

(ii)   Draft an appropriate note to the accounts and/or state the adjustment that would be made to items in the accounts as required.

Each of the items (a) to (d) carries equal marks.   **(25 marks)**

B5 Cohort   **45 mins**

ACR, 6/02

Cohort is a private limited company and has two 100% owned subsidiaries, Legion and Air, both themselves private limited companies. Cohort acquired Air on 1 January 20X2 for £5 million when the fair value of the net assets was £4 million, and the carrying value of the net assets was £3.5 million. The acquisition of Air and Legion was part of a business strategy whereby Cohort would build up the 'value' of the group over a three year period and then list its existing share capital on the Stock Exchange.

(a)   The following details relate to the acquisition of Air, which manufactures electronic goods.

(i)   Part of the purchase price has been allocated to intangible assets because it relates to the acquisition of a database of key customers from Air. The recognition and measurement criteria for an intangible asset under FRS 10 *Goodwill and intangible assets* do not appear to have been met but the directors feel that the intangible asset of £0.5 million will be allowed for tax purposes and have completed the tax provision accordingly. However, the tax authorities could possibly challenge this opinion.

(ii)   Air has sold goods worth £3 million to Cohort since acquisition and has made a profit of £1 million on the transaction. The stock of these goods recorded in Cohort's balance sheet at the year end of 31 May 20X2 was £1.8 million.

(iii) The balance on the profit and loss account of Air at acquisition was £2 million. The directors of Cohort have decided that, during the three years to the date that they intend to list the shares of the company, they will realise earnings through future dividend payments from the subsidiary amounting to £500,000 per year. No dividends have been declared for the current year.

(b)   Legion was acquired on 1 June 20X1 and is a company which undertakes various projects ranging from debt factoring to investing in property and commodities. The following details relate to Legion for the year ending 31 May 20X2.

(i)   Legion has a market portfolio of readily marketable government securities which are held as current assets. These investments are stated at market value in the balance sheet with any gain or loss taken to the profit and loss account. These gains and losses are taxed when the investments are sold. Currently the accumulated unrealised gains are £4 million.

(ii)   Legion has calculated that it requires a general provision of £2 million against its total loan portfolio. Tax relief is available when the specific loan is written off. Management feel that this part of the business will expand and thus the amount of the general provision will increase.

(iii)   When Cohort acquired Legion it had unused tax losses brought forward. At 1 June 20X1, it appeared that Legion would have sufficient taxable profit to realise the deferred asset created by these losses but subsequent events have proven that the future taxable profit will not be sufficient to realise all of the unused tax loss.

The current tax rate for Cohort is 30% and for public companies is 35%.

Required

Write a note suitable for presentation to the partner of an accounting firm setting out:

(a)   The general impact of FRS 19 *Deferred tax* on the financial statements of Cohort.   **(4 marks)**

(b)   the deferred tax implications of the above information for the Cohort group of companies.   **(21 marks)**

(Total = 25 marks)

B6 Panel   **45 mins**

ACR,12/05

The directors of Panel, a public limited company, are reviewing the procedures for the calculation of the deferred tax provision for their company. They are quite surprised at the impact on the provision caused by changes in accounting standards such as FRS 20 *Share-based payment*. Panel is considering adopting International Financial Reporting Standards (IFRS) for the first time as at 31 October 2005 and the directors are unsure how the deferred tax provision would be calculated in its financial statements ended on that date including the opening provision at 1 November 2003.

Required

(a)   (i)   Explain how changes in accounting standards are likely to have an impact on the provision for deferred taxation under FRS 19 *Deferred tax*.   **(5 marks)**

        (ii)   Describe the basis for the calculation of the provision for deferred tax on first time adoption of IFRSs including the provision in the opening IFRS balance sheet.   **(4 marks)**

Additionally the directors wish to know how the provision for deferred taxation would be calculated in the following situations under FRS 19 *Deferred tax*.

(i)   On 1 November 2003, the company had granted ten million share options worth £40 million subject to a two year vesting period. Assume tax law allows a tax deduction at the exercise date of the intrinsic value of the options. The intrinsic value of the 10 million share options at 31 October 2004 was £16 million and at 31 October 2005 was £46 million. The increase in the share price in the year to 31 October 2005 could not be foreseen at 31 October 2004. The options were exercised at 31 October 2005. The directors are unsure how to account for deferred taxation on this transaction for the years ended 31 October 2004 and 31 October 2005 as they wish to apply FRS 20 early.

(ii)   Panel is leasing a fixed asset under a finance lease over a five-year period. The asset was recorded at the present value of the minimum lease payments of £12 million at the inception of the lease which was 1 November 2004. The asset is depreciated on a straight line basis over the five years and has no residual value. The annual lease payments are £3 million payable in arrears on 31 October and the effective interest rate is 8% per annum. The directors have not leased an asset under a finance lease before and are unsure as to its treatment for deferred taxation. The company can claim a tax deduction for the annual rental payments as the finance lease does not qualify for capital allowances.

(iii)   A wholly owned overseas subsidiary, Pins, a private limited company, sold goods costing £7 million to Panel on 1 September 2005, and these goods have not been sold by Panel before the year end. Panel had paid £9 million for these goods. The directors do not understand how this transaction should be dealt with in the financial statements of the subsidiary and the group for taxation purposes. Pins pays tax locally at 30%.

(iv)   Nails, a private limited company, is a wholly owned subsidiary of Panel, and is an income generating unit in its own right. The value of the fixed assets of Nails at 31 October 2005 was £6 million and purchased goodwill was £1 million before any impairment loss. The company had no other assets or liabilities. An impairment loss of £1.8 million had occurred at 31 October 2005. The tax written down value of the fixed asset of Nails was £4 million as at 31 October 2005. The directors wish to know how the impairment loss will affect the deferred tax provision for the year. The impairment losses are not an allowable expense for taxation purposes.

Assume a tax rate of 30%.

Required

(b)   Discuss, with suitable computations, how the situations (i) to (iv) above will impact on the accounting for deferred tax under FRS 19 *Deferred tax* in the group financial statements of Panel.   **(16 marks)**

(The situations in (i) to (iv) above carry equal marks.)   **(Total = 25 marks)**

B7 Preparation question: Defined benefit scheme

Lewis Ltd has a defined benefit plan for its employees. The present value of the future benefit obligations and the fair value of the plan assets at 1 January 20X7 were both £1,000 million.

Further data concerning the years ended 31 December 20X7 and 20X8 are as follows:

	20X7 £m	20X8 £m	
Current service cost	130	140	
Benefit paid to former employees	150	180	
Contributions paid to plan	90	100	
Present value of benefit obligations at 31 December	1,100	1,380	} As valued by
Fair value of plan assets at 31 December	1,190	1,372	} professional actuaries
Gross yield on 'blue chip' Corporate bonds	10%	9%	
Expected return on plan assets	12%	10%	

In 20X8 the plan was amended to provide additional benefits from 1 January 20X8. The present value of the additional benefits was calculated by actuaries at £10 million with respect to current employees and £50 million for former employees.

Required

Calculate the amounts to be recognised in the profit and loss account, balance sheet and statement of total recognised gains and losses for 20X7 and 20X8 and prepare the 'movement in surplus' note.

B8 Retirement benefits

45 mins

(a) Accounting for retirement benefits remains one of the most challenging areas in financial reporting. The values being reported are significant, and the estimation of these values is complex and subjective. Standard setters and preparers of financial statements find it difficult to achieve a measure of consensus on the appropriate way to deal with the assets and costs involved. SSAP 24 *Accounting for pension costs* focused on the profit and loss account, viewing retirement benefits as an operating expense. However, FRS 17 *Retirement benefits* concentrates on the balance sheet and the valuation of the pension fund. The philosophy and rationale of the two statements are fundamentally different.

Required

(i) Describe four key issues in the determination of the method of accounting for retirement benefits in respect of defined benefit plans. **(6 marks)**

(ii) Discuss how FRS 17 *Retirement benefits* deals with these key issues and to what extent it provides solutions to the problems of accounting for retirement benefits. **(8 marks)**

(b) A, a public limited company, operates a defined benefit pension scheme. A full actuarial valuation by an independent actuary revealed that the value of the pension liability at 31 May 20X0 was £1,500 million. This was updated to 31 May 20X1 by the actuary and the value of the pension liability at that date was £2,000 million. The pension scheme assets comprised mainly UK bonds and equities and the market value of these assets was as follows.

	31 May 20X0	31 May 20X1
	£m	£m
Fixed interest and index linked bonds (UK)	380	600
Equities (UK)	1,300	1,900
Other investments	290	450
	1,970	2,950

The pension scheme had been altered during the year with improved benefits arising for the employees and this alteration had been taken into account by the actuaries. The increase in the actuarial liability in respect of employee service in prior periods was £25 million (past service cost). The increase in the actuarial liability resulting from employee service in the current period was £70 million (current service cost).

The company had paid contributions of £60 million to the scheme during the period. The company expects its return on the pension scheme assets at 31 May 20X1 to be £295 million and the interest on pension liabilities to be £230 million.

The company anticipates that a deferred tax liability will arise on the surplus in the scheme. Assume corporation tax is at a rate of 30 per cent.

Required

(i) Show the amount which will be shown as the net pension asset/pension reserve in the balance sheet of A plc as at 31 May 20X1 under FRS 17 *Retirement benefits*. (Comparative figures are not required.) **(4 marks)**

(ii) Show a reconciliation of the movement in the pension surplus during the year stating those amounts which would be charged to operating profit and the amounts which would be recognised in the statement of total recognised gains and losses (STRGL), utilising FRS 17 *Retirement benefits*. **(7 marks)**

(Total = 25 marks)

B9 Savage

45 mins

ACR, 12/05

Savage, a public limited company, operates a funded defined benefit plan for its employees. The pension plan provides a pension of 1% of the final salary for each year of service. The cost for the year is determined using the projected unit credit method. This reflects service rendered to the dates of valuation of the plan and incorporates actuarial assumptions primarily regarding discount rates, which are based on the market yields of high quality corporate bonds.

The directors have provided the following information about the defined benefit plan for the current year (year ended 31 October 20X5).

(a) The actuarial cost of providing benefits in respect of employees' service for the year to 31 October 2005 was £40 million. This is the present value of the pension benefits earned by the employees in the year.

(b) The pension benefits paid to former employees in the year were £42 million.

(c) Savage should have paid contributions to the fund of £28 million. Because of cash flow problems, £8 million of this amount had not been paid at the financial year end of 31 October 20X5.

(d) The present value of the obligation to provide benefits to current and former employees was £3,000 million at 31 October 20X4 and £3,375 million at 31 October 20X5.

(e) The fair value of the plan assets was £2,900 million at 31 October 20X4 and £3,170 million (including the contributions owed by Savage) at 31 October 20X5. The actuarial gains recognised at 31 October 20X4 were £336 million.

With effect from 1 November 20X4, the company has amended the plan so that the employees were now provided with an increased pension entitlement. The benefits became vested immediately and the actuaries computed that the present value of the cost of these benefits at 1 November 2004 was £125 million. The discount rates and expected rates of return on the plan assets were as follows.

	31 October 20X4	31 October 20X5
Discount rate	6%	7%
Expected rate of return on plan assets	8%	9%

Required

(a) Show the amounts which will be recognised in the balance sheet, profit and loss account and the statement of total recognised gains and losses of Savage for the year ended 31 October 2005 under FRS 17 *Retirement benefits*, and the movement in the net liability in the balance sheet. (Your calculations should show the changes in the present value of the obligation and the fair value of the plan assets during the year. Ignore any deferred taxation effects and assume that pension benefits and the contributions paid were settled at 31 October 20X5.) **(21 marks)**

(b) Explain how the non-payment of contributions and the change in the pension benefits should be treated in the financial statements of Savage for the year ended 31 October 20X5. **(4 marks)**

(Total = 25 marks)

B10 Issue

45 mins

ACR, 6/03

The managing partner has asked you, on behalf of a shareholder, to prepare a report on the financial and business position of Issue, a public limited company. There has been adverse press comment on the 'aggressive management of earnings' by the company and criticism of the management. Information about Issue has been gathered by the partner and this is set out below.

Business and financial environment

Issue provides internet-based electronic hosting, delivery and marketing services. The company was formed four years ago with the Board promising to take the company to the top 10% of listed companies within five years. Management are highly motivated and are compensated in part via share/stock options. Management work in a pressurised environment.

Issue makes use of different corporate entities in order to finance its business. The company has borrowed £40 million from twenty different entities which are owned by a bank, which itself owns twenty per cent of the shares of Issue. These entities have been set up as vehicles for the loans and do not trade. Issue had deposited £35 million with the entities with the balance being shown as a current liability. The management of Issue say that the entities are not under their control and that because each amount borrowed is individually immaterial there is no need to disclose the relationship in the financial statements. Additionally, it appears that in previous years a common practice was for Issue to invoice the same entities in the final week of the financial year for services and reverse the invoices once the company had filed its financial statements.

Financial statement information extracted from the published accounts for the years ended 31 January 20X3 and 31 January 20X2

(a)   ISSUE PLC

	31.1.X3 £m	31.1.X2 £m
Fixed assets at valuation		
Land and buildings	10	8
Plant and machinery	40	30
Intangibles	20	12
Current assets	230	240
Current liabilities	180	140
Long term liabilities	50	40
Share capital – £1 ordinary shares	30	30
Reserves: revaluation reserve	30	20
profit & loss account	10	60
Turnover	160	200
Profit before interest, tax, depreciation and amortisation	30	95
Profit/(loss) before tax	(10)	40
Extraordinary loss	(20)	(5)
Number of employees	150	250
Number of days after year end to publication of financial statements	65	25

(b)   The fixed assets have been revalued by one of the directors of Issue who holds no recognised professional qualification and has used estimated realisable value as the basis of valuation. The plant and machinery is of a highly specialised nature and is constructed by the company itself and is mainly computer hardware. The intangible assets are the data purchase and data capture costs of internally developed databases and are capitalised as development expenditure and written off over four years.

(c)   In the year to 31 January 20X2, a six year bond was issued by the company with a par value of £40 million for £42 million. The excess over par value was taken to the profit and loss account. In the year to 31 January 20X3, a further six year bond with a par value of £10 million was issued for £11 million and accounted for in the same manner. The investors may require redemption after three years or if the working capital ratio falls below 1.3. The bonds bear interest at 5% per annum and are redeemable at par.

(d)   Turnover represents the invoiced amount of goods sold and services provided and work undertaken during the year on long-term contracts after the deduction of trade discounts and sales related taxes.

(e)   Issue has published pro-forma financial statements for the four months to 31 May 20X3 showing profit before tax to be £20 million, long term liabilities reduced to £10 million, and the working capital ratio as being 1.5.

(f)   The extraordinary loss is the estimated impact of the terrorist attacks in the USA upon the business of Issue. These are sometimes referred to as the 'September 11 terrorist attacks'.

Required

Prepare a report for the managing partner on the business and financial position of Issue, setting out the implications of the financial and other information outlined above.

(25 marks)

B11 Tyre

45 mins

`ACR, 6/06`

Tyre, a public limited company, operates in the vehicle retailing sector. The company is currently preparing its financial statements for the year ended 31 May 20X6 and has asked for advice on how to deal with the following items.

(a)   Tyre requires customers to pay a deposit of 20% of the purchase price when placing an order for a vehicle. If the customer cancels the order, the deposit is not refundable and Tyre retains it. If the order cannot be fulfilled by Tyre, the company repays the full amount of the deposit to the customer. The balance of the purchase price becomes payable on the delivery of the vehicle when the title to the goods passes. Tyre proposes to recognise the revenue from the deposits immediately and the balance of the purchase price when the goods are delivered to the customer. The cost of sales of the vehicle is recognised when the balance of the purchase price is paid. Additionally, Tyre had sold a fleet of cars to Hub and gave Hub a discount of 30% of the retail price on the transaction. The discount given is normal for this type of transaction. Tyre has given Hub a buyback option which entitles Hub to require Tyre to repurchase the vehicles after three years for 40% of the purchase price. The normal economic life of the vehicles is five years and the buyback option is expected to be exercised.   **(8 marks)**

(b)   The land and buildings of the former administrative centre of Tyre are owned by the company. Tyre had decided in the year the that property was surplus to requirements and demolished the building on 10 June 20X6. After demolition, the company will have to carry out remedial environmental work, which is a legal requirement resulting from the demolition. It was intended that the land would be sold after the remedial work had been carried out. However, land prices are currently increasing in value. Therefore, the company has decided that it will not sell the land immediately but class the land as being 'held for sale' until such a time as it decides to sell it. Tyre values its land and buildings using historical cost and has owned the property for many years   **(7 marks)**

(c)   Tyre has entered into two new long lease property agreements for two major retail outlets. Annual rentals are paid under these agreements. Tyre has had to pay a premium to enter into these agreements because of the outlets' location. Tyre feels that the premiums paid are justifiable because of the increase in revenue that will occur because of the outlets' location. Tyre has analysed the leases and has decided that one is a finance lease and one is an operating lease but the company is unsure as to how to treat this premium.   **(5 marks)**

(d)   Tyre recently undertook a sales campaign whereby customers can obtain free car accessories by presenting a coupon, which has been included in an advertisement in a national newspaper, on the purchase of a vehicle. The offer is valid for a limited time period from 1 January 20X6 until 31 July 20X6. The management are unsure as to how to treat this offer in the financial statements for the year ended 31 May 20X6.

(5 marks)

Required

Advise the directors of Tyre on how to treat the above items in the financial statements for the year ended 31 May 20X6.

The mark allocation is shown against each of the above items. **(Total = 25 marks)**

B12 Preparation question: Leases

Biorocket is to sell its laboratory equipment on 1 January 20X5 for £17.5m to Funny Finance plc. Biorocket would then lease the equipment back at a rent (payable in arrears) of £1.75m a year for the next four years. On 1 January 20X5 the fair value of the laboratory equipment is estimated at £15m and the book value was £14m. (Assume an interest rate of 12%).

The DF for an annuity receivable for four years at 12% is 3.037.

Required

Indicate how the above transaction would be reflected in the financial statements of Biorocket for the year ended 31 December 20X5.

B13 AB
45 mins

(a) The development of conceptual frameworks for financial reporting by accounting standard setters could fundamentally change the way in which financial contracts such as leases are accounted for. These frameworks identify the basic elements of financial statements as assets, liabilities, equity, gains and losses and set down their recognition rules. In analysing the definitions of assets and liabilities one could conclude that most leases, including non-cancellable operating leases, qualify for recognition as assets and liabilities because the lessee is likely to enjoy the future economic benefit embodied in the leased asset and will have an unavoidable obligation to transfer economic benefits to the lessor. Because of the problems of accounting for leases, there have been calls for the capitalisation of all non-cancellable operating leases so that the only problem would be the definition of the term 'non-cancellable'.

Required

(i) Explain how leases are accounted for in the books of the lessee under SSAP 21 *Accounting for leases and hire purchase contracts.* **(7 marks)**

(ii) Discuss the current problems relating to the recognition and classification of leases in corporate financial statements. (Candidates should give examples where necessary.) **(8 marks)**

(b) (i) During the financial year to 31 May 20X8, AB plc disposed of electrical distribution systems from its electrical power plants to CD plc for a consideration of £198m. At the same time AB plc entered into a long-term distribution agreement with CD plc whereby the assets were leased back under a 10-year operating lease. The fair value of the assets sold was £98m and the carrying value based on the depreciated historic cost of the assets was £33m. The lease rental payments were £24m per annum which represented twice the normal payment for leasing this type of asset. **(5 marks)**

(ii) Additionally on 1 June 20X7, AB plc sold plant with a book value of £100m to EF plc when there was a balance on the revaluation reserve of £30m which related to the plant. The fair value and selling price of the plant at that date was £152m. The plant was immediately leased back over a lease term of four years which is the asset's remaining useful life. The residual value at the end of the lease period is estimated to be a negligible amount. AB plc can purchase the plant at the end of the lease for a nominal sum of £1. The lease is non-cancellable and requires equal rental payments of £43.5m at the commencement of each financial year. AB plc has to pay all of the costs of maintaining and insuring the plant. The implicit interest rate in the lease is 10% per annum. The plant is depreciated on a straight line basis. (The present value of an ordinary annuity of £1 per period for three years at 10% interest is £2.49.)   **(5 marks)**

Required

Show and explain how the above transactions should be dealt with in the financial statements of AB plc for the year ending 31 May 20X8 in accordance with SSAP 21 Accounting for leases and hire purchase contracts and FRS 5 Reporting the substance of transactions.

(Total = 25 marks)

B14 Preparation question: Financial instruments

(a)   Graben Co purchases a bond for £441,014 on 1 January 20X1. It will be redeemed on 31 December 20X4 for £600,000. The bond will be held to maturity and carries no coupon.

Required

Calculate the balance sheet valuation of the bond as at 31 December 20X1 and the finance income for 20X1 shown in the income statement.

Compound sum of £1: $(1 + r)^n$

Year	2%	4%	6%	8%	10%	12%	14%
1	1.0200	1.0400	1.0600	1.0800	1.1000	1.1200	1.1400
2	1.0404	1.0816	1.1236	1.1664	1.2100	1.2544	1.2996
3	1.0612	1.1249	1.1910	1.2597	1.3310	1.4049	1.4815
4	1.0824	1.1699	1.2625	1.3605	1.4641	1.5735	1.6890
5	1.1041	1.2167	1.3382	1.4693	1.6105	1.7623	1.9254

(b)   Baldie Co issues 4,000 convertible bonds on 1 January 20X2 at par. The bond is redeemable 3 years later at its par value of £500 per bond, which is its nominal value.

The bonds pay interest annually in arrears at an interest rate (based on nominal value) of 5%. Each bond can be converted at the maturity date into 30 £1 shares.

The prevailing market interest rate for three year bonds that have no right of conversion is 9%.

Required

Show the balance sheet valuation at 1 January 20X2.

Cumulative 3 year annuity factors:

(i)   5%   2.723
(ii)   9%   2.531

B15 Ambush

45 mins

ACR, 12/05

Ambush, a public limited company, is assessing the impact of implementing FRS 26 *Financial instruments: measurement*. The directors realise that significant changes may occur in their accounting treatment of financial instruments and they understand that on initial recognition any financial asset or liability can be designated as one and to be reassured at fair value through profit or loss (the fair value option). However, there are certain issues that they wish to have explained and these are set out below.

Required

(a) Outline in a report to the directors of Ambush the following information.

    (i) How financial assets and liabilities are measured and classified, briefly setting out the accounting method used for each category. (Hedging relationships can be ignored.) **(10 marks)**

    (ii) Why the 'fair value option' was initially introduced and why it has caused such concern. **(5 marks)**

(b) Ambush loaned £200,000 to Bromwich on 1 December 20X3. The effective and stated interest rate for this loan was 8%. Interest is payable by Bromwich at the end of each year and the loan is repayable on 30 November 20X7. At 30 November 20X5, the directors of Ambush have heard that Bromwich is in financial difficulties and is undergoing a financial reorganisation. The directors feel that it is likely that they will only receive £100,000 on 30 November 20X7 and no future interest payment. Interest for the year ended 30 November 20X5 had been received. The financial year end of Ambush is 30 November 20X5.

Required

    (i) Outline the requirements of FRS 26 as regards the impairment of financial assets. **(6 marks)**

    (ii) Explain the accounting treatment under FRS 26 of the loan to Bromwich in the financial statements of Ambush for the year ended 30 November 20X5. **(4 marks)**

(Total = 25 marks)

B16 Timber Products   45 mins

(a) (i) Explain briefly the objective of FRS 5 *Reporting the substance of transactions*.

    (ii) Explain the criteria for ceasing to recognise an asset and give an illustration of the application of each. **(7 marks)**

(b) Explain the appropriate accounting treatment for the following transactions and the entries that would appear in the balance sheet as at 31 October for transaction (i) and in the profit and loss account for the year ended 31 October 20X5 and balance sheet as at 31 October 20X5 for transactions (ii), (iii) and (iv).

    (i) Timber Products plc supplies large industrial and commercial customers direct on three month credit terms. On 1 November 20X4 it entered into an agreement with Ready Support plc whereby it transferred title to the debtors to that company subject to a reduction for bad debts based on Timber Products plc's past experience and in return received an immediate payment of 90% of the net debtor total plus rights to a future sum the amount of which depended on whether and when the debtors paid. Ready Support plc had the right of recourse against Timber Products plc for any additional losses up to an agreed maximum amount.

        The position at the year end, 31 October 20X5, was that title had been transferred to debtors with an invoice value of £15m less a bad debt provision of £600,000 and Timber Products plc was subject under the agreement to a maximum potential debit of £200,000 to cover losses.

    (ii) Timber Products plc imports unseasoned hardwood and keeps it for five years under controlled conditions prior to manufacturing high quality furniture. In the year ended 31 October 20X5 it imported unseasoned timber at a cost of £40m. It contracted to sell the whole amount for £40m and to buy it back in five years time for £56.10m.

    (iii) Timber Products plc manufactures and supplies retailers with furniture on a consignment basis such that either party can require the return of the furniture to the manufacturer within a period of six months from delivery. The retailers are required to pay a monthly charge for the facility to display the furniture. The manufacturer uses this monthly charge to pay for insurance cover and carriage costs. At the end of six months the retailer is required to pay Timber Products plc the trade price as at the date of delivery. No retailers have yet sent any goods back to Timber Products plc at the end of the six month period.

In the year ended 31 October 20X5, Timber Products plc had supplied furniture to retailers at the normal trade price of £10m being cost plus $33\frac{1}{3}\%$; received £50,000 in display charges; incurred insurance costs of £15,000 and carriage costs of £10,000; and received £6m from retailers.

(iv)   On 1 December 20X4 Timber Products plc sold a factory that it owned in Scotland to Inter plc a wholly owned subsidiary of Offshore Banking plc for £10m. The factory had a book value of £8.5m. Inter plc was financed by a loan of £10m from Offshore Banking plc. Timber Products plc was paid a fee by Inter plc to continue to operate the factory, such fee representing the balance of profit remaining after Inter plc paid its parent company loan interest set at a level that represented current interest rates. If there was an operating loss, then Timber Products plc would be charged a fee that would cover the operating losses and interest payable.

For the year ended 31 October 20X5 the fee paid to Timber Products plc amounted to £3m and the loan interest paid by Inter plc amounted to £1.5m.   **(14 marks)**

(c)   State what further information you would seek in order to determine the substance of the following transaction.

Timber Products plc has installed computer controlled equipment in its furniture making factory. This has created the need for large extractor fans to remove dust particles. The company has contracted with Extractor-Plus plc for that company to build and install extractor equipment. Timber Products plc will maintain and insure the equipment and make an annual payment to Extractor-Plus plc comprising a fixed quarterly rental and an hourly usage charge.

In the year ended 31 October 20X5 Timber Products plc has paid the fixed quarterly rentals totalling £80,000 and hourly charges totalling £120,000.   **(4 marks)**

(Total = 25 marks)

Compound interest table

Number of years	Interest rate per year				
	5%	6%	7%	8%	9%
1	1.050	1.060	1.070	1.080	1.090
2	1.102	1.124	1.143	1.166	1.188
3	1.158	1.191	1.225	1.260	1.295
4	1.216	1.262	1.311	1.360	1.412
5	1.276	1.338	1.403	1.469	1.539
6	1.340	1.419	1.501	1.587	1.677

REPORTING FINANCIAL PERFORMANCE

Questions C1 to C9 cover Reporting Financial Performance, the subject of Part C of the BPP Study Text for Paper P2.

C1 Mineral

45 mins

ACR, 12/01

Mineral plc has prepared its financial statements for the year ended 31 October 20X1. The following information relates to those financial statements.

	20X1	20X0
	£m	£m
Group turnover	250	201
Gross profit	45	35
Operating profit	10	9
Profit before taxation	12	8
Retained profit for year	5	4
Fixed assets	42	36
Current assets	55	43
Current liabilities	25	24
Long term liabilities: long term loans	13	9
Capital and reserves	59	46

The company expects to achieve growth in retained earnings of about 20% in the year to 31 October 20X2. Thereafter retained earnings are expected to accelerate to produce growth of between 20% and 25%. The growth will be generated by the introduction of new products and business efficiencies in manufacturing and in the company's infrastructure.

Mineral plc manufactures products from aluminium and other metals and is one of the largest producers in the world. Production for 20X1 increased by 18% through the acquisition of a competitor company, increased production at three of its plants and through the regeneration of old plants. There has been a recent growth in the consumption of its products because of the substitution of aluminium for heavier metals in motor vehicle manufacture. Cost reductions continued as a business focus in 20X1 and Mineral plc has implemented a cost reduction programme to be achieved by 20X4. Targets for each operation have been set.

Mineral plc's directors feel that its pricing strategy will help it compensate for increased competition in the sector. The company recently reduced the price of its products to the motor vehicle industry. This strategy is expected to increase demand and the usage of aluminium in the industry. However, in spite of the environmental benefits, certain car manufacturers have formed a cartel to prevent the increased usage of aluminium in car production.

In the period 20X1 to 20X3 Mineral plc expects to spend around £40 million on research and development and investment in fixed assets. The focus of the investments will be on enlarging the production capabilities. An important research and development project will be the joint project with a global car manufacturer to develop a new aluminium alloy car body.

In January 20X1, Mineral plc commenced a programme of acquisition of its own ordinary shares for cancellation. At 31 October 20X1, Mineral plc had purchased and cancelled five million ordinary shares of £1. In addition a subsidiary of Mineral plc had £4 million of convertible redeemable debentures outstanding. The debentures mature on 15 June 20X4 and are convertible into ordinary shares at the option of the holder. The competitive environment requires Mineral plc to provide medium and long-term financing to its customers in connection with the sale of its products. Generally the financing is placed with third party lenders but due to the higher risks associated with such financing, the amount of the financing expected to be provided by Mineral plc itself is likely to increase.

The directors of Mineral plc have attempted to minimise the financial risk to which the group is exposed. The company operates in the global market place with the inherent financial risk that this entails. The management have performed a sensitivity analysis assuming a 10% adverse movement in foreign exchange rates and interest rates applied to hedging contracts and other exposures. The analysis indicated that such market movement would not have a material effect on the company's financial position.

Mineral plc has a reputation for responsible corporate behaviour and sees the workforce as the key factor in the profitable growth of the business. During the year the company made progress towards the aim of linking environmental performance with financial performance by reporting the relationship between the eco-productivity index for basic production, and water and energy cost used in basic production. A feature of this index is that it can be segregated at site and divisional level and can be used in the internal management decision-making process.

The directors of Mineral plc are increasingly seeing their shareholder base widen with the result that investors are more demanding and sophisticated. As a result, the directors are uncertain as to the nature of the information which would provide clear and credible explanations for corporate activity. They wish their annual report to meet market expectations and not just the basic requirements of company law. They have heard that many companies deal with three key elements of corporate activity, namely reporting business performance, the analysis of the financial position and the nature of corporate citizenship, and have asked your firm's advice in drawing up the annual report.

Required

Draft a report to the directors of Mineral plc setting out the nature of information which could be disclosed in annual reports in order that there might be better assessment of the performance of the company.

Candidates should use the information in the question and produce their report under the headings:

(a)	Reporting business performance	**(10 marks)**
(b)	Analysis of financial position	**(6 marks)**
(c)	The nature of corporate citizenship	**(5 marks)**

Marks will be awarded for the presentation and style of the report. **(4 marks)**

(Total = 25 marks)

C2 Value relevance

45 mins

ACR, 12/02

The 'value relevance' of published financial statements is increasingly being called into question. Financial statements have been said to no longer have the same relevance to investors as they had in the past. Investment analysts are developing their own global investment performance standards which increasingly do not use historical cost as a basis for evaluating a company. The traditional accounting ratio analysis is outdated with a new range of performance measures now being used by analysts.

Companies themselves are under pressure to report information which is more transparent and which includes many non-financial disclosures. At the same time the move towards global accounting standards has become more important to companies wishing to raise capital in foreign markets. Corporate reporting is changing in order to meet the investors' needs. However, earnings are still the critical 'number' in both the company and the analysts' eyes.

In order to meet the increasing information needs of investors, standard setters are requiring the use of prospective information and current values more and more with the traditional historical cost accounts and related ratios seemingly becoming less and less important.

Required

(a)   Discuss the importance of published financial statements as a source of information for the investor, giving examples of the changing nature of the performance measures being utilised by investors.   **(11 marks)**

(b)   Discuss how financial reporting is changing to meet the information requirements of investors and why the emphasis on the earnings figure is potentially problematic.   **(8 marks)**

(c)   Discuss whether the intended use of fair values will reduce the importance of traditional historical cost information.   **(6 marks)**

(Total = 25 marks)

C3 Preparation question: Financial analysis

The following five year summary relates to Wandafood Products plc, and is based on financial statements prepared under the historical cost convention.

		20X5	*20X4*	*20X3*	*20X2*	*20X1*
Financial ratios						
Profitability margin						
Margin $\dfrac{\text{Trading profit}}{\text{Sales}}$	%	7.8	7.5	7.0	7.2	7.3
Return on assets $\dfrac{\text{Trading profit}}{\text{Net operating assets}}$	%	16.3	17.6	16.2	18.2	18.3
Interest and dividend cover						
Interest cover $\dfrac{\text{Trading profit}}{\text{Net finance charges}}$	times	2.9	4.8	5.1	6.5	3.6
Dividend cover $\dfrac{\text{Earnings per ordinary share}}{\text{Dividend per ordinary share}}$	times	2.7	2.6	2.1	2.5	3.1
Debt to equity ratios $\dfrac{\text{Net borrowings}}{\text{Shareholders funds}}$	%	65.9	61.3	48.3	10.8	36.5
$\dfrac{\text{Net borrowings}}{\text{Shareholders funds} + \text{minority interests}}$	%	59.3	55.5	44.0	10.1	33.9
Liquidity ratios						
Quick ratio $\dfrac{\text{Current assets less stock}}{\text{Current liabilities}}$	%	74.3	73.3	78.8	113.8	93.4
Current ratio $\dfrac{\text{Current assets}}{\text{Current liabilities}}$	%	133.6	130.3	142.2	178.9	174.7
Asset ratios						
Operating asset turnover $\dfrac{\text{Sales}}{\text{Net operating assets}}$	times	2.1	2.4	2.3	2.5	2.5
Working capital turnover $\dfrac{\text{Sales}}{\text{Working capital}}$	times	8.6	8.0	7.0	7.4	6.2
Per share						
Earnings per share – pre-tax basis	p	23.62	21.25	17.96	17.72	15.06
– net basis	p	15.65	13.60	10.98	11.32	12.18
Dividends per share	p	5.90	5.40	4.90	4.60	4.10
Net assets per share	p	102.10	89.22	85.95	85.79	78.11

Net operating assets include tangible fixed assets, stock, debtors and creditors. They exclude borrowings, taxation and dividends.

Required

Prepare a report on the company, clearly interpreting and evaluating the information given. Include comments on possible effects of price changes which may limit the quality of the report.

Helping hands

1   You must get used to questions where a load of information is thrown at you.

2   You should read the information once carefully and then skim through it again, marking off the important points.

3   Produce an answer plan first, otherwise your answer will lack structure.

C4 Rockby and Bye

45 mins

ACR, 6/04

Rockby, a public limited company, has committed itself before its year end of 31 March 20X4 to a plan of action to sell a subsidiary, Bye. The sale is expected to be completed on 1 July 20X4 and the financial statements of the group were signed on 15 May 20X4. The subsidiary, Bye, a public limited company, had net assets at the year end of £5 million and the book value of related goodwill is £1 million. Bye has made a loss of £500,000 from 1 April 20X4 to 15 May 20X4 and is expected to make a further loss up to the date of sale of £600,000. Rockby was at 15 May 20X4 negotiating the consideration for the sale of Bye but no contract has been signed.

Rockby expected to receive £4·5 million for the company after selling costs. The value-in-use of Bye at 15 May 20X4 was estimated at £3·9 million.

Further the fixed assets of Rockby include the following items of plant and head office land and buildings.

(i)   Fixed assets held for use in operating leases: at 31 March 20X4 the company has at carrying value £10 million of plant which has recently been leased out on operating leases. These leases have now expired. The company is undecided as to whether to sell the plant or lease it to customers under finance leases. The fair value less selling costs of the plant is £9 million and the value-in-use is estimated at £12 million.

Plant with a carrying value of £5 million at 31 March 20X4 has ceased to be used because of a downturn in the economy. The company had decided at 31 March 20X4 to maintain the plant in workable condition in case of a change in economic conditions. Rockby subsequently sold the plant by auction on 14 May 20X4 for £3 million net of costs.

(ii)   The Board of Rockby approved the relocation of the head office site on 1 March 20X3. The head office land and buildings were renovated and substantially improved in the year to 31 March 20X3 with a view to selling the site. During the renovations subsidence was found in the foundations of the main building. The work to correct the subsidence and the renovations were completed on 1 June 20X3. As at 31 March 20X3 the renovations had cost £2·3 million and the cost of correcting the subsidence was £1 million. The carrying value of the head office land and buildings was £5 million at 31 March 20X3 before accounting for the renovation. Rockby moved its head office to the new site in June 20X3 and at the same time, the old head office property was offered for sale at a price of £10 million.

However, the market for commercial property had deteriorated significantly and as at 31 March 20X4, a buyer for the property had not been found. At that time the company did not wish to reduce the price and hoped that market conditions would improve. On 20 April 20X4, a bid of £8.3 million was received for the property and eventually it was sold (net of costs) for £7·5 million on 1 June 20X4. The carrying value of the head office land and buildings was £7 million at 31 March 20X4.

Fixed assets are shown in the financial statements at historical cost.

Required

(a) Discuss the way in which the sale of the subsidiary, Bye, would be dealt with in the group financial statements of Rockby as at 31 March 20X4 under:

    (i) Current UK GAAP **(6 marks)**

    (ii) FRED 32 *Disposal of non-current assets and presentation of discontinued operations.*

        (7 marks)

(b) Discuss whether the following fixed assets would be classed as 'held for sale' if FRED 32 had been applied to:

    (i) The items of plant in the group financial statements at 31 March 20X4 **(7 marks)**

    (ii) The head office land and buildings in the group financial statements at 31 March 20X3 and 31 March 20X4. **(5 marks)**

(Total = 25 marks)

C5 Vident

45 mins

ACR, 6/05

The directors of Vident, a public limited company, are reviewing the impact of FRS 20 *Share-based payment* on the financial statements for the year ended 31 May 20X5 as they wish to adopt the FRS early. However, the directors of Vident are unhappy about having to apply the standard and have put forward the following arguments as to why they should not recognise an expense for share-based payments:

(i) They feel that share options have no cost to their company and, therefore, there should be no expense charged in the profit and loss account.

(ii) They do not feel that the expense arising from share options under FRS 20 actually meets the definition of an expense under the *Statement of Principles*.

(iii) The directors are worried about the dual impact of the FRS on earnings per share, as an expense is shown in the profit and loss account and the impact of share options is recognised in the diluted earnings per share calculation.

(iv) They feel that accounting for share-based payment may have an adverse effect on their company and may discourage it from introducing new share option plans.

The following share option schemes were in existence at 31 May 20X5:

Director's name	Grant date	Options granted	Fair value of options at grant date £	Exercise price £	Performance conditions	Vesting date	Exercise date
J. Van Heflin	1 June 20X2	30,000	4	3·50	A	6/20X5	6/20X6
	1 June 20X3	20,000	5	4·50	A	6/20X5	6/20X6
R. Ashworth	1 June 20X4	50,000	6	6	B	6/20X7	6/20X8

The price of the company's shares at 31 May 20X5 is £12 per share and at 31 May 20X4 was £12·50 per share.

The performance conditions which apply to the exercise of executive share options are as follows.

Performance Condition A

The share options do not vest if the growth in the company's earnings per share (EPS) for the year is less than 4%. The rate of growth of EPS was 4·5% (20X3), 4·1% (20X4), 4·2% (20X5). The directors must still work for the company on the vesting date.

Performance Condition B

The share options do not vest until the share price has increased from its value of £12·50 at the grant date (1 June 20X4) to above £13·50. The directors must still work for the company on the vesting date.

No directors have left the company since the issue of the share options and none are expected to leave before June 20X7. The shares vest and can be exercised on the first day of the due month.

The directors are unsure as to whether the share options granted to Van Heflin on 1 June 20X2 should be accounted for using FRS 20 as they were granted prior to the publication of the original Exposure Draft (7 November 20X2). Additionally the directors are also uncertain about the deferred tax implications of adopting FRS 20. A tax allowance will not arise until the options are exercised and the tax allowance will be based on the option's intrinsic value at the exercise date.

Assume a tax rate of 30%.

Required

Draft a report to the directors of Vident setting out:

(a)   The reasons why share-based payments should be recognised in financial statements and why the directors' arguments are unacceptable.   **(9 marks)**

(b)   A discussion (with suitable calculations) as to how the directors' share options would be accounted for in the financial statements for the year ended 31 May 20X5 including the adjustment to opening balances.   **(9 marks)**

(c)   The deferred tax implications (with suitable calculations) for the company which arise from the recognition of a remuneration expense for the directors' share options.   **(7 marks)**

(Total = 25 marks)

C6 Ashlee   **45 mins**

ACR, 6/05

Ashlee, a public limited company, is preparing its group financial statements for the year ended 31 March 20X5. The group comprises three companies, Ashlee, the holding company, and its 100% owned subsidiaries Pilot and Gibson, both public limited companies. The group financial statements at first appeared to indicate that the group was solvent and in a good financial position. However, after the year end, but prior to the approval of the financial statements, mistakes have been found which affect the financial position of the group to the extent that loan covenant agreements have been breached.

As a result the loan creditors require Ashlee to cut its costs, reduce its operations and reorganise its activities. Therefore, redundancies are planned and the subsidiary, Pilot, is to be reorganised. The carrying value of Pilot's net assets including allocated goodwill was £85 million at 31 March 20X5, before taking account of reorganisation costs. The directors of Ashlee wish to include £4 million of reorganisation costs in the financial statements of Pilot for the year ended 31 March 20X5. The directors of Ashlee have prepared cash flow projections which indicate that the net present value of future net cash flows from Pilot is expected to be £84 million if the reorganisation takes place and £82 million if the reorganisation does not take place.

Ashlee had already decided prior to the year end to sell the other subsidiary, Gibson. Gibson will be sold after the financial statements have been signed. The contract for the sale of Gibson was being negotiated at the time of the preparation of the financial statements and it is expected that Gibson will be sold in June 20X5. The carrying amounts of Gibson and Pilot including allocated goodwill were as follows at the year end.

	Gibson £m	Pilot £m
Goodwill	30	5
Property, plant and equipment		
Cost	120	55
Valuation	180	
Stock	100	20
Debtors	40	10
Creditors	(20)	(5)
	450	85

The fair value of the net assets of Gibson at the year end was £415 million and the estimated costs of selling the company were £5 million.

Part of the business activity of Ashlee is to buy and sell property. The directors of Ashlee had signed a contract on 1 March 20X5 to sell two of its development properties which are carried at the lower of cost and net realisable value under SSAP 9 *Stocks and long term contracts*. The sale was agreed at a figure of £40 million (carrying value £30 million). A debtor of £40 million and profit of £10 million were recognised in the financial statements for the year ended 31 March 20X5. The sale of the properties was completed on 1 May 20X5 when the legal title passed. The policy used in the prior year was to recognise revenue when the sale of such properties had been completed.

Additionally, Ashlee had purchased, on 1 April 20X4, 150,000 shares of a public limited company, Race, at a price of £20 per share. Ashlee had incurred transaction costs of £100,000 to acquire the shares. The company wishes to account for this transaction using the standards on financial instruments issued by the Accounting Standards Board but is unsure as to whether to classify this investment as 'available for sale' or 'at fair value through profit and loss' in the financial statements for the year ended 31 March 20X5. The quoted price of the shares at 31 March 20X5 was £25 per share. The shares purchased represent approximately 1% of the issued share capital of Race and are not classified as 'held for trading'.

There is no goodwill arising in the group financial statements other than that set out above.

Required

Discuss the implications, with suitable computations, of the above events for the group financial statements of Ashlee for the year ended 31 March 20X5 using current UK GAAP and FRED 32 *Disposal of non-current assets and presentation of discontinued operations*. **(25 marks)**

C7 Financial performance

45 mins

`ACR, 6/05`

The Accounting Standards Board (ASB) in the UK is currently in a joint project with the International Accounting Standards Board (IASB) and the Financial Accounting Standards Board (FASB) in the USA in the area of reporting financial performance/comprehensive income. The main focus of the project is the development of a single statement of comprehensive income to replace the profit and loss account and statement of total recognised gains and losses. The objective is to analyse all income and expenses and categorise them in a way that increases users' understanding of the results of an entity and assists in forming expectations of future income and expenditure. There seems to be some consensus that the performance statement should be divided into three components being the results of operating activities, financing and treasury activities, and other gains and losses.

The proposals will replace the current standard FRS 3 *Reporting financial performance* and build upon FRED 22 *Revision of FRS 3: Reporting financial performance*.

Required

(a) Describe the reasons why the three accounting standards boards have decided to cooperate and produce a single statement of financial performance. **(8 marks)**

(b) (i) Discuss the main factors that should be taken into account when determining how to treat gains and losses arising on tangible fixed assets in a single statement of financial performance. **(8 marks)**

(ii) Discuss whether gains and losses that have been reported initially in one section of the performance statement should be 'recycled' in a later period in another section and whether only 'realised' gains and losses should be included in such a statement. **(9 marks)**

(Total = 25 marks)

C8 Egin Group

45 mins

ACR, 6/06

On 1 June 20X5 Egin, a public limited company, was formed out of the re-organisation of a group of companies with foreign operations. The directors require advice on the disclosure of related party information but are reluctant to disclose information as they feel that such transactions are a normal feature of business and need not be disclosed.

Under the new group structure, Egin owns 80% of Briars, 60% of Doye and 30% of Eye. Egin exercises significant influence over Eye. The directors of Egin are also directors of Briars and Doye but only one director of Egin sits on the management board of Eye. The management board of Eye comprises five directors. Originally the group comprised the five companies but the fifth company, Tang, which was a 70% subsidiary of Egin, was sold on 31 January 20X6. The only transaction in the year to 31 May 20X6 between Egin and Tang was the purchase of machinery by Egin on 1 April 20X6. 30% of the shares of Egin are owned by another company, Atomic, which exerts significant influence over Egin. The remaining 40% of the shares of Doye are owned by Spade.

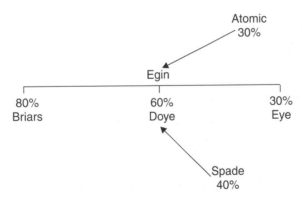

During the current financial year to 31 May 20X6, Doye has sold a significant amount of plant and machinery to Spade at the normal selling price for such items. The directors of Egin have proposed that where related party relationships are determined and sales are at normal selling price any disclosure will state that prices charged to related parties are made on an arm's length basis.

The directors are unsure how to treat certain transactions relating to their foreign subsidiary Briars. Egin purchased 80% of the ordinary share capital of Briars on 1 June 20X5 for 50 million euros when its net assets were fair valued at 45 million euros. Group policy is to amortise goodwill over five years. Additionally, at the date of acquisition, Egin had made an interest free loan to Briars of £10 million. The loan is to be repaid on 31 May 20X7. An equivalent loan would normally carry an interest rate of 6% taking into account Briars' credit rating. The exchange rates were as follows.

	Euros to £
1 June 20X5	2
31 May 20X6	2.5
Average rate for year	2.3

Financial liabilities of the group are normally measured at amortised cost.

One of the directors of Briars who is not on the management board of Egin owns the whole of the share capital of a company, Blue, that sells goods at market price to Briars. The director is in charge of the production at Briars and also acts as a consultant to the management board of the group.

Required

(a) (i) Discuss why it is important to disclose related party transactions explaining the criteria which determine a related party relationship. **(5 marks)**

(ii) Describe the nature of any related party relationships and transactions which exists:

- Within the Egin Group including Tang **(5 marks)**
- Between Spade and the Egin Group **(3 marks)**
- Between Atomic and the Egin Group **(3 marks)**

commenting on whether transactions should be described a being at 'arm's length'.

(b) Describe with suitable calculations how the goodwill arising on the acquisition of Briars will be dealt with in the group financial statements and how the loan to Briars should be treated in the financial statements of Briars for the year ended 31 May 20X6. **(9 marks)**

(Total = 25 marks)

C9 Engina

45 mins

ACR, Pilot Paper

Engina, a foreign company, has approached a partner in your firm to assist in obtaining a Stock Exchange listing for the company. Engina is registered in a country where transactions between related parties are considered to be normal but where such transactions are not disclosed. The directors of Engina are reluctant to disclose the nature of their related party transactions as they feel that although they are a normal feature of business in their part of the world, it could cause significant problems politically and culturally to disclose such transactions.

The partner in your firm has requested a list of all transactions with parties connected with the company and the directors of Engina have produced the following summary.

(a) Engina sells £50,000 of goods per month to Mr Satay, the financial director. The financial director has set up a small retailing business for his son and the goods are purchased at cost price for him. The annual turnover of Engina is £300 million. Additionally Mr Satay has purchased his company car from the company for £45,000 (market value £80,000). The director, Mr Satay, owns directly 10% of the shares in the company and earns a salary of £500,000 a year, and has a personal fortune of many millions of pounds.

(b) A hotel property had been sold to a brother of Mr Soy, the Managing Director of Engina, for £4 million (net of selling cost of £0.2 million). The market value of the property was £4.3 million but in the overseas country, property prices were falling rapidly. The carrying value of the hotel was £5 million and its value in use was £3.6 million. There was an over supply of hotel accommodation due to government subsidies in an attempt to encourage hotel development and the tourist industry.

(c)   Mr Satay owns several companies and the structure of the group is as follows.

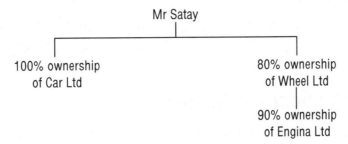

Engina earns 60% of its profit from transactions with Car and 40% of its profit from transactions with Wheel.

Required

Write a report to the directors of Engina setting out the reasons why it is important to disclose related party transactions and the nature of any disclosure required for the above transactions under the UK regulatory system before a Stock Exchange quotation can be obtained.   **(25 marks)**

The mark allocation will be as follows:

	Marks
Style/layout of report	4
Reasons	8
Transaction (a)	4
(b)	5
(c)	4
	25

GROUP FINANCIAL STATEMENTS

Questions D1 to D26 cover the Group Financial Statements, the subject of Part D of the BPP Study Text for Paper P2.

D1 Preparation question: Consolidation

FRS 7 *Fair values in acquisition accounting* contains provisions that govern the determination of the fair value of:

- The purchase consideration paid by the acquiring entity
- The net assets of the acquired entity

Purchase plc is a company incorporated in the United Kingdom. On 1 April 20X1, Purchase plc acquired 800,000 shares in Target Ltd. The balance sheet of Target Ltd on 1 April 20X1 showed the following balances.

	Note	£'000
Intangible fixed assets	1	500
Land and buildings	2	3,000
Plant and machinery	3	2,000
Stocks	4	900
Debtors	5	800
Cash at bank		200
Trade creditors		(350)
Taxation		(200)
Long-term loan	6	(2,500)
Provisions	7	(1,500)
		2,850
Share capital (£1 shares)		1,000
Share premium account		500
Profit and loss account		1,350
		2,850

Notes to the balance sheet

1 The intangible fixed assets represent the directors' valuation of the 'Bullseye' brand. Bullseye is a well-known product that is sold by Target Ltd. There is no readily ascertainable market value for the brand.

2 The land and buildings had a market value of £3.5 million at 1 April 20X1.

3 The plant and machinery has a total original cost of £3 million. It would cost £3.3 million to replace as new on 1 April 20X1.

4 The stocks of the company comprise the following.

   (i)   Stocks costing £100,000 that would cost £110,000 to replace and have a net realisable value of £75,000

   (ii) Stocks costing £800,000 that would cost £850,000 to replace and have a net realisable value of £950,000

5 At 1 April 20X1, Target Ltd was in the closing stages of a dispute with a supplier. Target Ltd was taking legal action against the supplier claiming damages of £150,000 in respect of the supply of defective products. On 1 April 20X1, the directors of Target Ltd had valid reasons for believing that the action would be successful. No entry had been made in the financial statements of Target Ltd in respect of this claim.

6 The long-term loan of Target Ltd is repayable on 31 March 20X6. The loan carries a rate of interest of 8% each year payable annually in arrears. The cost of raising similar finance on 1 April 20X1 would have been 10%.

7   The provisions of Target Ltd comprise the following.

(i)   £100,000 in respect of expected warranty claims relating to past sales

(ii)   £1,400,000 in respect of reorganisation costs that will be required following its incorporation into the Purchase plc group

The terms of agreement between Purchase plc and the shareholders of Target Ltd were that the shareholders of Target Ltd would receive:

(i)   On 1 April 20X1, 5 shares in Purchase plc for every share they owned in Target Ltd. The market value of a Purchase plc share on 1 April 20X1 was 90p

(ii)   A cash payment of 100p for every share they owned in Target Ltd. Of the cash payment of 100p, 40p is payable on 1 April 20X2 and 60p on 1 April 20X3.

Required

Compute the goodwill on the acquisition of Target Ltd by Purchase plc on 1 April 20X1. You should use a rate of 10% in any discounting calculations and give full explanations for all your workings.

D2 Preparation question: Consolidated profit and loss account

You are given the following information.

(a)   The details of the investments held by Orsino plc in Viola Ltd and Sebastian Ltd are as follows.

	Date	Price paid by Orsino plc £m	Ordinary share capital acquired* %	Retained profits at date of acquisition** £m	Share capital at date of acquisition** £m
Viola Ltd	1.1.20X2	34	80	10	20
Sebastian Ltd	1.1.20X4	10	$33^1/_3$	5	10

*   Each ordinary share has identical voting rights.

**   Share capital and retained profits represented the full amount of the shareholders' interest at these dates.

(b)   The summarised profit and loss accounts of Orsino plc, Viola Ltd and Sebastian Ltd for the year to 31 December 20X6 were as follows.

	Orsino plc £'000	Viola Ltd £'000	Sebastian Ltd £'000
Sales	290,000	110,000	60,000
Cost of sales	162,000	51,000	23,500
Gross profit	128,000	59,000	36,500
Administrative expenses	16,200	8,600	8,000
Distribution and selling expenses	48,800	12,400	9,000
Operating profit	63,000	38,000	19,500
Investment income	9,000	–	–
Profit before taxation	72,000	38,000	19,500
Taxation	25,000	12,000	9,000
Profit for the year	47,000	26,000	10,500

(c)   The investment income of Orsino plc came from dividends received from Viola Ltd and Sebastian Ltd.

(d)   Goodwill write-offs have not been made in the individual company accounts. It is a group accounting policy to write off all goodwill on a straight-line basis over five years. This write-off is treated as an administrative expense.

(e)   Details of inter-company trading profits in stocks were as follows.

Stock held by	Selling company	Date at which stock was held	Amount of profit in stock £m
Orsino plc	Viola Ltd	1.1.20X6	10
Orsino plc	Viola Ltd	31.12.20X6	20
Viola Ltd	Sebastian Ltd	31.12.20X6	30

It is the group's accounting policy to eliminate the intra-group stock profits made by the subsidiary against both the majority and minority interests.

Required

Prepare the consolidated profit and loss account for the Orsino Group for the year ended 31 December 20X6 for presentation to the shareholders.

D3 Preparation question: Status of investment

Both the *Statement of Principles for Financial Reporting* and individual accounting standards make it clear that the treatment in consolidated financial statements of investments in other undertakings is dependent on the extent of control or influence the investing entity is able to exercise over the other undertaking. Port plc has investments in three other undertakings.

(a)   On 15 May 20W0, Port plc purchased 40 million 50p equity shares in Harbour Ltd. The called-up equity share capital of Harbour Ltd on 15 May 20W0 was 50 million 50p equity shares.

(b)   On 15 June 20W1, Port plc purchased 30 million £1 equity shares in Inlet Ltd. The called-up equity share capital of Inlet Ltd on 15 June 20W1 was 75 million £1 equity shares. The remaining equity shares in Inlet Ltd are held by a large number of investors, none with more than 5 million equity shares.

(c)   On 15 July 20W2, Port plc purchased 25 million 50p equity shares in Bay Ltd. The called-up equity share capital of Bay Ltd on 15 July 20W2 was 80 million 50p equity shares. Another investor owns 50 million equity shares in Bay Ltd. This investor takes an active interest in directing the operating and financial policies of Bay Ltd and on a number of occasions has required Bay Ltd to follow policies that do not meet with the approval of Port plc.

Equity shares in all of the companies carry one vote per share at general meetings. No party can control or influence the composition of the board of directors of any of the companies other than through its ownership of equity shares. There have been no instances where shareholders in any of the companies have acted together to increase their control or influence. None of the companies has issued any additional equity shares since Port plc purchased its interests.

Extracts from the profit and loss accounts of the four companies for their year ended 30 June 20X1 are given below.

	Port plc £'000	Harbour Ltd £'000	Inlet Ltd £'000	Bay Ltd £'000
Turnover	65,000	45,000	48,000	40,000
Cost of sales	(35,000)	(25,000)	(26,000)	(19,000)
Gross profit	30,000	20,000	22,000	21,000

Note 1

Port plc manufactures a product that is used by Harbour Ltd and Inlet Ltd. During the year ended 30 June 20X1, sales of the product to Harbour Ltd and Inlet Ltd were:

- To Harbour Ltd – £8 million
- To Inlet Ltd – £7.5 million

Opening and closing stocks of this product in the financial statements of Harbour Ltd and Inlet Ltd (all purchased from Port plc at cost plus 25% mark up, unchanged during the year) were as follows.

Company	Closing stock	Opening stock
	£'000	£'000
Harbour Ltd	3,000	2,400
Inlet Ltd	2,500	Nil

At 30 June 20X1, there were no amounts payable by Harbour Ltd and Inlet Ltd in respect of stocks purchased from Port plc before 30 June 20X1.

Note 2

There was no other trading between the companies other than the payment of dividends.

Required

(a) State the alternative treatments of investments in consolidated financial statements that are set out in the *Statement of Principles for Financial Reporting* and UK accounting standards. Do **not** describe the mechanics of the methods.

(b) Identify the correct treatment of the investments in Harbour Ltd, Inlet Ltd and Bay Ltd in the consolidated financial statements of Port plc.

(c) Compute the consolidated turnover, cost of sales and gross profit of the Port group for the year ended 30 June 20X1. You should ensure that your computations are fully supported by relevant workings.

(d) Compute the adjustments that need to be made in respect of the transactions described in *Note 1* above when preparing the consolidated balance sheet of Port plc at 30 June 20X1. You should explain the rationale behind each adjustment you make.

D4 Preparation question: Associate

The balance sheets of J plc and its investee companies, P Ltd and S Ltd, at 31 December 20X5 are shown below.

BALANCE SHEETS AS AT 31 DECEMBER 20X5

	J Plc £'000	J Plc £'000	P Ltd £'000	P Ltd £'000	S Ltd £'000	S Ltd £'000
Tangible fixed assets						
Freehold property	1,950		1,250		500	
Plant and machinery	795		375		285	
		2,745		1,625		785
Investments		1,500		–		–
Current assets						
Stock	575		300		265	
Trade debtors	330		290		370	
Cash	50		120		20	
	955		710		655	
Creditors: due within one year						
Bank overdraft	560		–		–	
Trade creditors	680		350		300	
	1,240		350		300	
Net current (liabilities)/assets		(285)		360		355
Creditors: due after one year						
12% debentures		(500)		(100)		–
		3,460		1,885		1,140
Share capital (£1 ordinary shares)		2,000		1,000		750
Profit and loss account		1,460		885		390
		3,460		1,885		1,140

Additional information

(a)   J plc acquired 600,000 ordinary shares in P Ltd on 1 January 20X0 for £1,000,000 when the reserves of P Ltd were £200,000.

(b)   At the date of acquisition of P Ltd, the fair value of its freehold property was considered to be £400,000 greater than its value in P Ltd's balance sheet. P Ltd had acquired the property in January 20W0 and the buildings element (comprising 50% of the total value) is depreciated on cost over 50 years.

(c)   J plc acquired 225,000 ordinary shares in S Ltd on 1 January 20X4 for £500,000 when the reserves of S Ltd were £150,000.

(d)   P Ltd manufactures a component used by both J plc and S Ltd. Transfers are made by P Ltd at cost plus 25%. J plc held £100,000 stock of these components at 31 December 20X5 and S Ltd held £80,000 at the same date.

(e)   It is the policy of J plc to write off goodwill over a period of five years.

(f)   No entry has been made in the books of J plc for the dividends receivable from P Ltd or S Ltd at 31 December 20X5.

Required

Prepare, in a format suitable for inclusion in the annual report of the J Group, the consolidated balance sheet at 31 December 20X5.

D5 Baden
45 mins

(a) FRS 9 *Associates and joint ventures* deals not only with the accounting treatment of associated companies and joint venture operations but covers certain types of joint business arrangements not carried on through a separate entity. The main changes made by FRS 9 are to restrict the circumstances in which equity accounting can be applied and to provide detailed rules for accounting for joint ventures.

Required

(i)   Explain the criteria which distinguish an associate from ordinary fixed asset investment.   **(6 marks)**

(ii) Explain the principal difference between a joint venture and a 'joint arrangement' and the impact that this classification has upon the accounting for such relationships.   **(4 marks)**

(b) The following financial statements relate to Baden, a public limited company.

PROFIT AND LOSS ACCOUNT
FOR THE YEAR ENDED 31 DECEMBER 20X8

	£m	£m
Turnover		212
Cost of sales		(170)
Gross profit		42
Distribution costs	17	
Administrative costs	8	
		(25)
		17
Other operating income		12
Operating profit		29
Exceptional item		(10)
Interest payable		(4)
Profit on ordinary activities before tax		15
Taxation on profit on ordinary activities		(3)
		12
Ordinary dividend – paid		(4)
Retained profit for year		8

BALANCE SHEET AT 31 DECEMBER 20X8

	£m	£m
Fixed assets: tangible	30	
goodwill	7	
		37
Current assets	31	
Creditors: amounts falling due within one year	(12)	
Net current assets		19
Total assets less current liabilities		56
Creditors: amounts falling due after more than one year		(10)
		46
Capital and reserves		
Called up share capital		
Ordinary shares of £1		10
Share premium account		4
Profit and loss account		32
		46

(i)   Cable, a public limited company, acquired 30% of the ordinary share capital of Baden at a cost of £14 million on 1 January 20X7. The share capital of Baden has not changed since acquisition when the profit and loss reserve of Baden was £9 million.

(ii)   At 1 January 20X7 the following fair values were attributed to the net assets of Baden but not incorporated in its accounting records.

	£m	
Tangible fixed assets	30	(carrying value £20m)
Goodwill (estimate)	10	
Current assets	31	
Creditors: amounts falling due within one year	20	
Creditors: amounts falling due after more than one year	8	

(iii)   Guy, an associate company of Cable, also holds a 25% interest in the ordinary share capital of Baden. This was acquired on 1 January 20X8.

(iv)   During the year to 31 December 20X8, Baden sold goods to Cable to the value of £35 million. The inventory of Cable at 31 December 20X8 included goods purchased from Baden on which the company made a profit of £10 million.

(v)   The policy of all companies in the Cable Group is to amortise goodwill over four years and to depreciate tangible fixed assets at 20% per annum on the straight line basis.

(vi)   Baden does not represent a material part of the group and is significantly less than the 15% additional disclosure threshold required under FRS 9 *Associates and joint ventures.*

Required

(i)   Show how the investment in Baden would be stated in the consolidated balance sheet and profit and loss account of the Cable group under FRS 9 *Associates and joint ventures*, for the year ended 31 December 20X8 on the assumption that Baden is an associate. **(9 marks)**

(ii)   Show how the treatment of Baden would change if Baden was classified as an investment in a joint venture. **(6 marks)**

(Total = 25 marks)

D6 Preparation question: 'D' shaped group

Below are the balance sheets of three companies as at 31 December 20X9.

	Bauble Ltd £'000	Jewel Ltd £'000	Gem Ltd £'000
Fixed assets	720	60	70
Investments in group companies	185	100	–
Current assets	175	95	90
Creditors: amounts falling due within one year	(120)	(65)	(45)
	960	190	115
Share capital and reserves			
£1 ordinary shares	400	100	50
Profit and loss account	560	90	65
	960	190	115

You are also given the following information.

(a)   Bauble Ltd acquired 60% of the share capital of Jewel Ltd on 1 January 20X2 and 10% of Gem on 1 January 20X3. The cost of the investments were £142,000 and £43,000 respectively. Jewel Ltd acquired 70% of the share capital of Gem Ltd on 1 January 20X3.

(b)   The profit and loss account balances of Jewel Ltd and Gem Ltd were:

	1 January 20X2	1 January 20X3
Jewel Ltd	45	60
Gem Ltd	30	40

(c) Any goodwill is capitalised as an asset and reviewed annually for impairment. To date no write down has been considered necessary.

Required

(a) Prepare the consolidated balance sheet for Bauble Ltd and its subsidiary companies as at 31 December 20X9.

(b) Calculate the total goodwill arising on acquisition if Bauble Ltd had acquired its investments in Jewel and Gem on 1 January 20X3 at a cost of £142,000 and £43,000 respectively and Jewel Ltd had acquired its investment in Gem Ltd on 1 January 20X2.

D7 Question with analysis: X Group   45 mins

X, a public limited company, acquired 100 million ordinary shares of £1 in Y, a public limited company on 1 April 20X6 when the accumulated reserves were £120 million. Y acquired 45 million ordinary shares of £1 in Z, a public limited company, on 1 April 20X4 when the accumulated reserves were £10 million. On 1 April 20X4 there were no material differences between the carrying values and the fair values of Z. On 1 April 20X6, the accumulated reserves of Z were £20 million.

Y acquired 30% of the ordinary shares of W, a limited company, on 1 April 20X6 for £50 million when the accumulated reserves of W were £7 million. Y exercises significant influence over W and there were no material differences between the carrying values and the fair values of W at that date.

There had been no share issues since 1 April 20X4 by any of the group companies. The following balance sheets relate to the group companies as at 31 March 20X9.

	X £m	Y £m	Z £m	W £m
Fixed assets: tangible	900	100	30	40
intangible		30		
Investment in Y	320			
Investment in Z		90		
Investment in W		50		
Net current assets	640	360	75	73
Creditors: amounts falling due after one year	(200)	(150)	(15)	(10)
	1,660	480	90	103
Share capital	360	150	50	80
Share premium	250	120	10	6
Accumulated reserves	1,050	210	30	17
	1,660	480	90	103

(a) The following fair value table sets out the carrying values and fair values of certain assets and liabilities of the group companies together with any accounting policy adjustments required to ensure consistent group policies at 1 April 20X6.

	Carrying value		Accounting policy adj.		Fair Value adj.		New carrying value	
	£m Y	£m Z	£m Y	£m Z	£m Y	£m Z	£m Y	£m Z
Tangible fixed assets	90	20			30	10	120	30
Intangible fixed assets	30		(30)				–	
Stocks	20	12	2		(8)	(5)	14	7
Provision for bad debts	(15)				(9)		(24)	

These values had not been incorporated into the financial records. Group companies have consistent accounting policies as at 31 March 20X9.

(b) During the year ended 31 March 20X9 Z had sold goods to X and Y. At 31 March 20X9, there were £44 million of these goods in the stock of X and £16 million in the stock of Y. Z had made a profit of 25% on selling price on the goods.

(c) On 1 June 20X6, an amount of £36 million was received by Y from an arbitration award against Q. This receipt was secured as a result of an action against Q prior to Y's acquisition by X but was not included in the assets of Y at 1 April 20X6.

(d) The group charges depreciation on all tangible fixed assets on the straight line basis at 10% per annum. Goodwill is amortised over 11 years.

Required

Prepare a consolidated balance sheet as at 31 March 20X9 for the X group. **(25 marks)**

Analysis

> What percentage? What is the status?

X, a public limited company, acquired **100 million ordinary shares of £1 in Y**, a public limited company on 1 April 20X6 when the accumulated reserves were £120 million. Y acquired 45 million ordinary shares of £1 in Z, a public limited company, on 1 April 20X4 when the accumulated reserves were £10 million. On 1 April 20X4 there were no material differences between the carrying values and the fair values of Z. On 1 April 20X6, the accumulated reserves of Z were £20 million.

> What is the status? What does X control?

Y acquired 30% of the ordinary shares of W, a limited company, on 1 April 20X6 for £50 million when the accumulated reserves of W were £7 million. Y exercises significant influence over W and there were no material differences between the carrying values and the fair values of W at that date.

There had been no share issues since 1 April 20X4 by any of the group companies. The following balance sheets relate to the group companies as at 31 March 20X9.

	X £m	Y £m	Z £m	W £m
Fixed assets: tangible	900	100	30	40
intangible		30		
Investment in Y	320			
Investment in Z		90		
Investment in W		50		
Net current assets	640	360	75	73
Creditors: amounts falling due after one year	(200)	(150)	(15)	(10)
	1,660	480	90	103
Share capital	360	150	50	80
Share premium	250	120	10	6
Accumulated reserves	1,050	210	30	17
	1,660	480	90	103

> Use tables to work out total values for X and Z at acquisition and at the balance sheet date.

(a) **The following fair value table sets out the carrying values and fair values of certain assets and liabilities of the group companies together with any accounting policy adjustments required to ensure consistent group policies** at 1 April 20X6.

	Carrying value		Accounting policy adj.		Fair Value adj.		New carrying value	
	£m	£m	£m	£m	£m	£m	£m	£m
	Y	Z	Y	Z	Y	Z	Y	Z
Tangible fixed assets	90	20			30	10	120	30
Intangible fixed assets	30		(30)				-	
Stocks	20	12	2		(8)	(5)	14	7
Provision for bad debts	(15)				(9)		(24)	

These values had not been incorporated into the financial records. Group companies have consistent accounting policies as at 31 March 20X9.

Straightforward intragroup trading.

(b) During the year ended 31 March 20X9 **Z had sold goods to X and Y**. At 31 March 20X9, there were £44 million of these goods in the stock of X and £16 million in the stock of Y. Z had made a profit of 25% on selling price on the goods.

A contingent asset?

(c) On 1 June 20X6, an amount of £36 million was received by Y from an arbitration award against Q. This **receipt was secured as a result of an action** against Q prior to Y's acquisition by X but was not included in the assets of Y at 1 April 20X6.

(d) The group charges depreciation on all tangible fixed assets on the straight line basis at 10% per annum. Goodwill is amortised over 11 years.

Required

Prepare a consolidated balance sheet as at 31 March 20X9 for the X group.

D8 Largo

45 mins

ACR, 12/03

The following draft balance sheets relate to Largo, a public limited company, Fusion, a public limited company and Spine, a public limited company, as at 30 November 20X4

	Largo £m	Fusion £m	Spine £m
Fixed assets			
Tangible fixed assets	329	185	64
Investment in Fusion	150		
Investment in Spine	30	50	
Investment in Micro	11		
	520	235	64
Net current assets	110	53	36
Total assets less current liabilities	630	288	100
Provision for liabilities (deferred tax)	(20)	(20)	(5)
	610	268	95
Capital and reserves			
Called up ordinary share capital of £1	460	110	50
Share premium account	30	20	10
Profit and loss account	120	138	35
	610	268	95

The following information is relevant to the preparation of the group financial statements.

(a) Largo acquired ninety per cent of the ordinary share capital of Fusion and twenty-six per cent of the ordinary share capital of Spine on 1 December 20X3 in a share for share exchange when the profit and loss reserves were Fusion £136 million and Spine £30 million. The fair value of the net assets at 1 December 20X3 was

Largo £650 million, Fusion £300 million and Spine £110 million. Any increase in the fair value of the net assets over the carrying value is attributable to property held by the companies. There had been no new issue of shares since 1 December 20X3.

(b)   In arriving at the fair value of net assets acquired at 1 December 20X3, Largo has deducted deferred tax arising on the increase in the value of the property of both Fusion and Spine. The carrying value of the property of Fusion at 1 December 20X3 was £100 million and of Spine was £40 million. The fair value of the properties was Fusion £150 million and Spine £70 million. Assume a taxation rate of 30%.

(c)   Fusion had acquired a sixty per cent holding in Spine on 1 December 20X0 for a consideration of £50 million when the profit and loss reserve of Spine was £10 million. The fair value of the net assets at that date was £80 million with the increase in fair value attributable to property held by the companies. Property is depreciated within the group at five per cent per annum.

(d)   The directors of Largo wish to account for the business combination as a merger. On 1 December 20X3 before the share exchange the market capitalisation of the companies was £644 million: Largo, £310 million: Fusion; and £130 million: Spine. The number of employees of Largo was fifty per cent more than the combined total of the employees of both Fusion and Spine. The new board of directors will comprise ten directors, seven of whom will be nominated by Largo. As a result of the directors' wish to use merger accounting, the cost of the investment in Fusion and Spine, shown in the financial statements of Largo, is simply the nominal value of the share capital issued. The directors feel that merger accounting is appropriate as former institutional shareholders of Fusion own a substantial amount of equity in the new business combination with the result that Largo cannot dominate the new business combination because of their influence over the management of the new entity.

(e)   Largo purchased a forty per cent interest in Micro Ltd, an investment company on 1 December 20X2. The only asset of the company is a portfolio of investments which is held for trading purposes. The stake in Micro was purchased for cash for £11 million. The carrying value of the net assets of Micro on 1 December 20X2 was £18 million and their fair value was £20 million. On 30 November 20X4, the fair value of the net assets was £24 million, Largo exercises significant influence over Micro. Micro values the portfolio on a 'mark to market' basis.

(f)   Fusion has included a brand name in its tangible fixed assets at the cost of £9 million. The brand earnings can be separately identified and could be sold separately from the rest of the business. The fair value of the brand at 30 November 20X4 was £7 million and the brand is not amortised as it is considered that it has an unlimited useful life. This opinion has been accepted by the auditors. Group policy is to amortise goodwill over three years and the fair value of the brand at the date of Largo's acquisition of Fusion was £9 million.

Required

Prepare the consolidated balance sheet of the Largo Group at the year ended 30 November 20X4 in accordance with UK Generally Accepted Accounting Practice, explaining the reasons why the merger accounting method cannot be used for the business combination.

(25 marks)

D9 Case study question: Rod

90 mins

The following draft balance sheets relate to Rod, a public limited company, Reel, a public limited company, and Line, a public limited company, as at 30 November 20X3.

	Rod £m	Reel £m	Line £m
Fixed assets			
Tangible fixed assets – cost/valuation	1,230	505	256
Investment in Reel	640		
Investment in Line	160	100	
	2,030	605	256
Current assets			
Stocks	300	135	65
Debtors	240	105	49
Cash at bank and in hand	90	50	80
	630	290	194
Creditors: amounts falling due within one year	(100)	(70)	(50)
Net current assets	530	220	144
Total assets less current liabilities	2,560	825	400
Provisions for liabilities	(135)	(25)	(20)
	2,425	800	380
Capital and reserves			
Called up share capital	1,500	500	200
Share premium account	300	100	50
Revaluation reserve			70
Profit and loss account	625	200	60
	2,425	800	380

The following information is relevant to the preparation of the group financial statements.

(i) Rod had acquired eighty per cent of the ordinary share capital of Reel on 1 December 20X0 when the profit and loss reserve of Reel was £100 million. The fair value of the net assets of Reel was £710 million at 1 December 20X0. Any fair value adjustment related to net current assets and these net current assets had been realised by 30 November 20X3. There has been no new issue of shares in the group since the current group structure was created.

(ii) Rod and Reel had acquired their holdings in Line on the same date as part of an attempt to mask the true ownership of Line. Rod acquired forty per cent and Reel acquired twenty-five per cent of the ordinary share capital of Line on 1 December 20X1. The profit and loss reserves of Line on that date were £50 million and those of Reel were £150 million. There was no revaluation reserve in the books of Line on 1 December 20X1. The fair values of the net assets of Line at 1 December 20X1 were not materially different from their carrying values.

(iii) The group operates in the pharmaceutical industry and incurs a significant amount of expenditure on the development of products. These costs were formerly written off to the profit and loss account as incurred but then reinstated when the related products were brought into commercial use. The reinstated costs are shown as 'development stocks' and are included in stocks and work-in-progress. In the current year, Reel has included £20 million of these costs in stocks and work-in-progress. Of these costs £5 million relates to expenditure on a product written off in periods prior to 1 December 20X0. Commercial sales of this product had commenced during the current period. The accountant now wishes to comply strictly with accounting standards as regards development costs and feels that the criteria for the deferral of such costs have not been met.

(iv) Reel had purchased a significant amount of new production equipment during the year. The cost before trade discount of this equipment was £50 million. The trade discount of £6 million was taken to the profit and loss account. Depreciation is charged on the straight line basis over a six year period.

(v)   The policy of the group is now to state tangible fixed assets at depreciated historical cost. The group implemented FRS 15 *Tangible fixed assets* in the year ended 30 November 20X3 and restated all of its tangible fixed assets to historical cost in that year, except for the tangible fixed assets of Line which had been revalued by the directors of Line on 1 December 20X2. The values were incorporated in the financial records creating a revaluation reserve of £70 million. The tangible fixed assets of Line were originally purchased on 1 December 20X1 at a cost of £300 million. The assets are depreciated over six years on the straight line basis. The group does not make an annual transfer from revaluation reserves to the profit and loss reserve in respect of excess depreciation charged on revalued tangible fixed assets. There were no additions or disposals of the fixed assets of Line for the two years ended 30 November 20X3.

(vi)   During the year the directors of Rod decided to form a defined benefit pension scheme for the employees of the holding company and contributed cash to it of £100 million. The following details relate to the scheme at 30 November 20X3.

	£m
Present value of obligation	130
Fair value of plan assets	125
Current service cost	110
Interest cost – scheme liabilities	20
Expected return on pension scheme assets	10

The only entry in the financial statements made to date is in respect of the cash contribution which has been included in Rod's debtors. The directors have been uncertain as to how to deal with the above pension scheme in the consolidated financial statements.

(vii)   Goodwill is written off over four years on the straight line basis. Candidates should ignore any deferred tax implications relating to the pension scheme.

Required

(a)   Show how the defined benefit pension scheme should be dealt with in the consolidated financial statements.
(5 marks)

(b)   Prepare a consolidated balance sheet of the Rod Group as at 30 November 20X3 in accordance with UK Generally Accepted Accounting Practice.   **(22 marks)**

(c)   You are now advising the financial director of Rod about certain aspects of the financial statements for the year ended 30 November 20X4. The director has summarised these points as follows.

    (i)   **Restructuring of the group**. A formal announcement for a restructuring of the group was made after the year end on 5 December 20X4. No provision has been made in the financial statements as a public issue of shares is being planned and the company does not wish to lower the reported profits. Prior to the year end, the company has sold certain plant and issued redundancy notices to some employees in anticipation of the formal commencement of the restructuring. The company prepared a formal plan for the restructuring which was approved by the board and communicated to the trade union representatives prior to the year end. The directors estimate the cost of the restructuring to be £60 million, and it could take up to two years to complete the restructuring. The estimated cost of restructuring includes £10 million for retraining and relocating existing employees and the directors feel that costs of £20 million (of which £5 million is relocation costs) will have been incurred by the time that the financial statements are approved.   **(7 marks)**

    (ii)   **Fine for illegal receipt of a state subsidy**. The company was fined on 10 October 20X4 for the receipt of 'illegal' state subsidies that were used to offset trading losses in previous years. The European Union has informed Rod that it has to immediately repay to the government £300 million plus interest of £160 million. The total repayment has been treated as an intangible asset which is being amortised over twenty years with a full year's charge in the current year.   **(5 marks)**

(d)   Rod spends many millions of pounds on research in innovative areas. Often the research and development expenditure does not provide a revenue stream for many years. The company has gained a significant expertise in this field and is frustrated by the fact that the value which is being created is not shown on the balance sheet, but the cost of the innovation is charged to the profit and loss account. The knowledge gained by the company is not reported in the financial statements.

Advise the directors on the current problems of reporting financial performance in the case of a 'knowledge led' company such as Rod. **(8 marks)**

(e) In many organisations, bonus payments related to annual profits form a significant part of the total remuneration of all senior managers, not just the top few managers. The directors of Rod feel that the chief internal auditor makes a significant contribution to the company's profitability, and should therefore receive a bonus based on profit.

Advise the directors as to whether this is appropriate. **(3 marks)**

(Total = 50 marks)

D10 Case study question: Exotic   90 mins

The Exotic Group carries on business as a distributor of warehouse equipment and importer of fruit into the United Kingdom. Exotic plc was incorporated in 20X1 to distribute warehouse equipment. It diversified its activities during 20X3 to include the import and distribution of fruit, and expanded its operations by the acquisition of shares in Madeira plc in 20X2, in Melon plc in 20X5 and in Kiwi plc in 20X7.

Accounts for all companies are made up to 31 December.

The draft profit and loss accounts for Exotic plc, Melon plc and Kiwi plc for the year ended 31 December 20X9 are as follows.

	Exotic plc £'000	Melon plc £'000	Kiwi plc £'000
Turnover	45,600	24,700	22,800
Cost of sales	18,050	5,463	5,320
Gross profit	27,550	19,237	17,480
Distribution costs	3,325	2,137	1,900
Administrative expenses	3,475	950	1,900
Operating profit	20,750	16,150	13,680
Interest paid	325	–	–
Profit before tax	20,425	16,150	13,680
Taxation	8,300	5,390	4,241
Profit after tax	12,125	10,760	9,439
Retained profit brought forward	20,013	13,315	10,459
Retained profit carried forward	32,138	24,075	19,898

The draft balance sheets as at 31 December 20X9 are as follows.

	Exotic plc £'000	Melon plc £'000	Kiwi plc £'000
Fixed assets (NBV)	35,483	24,273	13,063
Investments			
Shares in Melon plc	6,650		
Shares in Kiwi plc		3,800	
Current assets	1,568	9,025	8,883
Current liabilities	(3,563)	(10,023)	(48)
	40,138	27,075	21,898
Share capital and reserves			
Ordinary £1 shares	8,000	3,000	2,000
Profit and loss account	32,138	24,075	19,898
	40,138	27,075	21,898

The following information is available relating to Exotic plc, Melon plc and Kiwi plc.

(a)   On 1 January 20X5 Exotic plc acquired 2,700,000 £1 ordinary shares in Melon plc for £6,650,000 at which date there was a credit balance on the profit and loss account of Melon plc of £1,425,000. No shares have been issued by Melon plc since Exotic plc acquired its interest.

(b)   On 1 January 20X7 Melon plc acquired 1,600,000 £1 ordinary shares in Kiwi plc for £3,800,000 at which date there was a credit balance on the profit and loss account of Kiwi plc of £950,000. No shares have been issued by Kiwi plc since Melon plc acquired its interest.

(c)   During 20X9, Kiwi plc had made inter-company sales to Melon plc of £480,000 making a profit of 25% on cost and £75,000 of these goods were in stock at 31 December 20X9.

(d)   During 20X9, Melon plc had made inter-company sales to Exotic plc of £260,000 making a profit of $33^1/_3$% on cost and £60,000 of these goods were in stock at 31 December 20X9.

(e)   On 1 November 20X9 Exotic plc sold warehouse equipment to Melon plc for £240,000 from stock. Melon plc has included this equipment in its fixed assets. The equipment had been purchased on credit by Exotic plc for £200,000 in October 20X9 and this amount is included in its current liabilities as at 31 December 20X9.

(f)   Melon plc charges depreciation on its warehouse equipment at 20% on cost. It is company policy to charge a full year's depreciation in the year of acquisition to be included in the cost of sales.

(g)   Goodwill arising on consolidation was deemed to have an indefinite life and is to remain in the balance sheet.

The following information is available relating to Madeira plc.

(a)   In 20X2 Madeira plc was incorporated as a wholly owned subsidiary of Exotic plc to carry on business importing bananas from Madeira to the United Kingdom. Increased competition from growers in other world markets has resulted in recurring trade losses.

(b)   In 20X7 the directors of the parent company arranged for all warehousing and distribution for Madeira plc to be physically handled by Melon plc. Madeira plc retained its office accommodation.

(c)   In the financial year ended 31 December 20X8 Exotic plc wrote off its investment in Madeira plc in its accounts.

(d)   In 20X8 Exotic plc decided to discontinue the trade carried on in Madeira plc's name as early as possible in 20X9. However, due to protracted negotiations with employees, the termination was not completed until November 20X9.

(e)   The following data relates to Madeira plc in 20X9.

	£'000
Turnover	2,000
Cost of sales	(2,682)
Distribution costs	(18)
Administrative expenses	(100)
Redundancy costs	(427)
Profit on sale of fixed assets	115
Loss on sale of net current assets	(36)

Required

(a)   Excluding Madeira plc:

  (i)   Prepare a consolidated profit and loss account, including brought forward reserves, for the Exotic Group plc for the year ended 31 December 20X9   **(13 marks)**

  (ii)   Prepare a consolidated balance sheet as at that date   **(10 marks)**

(b)   Show the accounting treatment for Madeira plc in the consolidated profit and loss account of the Exotic Group for the year ended 31 December 20X9 in accordance with FRS 3 on the assumption that there has been a discontinuance and that a provision of £500,000 had been created in 20X8 in expectation of trading losses. **(5 marks)**

(c) The following year, Exotic acquired the whole of the share capital of Zest Software, a public limited company, and merged Zest Software with its existing business. The directors feel that the goodwill (£10 million) arising on the purchase has an indefinite economic life, and therefore no amortisation has been provided as the goodwill is an inseparable part of the value of the business acquired. Additionally, Exotic acquired a 50% interest in a joint venture which gives rise to a net liability of £3 million. The reason for this liability is the fact that the negative goodwill (£6 million) arising on the acquisition of the interest in the joint venture was deducted from the interest in the net assets (£3 million). Exotic is proposing to net the liability of £3 million against a loan made to the joint venture by Exotic of £5 million, and show the resultant balance in tangible fixed assets. **(11 marks)**

(d) Advise the directors of Exotic on the issues relating to the reporting of environmental information in financial statements and the current reporting requirements in the UK. **(11 marks)**

(Total = 50 marks)

D11 Preparation question: Part disposal

Angel Ltd bought 70% of the share capital of Shane Ltd for £120,000 on 1 January 20X6. At that date Shane Ltd's profit and loss account balance stood at £10,000.

The balance sheets at 31 December 20X8, summarised profit and loss accounts to that date and movement on reserves are given below:

	Angel Ltd Group £'000	Shane Ltd £'000
Fixed assets	200	80
Investment in Shane Ltd	120	–
Net current assets	580	110
	900	190
Share capital and reserves		
£1 ordinary shares	500	100
Profit and loss account	400	90
	900	190

	Angel Ltd Group £'000	Shane Ltd £'000
Operating profit	110	30
Tax	(40)	(12)
Retained profit	70	18
Reserves		
As at 1 January 20X8	330	72
Profit for the year	70	18
As at 31 December 20X8	400	90

No entries have been made in the accounts for any of the following transactions.

Assume that profits accrue evenly throughout the year. Ignore tax.

Required

Prepare the consolidated balance sheet, profit and loss account and statement of reserves at 31 December 20X8 in following circumstances:

Angel Ltd sells one half of its holding in Shane Ltd for £160,000 on 30 June 20X8, and the remaining holding is to be dealt with as an associate. This will not be a discontinued activity. Angel's accounting policy is to capitalise goodwill as an asset and review for impairment. To date no write down has been considered necessary.

D12 Plans

45 mins

ACR, Pilot Paper

X, a public limited company, owns 100 per cent of companies Y and Z which are both public limited companies. The X group operates in the telecommunications industry and the directors are considering three different plans to restructure the group. The directors feel that the current group structure is not serving the best interests of the shareholders and wish to explore possible alternative group structures.

The balance sheets of X and its subsidiaries Y and Z at 31 May 20Y1 are as follows:

	X plc £m	Y plc £m	Z plc £m
Tangible fixed assets	600	200	45
Cost of investment in Y	60		
Cost of investment in Z	70		
Net current assets	160	100	20
	890	300	65
Share capital – ordinary shares of £1	120	60	40
Profit and loss account	770	240	25
	890	300	65

X acquired the investment in Z on 1 June 20X5 when the profit and loss account balance was £20 million. The fair value of the net assets of Z on 1 June 20X5 was £60 million. Company Y was incorporated by X and has always been a 100 per cent owned subsidiary. Goodwill is written off over four years. The fair value of the assets of Y at 31 May 20Y1 is £310 million and of Z is £80 million.

The directors are unsure as to the impact or implications that the following plans are likely to have on the individual accounts of the companies and the group accounts.

The three different plans to restructure the group are as follows.

Plan 1

Y is to purchase the whole of X's investment in Z. The directors are undecided as to whether the purchase consideration should be 50 million £1 ordinary shares of Y or a cash amount of £75 million.   **(10 marks)**

Plan 2

A new company, W, is to be formed which will issue shares to the shareholders of X in exchange for X's investment in Y and Z. W is to issue 130 million ordinary shares of £1 to the shareholders of X in exchange for their shares held in Y and Z. The group is being split into two separate companies W and X which will be quoted on the Stock Exchange.   **(8 marks)**

Plan 3

The assets and trade of Z are to be transferred to Y. Company Z would initially become a non-trading company. The assets and trade are to be transferred at their book value. The consideration for the transfer will be £60 million which will be left outstanding on the inter company account between Y and Z.   **(7 marks)**

Required

Discuss the key considerations and the accounting implications of the above plans for the X group. Your answer should show the potential impact on the individual accounts of X, Y and Z and the group accounts after each plan has been implemented.

(The mark allocation is shown in brackets next to each 'plan'.)   **(Total = 25 marks)**

D13 Ejoy

45 mins

ACR, 6/06

Ejoy, a public limited company, has acquired two subsidiaries and recently entered into a joint venture with another company. The details of the acquisitions are as follows:

Company	Date of acquisition	Ordinary share capital of £1 £m	Reserves at acquisition £m	Fair value of net assets at acquisition £m	Cost of investment £m	Ordinary share capital of £1 acquired £m
Zbay	1 June 20X4	200	170	600	520	160
Tbay	1 December 20X5	120	80	310	221	72

The draft profit and loss accounts for the year ended 31 May 20X6 are:

	Ejoy £m	Zbay £m	Tbay £m	Ivee £m
Turnover	2,500	1,500	800	20
Cost of sales	(1,800)	(1,200)	(600)	(12)
Gross profit	2,700	300	200	18
Other income	70	10	–	–
Distribution costs	(130)	(120)	(70)	(3)
Administrative expenses	(100)	(90)	(60)	(1)
Finance costs	(50)	(40)	(20)	
Profit before tax	490	60	50	4
Taxation	(200)	(26)	(20)	(2)
Profit for the period	290	34	30	2
Profit for year ended 31 May 20X5	190	20	15	–

The following information is relevant to the preparation of the group financial statements:

(a)   Tbay was acquired exclusively with a view to resale and at 31 May 20X6 the directors still intended to sell the company. The investment in Tbay is stated at £221 million in the financial statements of Ejoy. The shares of Tbay are quoted on the Stock Exchange. The share prices of Tbay were £3 per share at 1 December 20X5 and £3·10 per share at 31 May 20X6. The cost of purchasing the shares of Tbay was £5 million and this has been included in the cost of the investment.

(b)   Ejoy entered into a joint venture with another company on 31 March 20X6. The joint venture (Ivee) is a limited company and Ejoy has contributed assets at fair value of £20 million (carrying value £14 million). Each party will hold five million ordinary shares of £1 in the joint venture. The gain on the disposal of the assets to the joint venture (£6 million) has been included in 'other income'.

(c)   On acquisition, the financial statements of Tbay included a large cash balance. Immediately, Tbay paid a dividend of £40 million for the year. The whole of the dividend (£40 million) is included in other income in the profit and loss account of Ejoy. Since the acquisition of Zbay and Tbay, there have been no further dividend payments by these companies.

(d)   Zbay has a loan asset which is being carried at £60 million in the draft financial statements for the year ended 31 May 20X6. The loan's effective interest rate is six per cent. On 1 June 20X5 the company felt that because of the borrower's financial problems, it would receive £20 million in approximately two years time, on 31 May 20X7. At 31 May 20X6, the company still expects to receive the same amount on the same date. The loan asset is classified as 'loans and receivables'.

(e)   On 1 June 20X5, Ejoy purchased a five year bond with a principal amount of £50 million and a fixed interest rate of five per cent which was the current market rate. The bond is classified as an 'available for sale' financial asset. Because of the size of the investment, Ejoy has entered into a floating interest rate swap. Ejoy has designated the swap as a fair value hedge of the bond. At 31 May 20X6, market interest rates were six per cent. As a result, the fair value of the bond has decreased to £48·3 million. Ejoy has received £0·5 million in net interest payments on the swap at 31 May 20X6 and the fair value hedge has been 100% effective in the period. No entries have been made in the profit and loss account to account for the bond or the hedge.

(f) No impairment of the goodwill arising on the acquisition of Zbay had occurred at 1 June 20X5. However goodwill was to be impairment tested at 31 May 20X6 with no amortisation charged in the current year. The recoverable amount of the group's investment in Zbay was £521 million at 31 May 20X6 based upon its 'value in use'. Group policy is to amortise goodwill over eight years commencing on the day of acquisition. Impairment losses on goodwill and investments are charged to cost of sales.

(g) Assume that profits accrue evenly throughout the year and ignore any taxation effects. The Group wishes only to apply accounting standards that have been issued and not exposure drafts. Financial assets and liabilities are normally designated as at fair value through profit or loss unless otherwise stated.

Required

Prepare a consolidated profit and loss account for the Ejoy Group for the year ended 31 May 20X6 in accordance with UK accounting standards.

(25 marks)

D14 Case study question: Base Group   90 mins

(a) Base, a public limited company, acquired two subsidiaries, Zero and Black, both public limited companies, on 1 June 20X1. The details of the acquisitions at that date are as follows.

Subsidiary	Ordinary share capital of £1	Reserves	Fair value of net assets at acquisition	Cost of investment	Ordinary share capital acquired
	£m	£m	£m	£m	£m
Zero	350	250	770	600	250
Black	200	150	400	270	120

The draft profit and loss accounts for the year ended 31 May 20X3 are:

	Base	Zero	Black
	£m	£m	£m
Turnover	3,000	2,300	600
Cost of sales	(2,000)	(1,600)	(300)
Gross profit	1,000	700	300
Distribution costs	(240)	(230)	(120)
Administrative expenses	(200)	(220)	(80)
Operating profit	560	250	100
Interest payable	(20)	(10)	(12)
Investment income receivable (including inter company dividends paid May 20X3)	100	–	–
Profit before taxation	640	240	88
Tax	(130)	(80)	(36)
Profit after taxation	510	160	52
Dividends paid	(50)	(70)	–
Profit and loss reserves at 1 June 20X2	1,400	400	190

The following information is relevant to the preparation of the group financial statements.

(i) On 1 December 20X2, Base sold 50 million £1 ordinary shares in Zero for £155 million. The only accounting entry made by Base was to record the receipt of the cash consideration in the cash account and in a suspense account.

(ii) On 1 March 20X3, Black issued 100 million ordinary shares of £1 at a price of £2.65 per share. It was fully subscribed and paid up on that day. Base decided not to subscribe for the shares but the directors of Base had significant influence over the decision to issue the shares. The directors of Black had prepared financial information as at 28 February 20X3 for the purpose of the new issue of shares showing the carrying values of the net assets of Black to be £480 million.

(iii) Black had sold £150 million of goods to Base on 30 April 20X3. There was no opening stock of inter-company goods but the closing stock of these goods in Base's financial statements was £90 million. The profit on these goods was 30% on selling price.

(iv) Base has implemented in full FRS 17 *Retirement benefits* in its financial statements for the first time. The directors have included the following amounts in the figure for cost of sales.

	£m
Current service cost	4
Actuarial loss	5
Net amount of interest cost and expected return on assets	(3)
Charged to cost of sales	6

They are unsure as to whether they have treated these amounts correctly. Any prior year amounts relating to the adoption of FRS 17 have been adjusted on the opening profit and loss reserve.

(v) Base invested on 21 June 20X2 in a convertible debt instrument at a cost of £20 million. The debt is repayable in four years at £16 million but the conversion terms are extremely favourable. Base has included the convertible debt instrument in its balance sheet at £20 million.

(vi) Base had carried out work for a group of companies (Drum Group) during the financial year to 31 May 20X2. Base had accepted one million share options of the Drum Group in full settlement of the debt owed to them. At 1 June 20X2 these share options were valued at £3 million which was the value of the outstanding debt. The following table gives the prices of these shares and the fair value of the option.

	Share price	Fair value of option
31 May 20X2	£13	£3
31 May 20X3	£10	£1

The options had not been exercised during the year and remained at £3 million in the balance sheet of Base. The options can be exercised at any time after 31 May 20X5 for £8.50 per share.

(vii) The fair value adjustments have been incorporated into the subsidiaries' records. Amortisation of goodwill is charged to cost of sales over a period of five years.

(viii) Ignore the implications of capital gains tax for the purpose of the above information and assume profits accrue evenly throughout the year.

Required

Prepare a consolidated profit and loss account for the Base Group plc for the year ended 31 May 20X3 in accordance with the UK Companies Acts and Accounting Standards. (The amount of the consolidated profit dealt with in the holding company's accounts is not required.)

(26 marks)

(b) The turnover of the group results partly from the sale of software under licences which provide customers with the right to use these products. Base has stated that it follows emerging best practice in terms of its revenue recognition policy which it regards as US GAAP. It has stated that the Accounting Standards Board has been slow in developing a standard and the company has therefore adopted the US standard SAB101 *Revenue recognition in financial statements*. The group policy is as follows.

(i) If services are essential to the functioning of the software (for example setting up the software) and the payment terms are linked, the revenue for both software and services is recognised on acceptance of the contract.

(ii)   Software rentals or licences paid in advance are recognised over the term of the agreement and any balance credited to deferred income in the balance sheet.   **(6 marks)**

(c)   The directors of the Base group feel that their financial statements do not address a broad enough range of users' needs. They have reviewed the published financial statements and have realised that there is very little information about the corporate environmental governance. Base discloses the following environmental information in the financial statements.

    (i)   The highest radiation dosage to a member of the public
    (ii)   Total acid gas emissions and global warming potential
    (iii)   Contribution to clean air through emissions savings

Required

(i)   Explain the factors which provide encouragement to companies to disclose social and environmental information in their financial statements, briefly discussing whether the content of such disclosure should be at the company's discretion.   **(11 marks)**

(ii)   Describe how the current disclosure by the Base Group of 'corporate environmental governance' could be extended and improved.   **(7 marks)**

    (Total = 50 marks)

D15 Hyperinflation   45 mins

FRS 23 *The effects of changes in foreign exchange rates* states that where an entity has foreign operations, such as overseas subsidiaries, branches, joint ventures or associates, it should determine the functional currency of that foreign operation. The functional currency is the currency of the primary economic environment in which the entity operates. Where a foreign operation has a functional currency that is different from that of the reporting entity, it will be necessary to translate the financial statements of the foreign operation into the currency in which the reporting entity presents its financial statements.

However, where the foreign operation is located in a country with a high rate of inflation, the translation process may not be sufficient to present fairly the financial position of the foreign operation. Some adjustment for inflation should be undertaken to the local currency financial statements before translation. FRS 24 *Financial reporting in hyper-inflationary economies* deals with this issue.

Required

(a)   Explain the factors which should be taken into account in determining whether or not the functional currency of a foreign operation is the same as that of its parent.   **(10 marks)**

(b)   Discuss the effects that hyper-inflation can have on the usefulness of financial statements, and explain how entities with subsidiaries that are located in hyper-inflationary economies should reflect this fact in their consolidated financial statements. You should restrict your discussion to financial statements that have been prepared under the historical cost convention.   **(7 marks)**

(c)   On 30 November 20X3 Gold Co set up a subsidiary in an overseas country where the local currency is effados. The principal assets of this subsidiary were a chain of hotels. The value of the hotels on this date was 20 million effados. The rate of inflation for the period 30 November 20X3 to 30 November 20X7 has been significantly high. The following inflation is relevant to the economy of the overseas country.

	Effados in exchange for £	Consumer price index in overseas country
30 November 20X3	1.34	100
30 November 20X7	17.87	3,254

There is no depreciation charged in the financial statements as the hotels are maintained to a high standard.

Required

(i) Calculate the value at which the hotels would be included in the group financial statements of Gold Co on the following dates.

(1) At 30 November 20X3 and 30 November 20X7.

(2) At 30 November 20X7 after adjusting for current price levels. **(4 marks)**

(ii) Discuss the results of the valuations of the hotels, commenting on the validity of the different bases outlined above. **(4 marks)**

(Total = 25 marks)

D16 Question with helping hands: Zetec
45 mins

ACR, 12/01

Zetec, a public limited company, owns 80% of the ordinary share capital of Aztec, a public limited company which is a foreign operation. Zetec acquired Aztec on 1 November 20X1 for £44 million when the retained profits of Aztec were 98 million Krams (Kr). Aztec has not issued any share capital, nor revalued any assets since acquisition. The following financial statements relate to Zetec and Aztec.

BALANCE SHEET AT 31 OCTOBER 20X2

	Zetec £m	Aztec Krm
Fixed assets		
Tangible assets (including investments)	180	380
Investment in Aztec	44	
Intangible assets		12
Net current assets	146	116
Creditors falling due after one year	(74)	(320)
	296	188
Capital and reserves		
Ordinary shares of £1/1Kr	65	48
Share premium	70	18
Revaluation reserves	–	12
Retained earnings	161	110
	296	188

PROFIT AND LOSS ACCOUNTS FOR THE YEAR ENDED 31 OCTOBER 20X2

	Zetec £m	Aztec Krm
Turnover	325	250
Cost of sales	(189)	(120)
Gross profit	136	130
Distribution and administrative expenses	(84)	(46)
Operating profit	52	84
Interest payable	(2)	(20)
Profit before taxation	50	64
Taxation	(15)	(30)
Profit on ordinary activities after taxation	35	34
Extraordinary items	–	(22)
Dividends paid	(4)	–
Retained profit for the year	31	12

The directors of Zetec have not previously had the responsibility for the preparation of consolidated financial statements and are a little concerned as they understand that the financial statements of Aztec have been prepared under local accounting standards which are inconsistent in some respects with UK Generally Accepted Accounting

Practice (UK GAAP). They wish you to prepare the consolidated financial statements on their behalf and give you the following information about the financial statements of Aztec.

(a)   Under local accounting standards, Aztec had capitalised 'market shares' under intangible assets. Aztec acquired a company in the year to 31 October 20X2 and merged its activities with its own. The acquisition allowed the company to obtain a significant share of a specific market and, therefore, the excess of the price paid over the fair value of assets is allocated to 'market shares'. The amount capitalised was Kr12 million.

Further, under local accounting standards, from 1 November 20X1 Aztec classified revaluation gains and losses and the effects of changes in accounting policies as extraordinary items. During the year, the amounts classified as extraordinary items were as follows.

Revaluation loss

A fixed asset was physically damaged during the year and an amount of Kr9 million was written off its carrying value as an impairment loss. This asset had been revalued on 31 October 20X0 and a credit of Kr6 million still remains in revaluation reserve in respect of this asset.

Changes in accounting policy

A change in the accounting policy for research expenditure has occurred during the period, in an attempt to bring Aztec's policies into line with UK GAAP. Prior to November 20X1, research expenditure was capitalised and amortised. The amount included in extraordinary items as a prior year adjustment was Kr13 million.

(b)   The fair value of the net assets of Aztec at the date of acquisition was Kr240 million after taking into account any changes necessary to align the financial statements with UK GAAP. The directors do not know how to calculate the amount of goodwill. The increase in the fair value of Aztec over the net assets' carrying value relates to a stock market portfolio (included in tangible assets) held by Aztec. The value of these investments (in Krs) has not changed materially since acquisition.

(c)   Zetec sold £15 million of components to Aztec and these goods were shipped free on board (fob) on 31 May 20X2. The goods were received by Aztec on 30 June 20X2 as there had been a problem in the shipping of the goods. Zetec made a profit of 20% on selling price on the components. All of the goods had been utilised in the production process at 31 October 20X1 but none of the finished goods had been sold at that date. Aztec had paid for the goods on 31 July 20X2. This was the only inter company transaction in the year. Foreign exchange gains/losses on such transactions are included in cost of sales by Aztec.

(d)   The following exchange rates are relevant to the financial statements.

	Krams to the £
31 October 20X0	5
1 November 20X1	6
1 April 20X2	5.3
31 May 20X2	5.2
30 June 20X2	5.1
31 July 20X2	4.2
31 October 20X2	4
Weighted average for year to 31 October 20X2	5

(e)   Goodwill is capitalised and reviewed annually for impairment. There was no impairment in the value of goodwill.

Required

Prepare a consolidated profit and loss account (income statement) for the year ended 31 October 20X2 and a balance sheet as at that date for the Zetec group.

(Candidates should show any exchange gains or losses arising in the consolidated financial statements).

(25 marks)

Helping hands

1   Learn our format for translation of the profit and loss account and balance sheet.

2   It is best to do workings for tangible fixed assets and net current assets on the face of the P&L and balance sheet with reference to supporting workings where appropriate.

3   Remember that goodwill is translated at the closing rate, which means that there will be an exchange difference. The best and neatest way to calculate this difference is to set out your goodwill working as we have done.

D17 Memo

45 mins

ACR, 6/04

Memo, a public limited company, owns 75% of the ordinary share capital of Random, a public limited company which is situated in a foreign country. Memo acquired Random on 1 May 20X3 for 120 million crowns (CR) when the retained profits of Random were 80 million crowns. Random has not revalued its assets or issued any share capital since its acquisition by Memo. The following financial statements relate to Memo and Random.

BALANCE SHEETS AT 30 APRIL 20X4

	Memo £m	Random CRm
Tangible fixed assets	297	146
Investment in Random	48	
Loan to Random	5	
Current assets	355	102
Current liabilities	(205)	(60)
Creditors: amount falling due after one year	(30)	(41)
	470	147
Capital and reserves		
Ordinary shares of £1/1CR	60	32
Share premium account	50	20
Profit and loss account	360	95
	470	147

PROFIT AND LOSS ACCOUNTS
FOR YEAR ENDED 30 APRIL 20X4

	Memo £m	Random CRm
Turnover	200	142
Cost of sales	(120)	(96)
Gross profit	80	46
Distribution and administrative expenses	(30)	(20)
Operating profit	50	26
Interest receivable	4	–
Interest payable	–	(2)
Profit before taxation	54	24
Taxation	(20)	(9)
Profit after taxation	34	15

The following information is relevant to the preparation of the consolidated financial statements of Memo.

(a)   The directors wish to treat goodwill in accordance with FRS 23 as a foreign currency asset. Goodwill is written off over five years and the profit and loss account is translated at the average rate of exchange for the year.

(b) During the financial year Random has purchased raw materials from Memo and denominated the purchase in crowns in its financial records. The details of the transaction are set out below.

	Date of transaction	Purchase price £m	Profit percentage on selling price
Raw materials	1 February 20X4	6	20%

At the year end, half the raw materials purchased were still in the stock of Random. The inter-company transactions have not been eliminated from the financial statements and the goods were recorded by Random at the exchange rate ruling on 1 February 20X4. A payment of £6 million was made to Memo when the exchange rate was 2.2 Crowns to £1. Any exchange gain or loss on the transaction is still held in the current liabilities of Random.

(c) Memo had made an interest free loan to Random of £5 million on 1 May 20X3. The loan was repaid on 30 May 20X4. Random had included the loan in creditors of more than one year and had recorded it at the exchange rate at 1 May 20X3.

(d) The fair value of the net assets of Random at the date of acquisition is to be assumed to be the same as the carrying value.

(e) The functional currency of Random is the Crown.

(f) The following exchange rates are relevant to the financial statements.

	Crowns to £
30 April/1 May 20X3	2.5
1 November 20X3	2.6
1 February 20X4	2
30 April 20X4	2.1
Average rate for year to 30 April 20X4	2

(g) Memo has paid a dividend of £8 million in the financial year and this is not included in the profit and loss account.

Required

Prepare a consolidated profit and loss account for the year ended 30 April 20X4 and a consolidated balance sheet at that date in accordance with UK Generally Accepted Accounting Practice.

(Candidates should round their calculations to the nearest £100,000.) **(25 marks)**

D18 Preparation question: Cash flow statement

The following information relates to the draft financial statements of Lorna plc.

LORNA PLC: PROFIT AND LOSS ACCOUNT YEAR TO 30 SEPTEMBER 20X9

	£'000	£'000
Turnover		3,536
Materials consumed	1,079	
Labour costs	758	
Production overheads	453	
Cost of sales		(2,290)
Gross profit		1,246
Selling and distribution costs	(221)	
Administration	(252)	
		(473)
Interest payable	(85)	
Dividends receivable	24	
		(61)
		712
Taxation		(210)
Profit after tax		502

Dividends paid and payable for the year were £350,000.

LORNA PLC BALANCE SHEET AS AT:

	30 September 20X9			30 September 20X8		
	Cost £'000	Dep'n £'000	NBV £'000	Cost £'000	Dep'n £'000	NBV £'000
Fixed assets						
Tangible						
Land and buildings	2,000	750	1,250	1,700	745	955
Plant	1,368	525	843	940	310	630
	3,368	1,275	2,093	2,640	1,055	1,585
Investments						
Shares in						
Unquoted company			800			nil
			2,893			1,585
Current assets						
Stocks		758			628	
Debtors – all trade		260			194	
Dividend receivable		15			–	
Bank		22			–	
		1,055			822	
Creditors: amounts falling due within one year						
Creditors – all trade		234			253	
Dividends payable		200			180	
Taxation		251			204	
Government grants		125			75	
Overdraft		–			28	
		810			740	
Net current assets			245			82
Creditors: amounts falling due after more than one year						
Deferred tax		252			141	
Government grants		220			160	
7% debenture		968			Nil	
			(1,440)			(301)
			1,698			1,366

	30 September 20X9			30 September 20X8		
	Cost £'000	Dep'n £'000	NBV £'000	Cost £'000	Dep'n £'000	NBV £'000
Share capital and reserves						
Ordinary shares of £1 each			1,100			1,000
Reserves						
Share premium		180			100	
Profit and loss account		418			266	
			598			366
			1,698			1,366

Notes

1   Included in turnover are sales of £500,000 to Doon, a company located in Ruritania. This figure consists of two separate sales transactions, both of which have been translated into sterling. The first transaction, translated at £200,000 was paid in Rurits, the local currency. Lorna plc had difficulties in converting the Rurits into sterling. Doon's main activity relates to the extraction of crude oil, and as a result of previous exchange difficulties, it was agreed that Doon would pay for the second transaction in barrels of oil. The spot rate for the crude oil at the date it was shipped to Lorna was £10 per barrel. Lorna plc later used the crude oil in one of its manufacturing processes.

2   All depreciation charges and a credit of £80,000 relating to the amortisation of government grants have been included in production overheads. There were no disposals of fixed assets during the year.

3   During the year 10,000 ordinary shares were issued to employees under the company's employee share purchase scheme. The market value of these shares was £50,000. This amount has been correctly recorded in share capital and share premium. The terms of the share scheme meant that the employees were required to contribute only the nominal value of the shares. The net cost to the company of this transaction has been included in labour costs.

4   On 1 October 20X8 Lorna plc issued a £1,000,000 7% debenture at a discount of 5%. The debenture is redeemable on 30 September 20Y3 at a premium of 4%. Lorna plc has amortised the discount and premium on this financial instrument equally (straight-line) over its five-year life and included the amortisation charge in the interest payable figure.

5   On 1 October 20X8 Lorna plc acquired 15% of the share capital of Blackmore Ltd, one of its major materials suppliers. It has treated this as a fixed asset investment. Lorna plc has recently received the financial statements of Blackmore Ltd for the year to 30 September 20X9. These show an interim dividend paid of £60,000 and proposed final dividend of £100,000. Lorna plc received an interim dividend from Blackmore Ltd in March 20X9, and has accrued for its share of the proposed dividend.

Required

Prepare the cash flow statement for Lorna plc for the year to 30 September 20X9.

Note. The cash flow from operations must be prepared using the direct method; you are not required to prepare the reconciliation to operating profit nor the notes relating to net debt.

D19 Preparation question: Consolidated cash flow statement

On 1.9.20X5 Swing plc acquired 100% of Slide Ltd for £5,000 comprising £1,000 cash and 1,500 £1 shares. The balance sheet of Slide Ltd at acquisition was as follows:

	£
Fixed assets	2,000
Stock	1,300
Cash	200
	3,500

The consolidated balance sheet of Swing plc as at 31 December 20X5 was as follows:

	20X5		20X4	
	£	£	£	£
Goodwill		1,500		
Tangible assets		35,000		25,000
Current assets				
Stock	15,700		10,000	
Debtors	9,200		7,500	
Cash	3,800		1,500	
	28,700		19,000	
Creditors: amounts falling due within one year				
Trade creditors	7,300		6,100	
Tax	5,000		4,000	
	12,300	16,400	10,100	8,900
		52,900		33,900

	£	£
Share capital	11,500	10,000
Share premium	4,500	2,000
P&L a/c reserves	36,900	21,900
	52,900	33,900

The consolidated profit and loss account of Swing plc for the year ended 31 December 20X5 was as follows:

	20X5
	£
Operating profit	20,000
Tax	5,000
Profit after tax	15,000

Notes

1   Depreciation charged for the year was £5,000. The group made no disposals of fixed assets.
2   Goodwill on the acquisition of £1,500 has been capitalised as an asset.

Required

Prepare the consolidated cash flow statement of Swing plc for the year ended 31 December 20X5.

D20 Portal

45 mins

ACR, Pilot paper

Portal Group, a public limited company, has prepared the following group cash flow statement for the year ended 31 December 20X0.

PORTAL GROUP PLC
GROUP STATEMENT OF CASH FLOWS
FOR THE YEAR ENDED 31 DECEMBER 20X0 (DRAFT)

	£m	£m
Net cash inflow from operating activities		875
Returns on investments and servicing of finance		
Interest received	26	
Interest paid	(9)	
Minority interest	(40)	
		(23)
Taxation		31
Capital expenditure		
Purchase of tangible fixed assets	(380)	
Disposals and transfers of fixed assets at carrying value	1,585	
		1,205
Acquisitions and disposals		
Disposal of subsidiary	(25)	
Purchase of interest in joint venture	(225)	
		(250)
Net cash inflow before management of liquid resources and financing		1,838
Management of liquid resources		
Increase in short term deposits		(143)
Increase in cash in the period		1,695

The accountant has asked your advice on certain technical matters relating to the preparation of the group cash flow statement. Additionally the accountant has asked you to prepare a presentation for the directors on the usefulness and meaning of cash flow statements generally and specifically on the group cash flow statement of Portal.

The accountant has informed you that the actual change in the cash balance for the period is £165 million, which does not reconcile with the figures in the draft group cash flow statement above of £1,695 million.

The accountant feels that the reason for the difference lies in the incorrect treatment of several elements of the cash flow statement of which he had little technical knowledge. The following information relates to these elements.

(a)   Portal has disposed of a subsidiary company, Web plc, during the year. At the date of disposal (1 June 20X0) the following balance sheet was prepared for Web plc.

	£m	£m
Tangible fixed assets: valuation		340
depreciation		(30)
		310
Stocks	60	
Debtors	50	
Cash at bank and in hand	130	
	240	
Creditors: amounts falling due within one year (including taxation £25 million)	(130)	
		110
		420
		£m
Called up share capital		100
Profit and loss account		320
		420

The loss on the sale of the subsidiary in the group accounts comprised:

	£m
Sales proceeds: ordinary shares	300
cash	75
	375
Net assets sold (80% of 420)	(336)
Goodwill	(64)
Loss on sale	(25)

The accountant was unsure as to how to deal with the above disposal and has simply included the above loss in the cash flow statement without further adjustments.

(b)   During the year, Portal has transferred several of its tangible assets to a newly created company, Site plc, which is owned jointly with another company.

The following information relates to the accounting for the investment in Site plc.

	£m
Purchase cost: fixed assets transferred	200
cash	25
	225
Dividend received	(10)
Profit for year on joint venture after tax	55
Revaluation of fixed assets	30
Closing balance per balance sheet – Site plc	300

The cash flow statement showed the cost of purchasing a stake in Site plc of £225m.

(c)   The taxation amount in the cash flow statement is the difference between the opening and closing balances on the taxation account. The charge for taxation in the profit and loss account is £191 million of which £20 million related to the taxation on the joint venture.

(d)   Included in the cash flow figure for the disposal of tangible fixed assets is the sale and leaseback of certain land and buildings. The sale proceeds of the land and buildings were £1,000 million in the form of an 8% loan note repayable in 20Y2 at a premium of 5%. The total profit on the sale of fixed assets, including the land and buildings, was £120 million.

(e)   The minority interest figure in the statement comprised the difference between the opening and closing balance sheet totals. The profit attributable to the minority interest for the year was £75 million.

(f)   The net cash inflow from operating activities is the profit on ordinary activities before taxation adjusted for the balance sheet movement in stocks, debtors and creditors and the depreciation charge for the year. The interest receivable credited to the profit and loss account was £27 million and the interest payable was £19 million.

Required

(a)   Prepare a revised group cash flow statement for Portal plc, taking into account notes (a) to (f) above.

(18 marks)

(b)   Prepare a brief presentation on the usefulness and information content of group cash flow statements generally and specifically on the group cash flow statement of Portal.

(7 marks)

(Total = 25 marks)

D21 Case study question: Andash   **90 mins**

(a)   The following group draft financial statements relate to Andash, a public limited company:

ANDASH
DRAFT GROUP BALANCE SHEETS AT 31 OCTOBER

	20X6 £m	20X5 £m
Fixed assets		
Plant and machinery	5,170	4,110
Goodwill	111	130
Investment in associate	60	–
	5,341	4,240
Current assets		
Stocks	2,650	2,300
Debtors	2,400	1,500
Cash at bank and in hand	140	300
	5,190	4,100
Creditors: amounts falling due within one year		
Creditors	(4,700)	(2,800)
Interest payable	(70)	(40)
Current tax payable	(300)	(770)
	(5,070)	(3,610)
Net current assets	120	490
Total assets less current liabilities	5,461	4,730
Creditors: amounts falling due after more than one year:		
Long-term borrowings	(3,100)	(2,700)
Deferred tax	(400)	(300)
	(3,500)	(3,000)
Net assets	1,961	1,730
Capital and reserves		
Share capital – ordinary shares	400	370
Other reserves	120	80
Profit and loss account	1,241	1,100
	1,761	1,550
Minority interest	200	180
Capital employed	1,961	1,730

ANDASH
DRAFT CONSOLIDATED PROFIT AND LOSS ACCOUNT
FOR THE YEAR ENDED 31 OCTOBER 20X6

	£m
Turnover	17,500
Cost of sales	(14,600)
Gross profit	2,900
Distribution costs	(1,870)
Administrative expenses	(499)
Finance costs – interest payable	(148)
Gain on disposal of subsidiary	8
Profit before tax	391
Taxation	(160)
Profit after taxation	231
Equity minority interests	(40)
Profit for financial year	191

RECONCILIATION OF MOVEMENTS IN GROUP SHAREHOLDERS' FUNDS
FOR THE YEAR ENDED 31 OCTOBER 20X6

	Share capital £m	Other reserves £m	Profit and loss account £m	Total £m
Shareholders' funds at 31 October 20X5	370	80	1,100	1,550
Profit for period			191	191
Dividends			(50)	(50)
Issue of share capital	30	30		60
Share options issued				10
Shareholders' funds at 31 October 20X6	400	120	1,241	1,761

The following information relates to the draft group financial statements of Andash:

(i) There had been no disposal of plant and machinery during the year. The depreciation for the period included in cost of sales was £260 million. Andash had issued share options on 31 October 20X6 as consideration for the purchase of plant. The value of the plant purchased was £9 million at 31 October 20X6 and the share options issued had a market value of £10 million. The market value had been used to account for the plant and share options.

(ii) Andash had acquired 25 per cent of Joma on 1 November 20X5. The purchase consideration was 25 million ordinary shares of Andash valued at £50 million and cash of £10 million. Andash has significant influence over Joma. The investment is stated at cost in the draft group balance sheet. The reserves of Joma at the date of acquisition were £20 million and at 31 October 20X6 were £32 million. Joma had sold stock in the period to Andash at a selling price of £16 million. The cost of the stock was £8 million and the stock was still held by Andash at 31 October 20X6. There was no goodwill arising on the acquisition of Joma.

(iii) Andash purchased 100 per cent of a subsidiary Broiler, a public limited company on 1 November 20X4. The goodwill arising on acquisition was £90 million. The carrying value of Broiler's identifiable net assets (excluding goodwill arising on acquisition) in the group consolidated financial statements is £266 million at 31 October 20X6. The recoverable amount of Broiler is expected to be £260 million and no impairment loss has been recorded at 31 October 20X5. Goodwill is amortised over ten years using the straight line method.

(iv) On 30 April 20X6 a wholly owned subsidiary, Chang, had been disposed of. Chang prepared interim financial statements on that date which are as follows:

	£m
Plant and machinery	10
Stock	8
Debtors	4
Cash at bank and in hand	5
Creditors	(6)
Current tax payable	(7)
	14
Share capital	10
Profit and loss account	4
	14

The consolidated carrying values of the assets and liabilities at that date were the same as above. The group received cash proceeds of £32 million and the carrying amount of goodwill was £10 million.

(Ignore any taxation effects of the above adjustments required to the group financial statements and round all calculations to the nearest £million.)

BPP note. Assume no dividend has been received during the year from Joma Ltd.

Required

Prepare a group cash flow statement using the indirect method for the Andash Group for the year ended 31 October 20X6 in accordance with FRS 1 *Cash flow statements* after making any necessary adjustments required to the draft group financial statements of Andash as a result of the information above.

(Candidates are not required to produce the adjusted group financial statements of Andash)

(25 marks)

(b) Andash manufactures mining equipment and extracts natural gas. You are advising the directors on matters relating to the year ended 31 October 20X7.

The Directors are uncertain about the role of the Accounting Standards Board's *Statement of Principles for Financial Reporting*. Their view is that accounting is based on the transactions carried out by the company and these transactions are allocated to the company's accounting periods by using the matching and prudence concepts. The argument put forward by the directors is that the *Statement of Principles* does not take into account the business and legal constraints within which companies operate. Further they have given two situations which have arisen in the current financial statements where they feel that the current accounting practice is inconsistent with the *Statement of Principles*.

Situation 1

Andash has recently constructed a natural gas extraction facility and commenced production one year ago (1 November 20X6). There is an operating licence given to the company by the government which requires the removal of the facility at the end of its life which is estimated at 20 years. Depreciation is charged on the straight line basis. The cost of the construction of the facility was £200 million and the net present value at 1 November 20X6 of the future costs to be incurred in order to return the extraction site to its original condition are estimated at £50 million (using a discount rate of 5% per annum). 80% of these costs relate to the removal of the facility and 20% relate to the rectification of the damage caused through the extraction of the natural gas. The auditors have told the company that a provision for decommissioning has to be set up.

Situation 2

Andash purchased a building on 1 November 20X6 for £10 million. The building qualified for a grant of £2 million which has been treated as a deferred credit in the financial statements. The capital allowances for tax purposes are reduced by the amount of the grant. There are additional timing differences of £40 million in respect of deferred tax liabilities at the year end. Also the company has sold extraction equipment which carries a five year warranty. The directors have made a provision for the warranty of £4 million at 31 October 20X7 which is deductible for tax when costs are incurred under the warranty. In addition to the warranty provision the company has unused tax losses of £70 million. The directors of the company are unsure as to whether a provision for deferred taxation is required.

(Assume that the company is not discounting the deferred tax provision, depreciation of the building is straight line over ten years, and an initial capital allowance of 25% has been claimed on the building. Tax is payable at 30%)

Required

(i)   Explain the importance of the *Statement of Principles* to the reporting of corporate performance and whether it takes into account the business and legal constraints placed upon companies.   **(6 marks)**

(ii)   Explain with reasons and suitable extracts/computations, the accounting treatment of the above two situations in the financial statements for the year ended 31 October 20X7 under UK GAAP.

(14 marks)

(iii)   Discuss whether the treatment of the items appears consistent with the *Statement of Principles*.

(5 marks)

(Total = 50 marks)

D22 Case study question: Squire

90 mins

(a)   The following draft financial statements relate to Squire, a public limited company.

DRAFT GROUP BALANCE SHEET AT 31 MAY 20X2

	20X2 £m	20X1 £m
Fixed assets		
Intangible assets	80	65
Tangible assets	2,639	2,010
Investment in associate	545	550
	3,264	2,625
Current assets		
Stocks	1,300	1,160
Debtors	1,220	1,060
Cash at bank and in hand	90	280
	2,610	2,500
Creditors: amounts falling due within one year	(2,620)	(2,310)
Net current (liabilities) assets	(10)	190
Total assets less current liabilities	3,254	2,815
Creditors: amounts falling due after more than one year	(1,675)	(1,320)
Provisions for liabilities and charges – deferred tax	(200)	(175)
Minority interests – equity	(525)	(345)
	854	975
Pension asset	22	16
	876	991

	20X2 £m	20X1 £m
Capital and reserves		
Called up share capital	200	170
Share premium account	60	30
Revaluation reserve	66	286
Profit and loss account	550	505
	876	991

DRAFT GROUP PROFIT AND LOSS ACCOUNT
FOR THE YEAR ENDED 31 MAY 20X2

		£m	£m
Turnover:	continuing operations	6,674	
	acquisitions	2,100	
			8,774
Cost of sales			(7,310)
			1,464
Distribution and administrative expenses			(1,030)
Share of operating profit in associate			65
Operating profit:	continuing operations	324	
	acquisitions	175	
			499
Interest payable			(75)
Profit before taxation			424
Tax (including tax on income from associate £20 million)			(225)
Profit on ordinary activities after taxation			199
Minority interests: equity			(95)
Profit attributable to members of parent company			104

Equity dividends paid and payable for the period were £85,000.

DRAFT GROUP STATEMENT
OF TOTAL RECOGNISED GAINS AND LOSSES
FOR THE YEAR ENDED 31 MAY 20X2

	£m
Profit attributable to members of parent company	104
Actuarial gain on pension scheme	26
Impairment losses on fixed assets that do not represent consumption of economic benefits	(220)
	(90)

DRAFT RECONCILIATION OF SHAREHOLDERS' FUNDS
FOR THE YEAR ENDED 31 MAY 20X2

	£m
Total recognised gains and losses	(90)
Dividends	(85)
New shares issued	60
Total movements during the year	(115)
Shareholders' funds at 1 June 20X1	991
Shareholders' funds at 31 May 20X2	876

The following information relates to Squire.

(i)   Squire acquired a seventy per cent holding in Hunsten Holdings, a public limited company, on 1 June 20X1. The fair values of the net assets acquired were as follows.

	£m
Tangible fixed assets	150
Stocks and work in progress	180
Provisions for onerous contracts	(30)
	300

The purchase consideration was £200 million in cash and £50 million (discounted value) deferred consideration which is payable on 1 June 20X3. The provision for the onerous contracts was no longer required at 31 May 20X2 as Squire had paid compensation of £30 million in order to terminate the contract on 1 December 20X1. The group amortises goodwill over five years. The intangible asset in the group balance sheet comprises goodwill only. The difference between the discounted value of the deferred consideration (£50 million) and the amount payable (£54 million) is included in 'interest payable'.

(ii)   There had been no disposals of tangible fixed assets during the year. Depreciation for the period charged in cost of sales was £129 million.

(iii)   Creditors: amounts falling due within one year comprised the following items.

	20X2 £m	20X1 £m
Trade creditors	2,310	2,075
Interest payable	65	45
Corporation tax	200	160
Dividends payable	45	30
	2,620	2,310

(iv)   Creditors: amounts falling due after more than one year comprised the following.

	20X2 £m	20X1 £m
Deferred consideration – purchase of Hunsten	54	–
Creditors – purchase of fixed assets	351	–
Loans repayable	1,270	1,320
	1,675	1,320

(v)   The pension asset comprises the following.

	20X2 £m	20X1 £m
Surplus in scheme	35	23
Deferred tax liability	(13)	(7)
	22	16

	£m
Movement in year	
Surplus at 1 June 20X1	23
Current and past service costs charged to profit and loss account	(20)
Contributions paid to pension scheme	6
Actuarial gains	26
Surplus at 31 May 20X2	35

Required

Prepare a group cash flow statement using the indirect method for Squire Group plc for the year ended 31 May 20X2 in accordance with FRS 1 (revised) *Cash flow statements*. Your answer should include the following.

(i)   A reconciliation of operating profit to operating cash flows.
(ii) An analysis of cash flows for any headings netted in the cash flow statement.

The notes regarding the acquisition of the subsidiary and a reconciliation of net cash flow to movement in net debt are not required.   **(27 marks)**

You have been asked to conduct an environmental audit for the Squire Group to assess how 'green' it is in terms of energy consumption, use of renewable resources, and employee awareness of these issues.

(b)   Describe the information you would seek when planning the audit.   **(8 marks)**

(c)   Explain how would you test for employee awareness, and how would you involve all employees in the initiative.   **(6 marks)**

(d)   Discuss the reasons why companies wish to disclose environmental information in their financial statements. Discuss whether the content of such disclosure should be at the company's discretion.
                                                                                         (9 marks)
                                                                              (Total marks = 50)

D23 Baron   45 mins

The following draft financial statements relate to the Baron Group plc.

DRAFT GROUP PROFIT AND LOSS ACCOUNT
FOR THE YEAR ENDED 30 NOVEMBER 20X7

	£m	£m
Turnover		
Continuing operations	4,458	
Discontinued operations	1,263	
		5,721
Cost of sales		(4,560)
Gross profit		1,161
Distribution costs	309	
Administration expenses	285	
		(594)
		567
Income from interests in joint venture		75
Defence costs of take-over bid		(20)
Operating profit		
Continuing operations	438	
Discontinued operations	184	
		622
Loss on disposal of tangible fixed assets	(7)	
Loss on disposal of discontinued operations (note (a))	(25)	
		(32)
Interest receivable	27	
Interest payable	(19)	
		8
Profit on ordinary activities before taxation		598
Tax on profit on ordinary activities (note (c))		(191)
Profit on ordinary activities after taxation		407
Minority interests – equity		(75)
Profit attributable to members of the parent company		332

Dividends for the period amounted to £130m.

GROUP STATEMENT OF TOTAL RECOGNISED GAINS AND LOSSES
FOR THE YEAR ENDED 30 NOVEMBER 20X7

	£m
Profit attributable to members of the parent company	332
Deficit on revaluation of land and buildings	(30)
Deficit on revaluation of land and buildings in joint venture	(15)
Gain on revaluation of loan	28
Total recognised gains and losses relating to the year	315

DRAFT GROUP BALANCE SHEET AS AT 30 NOVEMBER 20X7

	20X7 £m	20X6 £m
Fixed assets		
Intangible assets	60	144
Tangible fixed assets (note (d))	1,415	1,800
Investments (notes (b) and (e))	600	–
	2,075	1,944
Current assets		
Stocks	720	680
Short term investments (note (e))	152	44
Debtors (note (f))	680	540
Cash at bank and in hand	24	133
	1,576	1,397
Creditors: amounts falling due within one year (note (g))	(1,601)	(1,223)
Net current assets	(25)	174
Total assets less current liabilities	2,050	2,118
Creditors: amounts falling due after more than one year	(186)	(214)
Provision for liabilities and charges – bid defence costs	(30)	(15)
Minority interests – equity	(330)	(570)
	1,504	1,319
Capital and reserves		
Called up share capital	440	440
Share premium account	101	101
Revaluation reserve	33	50
Profit and loss account	930	728
Total shareholders' funds – equity	1,504	1,319

The following information is relevant to the Baron Group plc.

(a)   The group disposed of a major subsidiary Piece plc on 1 September 20X7. Baron held an 80% interest in the subsidiary at the date of disposal. Piece plc's results are classified as discontinued in the profit and loss account.

The group required the subsidiary Piece plc to prepare an interim balance sheet at the date of the disposal and this is as follows.

	£m	£m
Tangible fixed assets (depreciation 30)		310
Current assets		
Stocks	60	
Debtors	50	
Cash at bank and in hand	130	
	240	
Creditors: amounts falling due within one year (including corporation tax – £25m)	(130)	
		110
		420
Called up share capital		100
Profit and loss account		320
		420

The consolidated carrying values of all the assets and liabilities at that date are as above. The depreciation charge in the profit and loss account for the period was £9 million. The carrying amount relating to goodwill in the group accounts arising on the acquisition of Piece plc was £64 million at 1 December 20X6. The loss on sale of discontinued operations in the group accounts comprises:

	£m
Sale proceeds	375
Net assets sold (80% × £420m)	(336)
Goodwill	(64)
	(25)

The consideration for the sale of Piece plc was 200 million ordinary shares of £1 in Meal plc, the acquiring company, at a value of £300 million and £75 million in cash. The group's policy is to amortise goodwill arising on acquisition but not in the year of sale of a subsidiary. The amortisation for the year was £20 million on other intangible assets.

(b) During the year, Baron plc had transferred several of its tangible assets to a newly created company, Kevla Ltd, which is owned jointly by three parties. The total investment at the date of transfer in the joint venture by Baron plc was £225 million at carrying value comprising £200 million in tangible fixed assets and £25 million in cash. The group has used equity accounting for the joint venture in Kevla Ltd. No dividends have been received from Kevla Ltd but the land and buildings transferred have been revalued at the year end.

(c) The taxation charge in the profit and loss account is made up of the following items.

	£m
Corporation tax	171
Tax attributable to joint venture	20
	191

(d) The movement on tangible fixed assets of the Baron Group plc during the year was as follows.

	£m
Cost or valuation 1 December 20X6	2,100
Additions	380
Revaluation	(30)
Disposals and transfers	(680)
At 30 November 20X7	1,770
Depreciation	
1 December 20X6	300
Provided during year	150
Disposals and transfers	(95)
At 30 November 20X7	355
Carrying value at 30 November 20X7	1,415
Carrying value at 1 December 20X6	1,800

(e) The investments included under fixed assets comprised the joint venture in Kevla Ltd (£265 million), the shares in Meal plc (£300 million), and investments in corporate bonds (£35 million). The bonds had been purchased in November 20X7 and were deemed to be highly liquid, although Baron plc intended to hold them for the longer term as their maturity date is 1 January 20X9.

The short term investments comprised the following items.

	20X7	20X6
	£m	£m
Government securities (Repayable 1 April 20X8)	51	23
Cash on seven day deposit	101	21
	152	44

(f) A prepayment of £20 million has been included in debtors against an exceptional pension liability which will fall due in the following financial year. Interest receivable included in debtors was £5 million at 30 November 20X7 (£4 million at 30 November 20X6).

(g)   Creditors: amounts falling due within one year comprise the following items.

	20X7 £m	20X6 £m
Trade creditors	1,300	973
Corporation tax	181	150
Dividends payable	80	70
Accrued interest	40	30
	1,601	1,223

Required

Prepare a group cash flow statement using the 'indirect method' for the Baron Group plc for the year ended 30 November 20X7 in accordance with the requirements of FRS 1 *Cash flow statements*. Your answer should include the following.

(a)   Reconciliation of operating profit to operating cash flows
(b)   An analysis of cash flows for any headings netted in the cash flow statement

(Candidates should distinguish net cash flows from continuing and discontinued operations.)   **(25 marks)**

The notes regarding the sale of the subsidiary and a reconciliation of net cash flow to movement in net debt are not required.

D24 George   45 mins

The balance sheets of George plc and its subsidiary companies Zippy Ltd and Bungle Ltd at 30 June 20X3 (the accounting date for all three companies) are given below:

	George plc £'000	£'000	Zippy Limited £'000	£'000	Bungle Limited £'000	£'000
Fixed assets						
Tangible assets (Note 3)	45,000		25,000		20,000	
Investments (Notes 1 and 2)	20,000		Nil		Nil	
		65,000		25,000		20,000
Current assets						
Stocks (Notes 3 and 4)	18,000		12,000		11,000	
Debtors (Notes 3 and 4)	15,000		10,000		9,000	
	33,000		22,000		20,000	
Creditors: amounts falling due within one year						
Trade creditors (Note 4)	10,000		6,500		6,000	
Tax payable	2,000		1,500		1,000	
Declared dividend payable (Note 5)	Nil		1,000		Nil	
Bank overdraft	5,000		4,000		3,000	
	17,000		13,000		10,000	
Net current assets		16,000		9,000		10,000
Total assets less current liabilities		81,000		34,000		30,000
Creditors: amounts falling due after more than one year						
Long-term loan (Note 3)		(20,000)		Nil		(4,000)
Provisions for liabilities						
Deferred tax	(2,000)		(1,000)		(1,500)	
Other (Note 3)	Nil		Nil		(1,200)	
		(2,000)		(1,000)		(2,700)
		59,000		33,000		23,300

Capital and reserves

Ordinary share capital (£1 shares)	25,000	15,000	10,000
10% £1 preference shares	Nil	10,000	Nil
Share premium account	10,000	Nil	4,000
Profit and loss account	24,000	8,000	9,300
	59,000	33,000	23,300

Notes to the balance sheets

1   On 1 July 20W0 (13 years ago), the date of incorporation of Zippy Ltd, George plc subscribed for all the ordinary shares of Zippy Ltd at par. Then on 1 July 20W5 (eight years ago), when its profit and loss account balance was £3 million, Zippy Ltd issued 10 million £1 preference shares at par. George plc subscribed for 50% of these shares.

2   On 30 June 20X3, George plc purchased 8 million £1 shares in Bungle Ltd. The terms of the purchase consideration were as follows.

   (a)   On 30 June 20X3, George plc issued 3 £1 ordinary shares for every 4 shares purchased in Bungle Ltd. The market value of the George plc ordinary shares at 30 June 20X3 was £4 per share.

   (b)   On 30 June 20X5, George plc will pay the former shareholders of Bungle Ltd £1 in cash for every share in Bungle Ltd they have purchased. This payment is contingent on the cumulative profits after tax of Bungle Ltd for the two years ending 30 June 20X5 being at least £3 million. At the date of carrying out the fair value exercise (see Note 3 below), the directors of George plc considered it probable that this cash payment would be made.

   (c)   No entries in respect of the purchase of shares in Bungle Ltd have been made in the balance sheet of George plc shown above.

3   Following the acquisition of Bungle Ltd, the directors of George plc carried out a fair value exercise as required by FRS 7 *Fair values in acquisition accounting*. The following matters are relevant and all potential fair value adjustments are material.

   (a)   Tangible fixed assets comprise land and buildings and plant and machinery. At 30 June 20X3, the land and buildings had a carrying value of £12 million and a market value of £15 million. The plant and machinery has a carrying value of £8 million. All the plant and machinery was purchased on 30 June 20X0 and was being depreciated on a straight-line basis over 8 years. No reliable estimate was available of the current market value of the plant and machinery, but, at 30 June 20X3, the plant would have cost £22 million to replace with new plant.

   (b)   The stock in hand at 30 June 20X3 would have cost £12 million to replace. This included a consignment of stock with an estimated replacement cost of £500,000 that had been damaged and could only be sold for scrap (estimated proceeds £100,000).

   (c)   Debtors include an amount of £400,000 that the directors of George plc consider doubtful.

   (d)   The long-term loan of Bungle Ltd is repayable at par on 30 June 20X6. Interest at 10% per annum is payable annually in arrears and the payment due on 30 June 20X3 has already been made. The relevant discount rate is 7%.

   (e)   The other provisions of Bungle Ltd comprise:

      (i)   £400,000 in respect of the closure of various retail outlets to which the directors of Bungle Ltd became committed prior to entering into acquisition negotiations with the directors of George plc

      (ii)   £800,000 in respect of the estimated cost of integrating Bungle Ltd into the George plc group. No detailed integration plans had been formulated by 30 June 20X3

4   George plc supplies a component to Zippy Ltd at cost plus a mark up of 20%. At 30 June 20X3, the stocks of Zippy Ltd included £1.5 million in respect of this component. At 30 June 20X3, the debtors of George plc showed an amount receivable from Zippy Ltd of £1.2 million, while the trade creditors of Zippy Ltd showed an amount payable to George plc of £600,000. On 29 June 20X3, George plc sent a consignment of components to Zippy Ltd at an invoiced price of £600,000. The consignment was received and recorded by Zippy Ltd on 2 July 20X3.

5   On 15 July 20X3, Zippy Ltd paid its preference dividend for the year ended 30 June 20X3. George plc made no entries in its financial statements in respect of this dividend until it was received in cash.

6   Goodwill on consolidation is amortised over its estimated useful economic life of 20 years. The amortisation of goodwill on consolidation of Bungle Ltd commences on 1 July 20X3.

Required

(a)   Compute the goodwill on consolidation of Bungle Ltd that will be shown in the consolidated balance sheet of George plc at 30 June 20X3. Provide justification for your figures where you consider this is needed.

(12 marks)

(b)   Prepare the consolidated balance sheet of George plc at 30 June 20X3.

(13 marks)

(Total = 25 marks)

D25 A Group

45 mins

The balance sheets of A plc, B Ltd, C Ltd and D Ltd at 31 December 20X8, the accounting date for all four companies, were as follows.

	A Ltd		B Ltd		C Ltd		D Ltd	
	£'000	£'000	£'000	£'000	£'000	£'000	£'000	£'000
Fixed assets								
Tangible assets	56,000		50,000		45,000		42,000	
Investments	90,000		71,200		nil		nil	
		146,000		121,200		45,000		42,000
Current assets								
Stocks	25,000		26,000		22,000		24,000	
Trade debtors	20,000		20,000		19,000		21,000	
Bank balances	6,000		nil		5,000		nil	
	51,000		46,000		46,000		45,000	
Creditors: amounts falling due within one year								
Trade creditors	12,000		13,000		12,000		11,000	
Taxation	6,000		6,500		6,000		4,500	
Bank overdrafts	nil		2,000		nil		1,000	
	18,000		21,500		18,000		16,500	
Net current assets		33,000		24,500		28,000		28,500
Creditors: amounts falling due after more than one year								
Long-term loans		(25,000)		(20,000)		nil		nil
		154,000		125,700		73,000		70,500
Capital and reserves								
Called up share capital (£1 shares)	80,000		75,000		45,000		40,000	
Share premium account	15,000		5,000		6,000		8,000	
Profit and loss account	59,000		45,700		22,000		22,500	
		154,000		125,700		73,000		70,500

Note 1 – Investments by A plc

On 1 January 20X2, A plc purchased 60 million shares in B Ltd for £1.50 per share. At that date, the profit and loss account of B Ltd showed a credit balance of £15 million and the profit and loss account of C Ltd showed a credit balance of £13 million.

Note 2 – Investments by B Ltd

- On 1 January 20X0, when the profit and loss account of C Ltd showed a credit balance of £10 million, B Ltd purchased 27 million shares in C Ltd for £1.60 per share.

- On 1 January 20X3, when the profit and loss account of D Ltd showed a credit balance of £12 million, B Ltd purchased 16 million shares in D Ltd for £1.75 per share. The remaining 24 million shares in D Ltd are held by a wide variety of investors.

Note 3 – Other details regarding share capital

All shares carry one vote at general meetings. The share premium accounts of all companies arose more than ten years ago. None of the companies has proposed any dividends at 31 December 20X8.

Note 4 – Amortisation of goodwill

The group amortises all goodwill on acquisition over 20 years.

Note 5 – Intra-group trading

B Ltd supplies a component that is used by the other three companies. B Ltd adds 20% to its production cost when setting a price for the product. Details of purchases of the product for 20X8, together with closing stocks, are as follows.

Company	Purchases from B Ltd	Amount in company stock at 31 December 20X8
	£'000	£'000
A plc	39,000	8,400
C Ltd	36,000	7,200
D Ltd	37,000	7,800

The following agreed amounts remain outstanding at 31 December 20X8 in respect of the purchases of the components:

- In creditors of A Ltd – £4 million
- In creditors of C Ltd – £2 million
- In creditors of D Ltd – £1.5 million

The equivalent amounts are included in the trade debtors of B Ltd at 31 December 20X8.

Note 6 – Fair value adjustments

- On 1 January 20X0 and 1 January 20X3, when B Ltd made its investments in C Ltd and D Ltd respectively, the directors of B Ltd carried out a fair value exercise and concluded that no fair value adjustments were necessary at either date.

- On 1 January 20X2, when A plc made its investment in B Ltd, the directors of A plc carried out a fair value exercise and concluded that the following fair value adjustments were necessary to the net assets of B Ltd and C Ltd.

	B Ltd		C Ltd	
	Carrying value	Fair value	Carrying value	Fair value
	£'000	£'000	£'000	£'000
Freehold land	22,000	25,000	15,000	16,000
Plant and machinery	24,000	26,000	18,000	19,000
Stocks	16,000	17,000	15,000	15,500

Freehold land is not depreciated. The estimated remaining useful life of the plant that was subject to the fair value adjustment was 10 years from 1 January 20X2. None of the fixed assets that were subject to fair value adjustments on 1 January 20X2 had been sold by 31 December 20X8. All the stock that was included in the balance sheets of B Ltd and C Ltd on 1 January 20X2 was sold in the following year.

On 30 June 20X1, B Ltd commenced legal action against a supplier in respect of financial losses incurred following the supply of faulty products. B Ltd was seeking damages of £2 million. In the event, the supplier (by making a payment of £1.5 million on 31 March 20X2) settled the action out of court. The payment of £1.5 million was the net amount receivable after tax implications. The balance sheet of B Ltd at 1 January 20X2 did not include any asset in respect of the contingent gain arising out of the legal action.

Required

(a) Explain how each of the investments in B Ltd, C Ltd and D Ltd will be treated in the consolidated financial statements of A plc for the year ended 31 December 20X8. You should provide a full justification of your answer in each case but *not* explain the consolidation method used.   **(4 marks)**

(b) Prepare the consolidated balance sheet of the A plc group at 31 December 20X8 in accordance with relevant accounting standards.   **(21 marks)**

(Total = 25 marks)

D26 A, B, C and D

45 mins

ACR, 12/04

The following balance sheets relate to A, B, C and D, all public limited companies, as at 30 November 20X4.

	A	B	C	D
	£m	£m	£m	£m
Tangible fixed assets	1,700	1,000	500	300
Investment in B at cost	1,250			
Investment in C at cost	800			
Investment in D at cost	450			
Net current assets	1,400	800	350	100
	5,600	1,800	850	400
Capital and reserves				
Called up share capital of £1	1,000	500	300	200
Share premium account	1,950	200	150	125
Profit and loss account	2,650	1,100	400	75
	5,600	1,800	850	400

The directors of A have decided to restructure the group at 30 November 20X4 and have agreed upon the following plan.

(a) A is to sell its holding in D to B in exchange for 110 million shares of B, plus a cash consideration of £50 million. The current value of the shares of the four companies is as follows as at 29 November 20X4.

	£
A	6
B	3.85
C	2.90
D	2.10

(b) C is to be demerged from the group and a new public limited company E formed. E will issue shares to the shareholders of A in exchange for A's investment in C. E issued 300 million ordinary shares of £1 to the shareholders of A.

(c) Goodwill arising on consolidation was impairment tested at 30 November 20X4 because of the impending move to International Financial Reporting Standards by the Group. The impairment loss when allocated only affected goodwill. Goodwill is currently amortised over five years.

(d)   The following information is also relevant to the group reconstruction. The subsidiaries were all 100% owned by A at the date of the reconstruction and the acquisition details are set out below.

Subsidiary	Profit/loss account at acquisition £m	Date of acquisition	Fair value of net assets at acquisition £m	Carrying value of goodwill at 30 November 20X4 after impairment test £m
B	450	01.12.X2	1,200	30
C	250	01.12.X2	700	20
D	50	01.12.X3	420	15

(e)   Any increase in the fair value of the net assets at acquisition is attributable to non-depreciable land. B, C and D have not issued any shares since acquisition other than the share issue proposed in the restructuring plan.

Required

(a)   (i)   Explain the impact of the group reconstruction on the individual accounts of A, B, C and D, showing suitable calculations.   **(7 marks)**

        (ii)   Prepare the individual balance sheets of A, B and D, and a consolidated balance sheet of the A group after the group reconstruction at 30 November 20X4.   **(14 marks)**

(b)   Prepare an analysis showing the composition of the group reserves of A at 30 November 20X4 after the reconstruction, showing the impact of the demerging of C.   **(4 marks)**

E1 Accounting framework for SMEs

45 mins

`ACR, 6/06`

The application of accounting standards to small and medium sized companies has been the subject of debate for several years. The Accounting Standards Board recently issued a revised *Financial Reporting Standard for Smaller Entities* (FRSSE) whose purpose is to simplify the reporting requirements for entities which satisfy certain size criteria. The debate has recently widened to include discussion as to whether there is a need for a set of *International Financial Reporting Standards* (IFRSs) which are specifically designed for small and medium sized entities (SMEs).

Required

(a)   Discuss the nature of the following issues in developing an accounting framework for SMEs with reference to the *Financial Reporting Standard for Smaller Entities*.

    (i)   The purpose of a framework and the type of entity to whom it should apply   **(7 marks)**

    (ii)   How existing standards should be modified to meet the needs of SMEs.   **(6 marks)**

    (iii)   How items not dealt with by the FRSSE should be treated.   **(5 marks)**

(b)   Discuss whether there is a need to develop a set of IFRSs specifically for SMEs.   **(7 marks)**

(Total = 25 marks)

E2 Seejoy

`ACR, 12/06`

Seejoy is a famous football club but has significant cash flow problems. The directors and shareholders wish to take steps to improve the club's financial position. The following proposals had been drafted in an attempt to improve the cash flow of the club. However, the directors need advice upon their implications.

(a)   **Sale and leaseback of football stadium (excluding the land element)**

The football stadium is currently accounted for using historical cost. The carrying value of the stadium will be £12 million at 31 December 20X6. The stadium will have a remaining life of 20 years at 31 December 20X6, and the club uses straight line depreciation. It is proposed to sell the stadium to a third party institution on 1 January 20X7 and lease it back under a 20 year finance lease. The sale price and fair value are £15 million which is the present value of the minimum lease payments. The agreement transfers the title of the stadium back to the football club at the end of the lease at nil cost. The rental is £1.2 million per annum (in advance) commencing on 1 January 20X7. The directors do not wish to treat this transaction as the raising of a secured loan.

The implicit interest rate on the finance in the lease is 5.6%   **(9 marks)**

(b)   **Player registrations**

The club capitalises the unconditional amounts (transfer fees) paid to acquire players.

The club proposes to amortise the cost of the transfer fees over ten years instead of the current practice which is to amortise the cost over the duration of the player's contract. The club has sold most of its valuable players during the current financial year but still has two valuable players under contract.

Player	Transfer fee capitalised £m	Amortisation to 31 December 20X6 £m	Contract commenced	Contract expires
A. Steel	20	4	1 January 20X6	31 December 20Y0
R. Aldo	15	10	1 January 20X5	31 December 20X7

If Seejoy win the national football league, then a further £5 million will be payable to the two players' former clubs. Seejoy are currently performing very poorly in the league. **(5 marks)**

(c) **Issue of bond**

The club proposes to issue a 7% bond with a face value of £50 million on 1 January 20X7 at a discount of 5% that will be secured on income from future ticket sales and corporate hospitality receipts, which are approximately £20 million per annum. Under the agreement the club cannot use the first £6 million received from corporate hospitality sales and reserved tickets (season tickets) as this will be used to repay the bond. The money from the bond will be used to pay for ground improvements and to pay the wages of players.

The bond will be repayable, both capital and interest, over 15 years with the first payment of £6 million due on 31 December 20X7. It will have an effective interest rate of 7.7%. There will be no active market for the bond and the company does not wish to use valuation models to value the bond. **(6 marks)**

(d) **Player trading**

Another proposal is for the club to sell its two valuable players, Aldo and Steel. It is thought that it will receive a total of £16 million for both players. The players are to be offered for sale at the end of the current football season on 1 May 20X7. **(5 marks)**

Required

Discuss how the above proposals would be dealt with in the financial statements of Seejoy for the year ending 31 December 20X7, setting out their accounting treatment and appropriateness in helping the football club's cash flow problems.

(Candidates do not need knowledge of the football finance sector to answer this question.)

(Total = 25 marks)

EVALUATING CURRENT DEVELOPMENTS

Questions F1 and F2 cover the Evaluating Current Developments, the subject of Part F of the BPP Study Text for Paper P2.

F1 Handrew

45 mins

ACR, 6/05

Handrew, a public limited company, is looking at the effect of adopting International Financial Reporting Standards (IFRS) on its financial statements for the year ended 31 May 2005. The directors of the company are worried about the effect of the move to IFRS on their financial performance and the views of analysts. The directors have highlighted some 'headline' differences between IFRS and current UK GAAP and require a report on the impact of a move to IFRS on the key financial ratios for the current period.

Differences between UK Generally Accepted Accounting Practice (UK GAAP) and IFRS

Leases

Long-term property leases are accounted for as operating leases in the financial statements of Handrew under UK GAAP.

IFRS requires property leases to be separated into land and building components with the elements being accounted for separately. The criteria under IFRS for the categorisation of leases into operating and finance are very similar to UK GAAP but are based on the substance of the transaction. Under the terms of the contract, the title to the land does not pass to Handrew but the title to the building passes to the company.

The company has produced a schedule of future minimum operating lease rentals and allocated these rentals between land and buildings based on their relative fair value at the start of the lease period. The operating leases commenced on 1 June 2004 when the value of the land was £270 million and the building was £90 million. Annual operating lease rentals paid in arrears commencing on 31 May 20X5 are land £30 million and buildings £10 million. These amounts are payable for the first five years of the lease term after which the payments diminish. The minimum lease term is 40 years.

The net present value of the future minimum operating lease payments as at 1 June 2004 was land £198 million and buildings £86 million. The interest rate used for discounting cash flows is 6%. Buildings are depreciated on a straight line basis over 20 years and at the end of this period, the building's economic life will be over. The lessor intends to redevelop the land at some stage in the future. Assume that the tax allowances on buildings are given to the lessee on the same basis as the depreciation charge. Under IFRS, a finance lease is initially recognised at the lower of the fair value of the asset and the present value of the minimum lease payments.

Plant and equipment

IFRS requires the residual value of a fixed asset to be reviewed at each balance sheet date based on current prices and the depreciation charge to be adjusted prospectively for any change in the residual value. The adjustment is treated in the same way as any change in an accounting estimate. The residual value of much of the plant and equipment is deemed to be negligible. However, certain plant (cost £20 million and carrying value £16 million at 31 May 2005) has a high residual value. At the time of purchasing this plant (June 2003) the residual value was thought to be approximately £4 million. However, the value of an item of an identical piece of plant already of the age and in the condition expected at the end of its useful life is £8 million at 31 May 2005 (£11 million at 1 June 2004). Plant is depreciated on a straight line basis over eight years.

Investment properties

IFRS requires investment property to be measured at fair value with gains on fair value reported in the profit and loss account or on a 'cost' basis similar to that in FRS 15 *Tangible fixed assets*. Fair value is the price at which the property can be exchanged between knowledgeable parties in an arm's length transaction and generally means the best value that can be gained for the asset. The company owns a hotel which consists of land and buildings and it has been designated as an investment property. The property was purchased on 1 June 2004. The carrying value of the hotel at market value at 31 May 2005 on an existing use basis is £40 million (land valuation £30 million, building £10 million). A revaluation gain of £5 million for the current year has been recognised in equity and no deferred tax has been provided on this gain. The company could sell the land for redevelopment for £50 million although it has no intention of doing so at the present time. The company wants to recognise holding gains/losses in profit and loss.

The directors have calculated the following ratios based on the UK GAAP financial statements for the year ended 31 May 2005.

Return on capital employed

$$\frac{\text{Profit before interest and tax}}{\text{Share capital, reserves and long term liabilities}} \quad \frac{£130m}{£520m} \times 100\% \quad \text{ie } 25\%$$

Gearing ratio

$$\frac{\text{Long term liabilities}}{\text{Share capital and reserves}} \quad \frac{£40m}{£480m} \times 100\% \quad \text{ie } 8.3\%$$

Price earnings ratio

$$\frac{\text{Market price per share}}{\text{Earnings per share}} \quad \frac{£6 \text{ per share}}{£0.5 \text{ per share}} \quad \text{ie } 12$$

The issued share capital of Handrew is 200 million ordinary shares of £1. There is no preference capital. The interest charge and tax charge in the profit and loss account are £5 million and £25 million respectively. Under IFRS, deferred tax is provided for on gains on the revaluation of fixed assets. Assume taxation is 30%.

Required

Write a report to the directors of Handrew:

(a)   Discussing the impact of the change to IFRS on the reported profit and balance sheet of Handrew at 31 May 2005.   **(18 marks)**

(b)   Calculate and briefly discuss the impact of the change to IFRS on the three performance ratios.   **(7 marks)**

(Candidates should show in an appendix calculations of the impact of the move to IFRS on profits, taxation and the balance sheet. Candidates do not need a knowledge of IFRS other than the information on IFRS provided in the question and need not take into account IFRS 1 *First-time adoption of International Financial Reporting Standards*.)

(Total = 25 marks)

F2 Guide

ACR, 12/04

Guide, a public limited company, is a leading international provider of insurance and banking services. It currently prepares its financial statements using UK GAAP and is concerned about the impact of the change to International Financial Reporting Standards (IFRS) from 2005.

The company is particularly worried about the impact of IFRS in the following areas.

(a)   The practical factors it will need to consider in implementing the change to IFRS   **(10 marks)**

(b)   Debt covenants   **(5 marks)**

(c)   Performance related pay   **(5 marks)**

(d)   The view of financial analysts   **(5 marks)**

Required

Draft a report to the directors Guide plc setting out your views and advice on the potential impact in each of the above four areas of a move to reporting under International Financial Reporting Standards.

(Total = 25 marks)

Answers

BPP LEARNING MEDIA

A1 Barriers to ethical standards

> **Top tips.** This question requires thought; the important elements of the answer are the problems of coming up with a clear definition, how much cultural factors should be allowed to influence ethical thinking and the need for the ethical framework to be more than a superficial gloss. The compatibility of ethical and commercial concerns is also an important issue to raise.

(a) **Problems with ethical framework**

Over the past few years the topic of business ethics has been examined and debated by many writers and academics. Although many organisation world-wide have adopted or redefined their business with ethics in mind, there are many people both in business and who study the area who see many barriers to businesses implementing an ethical framework.

What constitutes ethics

Defining 'what we mean by ethics' is for the most part easy to understand (inappropriate gifts, accepting money, environmental protection are all ethical issues). More **contentious issues** are topics such as workplace safety, product safety standards, advertising content and whistle-blowing which are areas where some businesses have been considered less ethical.

Necessity for action

Actions speak **louder than words.** Ethics are guidelines or rules of conduct by which we aim to live by. It is the actual conduct of the people in the organisation that, collectively, determines the organisation's standards – in other words it is not what the organisations 'says', but rather what it 'does' which is the real issue. It is no good having a code of ethics that is communicated to the outside world, but is ignored and treated with disdain by those inside the organisation.

Varying cultures

Globalisation and the resultant need to operate within different ethical frameworks has **undermined the idea** that ethical guidance can be defined in simple absolute terms. It may be culturally acceptable to promote by merit in one country, or by seniority in another. Paying custom officials may be acceptable in some cultures, but taboo in others.

Ethical versus commercial interests

Ethical and commercial interests have, it is argued, always diverged to some extent. Some organisations have seen for example the issues of **'being seen to be ethical'** as a good business move. However this viewpoint is pragmatic rather than idealistic; being ethical is seen as a means towards the end of gaining a better reputation and hence increasing sales.

Policies of others

Modern commercialism places great demands on everyone in organisations to succeed and provide the necessary revenues for the future growth and survival of the business. Acting with social responsibility can be hard, as not everyone plays by the same rules.

(b) **Need for practical steps**

If organisations are to **achieve a more ethical stance** they **need to put into place a range of practical steps** that will achieve this. Developing an ethical culture within the business will require the organisation to communicate to its workforce the 'rules' on what is considered to be ethical and is not. Two approaches have been identified to the management of ethics in organisations.

Rules-based approach

This is primarily designed to ensure that the organisation acts within the letter of the law, and that violations are **prevented, detected and punished.** This is very much the case in the US, where legal compliance is very much part of the business environment. The problem here is that legislation alone will not have the desired effect, particularly for those businesses who operate internationally and therefore may not be subject to equivalent legislation in other jurisdictions.

Integrity-based programmes

Here the concern is not for any legal control, but with developing an **organisational culture.** The task of ethics management is to define and give life to an organisation's **defining values** and to create an environment that supports ethical behaviour and to instil a sense of **shared accountability** among all employees. Integrity-based programmes require not just words or statements, but on seeing and doing and action. The purpose with this approach is not to exact revenge through legal compliance but the develop within the workforce a **culture of ethics** that has **value and meaning** for those in it.

The integrity-based approach encompasses all aspects of the business – **behavioural assumptions** of what is right or is wrong; staffing, education and training, audits and activities that promote a social responsibility across the workforce.

Organisations can also take further steps to reinforce their values by adopting **ethical committees** who are appointed to rule on misconduct and to develop ethical standards for the business.

Kohlberg's framework

Kohlberg's ethical framework demonstrates how individuals advance through different levels of moral development, their advance relating to how their **moral reasoning develops.** Kohlberg's framework goes from individuals who see ethical decisions solely in terms of the good or bad consequences for themselves through to individuals who choose to follow universal ethical principles, even if these conflict with the values of the organisation for which they are working.

The importance of different components of an organisation's ethical framework can indicate the level of moral reasoning that staff are in effect expected to employ.

Pre-conventional reasoning

A rules-based framework that sets out **expected behaviour** in detail and has strong provisions for punishing breaches implies that staff are at the lowest stage of development – they define right or wrong solely in terms of expected rewards or punishments. An emphasis on bureaucratic controls, including the reporting of all problems that occur with staff, would be designed to prevent 'You scratch my back, I scratch yours' behaviour that is also part of moral reasoning at this level.

Conventional reasoning

An emphasis on a **strong ethical culture** would indicate staff are expected to adopt the intermediate stage of Kohlberg's framework. **Peer pressure**, also the concepts that managers should set an **example**, are features of this sort of ethical approach; if also the organisation appears to be responding to **pressures from outside** to behave ethically, this suggests higher level reasoning within this stage

Post-conventional reasoning

An ethical approach based on staff using post-conventional reasoning would be likely to emphasise adherence to an ethical code. A detailed code based on rights and values of society would imply ethical reasoning based on the idea of the organisation **enforcing a social contract.** Higher-level reasoning would be expected if the code was framed in terms of more abstract principles such as justice or equality.

A2 Question with answer plan: Glowball

Top tips. A good test of report writing skills. To produce a good answer here you need to be able to explain the main issues in environmental reporting and to identify these in a scenario. Don't forget to think about FRSs, especially FRS 12 when reading the scenario. Your answer should read well as a report to the directors, as well as addressing all the technical issues.

Answer plan

Current disclosures – mention

Current disclosures are voluntary

Guidelines and Codes of Practice – list a few especially the Global Reporting Initiative

Environmental events:

(a)   FRS 12.
        No legal obligation but may be a constructive obligation.

(b)   Set up as provision for fine.
        Put in context in the environmental report.

(c)   Emphasise accurate but fair reporting.
        No provision.

(d)   Environmental report to mention steps taken to rectify the problem.
        Provision must be made in full.

Marking scheme

			Marks
(a)	Current reporting requirements		10
(b)	Restoration		5
	Infringement of law		4
	Emissions		4
	Decommissioning activities		4
	Report		4
		Available	31
		Maximum	25

REPORT

To: The Directors
          Glowball plc
From: A N Accountant
Date: 12 May 20X1

Environmental Reporting

Introduction

The purpose of this report is to provide information about current reporting requirements and guidelines on the subject of environmental reporting, and to give an indication of the required disclosure in relation to the specific events which you have brought to my attention. We hope that it will assist you in preparing your environmental report.

Current reporting requirements and guidelines

Most businesses, certainly those in the UK, have generally ignored environmental issues in the past. However, the use and misuse of natural resources all lead to environmental costs generated by businesses, both large and small.

There are very few rules, legal or otherwise, to ensure that companies disclose and report environmental matters. Any **disclosures tend to be voluntary**, unless environmental matters happen to fall under standard accounting principles. Environmental matters may be reported in the accounts of companies in the following areas.

- Contingent liabilities
- Exceptional charges
- Operating and financial review comments
- Profit and capital expenditure focus

The voluntary approach contrasts with the position in the United States, where the SEC/FASB accounting standards are obligatory.

While nothing is compulsory, there are a number of **published guidelines** and **codes of practice**, including:

- The *Valdez Principles*
- The Confederation of British Industry's guideline *Introducing Environmental Reporting*
- The ACCA's *Guide to Environment and Energy Reporting*
- The Coalition of Environmentally Responsible Economies (CERES) formats for environmental reports
- The Friends of the Earth *Environmental Charter for Local Government*
- The Eco Management and Audit Scheme Code of Practice

The question arises as to verification of the environmental information presented. Companies who adopt the Eco Management and Audit Scheme must have the report validated by an external verifier. In June 1999, BP Amoco commissioned KPMG to conduct an independent audit of its greenhouse gas emissions in the first ever **environmental audit**.

Comments on 'environmental events'

(a)   Of relevance to the farmland restoration is FRS 12 *Provisions, contingent liabilities and contingent assets*. Provisions for environmental liabilities should be recognised where there is a **legal or constructive obligation** to rectify environmental damage or perform restorative work. The mere existence of the restorative work does not give rise to an obligation and there is no legal obligation. However, it could be argued that there is a constructive obligation arising from the company's approach in previous years, which may have given rise to an **expectation** that the work would be carried out. If this is the case, a provision of £150m would be required in the financial statements. In addition, this provision and specific examples of restoration of land could be included in the environmental report.

(b)   The treatment of the **fine** is straightforward: it is an obligation to transfer economic benefits. An estimate of the fine should be made and a **provision** set up in the financial statements for £5m. This should be mentioned in the environmental report. The report might also **put the fines in context** by stating how many tests have been carried out and how many times the company has passed the tests. The directors may feel that it would do the company's reputation no harm to point out the fact that the number of prosecutions has been falling from year to year.

(c)   These statistics are good news and need to be covered in the environmental report. However, the emphasis should be on **accurate factual reporting** rather than boasting. It might be useful to provide target levels for comparison, or an industry average if available. The emissions statistics should be split into three categories:

- Acidity to air and water
- Hazardous substances
- Harmful emissions to water

As regards the aquatic emissions, the £70m planned expenditure on **research** should **be mentioned in the environmental report**. It shows a commitment to benefiting the environment. However, **FRS 12 would not permit a provision** to be made for this amount, since an obligation does not exist and the **expenditure is avoidable**. Nor does it qualify as development expenditure under SSAP 13.

(d)   The environmental report should mention the steps the company is taking to minimise the harmful impact on the environment in the way it sites and constructs its gas installations. The report should also explain the policy of dismantling the installations rather than sinking them at the end of their useful life.

Currently the company builds up a provision for decommissioning costs over the life of the installation. However, FRS 12 does not allow this. Instead, the **full amount must be provided** as soon as the obligation to transfer economic benefits exists. The obligation exists right at the beginning of the installation's life, and so the full £407m must be provided for. A corresponding asset is created.

B1 Prochain

Top tips. This question was a case study that dealt with the accounting issues for an entity engaged in the fashion industry. The areas examined were fundamental areas of the syllabus: fixed assets, intangible assets, determination of the purchase consideration for the subsidiary, and research and development expenditure. Tricky bits to get right were:

- A provision for dismantling the 'model areas' would need to be set up and discounted back to the present.
- Contingent consideration that is not probable would not be included in the cost of acquisition.
- Investment properties do not include properties owned and occupied by the entity.

Easy marks. Stating the obvious – that the model areas are tangible fixed assets and need to be depreciated will earn you easy marks, as will mentioning the basic distinction between research and development expenditure and listing the criteria when talking about the brand.

Examiner's comment. Generally, candidates answered the question quite well, obtaining a pass mark, although accounting for the non-current (fixed) assets did confuse some candidates.

Marking scheme

	Marks
Model areas	7
Purchase of Badex	8
Research and Development	6
Apartments	4
	25

Model areas

FRS 15 *Tangible fixed assets* is the relevant standard here. The model areas have physical substance, are held for use in the supply of goods and are used on a continuing basis in the entity's activities. The company should recognise the costs of setting up the model areas as **tangible fixed assets** and should **depreciate** the costs over their useful economic lives. **Subsequent measurement should be based on cost**. In theory the company could revalue the model areas, but it would be difficult to arrive at a reliable valuation.

FRS 15 states that the initial cost of an asset **should include** the initial estimate of the **costs of dismantling and removing the item and restoring the site** where the entity has an obligation to do so. **A present obligation appears to exist**, as defined by FRS 12 *Provisions, contingent liabilities and contingent assets* and therefore the entity should also **recognise a provision** for that amount. The provision should be **discounted to its present value** and the unwinding of the discount recognised in the profit and loss account.

At 31 May 20X6, the entity should recognise a tangible fixed asset of £15.7 million (cost of £23.6 million (W) less accumulated depreciation of £7.9 million (W)) and a provision of £3.73 million (W).

Working

	£m
Cost of model areas	20.0
Plus provision ($20 \times 20\% \times \dfrac{1}{1.055^2}$ (=0.898)	3.6
Cost on initial recognition	23.6
Less accumulated depreciation ($23.6 \times 8/24$)	(7.9)
Net book value at 31 May 2006	15.7
Provision: on initial recognition ($20 \times 20\% \times 0.898$)	3.60
Plus unwinding of discount ($3.6 \times 5.5\% \times 8/12$)	0.13
Provision at 31 May 20X6	3.73

Purchase of Badex

FRS 7 *Fair values in acquisition accounting* states that the cost of an acquisition is the amount of **cash paid**, plus the **fair value of any other consideration** given plus the **expenses incurred directly** in making the acquisition. Fair value is measured at the date on which control passes to the acquirer. Where any of the consideration is **deferred,** the amount should be **discounted to its present value**. Where the amount of consideration is **contingent on one or more future events**, the cost should include a **reasonable estimate** of the **amount expected to be payable** in future and these estimates should be **adjusted** as more certain information becomes available.

The purchase consideration consists of **£100 million paid on the acquisition date** plus a **further £25 million payable on 31 May 20X7**, including **£15 million payable only if profits exceed forecasts.** At the acquisition date it appeared that **profit forecasts would not be met** and that therefore payment of the contingent consideration of £15 million was **not probable**. This situation had not changed by 31 May 20X6. Therefore the **cost of the acquisition** at both dates is **£109 million** ($100 + 10 \times 0.898$).

A further issue concerns the valuation and treatment of the 'Badex' brand name. The brand name is an internally generated intangible asset of Badex, and therefore it will not be recognised in the balance sheet of Badex. FRS 10 *Goodwill and intangible assets* states that intangible assets can only be recognised separately from goodwill if they are **identifiable** (separable), are **controlled** by the entity and their value can be **measured reliably**. Although Prochain controls the brand, it is **not clear** whether either of the other two criteria have been met, despite the valuation at £20 million for the purpose of the sale to Prochain. If the entity can **demonstrate that the criteria have been met**, the brand should be **recognised separately in the consolidated balance sheet**, otherwise it should be **subsumed within goodwill**.

Development of own brand

SSAP 13 *Accounting for research and development* makes a distinction between research and development activities. Research expenditure is part of an entity's continuing operations and it is normally impossible to demonstrate that it will generate economic benefits in future periods. Therefore expenditure on **research** must be **recognised as an expense when it occurs**.

Development expenditure is normally undertaken for commercial reasons and is expected to generate future economic benefits in the form of increased revenue or reduced costs. Therefore development expenditure **may be recognised** as an asset if it meets **all the following criteria**.

(a)   There is a **clearly defined project**.
(b)   The related **expenditure** is **separately identifiable**.
(c)   The project is **technically feasible** and **commercially viable**.
(d)   Total development **costs** are reasonably expected to be **exceeded by future revenue**.
(e)   Adequate **financial and other resources** to complete the project **will be available**.

Assuming that all these criteria are met, the entity may either defer development expenditure to future periods or charge it to the profit and loss account as it is incurred. SSAP 13 is silent on the type of expenditure that may be capitalised, but research and development activities do not normally include **market research** and **legal and**

administrative work and these costs **should not be included**. The **cost of upgrading** existing machinery can be recognised as part of **tangible fixed assets**. Therefore the expenditure on the project should be treated as follows:

	Expense (profit and loss account)	Recognised in balance sheet	
		Intangible assets	Tangible fixed assets
	£m	£m	£m
Research	3		
Prototype design		4	
Employee costs		2	
Development work		5	
Upgrading machinery			3
Market research	2		
Legal costs	1		
	6	11	3

Prochain can **recognise £11 million** as an intangible asset. If this treatment is adopted, the asset should be **amortised**. Amortisation should start when Prochain commences commercial production of the sports clothes.

Apartments

The apartments are leased to persons who are under contract to the company. Therefore they **cannot be classified as investment property**. SSAP 19 *Accounting for investment properties* specifically states that **property owned and occupied by a company for its own purposes** is not investment property. The apartments must be treated as **land and buildings**, carried at cost or a valuation and depreciated over their useful economic lives.

Although the rent is below the market rate the difference between the actual rent and the market rate is simply **income foregone** (or an opportunity cost). In order to recognise the difference as an employee benefit cost it would also be necessary to **gross up rental income** to the market rate. The financial statements would **not give a true and fair view** of the financial performance of the company. Therefore the company **cannot recognise the difference** as an employee benefit cost.

B2 Question with helping hands: Impairment of assets

Top tips. This question required you to discuss the impairment of assets in terms of the indicators of the impairment loss under FRS 11. The final part of the question required candidates to apply the principles of part (a) to two small cases. Part (b) is a good illustration of how the examiner could test your ability to apply an accounting standard by asking you to explain how certain events will be reflected in the financial statements. Notice that the requirement in part (b) asks you to 'describe' – number-crunching alone is not sufficient.

Review your answer carefully.

Examiner's comment. Candidates performed very well on this question, particularly parts (a) and (b)(i). In part (b)(ii) some candidates did not realise that the carrying amount of the asset should not be reduced below net realisable value.

(a)   (i)   **Indications** of an impairment loss include the following.

(1)   A significant **decrease in the market value** of an asset in excess of normal depreciation

(2)   Adverse, significant **changes in the value of the business** or market in which the asset is used

(3)   **Technological, economic, legal** or **environmental changes** affecting the business in which the asset is used

(4)   **Financial factors** such as interest rate changes, market profitability, current period operating losses and net cash outflows adversely affecting the entity which uses the asset

(5)   A major loss of **key employees**

(6)   Damage, obsolescence or other **physical changes** to the asset

(7)   An indication that construction or purchase **costs have increased** so that expected profits from new assets will not arise as originally expected

(8)   **Management commitment** to **reorganisation or redundancy programmes**

(9)   **Adverse changes in the fair value indicators** used to establish the fair value of an asset, eg multiples of turnover

(ii)   Under FRS 11 possible impairment losses are **treated** as follows.

(1)   If any of the above indicators suggest an impairment has occurred then an **impairment review** must be carried out.

(2)   The **carrying value** of an asset is **compared to its recoverable amount** (the higher of NRV and value in use).

(3)   For assets held at cost less depreciation if the **carrying amount exceeds** the **recoverable amount**, the asset is impaired and must be **written down** through the profit and loss account.

(4)   Where assets are held at **valuation impairment losses** are recognised in the **statement of total recognised gains and losses** until the carrying value falls below depreciated historical cost. Impairments below depreciated historical cost are recognised in profit and loss account.

(5)   It may be more convenient to test impairment for **groups of assets** known as **income generating units** (IGU). Impairment should be tested for the smallest IGU which produces an independent income stream. Impairment **losses** in an IGU should be **allocated firstly to goodwill, then capitalised intangibles and finally to tangible assets**.

(6)   **Past impairment losses may be reversed** if the recoverable amount increases because of changed economic conditions. The losses should only be reversed to the original carrying amount, ie the amount it would have been if the original impairment had not occurred.

(7)   When impairment losses arise on fixed assets, the **remaining useful economic life should be reviewed** and revised if necessary.

(b)   (i)   Impaired assets need to be written down to their recoverable amount, which is the higher of NRV and value in use.

For the productive assets:

Carrying value	£290,000
Value in use	£248,700
NRV	£120,000

Note. Value in use is calculated as the discounted present value of cash flows from use of the asset. The cash flows are three years of £100,000, therefore use a discount factor (from tables) of 2.487.

The impairment loss is therefore £(290,000 − 248,700) = £41,300.

This will be written off to the profit and loss account.

(ii)   Impairment losses should be recognised if the recoverable amount of the income generating unit is less than the carrying value of the unit (the taxi business).

At 1 February 20X8

	1.1.X8	Impairment loss	1.2.X8
	£'000	£'000	£'000
Goodwill (230 – 190)	40	(15)	25
Intangibles	30	-	30
Vehicles	120	(30)	90
Sundry net assets	40	–	40
	230	(45)	185

An impairment loss of £30,000 is recognised for the stolen vehicle; the balance of £15,000 attributable to the IGU is applied initially to goodwill.

At 1 March 20X8

	1.2.X8 £'000	Impairment loss £'000	1.3.X8 £'000
Goodwill (230 − 190 − 15)	25	(25)	-
Intangibles	30	(5)	25
Vehicles	90	–	90
Sundry net assets	40	–	40
	185		155

In this case, there is an indication that the value of the intangible asset, the licence, has fallen to £25,000 so an impairment loss of £5,000 is recognised. There is no indication that the other tangible assets are impaired but value in use has fallen to £150,000.

NRV is therefore assumed to be £185,000 − £25,000 (goodwill) − £5,000 (licence)= £155,000.

The carrying amount is reduced to the higher of NRV or value in use as the recoverable amount.

B3 Ryder

Top tips. This is a mixed standard question, of the kind that the examiner generally likes.

Easy marks. Part (a) is fairly straightforward. You should be familiar with FRS 11, even if you missed the FRED 32 aspect.

Examiner's comment. This question was generally well answered. The question was quite discriminating as there was in most cases a correct answer rather than an issue to discuss. Surprisingly many candidates did not know how to deal with a proposed dividend or how to deal with contingent consideration on the purchase of subsidiary. Candidates dealt well with the property intended for sale but many candidates did not realise that cash settled share based payments (share appreciation rights) are remeasured to fair value at each reporting date. There was some confusion in candidate's answers over what constitutes 'grant date' and 'vesting date' and the importance for the share based payment transactions. The question was quite discriminating as there was in most cases a correct answer rather than an issue to discuss. Surprisingly many candidates did not know how to deal with a proposed dividend or how to deal with contingent consideration on the purchase of subsidiary. Candidates dealt well with the property intended for sale but many candidates did not realise that cash settled share based payments (share appreciation rights) are remeasured to fair value at each reporting date. There was some confusion in candidate's answers over what constitutes 'grant date' and 'vesting date' and the importance for the share based payment transactions.

(a)   **Disposal of subsidiary**

The issue here is the value of the subsidiary at 31 October 20X5. The directors have stated that there has been no significant event since the year end which could have resulted in a reduction in its value. This, taken together with the loss on disposal, indicates that the subsidiary had **suffered an impairment at 31 October 20X5**. FRS 21 requires the sale to be treated as an **adjusting event** after the balance sheet date as it provides **evidence of a condition that existed at the balance sheet date.**

The assets of Krup should be **written down to their recoverable amount**. In this case this is the eventual sale proceeds. Therefore the value of the net assets and purchased goodwill of Krup should be **reduced by £11 million** (the loss on disposal of £9 million plus the loss of £2 million that occurred between 1 November 20X5 and the date of sale). FRS 11 *Impairment of fixed assets and goodwill* states that an impairment loss should be allocated to goodwill first and therefore the **purchased goodwill of £12 million is reduced to £1 million**. The impairment loss of £11 million is **recognised in the profit and loss account**. The disposal is **disclosed** in the notes to the financial statements in accordance with FRS 21.

(b)   **Issue of shares**

FRS 7 *Fair values in acquisition accounting* requires that where the amount of the purchase consideration is **contingent on one or more future events**, the cost of acquisition should include a **reasonable estimate of the fair value of amounts expected to be payable** in the future. Ryder has **correctly included** an estimate of the amount of consideration in the cost of the acquisition on 21 January 20X4, because the average profits of Metalic suggested that the payment of the additional consideration was probable. This estimate would have been based on the fair value of Ryder's ordinary shares at that date, which has since **increased from £10 per share to £11 per share**. Therefore the **cost of acquisition must be adjusted**, with a corresponding **adjustment to goodwill**. As a result, **goodwill increases by £300,000** (300,000 × 11 – 10). The adjustment is treated as a **change of accounting estimate** in accordance with FRS 18 *Accounting policies* and the change is **recognised in the current period.**

The value of the contingent shares should be included in a **separate category of shares to be issued within shareholders' funds** (equity) in the balance sheet at 31 October 20X5. They should be transferred to share capital and share premium after the actual issue of the shares on 12 November 20X5.

The other matter is whether the share issue and the bonus issue affect the calculation of earnings per share for the year ended 31 October 20X5. FRS 22 *Earnings per share* states that **contingently issuable shares should be included** in the calculation of basic and diluted earnings per share **only from the date that all conditions are met**. As the conditions **were met at 31 October 20X5**, the shares **should be included** in the calculation from that date, even though the shares were not issued until after the year end. FRS 22 also states that if there is a **bonus share issue after the year end but before the financial statements are authorised for issue**, the bonus shares **should be included** in the calculation (and in the calculation of earnings per share for all previous periods presented).

Both FRS 21 and FRS 22 require **disclosure of all material share transactions** or potential share transactions entered into after the balance sheet date, excluding the bonus issue. Therefore **details of the issue of the contingent shares should be disclosed** in the notes to the financial statements.

(c)   **Property**

The property appears to have been **incorrectly classified** as 'held for sale'. Although the company had always intended to sell the property, FRED 32 *Disposal of non-current assets and presentation of discontinued operations* states that in order to qualify as 'held for sale' an asset must be **available for immediate sale in its present condition**. Because **repairs were needed** before the property could be sold and these were **not completed until after the balance sheet date**, this was clearly **not the case at 31 October 20X5.**

In addition, even if the property had been correctly classified, it has been **valued incorrectly**. FRED 32 requires assets held for sale to be valued at **the lower of their carrying amount or fair value less costs to sell**. The property **should have been valued at its carrying amount of £20 million**, not at the eventual sale proceeds of £27 million.

The property **must be included within tangible fixed assets** and must be **depreciated**. Therefore its **carrying amount at 31 October 20X5 is £19 million** (£20 million less depreciation of £1 million). The **gain of £7 million** that the company has previously recognised **should be reversed**.

Although the property cannot be classified as 'held for sale' in the financial statements for the year ended 31 October 20X5, it **will qualify for the classification after the balance sheet date**. Therefore details of the sale should be **disclosed** in the notes to the financial statements as the company wishes to comply with FRED 32. This is also required by FRS 21 (the sale is a **non-adjusting event** after the balance sheet date).

(d)   **Share appreciation rights**

The granting of share appreciation rights is a **cash settled share based payment transaction** as defined by FRS 20 *Share based payment*. FRS 20 requires these to be **measured at the fair value of the liability** to pay cash. The liability should be **re-measured at each reporting date and at the date of settlement**. Any **changes in fair value** should be **recognised in the profit and loss account** for the period.

However, the company has **not remeasured the liability since 31 October 20X4**. Because FRS 20 requires the expense and the related liability to be recognised over the two-year vesting period, the rights should be measured as follows:

	£m
At 31 October 20X4: (£6 × 10 million × ½)	30
At 31 October 20X5 (£8 × 10 million)	80
At 1 December 20X5 (settlement date) (£9 × 10 million)	90

Therefore at 31 October 20X5 the liability **should be re-measured to £80 million** and an **expense of £50 million** should be recognised in the profit and loss account for the year.

The additional expense of £10 million resulting from the remeasurement at the settlement date is not included in the financial statements for the year ended 31 October 20X5, but is recognised the following year.

B4 Finaleyes

Top tips. This question covers a variety of post balance sheet events, but standards other than FRS 21 are involved and you should identify these where relevant. Make sure you identify the correct standard, for example in (c) SSAP 21 is not an issue, nor is FRS 26 in (a). Make sure you state the correct accounting treatment (with reasons) and then give the correct adjustments or disclosure. The examiner may not identify the relevant standard in the exam.

Examiner's comment. Candidates fared badly if they applied the inappropriate FRS or where the accounting entries were incorrect. However, there were some excellent answers with some candidates displaying a good range of knowledge and skills.

(a) **Share issue**

(i)   *Accounting treatment*

This is a **non-adjusting post balance sheet event** because, although the announcement was made before the year end, the conditions for receipt of the funds did not exist at the balance sheet date. Nor did the entitlement to receive the funds exist at the year end as the intention to issue the shares might not eventually have been carried out.

(ii) *Required adjustment/disclosure*

Disclosure should be by note, because of the **materiality** of the issue, giving the date of issue, the number of shares issued (£14m/£7.00 = 2m shares), the price at which they were issued (£7.00) and the total funds raised (£14m). The percentage increase in the company's share capital should be noted (2m/40m = 5%) and the use for which the funds were raised.

(b) **Acquisition of a plant**

(i)   *Accounting treatment*

Considering the definition of liabilities given by the ASB, the first part is satisfied in that it seems clear that in 15 years' time the company must replace the heating system, ie **transfer economic benefits**. The question of whether a liability arises out of past transactions or events is more vexed. Arguments could range from the extremes of full provision of £30,000 per year (anticipating all losses but no profits, ie prudence) to no provision at all because the 'past event' will be the actual replacement in 15 years' time.

When the system is replaced, the **assets** of the company will be **increased**, **not** its **liabilities**. Thus, the most sensible approach seems to be to make a provision for depreciation of £30,000 per year, thereby matching the cost of the heating system to the benefit received from it. The useful life should be 15 years, not the 40 year life of the buildings.

(ii) *Required adjustment/disclosure*

The company should not have depreciated the entire £4m over the 40 years and then made an additional provision of £30,000 for the heating system. Instead, depreciation should be calculated separately on buildings and plant and machinery.

$$\text{Depreciation on buildings} = \frac{\text{£4m} - \text{£0.45m}}{40} = \text{£88,750}$$

Total depreciation = £88,750 + £30,000 = £118,750

(c) **Sale and leaseback of factory**

(i) *Accounting treatment*

This is a **post balance sheet event which is non-adjusting** because it concerns conditions which did not exist at the balance sheet date. It must be disclosed by way of a note, however, because its materiality (£10m/£80m = 12.5% of net assets) is such that its non-disclosure would prevent users obtaining a true and fair view of the financial statements.

(ii) *Required adjustment/disclosure*

A note is required, as in (a) above, laying out the particulars of the transaction, namely: the sale price and book value of the factory (at 30 April 20X6), the intention to lease back over 20 years at market rents, and the date the contracts were signed.

(d) **Stock valuation errors**

(i) *Accounting treatment*

Prior year adjustments are defined by FRS 3 *Reporting financial performance* as material adjustments applicable to prior periods arising from changes in accounting policies or from the correction of fundamental errors.

The problem here is that the item is **not material** enough in relation to the company's overall results to be considered fundamental. In addition, because stock entries reverse each year, it is not the cumulative figure which should be adjusted, even if the item qualified as a prior year adjustment.

There has also been no change in accounting policy, only a failure to apply an existing one.

(ii) *Required adjustment/disclosure*

The prior year adjustment should be **reversed** and so should the stock valuation adjustment.

The stock valuation at 30 April 20X6 should be reduced by £115,000. For the profit and loss account the same amount should be debited to cost of sales.

B5 Cohort

Top tips. This question required a knowledge of deferred tax (FRS 19). The question focused on the key areas of the standard and required an understanding of those areas. It did not require detailed computational knowledge but the ability to take a brief outline scenario and advise the client accordingly. Rote knowledge would be of little use in this situation.

Examiner's comment. Some candidates scored quite well on the question but again guessing at the answer was a fruitless exercise. The key areas were intercompany profit in stock, unremitted earnings of subsidiaries, revaluation of securities, general provisions and tax losses. Basically an appreciation was required of how to deal with each of these areas but unfortunately most candidates struggled to deal with the issues involved.

Marking scheme

		Marks
Air	acquisition	5
	intangible asset	3
	inter-company profit	3
	unremitted earnings	3
Legion	long term investments	4
	loan provision	4
	deferred tax asset	4
	Available	26
	Maximum	25

(a) **General impact of FRS 19**

FRS 19 has now come into effect and Cohort will have to apply it for the first time in its financial statements for the year ended 31 May 20X2. FRS 19 requires deferred tax to be provided on a **full provision basis**, rather than a partial provision basis. This means that the **deferred tax liability will probably increase** significantly, particularly if Cohort currently has large amounts of unprovided deferred tax arising from accelerated capital allowances. In addition, **deferred tax assets can only be recognised if there is evidence of taxable future profits against which the assets can be recovered.**

(b) **Acquisition of the subsidiaries – general**

Fair value adjustments have been made for consolidation purposes in both cases, but these **will probably not affect the deferred tax charge for the year.** FRS 7 *Fair values in acquisition accounting* states that fair value adjustments are **treated in the same way as they would be if they were timing differences arising in the entity's own accounts.** For example, buildings are valued at market value on acquisition, but deferred tax is only recognised if the gain is certain to be realised (for example, because the acquired entity has entered into a binding agreement to sell the building).

Future listing

Cohort plans to seek a listing in three years time. Therefore it will become a **public company** and will be subject to a **higher rate of tax**. FRS 19 states that deferred tax should be measured at the **average tax rates expected to apply in the periods in which the timing differences are expected to reverse**, based on current enacted tax rates and laws. This means that Cohort may be paying tax at the higher rate when some of its timing differences reverse and this should be taken into account in the calculation.

Acquisition of Air

(i)   The directors have calculated the tax provision on the assumption that the intangible asset of £0.5 million will be allowed for tax purposes. However, this is not certain and the directors **may eventually have to pay the additional tax**. If the directors cannot be persuaded to adjust their calculations **a liability for the additional tax should be recognised.**

(ii)   The intra-group transaction has resulted in an **unrealised profit** of £0.6 million in the group accounts and this will be **eliminated on consolidation**. The tax charge in the group profit and loss account includes the tax on this profit, for which **the group will not become liable to tax until the following period. From the perspective of the group, there is a timing difference. Deferred tax should be provided** on this difference (an asset) using the rate of tax payable by Air.

(iii)   FRS 19 states **that deferred tax should not be recognised on the unremitted earnings of subsidiaries** unless dividends payable by the subsidiary have been accrued by the balance sheet date or a binding agreement to distribute future earnings has been made. It does not appear that any such agreement has been made and **no provision for deferred tax should be recognised.**

Acquisition of Legion

(i)   As stated above, deferred tax is not normally recognised on timing differences where non-monetary assets are revalued. However, FRS 19 states that **where assets are continuously revalued and the changes in value are recognised in the profit and loss account, deferred tax should be recognised on any timing differences**. The government securities are treated in this way and therefore the company **should recognise a provision for deferred tax on the accumulated unrealised gains of £4 million.**

(ii)   A timing difference arises when the provision for the loss on the loan portfolio is first recognised. The general provision is expected to increase and therefore it is unlikely that the timing difference will reverse in the near future. However, under the full provision basis a **provision for deferred tax should still be made**. The timing difference gives rise to a **deferred tax asset**. FRS 19 states that **deferred tax assets should not be recognised unless it is probable that taxable profits will be available** against which the taxable profits can be utilised. **This is affected by the situation in point (iii) below.**

(iii)   In theory, unused tax losses give rise to a deferred tax asset. However, FRS 19 states that **deferred tax assets should only be recognised to the extent that they are regarded as recoverable**. They should be regarded as recoverable to the extent that on the basis of all the evidence available it is **more likely than not that there will be suitable taxable profits against which the losses can be recovered**. The future taxable profit of Legion **will not be sufficient to realise all the unused tax loss**. Only tax losses made since the acquisition of Legion are available for group relief. **Therefore the deferred tax asset is reduced to the amount that is expected to be recovered.**

This reduction in the deferred tax asset implies that it was **overstated at 1 June 20X1**, when it was acquired by the group. As these are the first post-acquisition financial statements, **goodwill should also be adjusted**.

B6 Panel

> **Top tips.** This is a single topic question, which is a departure from the examiner's usual mixed standard question. The IFRS 1 aspects are likely to become less frequent over time.
>
> **Easy marks.** Part (b) (iii) and (iv) are easier than (i) and (ii), though they carry the same number of marks.
>
> **Examiner's comment.** Part (a) was quite well answered albeit often in a very general way. Part (b) was answered far better than when this area was tested in June 2005. The other three areas were a leasing transaction, an inter company sale and an impairment of property plant and equipment. These elements of the question were quite well answered although the discussion of the topic areas was generally quite poor whilst the computations were quite good. Deferred tax is a key area and must be understood.

(a)   (i)   **The impact of changes in accounting standards**

FRS 19 *Deferred tax* requires the recognition of the **future tax consequences of past transactions and events** as liabilities or assets in the financial statements. Where the recognition criteria in a standard are different from those in tax law, a **transaction or event occurs in a different accounting period from its tax consequences**. For example, income from interest receivable is recognised in the financial statements in one accounting period but it is only taxable when it is actually received in the following accounting period. These differences are known as **'timing differences'**.

FRS 19 requires a company to make **full provision** for the tax effects of timing differences which have originated but not reversed by the balance sheet date. Where a change in an accounting standard results in a change to the way in which income and expenditure is recognised in the financial statements, a **timing difference may arise**. Therefore the amount of the deferred tax provision is affected.

(ii)   **Calculation of deferred tax on first time adoption of IFRS**

IFRS 1 *First time adoption of International Financial Reporting Standards* requires a company to **prepare an opening IFRS balance sheet** and to **apply the standard on deferred taxation to temporary differences** between the carrying amounts of assets and liabilities and their tax bases at that date. Panel prepares its opening IFRS balance sheet **at 1 November 2003**. The carrying values of its assets and liabilities are **measured in accordance with IFRS 1** and **other applicable IFRSs** in force at 31 October 2005. The deferred tax provision is based on **tax rates that have been enacted or substantially enacted by the balance sheet date**. Any **adjustments** to the deferred tax liability under previous GAAP are **recognised directly in equity (opening retained profit)**.

(b)   (i)   **Share options**

Under FRS 20 *Share based payment* the company **recognises an expense** for the employee services received in return for the share options granted over the vesting period, but this is **not allowable for tax**. The related tax deduction **does not arise until the share options are exercised**. Therefore a **deferred tax asset arises**, based on the anticipated tax benefit on the exercise of the options.

Because the eventual tax benefit is based on the intrinsic value of the shares at 31 October 20X5 (the vesting date), an estimate will have to be made at 31 October 2004. The intrinsic value at that date can be used. FRS 20 also requires that the remuneration expense is spread over the two year vesting period.

Therefore the **timing difference is £8 million** (£16 million ÷ 2) and the **deferred tax asset is £2.4 million** (30% × 8). This is recognised at 31 October 2004 provided that taxable profit is available against which it can be utilised.

At 31 October 2005 there is **no longer a deferred tax asset** because the options have been exercised. The **tax benefit receivable is £13.8 million** (30% × £46 million).

(ii)   **Leased plant**

An asset leased under a finance lease is **recognised as an asset** owned by the company and the **related obligation** to pay lease rentals is **recognised as a liability**. Each instalment payable is treated partly as interest and partly as repayment of the liability. Depreciation is **not allowable** for tax, but the **lease rentals attract tax relief**. Therefore, at 31 October 2005 a **timing difference** arises as follows:

	£m	£m
Expense recognised in financial statements:		
Depreciation (12 ÷ 5)	2.4	
Interest (8% × 12)	0.96	
		3.36
Less: lease rental		(3)
Timing difference		0.36

A **deferred tax asset of £108,000** (30% × 360,000) arises.

(iii)   **Intra-group sale**

Pins has **made a profit of £2 million** on its sale to Panel. Tax is **payable on the profits of individual companies**. Pins is liable for tax on this profit in the current year and has provided for the related tax in its individual financial statements. However, **from the viewpoint of the group** the profit **will not be realised until the following year**, when the goods are sold to a third party and must be **eliminated** from the consolidated financial statements. Because the group **pays tax before the profit is realised** there is a **timing difference of £2 million** and a **deferred tax asset of £600,000** (30% × £2 million).

(iv)   **Impairment loss**

The impairment loss in the financial statements of Nails is effectively accelerated depreciation, which is **not allowable for tax**. However, the assets will still attract capital allowances based on their original cost. Therefore there is a **timing difference**.

Under FRS 11 *Impairment of fixed assets and goodwill* the impairment loss is allocated first to goodwill and then to other assets:

	Goodwill £m	Fixed assets £m	Total £m
Net book value at 31 October 2005	1	6	7
Impairment loss	(1)	(0.8)	(1.8)
	–	5.2	5.2

No deferred tax is recognised on goodwill and therefore only the impairment loss relating to the fixed assets affects the deferred tax position.

The effect of the impairment loss is as follows:

	Before impairment £m	After impairment £m	Difference £m
Net book value in financial statements	6.0	5.2	
Tax written down value	(4.0)	(4.0)	
Timing difference	2.0	1.2	0.8
Tax liability (30%)	0.6	0.36	0.24

Therefore the impairment loss reduces the tax liability by £240,000.

B7 Preparation question: Defined benefit scheme

PROFIT AND LOSS ACCOUNT (EXTRACT)

	20X7 £m	20X8 £m
Operating expenses		
Current service cost	130	140
Past service	–	60 (W5)
Other finance charges (W4)	(20) (cr)	(20) (cr)

BALANCE SHEET (EXTRACT)

	20X7 £m	20X8 £m
Pension asset/(liability) (W1)	90	(8)
Pension reserve	90	(8)
Statement of total recognised gains and losses		
Actual return less expected return on pension scheme assets (W3)	130	143
Experience gains and losses arising on the scheme liabilities (W2)	(20)	(161)

Movement in surplus during the year	£m	£m
Surplus in scheme at beginning of year		90
Movements in year		
Current cost	(130)	(140)
Contributions	90	100
Past service costs		(60)
Other finance income	20	20
Actuarial gain/loss	110	(18)
Surplus/deficit in scheme at end of year	90	(8)

Workings

1   *Balance sheet net asset/(liability)*

	£m
31.12.X7 (1,190 – 1,100)	90
31.12.X8 (1,372 – 1,380)	(8)

2   *Liability*

	£m
b/f 1.1.X7	1,000
Current service cost	130
Benefits paid	(150)
Interest (1,000 × 10%)	100
∴ experience loss on scheme liabilities	20
PV at 31.12.X7	1,100
Current service cost (X8)	140
Past service cost (W5)	60
Benefits paid	(180)
Interest (1,100 × 9%)	99
∴ experience loss on scheme liabilities	161
PV at 31.12.X8	1,380

BPP LEARNING MEDIA

3   *Fair value of assets*

		£m
b/f 1.1.X7		1,000
Benefits paid		(150)
Contributions paid		90
Expected return on assets (12% × 1,000)		120
∴ actual return less expected return		130
FV at 31.12.X7		1,190
Benefits paid		(180)
Contributions paid		100
Expected return on assets (10% × 1,190)		119
∴ Actual return less expected return		143
FV at 31.12.X8		1,372

4   *Other finance charges*

	20X7	20X8
	£m	£m
Finance charges		
Interest (W2)	100	99
Expected return on assets (W3)	(120)	(119)
	(20) credit	(20) credit

5   *Past service cost 20X8*

	£m	
Re former employees	50	(recognised immediately)
Re current employees ($100/10$)	10	(recognised over period until benefits vest)
	60	

B8 Retirement benefits

> **Top tips**. Review our solution carefully, it is fairly comprehensive.

(a)   (i)   There are many key issues in determining how accounting for retirement benefits is carried out in respect of a defined benefit plan.

(1)   The two main alternative approaches are what might be called the **profit and loss account approach** or the **balance sheet approach**. Under the profit and loss account approach the pension cost is seen as an operating cost and under the accruals or matching concept the attempt is made to spread the total pension cost over the service lives of the employees. The balance sheet approach however concentrates on the valuation of the assets and liabilities of the plan and the cost to the profit and loss account is the change in value of the plan net assets or liabilities.

(2)   Regarding the assets of the defined benefit plan there are two issues: **whether or not they should be included** on the balance sheet of the company and **how** they would be **valued**. Alternative valuation methods such as cost, market value and fair value are available.

(3)   How should scheme liabilities be valued? Should they be valued using an **actuarial valuation or a market value**? Usually actuarial techniques will have to be used as there is no market value for such liabilities but then there is an issue over which actuarial method should be used – accrued benefits or prospective benefits.

(4)   Should **discounting** be used when valuing the scheme liabilities in order to take account of the time value of money?

(5)   If **actuarial gains and losses** occur where should they be **recognised** – in the profit and loss account or in the statement of total recognised gains and losses? Should such gains and losses be recognised immediately or spread over the remaining service lives of the

employees? Or should the actuarial gains and losses only be recognised in the profit and loss account if they exceed a predetermined amount? The problem that faces standard setters is how to deal with the volatility of actuarial gains and losses.

(6) **How often** should **actuarial valuations** take place? In theory they should take place at each year end but the costs and practicalities of this makes it difficult and onerous.

(7) If there are **changes to the defined benefit plan** such as improvement of benefits or addition of new benefits in relation to past service how should these be accounted for? The alternatives are to recognise the cost immediately in the profit and loss account, spread it over the remaining service lives of employees or to offset it against any surplus in the scheme.

Note. Candidates are only required to describe **four** of the above.

(ii) FRS 17 *Retirement benefits* follows a **balance sheet approach** to accounting for defined benefit schemes in accordance with the *Statement of Principles*. The assets of the scheme are to be valued on an actuarial basis using the **projected unit credit method** and the liabilities should be discounted to reflect the time value of money and the particular characteristics of the liability. The discount rate to be used is the rate of return on high quality corporate bonds of equivalent currency and term as the scheme liabilities being valued.

The net amount of the fair value of the assets and the discounted value of the liabilities appears in the balance sheet as a **surplus or a deficit**. Full actuarial valuations should take place at intervals not exceeding three years to ensure that the financial statement amounts do not differ materially from the amounts that would be determined at the balance sheet date. Actuarial gains and losses should be recognised in the STRGL.

Past service costs for active employees are recognised in the profit and loss account over the period in which the increases in benefits vest (immediately if the benefits vest immediately).

FRS 17 does not provide a complete solution to all the problems regarding accounting for retirement benefits. The profit and loss account contains estimated figures (current and past service cost and net returns on the pension scheme); all experience gains are taken to the STRGL. Thus any **volatility** regarding actuarial gains and losses can be said to have been **displaced** rather than reduced. **Further volatility** is introduced into the profit and loss account in the form of the **'expected return on assets'**, which mirrors the volatility in the asset value of equities. In general, it could be argued that FRS 17 solves some problems while creating others.

(b) (i) *Net pension asset/pension reserve as at 31 May 20X1*

	£m
Fixed interest and index linked bonds	600
Equities	1,900
Other investments	450
	2,950
Actuarial value of liability	(2,000)
Surplus in pension scheme	950
Deferred tax liability (30%)	(285)
Net pension asset	665

The opposite side of the balance sheet would show 'pension reserve' of the same amount. The long term rate of return expected on the pension assets would be individually disclosed.

(ii) *Movement in surplus in the year*

	£m	£m
Surplus in scheme at 31 May 20X0 (1,970 – 1,500)		470
Current service cost	(70)	
Past service cost	(25)	
		(95)
Contributions to the scheme		60
Net interest/return on assets (295 – 230)		65
Actuarial gain/loss (difference)		450
Surplus in pension scheme		950

The **statement of total recognised gains and losses** will show the **actuarial** gain for the year to 31 May 20X1 of £450 million, and the **operating profit** will be charged with the **current and past service costs** of £95 million in total. The net interest/**return on the assets** of the pension scheme of £65 million will be shown as other **finance income**. The **past service cost** has been charged in full to the **profit and loss account** as the increased benefit has been vested.

B9 Savage

Top tips. A lot of the information is given to you in the question. You need to know how to present it.

Easy marks. Part (b), a test of knowledge is a source of easy marks.

Examiner's comment. In theory, this question should have had the highest average mark on the paper. In practice it was the poorest answered. The question was on employee benefits. The main problem for candidates is not the accounting process but understanding the terminology and what that means for the accounting process. An article has been prepared for *Student Accountant* which hopefully will help candidates.

Candidates had to calculate the expense recognised in profit or loss, the amount recognised in the balance sheet and the statement of total recognised gains and losses for the employee benefit transactions in the year. Candidates had very few calculations to make. Basically the only calculations were the interest cost and the expected return on the plan assets. The remainder of the question simply required candidates to enter the various transactions into the relevant accounts, but because of the problem of understanding the nature of the items, this proved to be a difficult exercise. Hopefully the article will help.

Part (b) of the question required candidates to explain how the non-payment of the contributions and change in the pension benefits should be treated. Many candidates did not attempt this part of the question which is not a good strategy even though the part only carried four marks.

(a) AMOUNTS RECOGNISED IN THE BALANCE SHEET

	31 October 20X5	31 October 20X4
	£m	£m
Present value of obligation	3,375	3,000
Less: fair value of plan assets	(3,170)	(2,900)
Liability	205	100

EXPENSE RECOGNISED IN THE PROFIT AND LOSS ACCOUNT
FOR THE YEAR ENDED 31 OCTOBER 20X5

	£m	£m
In operating expenses:		
Current service cost	40	
Past service cost	125	
		165
Finance income		
Interest cost	188	
Expected return on assets	(232)	
		(44)

AMOUNT RECOGNISED IN STATEMENT OF TOTAL RECOGNISED GAINS AND LOSSES
FOR THE YEAR ENDED 31 OCTOBER 20X5

	£m
Experience gains and losses arising on scheme liabilities	64
Actual return less expected return on scheme assets	(52)
Net actuarial loss recognised	(12)

MOVEMENT IN NET LIABILITY IN BALANCE SHEET

	£m
Net liability at 1 November 20X4	100
Movement in year:	
Current service cost	40
Past service cost	125
Contributions paid	(28)
Other finance income	(44)
Actuarial loss	12
Net liability at 31 October 20X5	205

Workings

1   *Changes in the present value of the obligation*

	£m
Present value of obligation at 1 November 20X4	3,000
Past service cost	125
Interest cost (6% × 3,125)	188
Current service cost	40
Benefits paid	(42)
Actuarial loss on obligation (balancing figure)	64
Present value of obligation at 31 October 20X5	3,375

Note: the past service costs of £125 million are recognised immediately because the benefits vest on 1 November 20X4. They are also included in opening scheme liabilities for the purpose of calculating interest.

2   *Changes in the fair value of plan assets*

	£m
Fair value of plan assets at 1 November 20X4	2,900
Expected return on plan assets (8% × 2,900)	232
Contributions	28
Benefits paid	(42)
Actuarial gain on plan assets (balancing figure)	52
Fair value of plan assets at 31 October 20X5	3,170

(b)   At 31 October 20X5, contributions of £8 million remain unpaid. These are included in scheme assets unless they are unlikely to be recovered. FRS 17 *Retirement benefits* states that any unpaid contributions should be presented in the balance sheet as a creditor due within one year. Therefore a creditor for £8 million should be recognised in the balance sheet at 31 October 20X5. This amount is payable to the Trustees.

FRS 17 also states that past service costs should be recognised immediately if the benefits have already vested. The benefits vested on 1 November 20X4 and therefore past service costs of £125 million should be recognised in the profit and loss account for the year ended 31 October 20X5.

B10 Issue

Top tips. This question required you to discuss the business and financial position of a company. It is not a ratio analysis question, but it involves the evaluation of the financial position taking into account all the available information.

Easy marks. There is a lot of information in the question, which you should make full use of in order to gain easy marks.

Examiner's comment. Some candidates' answers were quite narrow, showing that they had not seen the implications of the information provided. Others wasted time calculating ratios.

Marking scheme

	Marks
Environment – business	3
Special purpose entities	4
Related party and immateriality	3
Reversal of invoices	1
Fixed assets	2
Intangibles	2
Liquidity	4
Revenue recognition	2
Extraordinary items	2
Pro-forma information	2
Ratios	2
Conclusion: employees	1
publication lag	1
other	4
Report – style	1
Available	34
Maximum	25

REPORT

To: Managing Partner
From:
Subject: Financial and business position of Issue
Date: June 20X3

As requested, I report below on the business and financial position of Issue and on the implications of the financial information and the other information provided.

General business environment

Issue operates in a sector that has recently suffered an **economic downturn** and Issue's performance and financial position should be interpreted in this context.

There has been adverse press comment about **'aggressive earnings management'**. The company certainly operates under conditions that could **provide an incentive to adopt dubious accounting practices.** Management are partly **remunerated by means of share options**; this means that they personally **benefit from any increase in the share price**. In addition, the Board has promised to take the company into the top 10% of listed companies within its first five years; this period is now almost up. The company is **vulnerable** because it has issued bonds which are **redeemable if the working capital ratio falls below 1.3**. This means that **management may be under pressure to achieve unrealistic targets**.

There is evidence that management has adopted several **questionable accounting policies**.

Specific accounting policies

Special purpose entities

The company has borrowed £40 million from 20 different entities, all of which are owned by a bank. It has deposited £35 million of this with the entities, so that only £5 million is shown as actual debt in the financial statements. These entities are **Special Purpose Entities** (sometimes called quasi-subsidiaries or vehicle companies) which **appear to have been used to hide the true level of the company's indebtedness** from users of the financial statements. The economic substance of the arrangement is that the entities are **probably subsidiaries of Issue** rather than of the bank and if so, **consolidated financial statements should have been prepared** (although in practice these might not have provided much better information because intra-group balances would have been eliminated on consolidation).

It is necessary to **examine the detail of the arrangement** to determine whether the entities are subsidiaries of Issue or of the bank. If the bank controls the entities then the **long-term borrowings of Issue are understated by £35 million.**

Management **claims that each individual transaction is immaterial** and does not have to be disclosed. This is incorrect as **transactions of the same nature should be considered in aggregate**, rather than individually. In addition, because the bank owns 20% of the shares of Issue, it is **likely to be a related party** under FRS 8 *Related party disclosures*. This is a **further suggestion that the entities are vehicle companies.**

Issue has invoiced the entities for 'services' at each year end and has subsequently reversed the invoices after the company has filed its financial statements. Therefore it seems to be **using the entities to increase earnings (and possibly working capital ratios) artificially.**

Valuation of fixed assets

The valuation of the property, plant and equipment and intangible assets has been performed by **one of the directors of Issue** who is **not professionally qualified**. FRS 15 *Tangible fixed assets* states that a full valuation should be carried out by a **qualified valuer external to the business** or by a **qualified internal valuer provided that the valuation is subject to review by a qualified external valuer**. Even an interim valuation must be carried out by a qualified valuer. The fact that this requirement has not been followed **casts doubt on the legitimacy** of the valuation. It should be noted that the **revaluation reserve has increased by £10 million** during the year; an unexpectedly large amount, given that many of the assets are of a **specialised nature**.

In addition, the **basis for valuing the assets appears to be incorrect**. For properties, FRS 15 states that **current value is normally existing use value**, not net realisable value. **Market value** is normally used for plant and equipment. Where, as in this case, **assets are specialised** so that there is unlikely to be a reliable market value, **depreciated replacement cost should be used**. Revaluations of plant and equipment are **unusual** and there is no obvious reason for this one other than strengthening the balance sheet.

The intangible assets are data purchase and data capture costs of internally generated databases unless they have a readily ascertainable market value. FRS 10 *Goodwill and intangible assets* **does not permit internally generated intangible assets to be capitalised**. SSAP 13 *Accounting for research and development* states that **development costs should only be capitalised if they meet certain criteria**. These include **commercial viability** and **aggregate costs exceeding estimated future sales revenue**. Given the nature of the costs, this is **unlikely** and it appears that they **should have been written off** as they were incurred. However, further investigation of the reason for adopting this policy is needed.

Six year bonds

At first sight the accounting treatment adopted for the two bond issues **appears to be incorrect**. Under FRS 26 *Financial instruments: measurement*, this type of financial instrument is **normally measured at amortised cost**. This means that the finance credits of £2 million and £1 million **should not be recognised in the profit and loss account immediately**, but over the **shortest period** that the investor can require redemption (three years in this case). However, it could be argued that **there is a case for recognising the finance credits immediately**, because the holders can demand payment immediately if the working capital ratio falls below 1.3.

Revenue recognition

In practice information technology businesses use **a variety of different policies**, some acceptable and some not. Issue **has long-term contracts**, but it is **unclear exactly when amounts are invoiced and revenue recognised**. Is revenue recognised on completion, or in stages as the contract progresses? It should be noted that because there is **little adequate guidance**, many software companies have adopted **'aggressive earnings management'** by **invoicing and recognising revenue as early in a transaction as possible**, well before the company has performed any work under the contract. However, it is **not certain** that Issue has done this.

Extraordinary items

Issue has recognised an **extraordinary item** in the profit and loss account: losses caused by the terrorist attacks on New York on 11 September 2001. FRS 3 *Reporting financial performance* has effectively **prohibited the recognition of extraordinary items**. This is very clearly an attempt to manipulate the earnings figure and therefore **operating profit is actually £20 million lower** than reported.

The financial position

Like many other businesses in the same sector, the company is **clearly facing difficulties**. In the year ended 31 January 20X3 **revenue fell by 20%** and it **reported earnings** before interest, tax, depreciation and amortisation **of £10 million** (adjusted for the extraordinary item) **compared with £90 million the previous year**. It is possible that these figures are **considerably overstated. Return on shareholders' equity is now a negative figure of 42.9%** (compared with a positive figure of 31.8% the previous year). Staff numbers have **reduced by 40%,** indicating that the company has been **forced to cut costs.**

A further problem is the **level of indebtedness**. Gearing has **risen from 27% to 42%** and it is **possible that it should be still higher**, because of the £35 million debt that may be 'off balance sheet'. **Liquidity has also worsened**; the working capital (current) ratio fell from 1.71 in 20X2 to 1.28 in 20X3. Not only might this cause problems in itself, but **as the working capital ratio has fallen below 1.3 the bonds of £50 million may have to be repaid.** This would **probably be disastrous** as it is unlikely that the company has sufficient funds available to make the payments.

A further thing to note is the **increasing length of time** between the year-end and the publication of the financial statements. This suggests that in 20X3 the company **might have had to spend additional time finalising** the financial statements and **devising ways of making the company's performance appear better than it was.**

Issue has **published pro-forma information** for the four months to 31 May 20X3. This seems to indicate that **the situation has improved dramatically** and in particular that **gearing has reduced**. The working capital ratio has increased to 1.5. However, pro-forma financial statements should always be **interpreted with caution** as they are **notoriously unreliable**. Issue has probably provided this additional information in an **attempt to restore investor confidence** or to **prevent the redemption of the bonds**. Given the company's use of special purpose entities and its other questionable accounting policies, **there has to be a degree of suspicion** about the way in which the improvement has been managed.

Conclusion

There appear to be a **number of problems**, both with Issue's **management culture** and with the **financial information provided. Many of the company's accounting policies require further investigation.** It is possible that the figures for **turnover, tangible fixed assets and intangible assets are all overstated** and that the figures for

current liabilities and long-term borrowings are significantly understated. Even the figures as they stand suggest that the company's turnover and profits are falling, that liquidity is decreasing and gearing is increasing and that the company is in difficulties.

Given these problems, we **cannot recommend that you continue to invest in this company**.

Appendix

	20X3	20X2
Return on shareholders' equity (adjusted for extraordinary item)	$\frac{(30)}{70}$ = (42.9)%	$\frac{35}{110}$ = 31.8%
Working capital ratio	$\frac{230}{180}$ = 1.28	$\frac{240}{140}$ = 1.71
Gearing ratio	$\frac{50}{120}$ = 42%	$\frac{40}{150}$ = 27%

B11 Tyre

Top tips. This question required candidates to deal with issues surrounding revenue recognition, accounting for fixed assets, provisions for environmental costs, accounting for lease premiums, and provisioning under FRS 12 *Provisions, contingent liabilities and contingent assets*.

Easy marks. Although this is mainly about application of knowledge, there are easy marks for showing that you know what is going on. Credit will be given for different but sensible interpretations, for example, if you argued for a provision being made for the potential cost of the free car accessories.

Examiner's comment. The question was quite well answered, particularly the revenue recognition aspects.

Marking scheme

	Marks
Revenue recognition	8
Administration building	7
Lease agreements	5
Car accessories	5
	25

(a) **General sales to customers**

FRS 5 *Reporting the substance of transactions* (Application Note G) states that a seller recognises revenue when it obtains the right to consideration **in exchange for its performance**. Where a seller receives advance payments, it should normally **recognise a liability. Revenue should not be recognised until the seller has actually completed its performance under the contract**. A deposit should only be recognised as revenue if the seller has no further obligations in respect of that amount.

In this case, the seller **has not completed its performance** under the contract, because **ownership has not been transferred.** There is also a possibility that the **deposit might have to be returned** if Tyre does not eventually perform its part of the contract.

Therefore the deposit should be treated as a **liability** until the vehicle has been delivered to the customer and only then should revenue be recognised. If the customer cancels the order, the deposit should be recognised as revenue at the date of cancellation.

Sale of car fleet to Hub

A central principle of FRS 5 is that **a sale of an asset can only be recognised** if the significant **risks and rewards associated with ownership**, as well as the legal title, **have been transferred**. The buyback option is **expected to be exercised**. Therefore it is clear that the significant risks and rewards **have not been transferred** to Hub, because Tyre **retains an interest** in the residual value of the fleet.

The **substance** of the transaction is that Tyre has **leased the vehicles**, rather than sold them. Tyre **will only receive 60%** of the (heavily discounted) purchase price of the vehicles, meaning that the **present value** of the **minimum lease payments** will be considerably **less than their fair value.** In addition, Tyre will buy the vehicles back well **before the end** of their **economic life**. The **risks and rewards of ownership** have not been transferred in practice. All these factors indicate that the lease is an **operating lease.**

The fleet of vehicles will therefore continue to be recognised in **tangible fixed assets** and **depreciated** over their useful economic lives in accordance with FRS 15 *Tangible fixed assets*. Because the discount is normal for this type of transaction, the fair value of the vehicles will be measured at their actual purchase price, not the discounted price. **Income from the lease** should be **recognised over the lease term** on a straight line basis.

The **buyback option** may meet the definition of a **financial liability** under FRS 26 *Financial instruments: Recognition and measurement*. If this is the case, the liability should be **measured initially at its fair value** and subsequently at **amortised cost**.

(b) **Former administrative centre**

The land and the building must be considered separately. The decision to demolish the building was taken **during the year** and this indicates that it was **impaired** at 31 May 20X6. The **recoverable amount** of the building is **zero** and therefore it should be written down to that amount, and the **impairment loss recognised in the profit and loss account** for the year ended 31 May 20X6.

The **demolition costs** must be **charged** to the profit and loss account **in the period in which they occur** (the year ended 31 May 20X7). **No provision** for remedial environmental work **should be recognised at 31 May 20X6**, because the company **did not have an obligation** to incur costs at that date (the building had not yet been demolished).

Although the company has decided to sell the land, it **does not meet the definition** of an asset **'held for sale'** under FRED 32 *Disposal of non-current assets and presentation of discontinued operations*. In order to be treated as 'held for sale' the land would have to be **actively marketed** and **available for immediate sale in its present condition**. Remedial work must be carried out and the directors have decided to delay the sale to take advantage of rising prices. Therefore **the criteria have clearly not been met.**

The land is measured at **cost**. It was acquired many years ago and prices are rising, so it **cannot be impaired**. When the remedial work has been completed, it may be possible to treat the land as an **investment property** under SSAP 19 *Accounting for investment property*. The land would then be **measured at fair value** and **gains or losses on revaluation** would be **recognised in equity** (in an investment revaluation reserve).

(c) **Lease premiums**

Because one lease is a **finance lease** and the other is an **operating lease** the two lease premiums must be **treated differently**.

SSAP 21 *Accounting for leases and hire purchase contracts* states that costs that are **directly attributable to a finance lease** should be **added to the amount recognised as an asset**. Therefore the **amount capitalised** at the start of the finance lease should **include the premium**, which will then be **depreciated** over the lease term or the property's useful life (whichever is the shorter). The premium is also **included in the liability** for future payments under the lease.

The premium paid to enter into the **operating lease** is treated as **part of the lease rentals.** In effect, this is a prepayment of rent. Therefore the premium is **recognised as an expense** over the lease term on a **straight line basis** (unless some other systematic basis is more appropriate).

(d) **Car accessories**

The main issue here is whether the company has **incurred an obligation** to supply the free car accessories at 31 May 20X6 and therefore whether a **provision** should be recognised in the financial statements.

FRS 12 *Provisions, contingent liabilities and contingent assets* states that a provision should only be recognised if:

- There is a **present obligation** as the result of a **past event**
- An **outflow of economic benefit is probable**; and
- A **reliable estimate** of the amount can be made.

The accessories can only be obtained by presenting a coupon when a vehicle is purchased. The **purchase of the car is the obligating event** and an **outflow of economic benefit occurs at the same time**. The company does not have an obligation to provide free goods relating to sales that have not yet happened. **No provision should be recognised.**

The cost of the accessories is included in the **cost of sales**. The **revenue recognised should be the actual amount received** from the customer; the sales price of the car only, not including the accessories.

B12 Preparation question: Leases

Treat as a sale at fair value of £15m and loan of £2.5m ∴ recognise profit on sale of £1m immediately.

The rentals need to be split between the 'fair market rental' which is changed to the profit and loss account immediately and repayment of the loan plus interest.

Repayment of loan = $\dfrac{\text{£2.5m}}{3.037}$ = £823,181

∴ Operating lease rentals = £(1,750,000 − 823,181 =) £926,819

Interest on £2.5m = at 12% £300,000 (Charge to P&L a/c)

∴ Repayment of capital = £(823,181 − 300,000=) £523,181

B/S liability = £2,500,000 − £523,181 = £1,976,819

B13 AB

Top tips. Part (a) of this question allows you to get easy marks for knowledge of the distinction between operating leases and finance leases. It also asks for some of the shortcomings in the way leases are currently accounted for. This area is being debated at the moment by the standard-setting bodies, and a Discussion Paper has recently been published. Part (b) of the question required an explanation of how certain sale and leaseback transactions should be dealt with.

Examiner's comment. Answers to part (a) showed that many candidates were not aware of current issues. In part (b) many candidates did not discuss the various elements of the question in sufficient detail, relying on a numerical answer.

(a) (i)   A distinction must be made between finance and operating leases.

A finance lease is one which transfers substantially all of the risks and rewards of ownership of an asset to a lessee. An operating lease is any other type of lease.

Finance leases are capitalised in the accounts at the present value of the minimum lease payments using the lease term and the interest rate implicit in the lease. Any residual payments guaranteed by the lessee should also be taken into account. Assets are depreciated over the shorter of the lease term or useful economic life. The interest and principal elements of the lease repayments must be identified and the interest element allocated to appropriate periods. The lease liability is then appropriately reduced for the capital element. Finance charges should produce a constant periodic rate of charge.

Operating lease rentals are simply charged to the profit and loss account on a straight line basis over the lease term regardless of when the payments are due. The charges reflect the pattern of benefits from the leased asset.

(ii)   Deficiencies in lease accounting are as follows.

(1)   The distinction between treatment as a finance or operating lease is determined by the **substantial transfer** of risks and rewards of ownership to a lessee. If this occurs, a recognisable asset and liability are created in the lessee accounts. (This is normally taken as being the case if the lease is non cancellable and the present value of the minimum lease payments is equal to or greater than 90% of the fair value of the leased asset.) In other words, 'substantial' is normally judged against **quantitative not qualitative** criteria.

(2)   Many operating leasing transactions have been **designed to fit** the **quantitative criteria**, while **in substance they are finance leases**. Typical areas of concern are responsibility for maintenance, insurance and so on.

(3)   The 90% present value criterion may be satisfied by using a **contingent rental clause**. Contingent rentals would not come into the present value calculation.

(4)   The **interest rate** implicit in the lease may not be available in which case an alternative **estimated** rate can be used. This again can lead to the present value criterion being circumvented.

(5)   **Leases of land and buildings can be distorted** because land normally has an indefinite life and its title will not pass to a lessee, so that the lessee does not receive the risks and rewards of ownership. Companies can therefore distort the accounting treatment by allocating as large a value as possible to the land element so the lease is classified as an operating lease rather than a finance lease.

(6)   The relative **ease of classifying a lease as operating** rather than finance by avoiding the criteria to determine the substantial transfer of risks and rewards of ownership is a **major deficiency of SSAP 21** leading to assets and liabilities not being recognised in the lessee's financial statements.

(b) (i)   Where a lessee enters a **sale and leaseback transaction** resulting in an **operating lease** then the original asset should be **treated as sold**. If the transaction is at **fair value** then **immediate recognition** of the profit or loss should occur. If the transaction is **above fair value**, the **profit based on fair value** (98 – 33) ie £65m may be recognised immediately. The balance of profit in **excess of fair value** (198 – 98) ie £100m should be **deferred and amortised** over the shorter of the lease term and the period to the next lease rental review. In this case this would be amortised over 10 years, ie £10m pa.

However, as the sales value is not the fair value, the operating lease rentals (£24m) are likely to have been adjusted for the excess price paid for the assets. For AB plc the sales value is more than twice the fair value, and according to FRS 5 the substance of the transaction is one of sale of asset and a loan equalling the deferred income element, ie £100m. Therefore at least half of the commitments under the agreement, £24m/2 ie £12m pa could be viewed as repayment of the loan plus interest. The company could show the excess over fair value as a loan and part of the operating lease cost as a repayment of capital and interest on this amount.

(ii) The sale and leaseback appears to create a **finance lease** as the present value of the minimum lease payments is greater than 90% of the fair value of the plant (£43.5m + £43.5m × 2.49 = £151.82m compared with £152m). AB has to pay all the costs of maintenance and insurance and the lease covers the remaining life of the plant after which it can be purchased at a nominal amount.

Under FRS 5 the asset should **remain in the lessee's balance sheet at carrying value** and the sale proceeds (£152m) are shown as a creditor representing the finance lease liability. As payments are made they are treated partly as a repayment of the creditor and partly as a finance charge against income.

The revaluation reserve will continue to be treated as before, and if it is transferred to the profit and loss reserve, this will done over the lease term/asset life of four years.

B14 Preparation question: Financial instruments

(a) PROFIT AND LOSS ACCOUNT

	£
Interest receivable and similar income	
(441,014 × 8% (W1))	35,281

BALANCE SHEET

	£
Fixed assets	
Financial asset (441,014 + 35,281)	476,295

Working: Effective interest rate

$$\frac{600,000}{441,014} = 1.3605$$

∴ From tables interest rate is 8%

(b)

	£
Proceeds of bond issue (4,000 × £500)	2,000,000
Less: liability component (W1)	(1,797,467)
Equity component	202,533

Working: Fair value of equivalent non-convertible debt

Present value of principal payable at end of 3 years

	£
$(£500 \times 4{,}000 \times \dfrac{1}{(1.09)^3})$	1,544,367
Present value of interest (annuity)	
[(5% × £500 × 4,000) × 2.531]	253,100
	1,797,467

B15 Ambush

> **Top tips.** A whole question on FRS 26 may appear daunting, but in fact this question is quite fair.
>
> **Easy marks.** These are available for the discursive aspects, which are most of the question.
>
> **Examiner's comment.** The first part of the question was well answered but candidates' answers on the fair value option and impairment were of poorer quality. Candidates often set out the requirement for the impairment of non current assets rather than financial instruments. There are some similarities but the conditions are different. The problems of the fair value option are well documented and some candidates answered this part of the question very well. However many candidates offered little in the way of logical argument as to why it has caused concern. Overall however the question was well answered.

REPORT

To: Directors of Ambush
From:
Subject: FRS 26 *Financial instruments: Measurement*
Date: December 20X5

As requested, this report outlines the way in which financial instruments are measured and classified and explains why the fair value option was initially introduced.

(a)   (i)   **How financial assets and liabilities are measured and classified**

FRS 26 states that all financial assets and liabilities should be **measured at fair value when they are first recognised**. This is normally their cost (the fair value of the consideration given or received). Fair value **includes transaction costs** unless the instrument is **classified as 'at fair value through profit or loss'**, in which case transaction costs are **recognised in the profit and loss account**.

The way in which an instrument is measured subsequently depends on its classification. There are four categories:

- Financial assets and liabilities at fair value through profit or loss
- Held to maturity investments
- Loans and receivables
- Available-for-sale financial assets

Financial assets and liabilities **at fair value through profit or loss** includes all items **held for trading** and all **derivative financial instruments**. In addition, it is possible to **designate any** financial asset or liability as 'at fair value through profit or loss', apart from equity instruments that **do not have a quoted market price** in an active market and whose **fair value cannot be reliably measured**. The designation must be adopted **on initial recognition** of the instrument.

Held to maturity investments have **fixed or determinable payments** and **fixed maturity.** The company must have the **positive intention and ability** to **hold them to maturity**. There are a number of detailed conditions that must be met before an instrument can be classified in this way. Equity instruments cannot be held to maturity investments.

Loans and receivables have fixed or determinable payments and are not quoted in an active market.

Available for sale financial assets are all **items that do not fall into the other categories**. Financial instruments not required to be classified as at fair value through profit or loss can be designated as available for sale.

FRS 26 **restricts reclassifications** between categories. Instruments cannot be reclassified into or out of 'at fair value through profit or loss'. There are penalties if held to maturity investments are reclassified or sold; a company cannot use this category again for two years.

Most financial assets are measured at fair value. Exceptions are **held to maturity investments** and **loans and receivables**, which are measured at **amortised cost**, using the **effective interest rate method**. This involves adjusting the cost of an instrument to reflect interest and repayments. The interest is allocated to accounting periods so as to achieve a **constant rate on the carrying amount** over the term of the instrument. Investments in **unquoted equity instruments** for which there is no reliable market value are measured at **cost**.

Financial **liabilities at fair value through profit or loss** are measured at **fair value. Other financial liabilities** are measured at **amortised cost**.

The way in which **gains and losses on remeasurement** are treated also depends upon the classification of the instruments. Gains and losses relating to instruments at **fair value through profit or loss** are **recognised in the profit and loss account**, even if they are unrealised. Gains and losses relating to changes in the fair value of **available for sale financial assets** are **recognised in the statement of total recognised gains and losses** and 'recycled' to the profit and loss account when the asset is sold. Changes in **amortised cost** are recognised in the **profit and loss account.**

(ii) **The fair value option**

The fair value option was originally introduced because the IASB believed that **fair value provides more relevant information** than historic cost and therefore it wished to encourage greater use of fair values. The fair value option also has specific advantages. It eliminates the burden of **separating embedded derivatives** and it **eliminates volatility** in profit and loss where matched positions of financial assets and financial liabilities are not measured consistently.

However, in practice the fair value option has **caused problems**. Fair value can be **used inappropriately**. For example:

- Companies can apply the fair value option to financial instruments whose fair value is **not verifiable**. Because the valuation is **subjective**, they then have scope to **manipulate profit or loss**.

- Use of fair values **can increase volatility** in profit and loss if the option is applied **selectively**.

- Where the fair value option is applied to **financial liabilities**, a company might recognise gains and losses as a result of **changes in its own creditworthiness**.

As a result of these problems, it is likely that FRS 26 will be amended to **restrict the use of the fair value option**. It should also be noted that UK companies applying FRS 26 **must still comply with the Companies Act**; this does not allow fair value accounting for some types of financial assets and financial liabilities.

(b) (i) **Impairment of financial assets**

FRS 26 states that **at each balance sheet date**, an entity should **assess** whether there is any **objective evidence that a financial asset or group of assets is impaired. Indications** of impairment include **significant financial difficulty** of the issuer; the probability that the borrower will **enter bankruptcy**; a **default** in interest or principal payments; or (for available for sale financial assets) a significant and prolonged **decline in fair value** below cost.

Where there is objective evidence of impairment, the entity should **determine the amount** of any impairment loss, which should be **recognised immediately in profit or loss**. Only losses relating to **past events** can be recognised. **Two conditions** must be met before an impairment loss is recognised:

- there is **objective evidence** of impairment as a result of one or more events that **occurred after the initial recognition** of the asset; and

- the **impact on the estimated future cash flows** of the asset can be **reliably estimated**.

For financial assets **carried at amortised cost** (held to maturity investments and loans and receivables) the impairment loss is the **difference** between the asset's **carrying amount** and its **recoverable amount**. The asset's recoverable amount is the **present value of estimated future cash flows**, discounted at the financial instrument's **original** effective interest rate.

For financial assets **carried at cost** because their fair value cannot be reliably measured, the impairment loss is the **difference** between the asset's **carrying amount** and the **present value of estimated future cash flows**, discounted at the **current market rate of return for a similar financial instrument.**

For **available for sale** financial assets, the impairment loss is the **difference** between the **acquisition cost** (net of any principal repayment and amortisation) and **current fair value** (for equity instruments) or **recoverable amount** (for debt instruments).

Assets at **fair value through profit or loss** are **not subject to impairment testing**, because changes in fair value are automatically recognised immediately in profit or loss.

(ii) **Loan to Bromwich**

The **financial difficulties** and **reorganisation** of Bromwich are **objective evidence of impairment**. The impairment loss is the **difference** between the **carrying amount** of the loan at 30 November 2005 and the **present value of the estimated future cash flows**, £100,000 on 30 November 2007, discounted at the **original effective interest rate of 8%.**

This is **£85,730** (100,000 × 0.8573). Therefore **the impairment loss is £114,270** (200,000 – 85,730) and this is **recognised immediately in the profit and loss account**.

B16 Timber Products

Top tips. This question covers all the major types of off balance sheet finance which appear in the application notes of FRS 5. You should therefore be familiar with the way each should be treated. Part (a) should earn you some easy marks.

Review your solution to check that for each part of the question you have:

Met the specific requirements for each part (eg. explain, entries in balance sheet and profit and loss accounts, giving reasons etc)

Demonstrated your technical knowledge of FRS 5

Clearly identified the issues in each of the transactions.

Examiner's comment. Part (a) was often well answered, as long as candidates didn't just write down all they knew on FRS 5. In part (b), candidates knew more about transactions (i) to (iii) than about transaction (iv), where they failed to identify the quasi subsidiary. Candidates approached part (c) as a finance vs operating lease decision and credit was given for this approach.

(a) (i) **FRS 5's objective** is:

'to ensure that the substance of an entity's transactions is reported in its financial statements. The commercial effect of the entity's transactions and any resulting assets, liabilities, gains or losses, should be faithfully represented in its financial statements.'

FRS 5's **fundamental principle** is that the substance of an entity's transactions should be reflected in its accounts, ie the substance of a transaction should be shown, not just its legal form. The key considerations are whether a transaction has given rise to new assets and liabilities, and whether it has changed any existing assets and liabilities. Sometimes there will be a series of connected transactions to be evaluated, not just a single transaction. It is necessary to identify and account for the substance of the series of transactions as a whole, rather than addressing each transaction individually.

The standard defines assets and liabilities and these definitions tie in to the *Statement of Principles*.

(ii)   There are two main types of transaction where the FRS states that derecognition would be appropriate.

Firstly, where a transaction results in the transfer to another party of all **significant benefits and risks** relating to an asset, the entire asset should cease to be recognised. An example here is the sale of photocopy paper and toner at list price to a customer in a shop.

Secondly, the standard deals with **partial derecognition** where, although not all significant benefits and risks have been transferred, the transaction is more than a mere financing and has transferred enough of the benefits and risks to warrant at least some derecognition of the asset. An example is the sale of a photocopier by a manufacturer under a residual value guarantee.

(b)   (i)   **Factored debts**

Linked presentation would seem to be appropriate in this situation according to FRS 5 because:

(1)   Some non-returnable proceeds have been received, but Timber Products has the right to further sums from Ready Support, the amounts of which depend on whether/when debtors will pay

(2)   Recourse for losses has a fixed monetary ceiling

(3)   Ready Support is paid only out of amounts collected from the factored debts and Timber Products has no right/obligation to repurchase the debts

The accounting treatment in the balance sheet will be as follows.

	£m	£m
Current assets: debtors subject to financing arrangements		
Gross debtors (15.0 – 0.6)		14.40
Non-returnable proceeds		
90% × net debtors	12.96	
Potential recourse	(0.20)	
		12.76
		1.64
Cash		12.96
Creditors		
Recourse under factored debts		0.20

(ii)   **Sale and repurchase agreement**

The characteristics of this transaction indicate that it is a secured loan, not a true sale of an asset, because Timber Products has not transferred the risks and benefits of ownership of the unseasoned hardwood to the buyer. FRS 5 therefore requires that the unseasoned hardwood should still be recognised as an asset (ie stock), that interest should be accrued, the carrying amount of the asset should be reviewed and that full disclosure should be made.

The accounting treatment is as follows.

	£m
Year ended 31 October 20X5	
Profit and loss account	
Interest payable (W)	2.8

	£m
Balance sheet	
Stock	40.0
Loan payable after more than one year (W)	42.8

Working: interest payable

You can work the interest rate on the loan from first principles without using the tables.

$40(1 + r)^5 = 56.10$

$(1 + r)^5 = \dfrac{56.1}{40} = 1.4025$ (see tables), *or*

$1 + r = \sqrt[5]{1.4025} = 1.07$

$r = 7\%$

∴ Interest for first year = 7% × £40m = £2.8m

∴ Balance outstanding = £42.8m

(iii)   **Consignment stock**

The characteristics of the consignment stock transaction indicate that the furniture is *not* an asset of the retailer on delivery, ie it remains an asset of Timber Products (mainly because the retailer has the right to return it). An indication that the stock *is* an asset of the retailer on delivery is the fact that the retailer is charged the price prevailing on the delivery date (rather than the date the stock is used by the retailer or the date the six month period expires).

On balance, the transaction should be treated as a genuine sale or return, with the price held for six months by the manufacturer. This is the more prudent view, indicating that the risks and benefits remain with Timber Products and this view is supported by the fact that retailers can return the stock just before the expiry of the six month period. The stock which has not been paid for should therefore be recognised by Timber Products at cost. The accounting treatment would therefore be as follows.

Year ended 31 October 20X5

Profit and loss account	£'000
Sales	6,000
Cost of sales (6,000 × 100/133¹/₃)	4,500
Gross profit	1,500
Other income	50
Other costs	
Insurance	15
Carriage	10
	25

Balance sheet	£'000
Stock at cost (4,000 × 100/133¹/₃)	3,000

Note. There is no absolute answer here. You could have argued that derecognition of the stock and recognition of the sale was more appropriate, in which case the figures would have been as follows.

Profit and loss account	£'000
Sales	10,000
Cost of sales	7,500
	2,500

Other income and cost figures as above.

Balance sheet	£'000
Debtors	4,000

A provision for returns would also be made based on past experience. A further point is that prudence might dictate that the stock should be recognised by both the retailer and Timber Products in their balance sheets.

(iv) **Quasi subsidiary**

The circumstances of this transaction are such that, in effect, Inter plc is acting as a subsidiary to Timber Products, ie it is a quasi subsidiary under FRS 5. The transaction has been set up this way in order to avoid the definition of a subsidiary in FRS 2.

The accounting treatment will show the results of Inter plc relating to the factory consolidated into Timber Products results. The factory will appear in the balance sheet at £8.5m (cost to the group) and the loan from Offshore Banking plc will be shown at £10m under creditors. The profit on the sale of the factory will be cancelled out, as will the fee, as intra-group transactions. The consolidated profit and loss account will include the profit or loss made by the plant and the interest of £1.5m paid to Offshore Banking plc.

(c) There are two aspects to examine in relation to this transaction.

(i) Is this transaction a **secured loan**? Timber Products is bearing risks in terms of insurance and maintenance payments. If it was also shown that Timber Products was paying a financing cost for the construction of the asset, then the equipment should be recognised as an asset in the Timber Product balance sheet with a loan for the same amount secured on the asset. More information is required in order to determine whether the amounts paid to Extractor-Plus represent a lender's return or whether they are market-rate rental amounts.

(ii) Is this a **leasing transaction**? The company may be attempting to circumvent the SSAP 21 definition of a finance lease. Information required would include the cost of the equipment, any minimum lease payments (if the hourly use falls below a certain level) and the length of the contract.

C1 Mineral

Top tips. This question required candidates to discuss the nature of information, which could be disclosed in annual reports in order to better assess the performance of a company. The question was case study based although many candidates ignored the information in the question. This type of question will arise regularly.

Examiner's comment. Too often candidates simply wrote about environmental reporting, or produced a ratio analysis type answer, or assessed the current performance of the company. The question was about the information content of published financial statements and how this might be improved. This was clearly set out in the question. Answers were often wide-ranging and irrelevant and candidates sometimes spent a disproportionate amount of time on this question. However, generally speaking the layout and style of the reports were quite good and marks were awarded accordingly. Overall this question was satisfactorily answered although it would be preferable if candidates used the facts in the scenario.

Marking scheme

		Marks
Reporting business performance:	Strategy and targets	3
	Operating performance	2
	Risks	2
	Investment	2
Analysis of financial position:	Long term capital structure	2
	Liquidity	2
	Treasury management	2
Corporate citizenship:	Corporate governance	2
	Ethics	1
	Employee reports	1
	Environment	1
Use of information in question		4
Style and layout		4
	Available	28
	Maximum	25

REPORT

To: The Directors
         Mineral plc

From: Accountant

Date: 12 November 20X1

Information to be disclosed in Annual Reports

In addition to the main financial statements, annual reports need to contain information about **key elements of corporate activity**. This report focuses on three main areas.

(a)   Reporting business performance
(b)   Analysis of the financial position
(c)   Nature of corporate citizenship

Reporting business performance

A report on business performance may include a ratio analysis, with a year on year comparison. The ratios commonly selected are those concerned with **profitability and liquidity:**

Profitability

	20X1	*20X0*
Return on capital employed	$\dfrac{10}{59+13} = 13.9\%$	$\dfrac{9}{46+9} = 16.4\%$
$\dfrac{\text{Gross profit}}{\text{sales}}$	$\dfrac{45}{250} = 18\%$	$\dfrac{35}{201} = 17.4\%$
$\dfrac{\text{Operating profit}}{\text{sales}}$	$\dfrac{10}{250} \times 100\% = 4\%$	$\dfrac{9}{201} \times 100\% = 4.5\%$

Long– and short-term liquidity

	20X1	*20X0*
$\dfrac{\text{Current assets}}{\text{Current liabilities}}$	$\dfrac{55}{25} = 2.2$	$\dfrac{43}{24} = 1.8$
$\dfrac{\text{Long - term liabilities}}{\text{Capital and reserves}}$	$\dfrac{13}{59} \times 100\% = 22\%$	$\dfrac{9}{46} \times 100\% = 19.6\%$

These ratios raise a number of questions.

(a)   Gross profit margin has risen, while operating profit margin and return on capital employed have fallen. Possible problems with **control of overheads?**

(b)   Short-term liquidity has improved, but gearing has deteriorated. Is the company using long-term loans to finance expansion? The company has **expanded**, both in turnover and fixed assets.

Standard ratios are a useful tool, but must be discussed in relation to the **specific circumstances of the company.** For example, the **impact of the increase in production** through the acquisition of the competitor company and the regeneration of old plants needs to be taken into account when considering turnover and fixed asset ratios and other comments in the report. When considering profit ratios, the **effectiveness of the cost control programme** can be assessed.

As well as year on year comparison, a report on business performance might usefully **compare actual performance against targets**. The company has in place some specific, measurable targets for growth in retained earnings, presumably based on the growth achieved from 20X0 to 20X1. Growth needs to be monitored to see if this target continues to be **realistic.**

No discussion of business performance would be complete without consideration of the **risks** that the business faces. In the context of Mineral plc, such a discussion would cover the proposed £40m **expenditure on research and development and investment in fixed assets.** Are the directors justified in assuming the predicted growth in retained earnings that this large expenditure is meant to bring about? The joint project to develop a new aluminium car body will be very lucrative if successful, but it is a risky undertaking.

Knowledge management is also an important issue where new processes and products are being developed.

Analysis of the financial position

Annual reports should contain a review of the company's financing arrangements and financial position as well as a review of its operating activities.

In the case of Mineral plc, such a review would note that **gearing has increased, but it is still low**, so the expenditure on research and development could be financed by borrowing, if not by retained earnings. In this connection it would also comment on the fact that, of the long-term loans of £13m, debentures of £4m could be converted into shares or redeemed. Current assets are comfortably in excess of current liabilities (by £30m), so the company should have little problem in redeeming the debentures. However, should the debentures be **converted**, the **existing shareholders' interest will be diluted**, and they should be made aware of this.

The report will need to disclose information about the **treasury management policies** of the company. This would cover such issues as the potential adverse movement in foreign exchange risk and details of the use of financial instruments for hedging. **Currency risk and interest rate risk** need to be managed and minimised, and the report needs to disclose the company's strategy for dealing with this. **Credit risk** is also an important issue, particularly as the company operates in the global market place.

A cash flow statement will be provided as part of the financial statements, but the annual report should also indicate the **maturity profile of borrowings**.

Finally, the financial analysis might benefit from the use of techniques such as **SWOT analysis,** covering potential liquidity problems and market growth. Reference would be made to the **cartel** of car manufacturers aiming to prevent the increased use of aluminium in the car industry.

Nature of corporate citizenship

Increasingly businesses are expected to be **socially responsible as well as profitable**. Strategic decisions by businesses, particularly global businesses nearly always have wider social consequences. It could be argued, as Henry Mintzburg does, that a company produces two outputs: goods and services, and the social consequences of its activities, such as pollution.

One major development in the area of corporate citizenship is the **environmental report.** While this is not a legal requirement, a large number of UK FTSE 100 companies produce them. Worldwide there are around 20 award schemes for environmental reporting, notably the ACCA's.

Mineral plc shows that it is responsible with regard to the environment by disclosing the following information.

(a) The use of the **eco-productivity index** in the financial performance of sites and divisions. This links environmental and financial performance

(b) The **regeneration of old plants**

(c) The development of **eco-friendly cars**. Particularly impressive, if successful, is the project to develop a new aluminium alloy car body. Aluminium is rust-free, and it is also lighter, which would reduce fuel consumption.

Another environmental issue which the company could consider is **emission levels** from factories. Many companies now include details of this in their environmental report.

The other main aspect of corporate citizenship where Mineral plc scores highly is in its **treatment of its workforce.** The company sees the workforce as the key factor in the growth of its business. The car industry had a reputation

in the past for **restrictive practices,** and the annual report could usefully discuss the extent to which these have been eliminated.

Employees of a businesses are **stakeholders** in that business, along with shareholders and customers. A company wishing to demonstrate good corporate citizenship will therefore be concerned with **employee welfare**. Accordingly, the annual report might usefully contain information on details of working hours, industrial accidents and sickness of employees.

In conclusion, it can be seen that the annual report can, and should go **far beyond the financial statements** and traditional ratio analysis.

C2 Value relevance

Top tips. This question required candidates to discuss the importance of published financial statements as a source of information, how financial reporting is changing to meet various needs, the problem of reliance on the earnings figure and the use of fair values. Part (c) of the question required a discussion about 'fair value' accounting.

Examiner's comment. The question was quite well answered but many candidates' answers were quite narrow, relying on traditional advantages and disadvantages of published financial statements. Again there was evidence of a lack of knowledge of current thinking and practice. Many candidates simply discussed the benefits of ratio analysis which is not sufficient for a Part 3 paper. Candidates would benefit from reading the scenario at the beginning of the question, as it often contains some guidance as regards the nature of the answer required. Part (c) was not well answered and candidates struggled to find examples of the use of 'fair value' accounting.

Marking scheme

		Marks
(a)	Subjective	11
(b)	Subjective	8
(c)	Subjective	6
		25

(a)   The importance of published financial statements

The objective of published financial statements is to satisfy the information needs of users. Some types of user will always need financial statements as their main source of information about a company. **Companies are required to file financial statements with the Registrar of Companies** so that a certain amount of information is available to the general public. The government uses financial statements in order to assess taxation and to regulate the activities of businesses.

Financial reporting has evolved to meet the needs of investors in large public companies and their advisers. Yet **published financial statements have serious limitations**: they are based on historic information and they only reflect the financial effects of transactions and events. **Investors need to predict a company's future performance**, including changes in shareholder value. These are affected by the development of new products, the quality of management, the use of new technology and the economic and political environment.

Traditional financial statements are **only one of many sources of information used by investors**. Other sources include **market data, product information, quarterly earnings announcements, press conferences and other briefings given by the directors to institutional investors, analysts and financial journalists**.

Traditional ratio analysis is becoming outdated. The Association for Investment Management and Research (AIMR) has developed global investment performance standards. These are based on 'total return', which includes realised and unrealised gains and income and rates of return that are adjusted for daily-weighted cash flows. **Earnings per share and the price earnings ratio continue to be important, but analysts now calculate a range of other measures. These include cash flow per share, market value per share and 'consensus earnings per share', which predicts future performance**.

Free cash flow is a key performance measure used by analysts to value a company. Free cash flow is cash revenues less cash expenses, taxation paid, cash needed for working capital and cash required for routine capital expenditure. **This can be compared with the cost of capital employed to assess whether**

shareholder value has increased or decreased. It can also be projected and discounted to provide an approximate market value.

(b) **How financial reporting is changing**

Financial reporting practice develops over time in response to changes in the business environment. For example, because businesses are entering into more sophisticated transactions, financial reporting **standards are now based on principles rather than rules**. Businesses increasingly operate across national boundaries and so there is an **emphasis on international convergence of accounting standards**. These developments improve the transparency and comparability of the information available to investors and other users of the financial statements.

Businesses increasingly recognise the **limitations of traditional financial statements** and **non-financial information is now routinely included in the annual report**. Companies disclose information about **risks and opportunities, long term goals, products, human resources, intangible assets and research and development activities**. They may also report the effects of their operations on the **natural environment** and on the **wider social community**. These disclosures reflect a growing awareness that **an entity's performance goes far beyond its earnings for the year**.

Despite this, **many users and preparers of financial statements still focus narrowly on the earnings figure**. As a result, earnings before interest, tax, depreciation and amortisation **(EBITDA) has been developed as a key performance measure. 'Aggressive earnings management' (inappropriate methods of revenue recognition) and other forms of 'creative accounting' may be used in an attempt to enhance EBITDA**. Emphasis on profits means that quite small changes in earnings can bring about major fluctuations in a company's share price.

(c) **The use of fair values**

Financial statements should provide information that helps users to predict the future performance of a company. Fair values are more relevant than historic costs for this purpose. In theory fair values reflect the present value of future cash flows and the fair value of an asset shows its potential contribution to future cash flows.

However, **there will always be a difference between the overall value of a company and the aggregate fair values of its assets and liabilities**. (This difference is often described as goodwill.) There may not be a direct relationship between future cash flows and the assets and liabilities on the balance sheet. In addition, **investors and others may use financial statements for purposes other than predicting future performance and cash flows**.

It can be difficult to arrive at a fair value for an asset or liability because there may not always be a reliable market price. If this is the case, (in theory) fair values are based on the company's own predictions of future cash flow and can only be subjective.

Historic cost accounting has the advantages of being **objective and reliable**. It is **based on actual transactions which can be verified**. Therefore **traditional historic cost financial statements may better meet the needs of users than financial statements based on fair values**.

C3 Preparation question: Financial analysis

Top tips. This is a straightforward question on interpretation of accounts, of a manageable size and providing you with all the ratios you need. You should, as with all interpretation questions, spend some time *thinking* about the ratios before you start writing. Mark what you think are the significant trends shown in the question and make brief notes which will serve as an answer plan. Then proceed to discuss each area, using sensible headings to break your report up, and including a brief introduction and conclusion.

WANDAFOOD PRODUCTS
FIVE YEAR SUMMARY: 20X1 TO 20X5

Prepared by: An Accountant
Date: 28 February 20X6

Introduction

This report discusses the trends shown in the five year summary prepared from the published accounts for the five years ended 31 December 20X5. It also considers how price changes over that period may have limited the usefulness of the historical cost data provided.

Profitability

The net profit margin has remained fairly constant, although it dropped in 20X3. Asset turnover has decreased over the five years, pulling back a little in 20X4. Return on capital (or return on assets), the primary ratio produced by combining these two secondary ratios, has therefore decreased over the period but was at its lowest in 20X3.

These findings seem to indicate that assets are not being used more efficiently and that this has caused the decrease in return on assets. Inflation may be responsible for increases in turnover which would mask even worse decreases in efficiency.

Interest and dividend cover

Interest cover improved markedly between 20X1 and 20X2, falling back a little in 20X3 and 20X4 but now below the 20X1 level, indicating increases in debt and/or interest rates. Dividend cover, however, after dropping below 20X1 levels for three years, has now recovered some lost ground. In both cases cover was adequate, even at the lowest points; however, since there has been a substantial increase in gearing, interest cover ought to be watched carefully. Profits may be available to cover interest and dividends but this must be matched by good cash flow.

Debt to equity

Debt: equity fell in 20X2 but has steadily increased until in 20X5 it was almost double its 20X1 level. Minority interests appear to have remained a relatively insignificant element in the group's funding. It is more likely that debt has increased than that equity has decreased (for example, because of a purchase or redemption of own shares). Interest cover has fallen in line with this increase in borrowing as a proportion of long-term capital.

Liquidity

Both the current and the quick ratios have declined over the period, although in 20X2 they both improved. However, they have been fairly constant between 20X3 and 20X5 and are quite high, although comments on the adequacy of these ratios are of very limited utility in the absence of information about the company's activities and industry averages.

The reduction may have been planned to reduce the costs involved in maintaining high levels of stock and allowing generous credit to customers. From the differential between the quick and current ratios it would seem that stock is a significant asset here. However, current liabilities must not be allowed to increase to the extent that current assets (and especially liquid assets) are insufficient to cover them, as this can lead to a liquidity crisis. Worsening liquidity ratios can be an indicator of overtrading but this most often arises when expansion is funded from short-term borrowings, whereas here new long-term capital in the form of debt appears to have been found.

Because working capital has fallen in size, it is now being used more efficiently, generating more sales from a reduced base. It would seem likely, given the slight fall in asset turnover, that fixed asset turnover has worsened considerably and that the improvement in working capital turnover has compensated for this in calculating total asset turnover. It may be that long-term borrowings have financed capital expenditure which has not yet affected operations. (An increase in the amount of fixed assets would decrease fixed asset turnover if turnover did not increase correspondingly.)

Investors' ratios

Earnings, dividends and net assets per share have all increased over the period. There has therefore been no need to increase dividends regardless of fluctuations in earnings.

The increase in net assets per share seems to indicate either that retained profits and borrowings have been used to increase fixed asset expenditure or (less likely) that assets have been revalued each year.

Inflation

Historical cost accounts do not show the effect on the group's operating capacity of rising prices over a period. The modest increases in EPS and dividend do not suggest that profit has increased sufficiently to compensate for more than a very low level of inflation. It is also possible that the value of assets is understated, so that ROCE and asset turnover measures are all understated. The underlying trends in real terms may be very much worse than those shown in historical cost terms.

Conclusion

The group would appear, from this superficial analysis, to be a steady performer but not expanding fast. This may be an advantage in times of recession: debt is probably not so high as to cause liquidity problems nor have shareholders come to expect a high payout ratio. However, inflation may be eroding its profits. The possible recent expansion of fixed assets may help it to grow in future, as will its improved working capital management.

C4 Rockby and Bye

> **Top tips.** This question required candidates to have knowledge of FRED 32 and discontinued operations. In part (b), you had to discuss whether certain assets would be considered to be 'held for sale'.
>
> **Easy marks.** The obvious easy marks are for Part (a), which is straight out of your Study Text. But as the examiner said, 'Often in questions of this nature, candidates assume certain facts about the scenario. If the assumptions are reasonable, due regard is taken and credit given.'
>
> **Examiner's comment.** This question was well answered, though candidates did not use the facts of the question in formulating their answer as much as they should have done.

(a) **Sale of the subsidiary under current UK GAAP**

The main issue is whether Bye is a **discontinued operation** as defined by FRS 3 *Reporting Financial Performance*. In order to meet the definition the sale of the operation must either be **completed in the period** or within the **earlier of three months after the beginning of the subsequent period and the date on which the financial statements are approved.** As the sale is not expected to be completed until 1 July 20X4 **this condition is not met** and Bye must be treated as a **continuing operation** in the financial statements for the year ended 31 March 20X4.

No contract has been signed for the sale and therefore **no provision for future losses** should be made. Although the group is effectively committed to the sale, FRS 3 states that there **should be a 'binding sale agreement'** before any provision can be made. FRS 12 *Provisions, contingent liabilities and contingent assets* also states that there is no obligation to dispose of the subsidiary unless there is a binding sale agreement and no provision can be made unless there is an obligation.

However, because Bye is **making losses**, the group should carry out an **impairment review** in accordance with FRS 11 *Impairment of fixed assets and goodwill*.

The impairment loss is calculated as follows:

	£'000
Net assets at 31 March 20X4	5,000
Goodwill	1,000
	6,000
Value in use at 15 May 20X4	3,900
Add losses incurred from 1 April 20X4 to 15 May 20X4	500
Value in use at 31 March 20X4	4,400
Net realisable value	4,500

Recoverable amount is the **higher of net realisable value** and **value in use**. In this case, recoverable amount **is net realisable value** and so there is an **impairment loss of £1.5 million.** This is allocated first to goodwill, then to any other intangible assets, then to tangible assets.

Sale of the subsidiary under FRED 32

FRED 32 *Disposal of non-current assets and presentation of discontinued operations* requires an asset or disposal group (such as a subsidiary) to be classified as held for sale in the following circumstances.

(i)   Management are **committed** to the sale.

(ii)   The asset is **available for immediate sale** in its **present condition** subject to **terms that are usual and customary**.

(iii)   An **active programme to locate a buyer** has been initiated.

(iv)   The sale is **highly probable** and **expected to be completed within one year** from the date of classification.

(v)   The **market price** is **reasonable** in relation to the asset's current fair value.

(vi)   There are **unlikely to be significant changes** to the plan.

The proposed sale of Bye **appears to meet these conditions**. Although the sale had not taken place by the time that the 20X4 financial statements were approved, **negotiations were in progress** and the sale is expected to take place on 1 July 20X4, well **within a year** after the decision to sell. Rockby had **committed** itself to the sale **before its year-end of 31 March 20X4.**

FRED 32 requires items held for sale to be measured at the **lower of their carrying amount and fair value less costs to sell** (net realisable value) and therefore Bye will be carried **at £4.5 million** in the balance sheet and the loss of £1.5 million will be recognised in the profit and loss account. The impairment loss is written off against fixed assets.

Where a subsidiary is held for sale it is **presented separately** from other assets and liabilities in the balance sheet and its assets and liabilities should not be offset. If Bye represents a **separate major line of business or geographical area** of operations it will also qualify as a **discontinued operation**, which means that on the **face of the profit and loss account** the group must disclose its **revenue, expenses, pre-tax profit or loss and income tax expense**. The group must also disclose the **gain or loss recognised on the remeasurement of Bye** and its net **cash flows.** The notes to the financial statements must also disclose a description of the facts and circumstances leading to the expected disposal and the expected manner and timing of the disposal.

(b)   **Items of plant**

If the items of plant are to be classified as 'held for sale', management must be **committed** to the sale and the sale must be **highly probable** and **expected to take place within one year**. The operating leases **do not appear to qualify** as the company is **undecided** as to whether to sell or lease the plant under finance leases. Therefore the company should **continue to treat them as fixed assets** and to depreciate them. The value in use of the items is greater than their carrying value and so they are **not impaired**.

The other items of plant will also **not be classified as 'held for sale'**. Although they were no longer in use at 31 March 20X4 and were sold subsequently, a **firm decision** to sell them **had not been made by the year-end**. FRED 32 **prohibits retrospective use** of the 'held for sale' classification if, as in this case, assets are sold after the year end but before the financial statements are authorised for issue, although the sale should be **disclosed as an event after the balance sheet date**.

Head office land and buildings

In order to qualify as 'held for sale' an asset must be **available for immediate sale** in its **present condition**, subject to the usual terms. Although the company had taken the decision to sell the property at 31 March 20X3, the **subsidence** would have meant that a buyer was **unlikely to be found** for the property until the renovations had taken place. Therefore the property **did not qualify as 'held for sale' at 31 March 20X3**.

At 31 March 20X4 the property **had been on the market for nine months** at the price of £10 million. **No buyer** had yet been found. Despite the fact that the **market had deteriorated significantly** the company had **not reduced the price**. The property was eventually sold for £7.5 million on 1 June 20X4. To qualify as being held for sale at the year-end the **market price must be reasonable** in relation to the asset's current fair value. It appears that the market price of £10 million is **not reasonable when compared with the eventual selling price** of £7.5 million, the **offer** of £8.3 million received on 20 April or the **carrying value** of £7 million. Therefore the property **should not be classified as 'held for sale' at 31 March 20X4**.

C5 Vident

Top tips. This question examined the topic of share-based payment. The first part of the question dealt with the reasons why a standard was needed in this area. This type of question will often appear when a new standard is issued. The other elements dealt with the accounting for a share-based payment transaction, and the deferred tax implications.

Easy marks. Part (a) is very straightforward and can be reproduced from the BPP Study Text. And nine marks is generous for a straightforward bit.

Examiner's comment. Candidates did not seem to know FRS 20 very well. Candidates managed to discuss the reasons behind the standard quite well but generally found it difficult to account for a transaction. The actual calculation of the expense/equity to be recognised was at a basic level, but candidates did not seem to be able to achieve the desired result – a discussion, and calculation, of the way a share-based transaction should be accounted for. Similarly, the deferred tax implications were generally not understood by candidates. The deferred tax aspect is important for companies adopting the standard, as in many regions a significant deferred tax asset may be created.

Marking scheme

		Marks
(a)	Discussion	9
(b)	Computation and discussion	9
(c)	Computation and discussion	7
		25

REPORT

To: Directors of Vident
From:
Subject: FRS 20 *Share based payment*
Date: June 20X5

As requested, this report explains why share based payments should be recognised in the financial statements. It also explains how the directors' share options should be accounted for in the financial statements for the year ended 31 May 20X5.

(a)   **Why share based payments should be recognised in the financial statements**

FRS 20 *Share based payment* applies to **all share option schemes granted after 7 November 20X2**. The directors have put forward several arguments for not recognising the expense of remunerating directors in this way.

Share options have no cost to the company

When shares are **issued for cash** or in a business acquisition, **an accounting entry is needed** to **recognise the receipt of cash** (or other resources) as consideration for the issue. Share options (the right to receive shares in future) **are also issued in consideration for resources**: services rendered by directors or employees. These resources are **consumed by the company** and it would be **inconsistent not to recognise an expense**.

Share issues do not meet the definition of an expense in the ASB's Statement of Principles

The *Statement of Principles* defines an expense (a gain) as a **decrease in ownership interest: a decrease in assets** or an **increase in liabilities**. It is not immediately obvious that employee services meet the definition of an asset and therefore **it can be argued that consumption of those services does not meet the definition of an expense**. However, share options **are issued for consideration in the form of employee services** so that **arguably there is an asset**, although it is **consumed at the same time that it is received**. Therefore the recognition of an expense relating to share based payment is **consistent with the *Statement of Principles***.

The expense relating to share options is already recognised in the diluted earnings per share calculation

It can be argued that to recognise an expense in the profit and loss account **would have the effect of distorting diluted earnings per share** as diluted earnings per share would then **take the expense into account twice**. This is not a valid argument. There are **two events** involved: **issuing the options**; and **consuming the resources** (the directors' services) received as consideration. The diluted earnings per share calculation **only reflects the issue of the options**; there is **no adjustment to basic earnings**. Recognising an expense reflects the consumption of services. There is **no 'double counting'**.

Accounting for share based payment may discourage the company from introducing new share option plans

This is quite **possibly true**. Accounting for share based payment **reduces earnings**. However, it **improves the information provided** in the financial statements, as these now make users aware of the **true economic consequences** of issuing share options as remuneration. The economic consequences are the reason why share option schemes may be discontinued. FRS 20 simply **enables management and shareholders** to **reach an informed decision** on the best method of remuneration.

(b)   Accounting for share options in the financial statements for the year ended 31 May 20X5

The basic principle of accounting for share options is that **an expense is recognised** for the **services rendered** by the directors and a **corresponding amount is credited to equity**. The transaction is **measured at the fair value of the options granted at the grant date** and fair value is taken to be the **market price**. Where (as is usual) options vest only after staff have completed a specified period of service, the expense is **allocated to accounting periods over this period of service**.

FRS 20 **does not apply to the share options granted to J. Van Heflin on 1 June 20X2** as this is before 7 November 20X2 (the date set for accounting for share options). It applies to the other share options.

Options granted to J. Van Heflin on 1 June 20X3

The **performance conditions have been met** and the director is **still working for the company** at 31 May 20X5. As the **number of shares** that will vest is **fixed**, the expense is **allocated on a straight line basis to the two years ended 31 May 20X5**.

Options granted to R. Ashworth on 1 June 20X4

The **performance conditions** (the increase in the share price to £13.50) **have not yet been met**. However, the director is **still working for the company** and **must work for the company for three years** before the options vest, so the **expense is recognised**. Again, the **number of shares is fixed**, so the expense is **allocated on a straight line basis over the three years to 31 May 20X7**.

The expense to be recognised is calculated as follows:

	At 1 June 20X4 (opening reserves)	Year ended 31 May 20X5
	£	£
J. Van Heflin (20,000 × £5 × ½)	50,000	50,000
R. Ashworth (50,000 × £6 × 1/3)		100,000
	50,000	150,000

At 1 June 20X4 the **opening reserves are reduced by £50,000 and a separate component of equity is increased by £50,000**.

An **expense of £150,000 is recognised** in the profit and loss account for the year ended 31 May 20X5. **Equity** (the same separate component as before) is **credited with £150,000**.

(c) **Deferred tax implications of the recognition of an expense for directors' share options**

The company will **recognise an expense** for the consumption of employee services given in consideration for share options granted, **but will not receive a tax deduction until the share options are actually exercised**. Therefore a timing difference arises and FRS 19 *Deferred tax* requires the recognition of deferred tax.

A **deferred tax asset** (a deductible timing difference) results from the **difference** between the **tax value of the services received** (a tax deduction in future periods) and the **carrying value of zero**. The future tax deduction should be based on the **intrinsic value of the options at the year end**. This is the **difference** between the **fair value of the share** and the **exercise price of the option**.

At 1 June 20X4

Deferred tax asset:

	£m
Fair value (20,000 × £12.50 × 1/2)	125,000
Exercise price of option (20,000 × £4.50 × ½)	(45,000)
Intrinsic value (estimated tax deduction)	80,000
Tax at 30%	24,000

Therefore:

- A deferred tax asset of £24,000 is recognised in the opening balance sheet.
- Opening reserves are increased by £24,000.

Year to 31 May 20X5

Deferred tax asset:

	£
Fair value:	
(20,000 × £12)	240,000
(50,000 × £12 × 1/3)	200,000
	440,000
Exercise price of options	
(20,000 × £4.50)	(90,000)
(50,000 × £6 × 1/3)	(100,000)
Intrinsic value (estimated tax deduction)	250,000
Tax at 30%	75,000
Less previously recognised	(24,000)
	51,000

Therefore:

- A deferred tax asset of £75,000 is recognised in the balance sheet at 31 May 20X5.
- There is potential deferred tax income of £51,000 for the year ended 31 May 20X5.

I hope that the above explanations and advice are helpful. Please do not hesitate to contact me should you require any further assistance.

C6 Ashlee

Top tips. This question was a case study which described mistakes or problems occurring in the financial statements of a company. Candidates had to discuss the implications for the financial statements. The case study dealt with going concern, reorganisation provisions, discontinuance, revenue recognition, impairment, financial instruments, and breach of loan covenants. The answer required a discussion of the implications of the events, together with relevant computations. In the answer, it is important to set out the basic principles relating to the event, then quantify (if possible) the impact on the financial statements and, finally, to discuss the implications/solutions to the problem.

Easy marks. There are no obviously easy marks in this question, which does not specify a mark allocation for each item. It is best to assume that marks are allocated equally.

Examiner's comment. The question was quite well-answered but candidates do not seem to be able to apply their knowledge to the case study. Instead, rote knowledge was set out in answers and not application of that knowledge. This is a continuing problem. In addition, the areas covered by this question appear frequently in this paper and yet the standard of answers is not really improving.

Marking scheme

		Marks
Introduction		3
Pilot		9
Gibson		8
Ashlee		6
	Available	26
	Maximum	25

General

The **mistakes** which have been found in the financial statements **must be adjusted** before the financial statements are approved by the directors and published.

Loan covenants have been breached. This means that **the directors should determine whether the company continues to be a going concern**. If this is not the case, the financial statements for the year ended 31 March 20X5 should not be prepared on a going concern basis. The company appears to have come to an arrangement with the loan creditors and this suggests that **in practice it will be able to carry on trading** at least in the short term. Any **material uncertainties** that **cast significant doubts on the company's ability to continue as a going concern** should be **disclosed** in the notes to the financial statements, as required by FRS 18 *Accounting policies*.

The fact that the loan covenants have been breached suggests that the **assets of the group may have become impaired**. An **impairment review should be carried out** in accordance with FRS 11 *Impairment of fixed assets and goodwill* and **any impairment loss should be recognised** in the financial statements for the year ended 31 March 20X5.

Pilot

FRS 12 *Provisions, contingent liabilities and contingent assets* states that **a provision for reorganisation costs cannot be recognised** unless the entity had a **constructive obligation** to carry out the reorganisation at the year end. The **decision** to reorganise Pilot **was not taken until after the year end**. Therefore the reorganisation costs of £4 million **cannot be recognised** in the financial statements for the year ended 31 March 20X5. The financial statements should **disclose** details of the planned reorganisation in the notes as it is a **non-adjusting event** as defined by FRS 21 *Events after the balance sheet date*.

A major reorganisation indicates that **the assets of Pilot may be impaired** and so an **impairment review is required**. Because the **reorganisation costs** cannot be recognised, these **should not be included in any calculation of recoverable amount**. The **recoverable amount** (value in use) of Pilot is **£82 million** without the reorganisation, this is **less than the carrying value of £85 million** and therefore the company should **recognise an impairment loss of £3 million**. This reduces the carrying value of Pilot's **goodwill**.

Gibson

The **decision** to sell Gibson was **made before the year end** and the sale is **expected to take place in June 20X5**. The issue here is whether the sale meets the definition of a **discontinued operation** in FRS 3 *Reporting financial performance*. This will be the case if:

- The sale is **completed** either **in the period** or before the **earlier of three months after the beginning of the subsequent period** and the **date on which the financial statements are approved**.

- It has a **material effect** on the nature and focus of the group's operations and represents a **material reduction** in its operating facilities.

- The assets, liabilities, results and activities are **clearly distinguishable**, physically, operationally and for financial reporting purposes.

The third condition and possibly the second condition are met, but the **first condition will not be met unless the sale is completed before 30 June 20X5**. Therefore Gibson is likely to be reported under **continuing operations for the year ended 31 March 20X5**. Again, the planned sale should be **disclosed** as a non-adjusting post balance sheet event. An **impairment review** is required (see below) because of the reorganisation and this would be the case even if there were no plans to sell Gibson.

The accounting treatment of Gibson **would be different under the proposals in FRED 32** *Disposal of non-current assets and presentation of discontinued operations*. The contract for sale **was being negotiated** at the time of preparation of the financial statements and the sale **appears to be certain**. Therefore Gibson **meets the definition of a 'disposal group'**: a group of assets to be disposed of in a single transaction.

A disposal group is **separately disclosed on the face of the balance sheet** and **details** of the disposal **are disclosed in the notes** to the financial statements.

Under FRED 32, a disposal group is **measured at the lower of its carrying amount and fair value less costs to sell**. The **carrying amount is £450 million** and **fair value less costs to sell is £410 million** (£415 million less selling costs of £5 million) and therefore **an impairment loss of £40 million is recognised**. This impairment loss will almost certainly be the same under current UK GAAP. As Gibson is being sold, it is unlikely that value in use is higher than net realisable value/fair value less costs to sell. The loss is **allocated as set out in FRS 11**: first to goodwill, then to the other fixed assets on a pro-rata basis.

Impairment calculation

	Before impairment £m	Impairment loss £m	After impairment £m
Goodwill	30	(30)	–
Property, plant and equipment at cost	120	(4)	116
Property, plant and equipment at valuation	180	(6)	174
Stock	100	–	100
Net current assets	20	–	20
	450	(40)	410

Revenue recognition

An Application Note to FRS 5 *Reporting the substance of transactions* states that revenue should be recognised when it obtains the right to consideration. **Where properties are sold**, this is normally **when title passes**. Ashlee has followed this policy in previous years and **the change seems questionable**. Therefore the **profit of £10 million on sale should not be recognised** in the profit and loss account statement and the properties should **continue to be recognised at their carrying value in the balance sheet**.

Financial instruments

FRS 26 *Financial instruments: measurement* allows some financial assets to be designated as 'at fair value through profit or loss'. The shares are **neither derivatives, nor held for trading** and so they are **not required to be classified as 'at fair value through profit or loss'**. Investments in equity instruments that **do not have a quoted market price** in an active market and **whose fair value cannot be reliably measured cannot be designated in this way**.

If the shares are **designated as 'at fair value through profit or loss'** the shares are **initially valued at £3 million** (150,000 × £20). **Transaction costs are charged to the profit and loss account**. At 31 March 20X5 the shares are **revalued to their fair value of £3.75 million** (150,000 × £25) and a **gain of £750,000 is recognised in the profit and loss account**.

If the shares are **classified as 'available for sale'** they are **also valued on a fair value basis**, except that **transaction costs are included in the initial measurement**. Therefore the shares are **initially valued at £3.1 million**. At the year end they are **remeasured to £3.75 million as before**. The **gain of £650,000 is recognised in the statement of total recognised gains and losses**, rather than as part of the profit for the year. When the shares are eventually **sold**, the cumulative **gains and losses on remeasurement are 'recycled'** from reserves to the profit and loss account.

A recent amendment to the equivalent international standard has **restricted the use of the fair value option**. It seems likely that FRS 26 will be similarly amended in due course. Given **the company's present circumstances** and the fact that the **financial statements are open to particular scrutiny**, it may be **prudent to classify the shares as 'available for sale'**.

C7 Financial performance

Top tips. The question required candidates to set out why a single statement of performance was being developed. Additionally, candidates had to discuss the issues surrounding the treatment of gains and losses on tangible non-current assets, and the recycling of gains and losses. Remember that it is the characteristics of the gains and losses that determines the accounting treatment.

Easy marks. Part (a) has some easy marks for listing arguments that will be in your text book. Likewise Part (b)(ii)

Examiner's comment. The question was quite well-answered but the answers demonstrated that many candidates do not read very widely. Many candidates did not have an understanding of the different nature of gains/losses. Many candidates did not understand the issues surrounding the recognition of a profit in the performance statement on more than one occasion. Examples of recycling were not often discussed in candidates' answers.

Marking scheme

				Marks
(a)		Reasons 2 marks per point	Maximum	8
(b)	(i)	Factors 2 marks per point	Maximum	8
	(ii)	Discussion		9
				25

(a) There are several reasons why the three accounting standards boards believe that a single statement of financial performance is needed. Most of these are a response to the problems of reporting performance under current accounting standards.

   (i) It is **difficult to compare** the financial performance of **entities in different countries**, because a variety of different formats are used. There are also a variety of different requirements relating to comparative information.

   (iii) Business practice is becoming more sophisticated and as a result **many see traditional performance measures such as profit before tax as too simplistic**. There is evidence that the **use of the traditional performance measures is decreasing**. The financial statements should provide users with the information that they need to arrive at key performance measures. Because the key measures used are changing and evolving it can be argued that increasingly they do not do this.

   (iii) There are a number of **different views** as to how an entity's **financial performance should be defined**. This means that there is no agreement on what the key performance measures should be and therefore no agreement about the information that should be provided in the financial statements.

   (iv) There is often **too much aggregation** of financial information. This prevents users from analysing an entity's performance effectively.

   (v) Information is often **inconsistently classified** within and outside totals and subtotals.

   (vi) **Some relevant items are not included in profit and loss.** For example, many countries require gains and losses on the retranslation of the net investment in a foreign subsidiary to be recognised in the statement of total recognised gains and losses (equity), rather than the profit and loss account. In contrast, **some questionable items may be included in profit and loss**. Some countries require proposed dividends to be shown on the face of the profit and loss account, although they are not an expense, but a transaction with the owners of the business.

(vii)   Current financial reporting uses a **mixed measurement model** in which some items are measured at historic cost and some at fair value/current value. Therefore users of the financial statements **need to be able to distinguish between items measured at historic cost and items measured at current or fair value** and to distinguish between **operating gains** and **revaluation gains**. Some countries, such as the UK, now use an additional performance statement (the statement of total recognised gains and losses) to record revaluation gains and losses, but reporting is inconsistent and sometimes confusing to users.

(viii) Financial instruments have caused particular problems. It is often **difficult for users to understand the effects of financial instruments on performance**, because the way in which gains and losses are reported depends upon the classification of the instrument.

(ix)   Some countries permit the **'recycling'** of certain gains and losses from equity (reserves) to the profit and loss account so that they are **effectively recognised twice**. Others prohibit it. These **inconsistencies are unhelpful to users**.

(b)   (i)   Determining how and where to report gains and losses arising on tangible fixed assets presents particular problems. Some assets are measured at historic cost while others are measured at current value or fair value. Gains and losses take a number of different forms: revaluation gains and losses, gains and losses on disposal, depreciation and impairment.

Revaluation gains and losses are **part of an entity's performance, but not part of its operating activities.** Users need to be able to appreciate this difference and therefore there is a need to **report them separately from operating activities**. There is also an argument that as they are **not certain until the asset is sold** they should be **reported outside the main performance statement** or in a separate section of it ('other gains and losses').

It is generally accepted that **depreciation** is not a loss in market value, but an **application of the accruals concept**. Depreciation reflects the consumption of an asset by the entity and for this reason it is **reported in operating activities**.

There are two possible views of **impairment.** One is that it is a form of **depreciation**; it arises because the **economic benefits relating to an asset have been consumed**. This type of impairment is clearly an **operating loss**. The other view of impairment is that it is a **holding loss** and this **should not be reported in operating activities**. Impairment that is effectively a holding loss may arise where an asset that has previously been revalued upwards becomes impaired. Under current accounting standards, the **impairment is set off against the revaluation surplus** relating to the asset. Any excess is treated as consumption of economic benefits and is reported in operating activities. There is an **argument that** because an asset is impaired if its carrying amount is above its recoverable amount, *all* **impairment losses represent consumption of economic benefits** and **all impairment losses should be reported within operating activities.**

Gains and losses on disposal are calculated as the difference between the sale proceeds and the asset's carrying amount. There are **several arguments** for **reporting these outside operating activities**. Selling assets is **not normally part of an entity's trading operations**. Where a gain or a loss is material, users of the financial statements need to be made aware that it will not recur (although this issue is partly one of separate presentation, rather than where to report particular gains and losses in the performance statement). Where a **gain** arises **on an asset that has been revalued**, that gain is a **holding gain, rather than an operating gain**.

There are also **arguments for reporting gains and losses on disposal within operating activities**. Where an asset is carried at historical cost, the gain or loss is **effectively an adjustment to depreciation** (for example, because the rate has been underestimated) and depreciation is an operating expense. The **same argument applies** where a loss on disposal has arisen **because the asset is impaired**. However, many would still take the view that there is such a thing as a holding loss (caused by a fall in market value) as distinct from an impairment loss (caused by consumption of economic benefits). A **holding loss should not be included in operating activities**. On the other hand it would **be difficult to clearly distinguish between a holding loss and an impairment loss** and this ambiguity would provide companies with a means of manipulating their operating profits.

One objective of a single performance statement is to enable users to **appreciate the various components of financial performance**. This will be achieved if **gains and losses with similar characteristics are reported together.** This will also improve the comparability of the financial statements.

(ii) **Recycling** occurs where an item of financial performance is **reported in more than one accounting period.** An item that is recycled is recognised in the financial statements twice. For example, current accounting standards require gains and losses on the retranslation of the net investment in a foreign operation to be reported in equity (the statement of total recognised gains and losses) when they occur and then to be reported again in the profit and loss account when the operation is eventually sold.

The main **argument for recycling** is that **all items are ultimately part of the operating or financing activities of an entity**. Therefore **all items should pass through the main performance statement** or be reported as part of earnings at some point in time, even if they have previously been recognised in equity. It has also been argued that when unrealised items become realised they should be reported again and when uncertain measurements become certain they should be reported again.

The **argument against recycling** is that **an item should only be recognised in the statement(s) of financial performance once**, regardless of whether it is realised or unrealised. If an item is recognised in the financial statements it is assumed that there is reasonable **certainty that it exists** and that it can be **measured reliably**. There is **no justification** for **recognising it in equity/'other gains and losses' in one period** and **recognising it again in profit and loss/operating activities in a subsequent period**.

The idea that an item should only be reported in the profit or loss account if it is **realised** (almost certain to result in a present or future inflow or outflow of cash) has **become outdated**. In many countries, **realisation is a legal concept**. Unrealised gains, such as revaluation gains, are subjective. **Only realised gains can be recognised in distributable profits** because they are **certain**. However, given the **increasing complexity of the business environment** and the **widespread use of financial instruments**, the distinction between realised and unrealised profits is **no longer a particularly useful basis** for **classifying elements of financial performance**. In practice, the effect of realised gains and losses is **shown in the cash flow statement. Unrealised items often form an important part of** an entity's **overall financial performance** and there is **no longer any real case for excluding them** from the performance statement.

C8 Egin Group

Top tips. This question dealt with the importance of the disclosure of related party transactions and the criteria determining a related party. Additionally, it required candidates to identify related parties, and to account for goodwill and a loan made to one of the related parties which was an overseas subsidiary. Don't forget, from your group accounting knowledge, that goodwill relating to the overseas subsidiary is treated as a foreign currency asset and translated at the closing rate of exchange.

Easy marks. Part (a) should earn you five very easy marks, as it is basic knowledge. Part (b) is application, but very straightforward. This leaves only nine marks for the more difficult aspects

Examiner's comment. The importance of related parties and their criteria was quite well answered, although candidates often quoted specific examples rather than the criteria for establishing related parties. The identification of related party relationships was well answered, but the accounting for the goodwill of the foreign subsidiary (and the loan made to it) were poorly answered.

			Marks
(a)	(i)	Reasons and explanation	5
	(ii)	Egin	5
		Spade	3
		Atomic	3
(b)		Goodwill	5
		Loan	5
		Available	26
		Maximum	25

(a) (i) **Why it is important to disclose related party transactions**

The directors of Egin are correct to say that related party transactions are a normal feature of business. However, where a company **controls** or can exercise **influence** over another the **financial performance and position of both companies can be affected**. For example, one group company can sell goods to another at artificially low prices. Even where there are no actual transactions between group companies, **a parent normally influences the way in which a subsidiary operates**. For example, a parent may instruct a subsidiary not to trade with particular customers or suppliers or not to undertake particular activities.

In the absence of other information, users of the financial statements **assume that a company pursues its interests independently** and undertakes transactions on an **arm's length basis** on terms that could have been obtained in a transaction with a third party. Knowledge of related party relationships and transactions affects the way in which users assess a company's operations and the risks and opportunities that it faces. Therefore **details of related party relationships and transactions should be disclosed.** Even if the company's transactions and operations have not been affected by a related party relationship, **disclosure puts users on notice that they may be affected in future.**

FRS 8 *Related party disclosures* states that two or more parties are related if:

(a) one party has **direct or indirect control** of the other party; or

(b) the parties are subject to **common control** from the same source; or

(c) one party has **influence** over the financial and operating policies of the other party to an extent that the other party might be inhibited from pursuing its own separate interests; or

(d) the parties are subject to **influence from the same source** to such an extent that one of the parties has subordinated its own separate interests.

Control is the **power to govern the financial and operating policies of an entity** so as to obtain benefits from its activities. FRS 8 does not define **influence**, but one party clearly influences another in situations where that other party might be **inhibited from pursuing its own interests.**

(ii) **Nature of related party relationships**

Within the Egin Group

Briars and Doye are related parties of Egin because they are **controlled** by Egin. **Eye is also a related party of Egin** because Egin has **significant influence** over it. **Briars and Doye** are also **related parties of each other** because they are under **common control** and have **directors in common.**

ANSWERS

Briars and Doye may not be related parties of Eye, as there is only one director in common and entities are not necessarily deemed related because they have a director in common. A related party relationship exists if any of the parties **subordinated their own interests** as a result of the **influence** of any of the others.

Although Tang was sold several months before the year end it was a **related party of Egin, Briars and Doye until then**. In these circumstances, FRS 8 requires the subsidiary to be treated as a related party for the **whole of the period**. The purchase of the machinery took place after Tang was sold and therefore it **will not be eliminated on consolidation**. Therefore this transaction **should be disclosed**.

Blue is a related party of Briars as a **director of Briars controls it**. Because the director is not on the management board of Egin it is **not clear whether Blue is also a related party of Egin**. This would depend on whether the director is considered key management personnel at a group level. The director's services as a consultant to the group may mean that a related party relationship exists.

Between Spade and the Egin Group

Spade is a related party of Doye because it holds **significant voting power** in Doye. This means that the **sale** of plant and machinery **to Spade must be disclosed**. **Egin is not necessarily a related party of Spade** simply because both have an investment in Doye. A related party relationship will only exist if one party **exercises influence** over another **in practice.**

The directors have proposed that disclosures should state that prices charged to related parties are set on an **arm's length basis**. Because the transaction took place **between related parties** by definition it **cannot have taken place on an arm's length basis** and this description would be **misleading**. Doye sold plant and machinery to Spade at **normal selling prices** and this is the information that should be disclosed.

Between Atomic and the Egin Group

Atomic is a related party of Egin because it can exercise **significant influence** over it. It is **also a related party of Briars and Doye** because **Egin controls Briars and Doye**. It is **unlikely that Eye is a related party of Atomic** because Eye is an associate of an associate. Atomic would have to be able to **exercise significant influence in practice** for a related party relationship to exist.

(b)   **Goodwill arising on the acquisition of Briars**

FRS 23 *The effect of changes in foreign exchange rates* states that goodwill arising on the acquisition of a foreign subsidiary should be expressed in the functional currency of the foreign operation and **retranslated at the closing rate at each year-end**. Goodwill is calculated and translated as follows:

	Euros m	Rate	£m
Cost of acquisition	50	2	25
Less fair value of identifiable net assets acquired			
(80% × 45)	(36)	2	(18)
Goodwill at acquisition	14		7
Amortisation (20% × 14)	(2.8)	2.5	(1.1)
Exchange loss (balancing figure)			(1.4)
At 31 May 20X6	11.2	2.5	4.5

Goodwill is measured at **£4.5 million** in the balance sheet. An amortisation charge of **£1.1 million** is **recognised in the profit and loss account, based on the average rate**. An **exchange loss of £1.4 million** is **recognised in equity** (taken to the translation reserve).

Loan to Briars

The loan is a **financial liability measured at amortised cost**. The loan is measured at **fair value** on initial recognition. Fair value is the amount for which the liability could be settled between **knowledgeable, willing parties on an arm's length basis**. This would normally be the actual transaction price. However, Egin and Briars are **related parties** and the transaction **has not taken place on normal commercial terms**.

164

FRS 26 *Financial instruments: Recognition and measurement* states that it is necessary to **establish what the transaction price would have been** in an arm's length exchange motivated by normal business considerations. The amount that will eventually be repaid to Egin is £10 million and the normal commercial rate of interest is 6%. Therefore the fair value of the loan is its **discounted present value**, which is **retranslated at the closing rate** at each year-end.

Therefore the loan is measured at the following amounts in the balance sheet:

	£'000	Rate	Euros '000
At 1/6/20X5 $(10 \times \frac{1}{1.06^2} \ 0.890)$	8,900	2	17,800
Unwinding of discount $(8,900 \times 6\%)$	534	2.3	1,228
Exchange loss			4,557
At 31/5/20X6 $(10 \times \frac{1}{1.06} \ 0.943)$	9,434	2.5	23,585

The **unwinding of the discount** is recognised as a **finance cost** in the profit and loss account and the **exchange loss** is also **recognised in the profit and loss account**.

Note. It would also be possible to calculate the finance cost for the year ended 31 May 20X6 at the closing rate. This would increase the exchange loss and the total expense recognised in profit and loss would be the same.

C9 Engina

Top tips. A good test of your ability to apply FRS 8 to a practical scenario.

Notice the mark allocation before starting to produce your answer. Take time to think about the presentation and structure of the report and ensure you allocate your time appropriately over the headings and keep sentences and paragraphs short to make your answer easy to mark.

When you review your answer, think about whether it is written in a good professional style as well as checking the technical details.

Marking scheme

	Marks
Style of letter/report	4
Reasons	8
Goods to directors	4
Property	5
Group	4
Available	25
Maximum	25

REPORT

To: The Directors
        Engina Co
        Zenda
        Ruritania

From: A N Accountant

Date: 12 May 20X1

Related Party Transactions

The purpose of this report is to explain why it is necessary to disclose related party transactions. We appreciate that you may regard such disclosure as politically and culturally sensitive. However, there are **sound reasons for the required disclosures**. It should be emphasised that related party transactions are a normal part of business life, and the disclosures are required to give a fuller picture to the users of accounts, rather than because they are problematic.

Prior to the issue of FRS 8, disclosures in respect of related parties were concerned with directors and their relationship with the group. The ASB extended this definition and also the required disclosures. This reflects the objective of the ASB to provide useful data for investors, not merely for companies to report on stewardship activities.

Unless investors know that transactions with related parties have not been carried out at **'arm's length'** between independent parties, they may fail to ascertain the true financial position.

Related party transactions typically take place on **terms which are significantly different** from those undertaken on normal commercial terms.

FRS 8 brings the UK more into line with **international practice** and requires all material related party transactions to be disclosed.

It should be noted that related party transactions are not necessarily fraudulent or intended to deceive. Without proper disclosures, investors may be disadvantaged – FRS 8 seeks to remedy this.

Sale of goods to the directors

Disclosure of related party transactions is only necessary when the transactions are **material.** FRS 8 applies only to material related party transactions. For the purposes of FRS 8, however, transactions are material when their disclosure might be expected to influence decisions made by users of the financial statements, irrespective of their amount. Moreover, the materiality of a related party transaction with an individual, for example a director, must be judged by reference to that individual and not just the company. In addition, disclosure of contracts of significance with directors is required by the Stock Exchange.

Mr Satay has purchased £600,000 (12 × £50,000) worth of goods from the company and a car for £45,000, which is just over half its market value. The transactions are not material to the company, and because Mr Satay has considerable personal wealth, they are not material to him either. However, **while not material**, any transactions with directors could be viewed as **sensitive**, and therefore ought to be disclosed in accordance with **best practice and good corporate governance.**

Hotel property

The hotel property sold to the Managing Director's brother is a **related party transaction**, and it appears to have been undertaken at **below market price**. FRS 8 requires disclosure of 'any other elements of the transactions necessary for an understanding of the financial statements'.

However, not only must the transaction be disclosed, but the question of **impairment** needs to be considered. The value of the hotel has become impaired due to the fall in property prices, so the carrying value needs to be adjusted in accordance with FRS 11 *Impairment of fixed assets and goodwill.* The hotel should be shown at the lower of carrying value (£5m) and the recoverable amount. The recoverable amount is the higher of net realisable value (£4.3m – £0.2m = £4.1m) and value in use (£3.6m). Therefore the hotel should be shown at £4.1m.

The sale of the property was for £100,000 below this impaired value, and it is this amount which needs to be disclosed.

Group structure

FRS 8 **exempts from the disclosure** requirements group companies where the parent company owns **90% or more** of the subsidiary's share capital. Engina does not therefore need to disclose transactions with Wheel Ltd, provided that Wheel Ltd prepares consolidated accounts.

However, Engina's transactions with Car Ltd will need to be disclosed. FRS 8 states that companies under **common control** are related parties, and the two companies are under the common control of Mr Satay. Car is not part of the Wheel group and so will not be entitled to exemption on that basis.

You should also be aware that companies legislation and the Stock Exchange require **disclosure of each director's interests** in a company's share capital. Thus Mr Satay would need to disclose his ownership of the share capital of Engina, being 10% direct and 90% through his ownership of Wheel.

D1 Preparation question: Consolidation

FAIR VALUE OF CONSIDERATION

	£	£
Shares (5 × 800,000 × 90p)		3,600,000
Cash (at present value):		
At 1 April 20X2 (800,000 × 40p × 0.909)	290,880	
At 1 April 20X3 (800,000 × 60p × 0.826)	396,480	
		687,360
		4,287,360

FAIR VALUE OF NET ASSETS ACQUIRED

	Note	£'000
Intangible fixed assets	1	–
Land and buildings	2	3,500
Plant and machinery	3	2,200
Stocks	4	925
Debtors	5	950
Cash at bank	6	200
Trade creditors	6	(350)
Taxation	6	(200)
Long term loan	7	(2,311)
Provisions	8	(100)
		4,814

Notes

The fair value of the net assets acquired has been calculated in accordance with the requirements of FRS 7 *Fair values in acquisition accounting*.

1   There is no readily ascertainable market value for the brand and therefore it must be treated as part of goodwill (FRS 10).

2   Land and buildings are stated at market value.

3   There is no market value for the plant and machinery and therefore it is stated at depreciated replacement cost (estimated at 2/3 × £3.3 million, based on the fact that net book value is 2/3 of cost).

4   Stocks are valued at the lower of replacement cost and net realisable value (75 + 850).

5   Trade debtors are valued at their carrying amount of £800,000 plus the contingent asset of £150,000. FRS 7 requires that monetary assets should be stated at the amount expected to be received or paid. Although FRS 12 does not allow the recognition of contingent assets unless recovery is virtually certain, FRS 7 allows their recognition at lesser certainty to avoid windfall gains relating to pre-acquisition events being recognised in post-acquisition profits.

6   The other monetary assets and liabilities are stated at the amount expected to be received or paid (ie, their carrying amounts).

7   Long term loans are stated at net present value (to reflect the timing of the payments):

	£
Interest (200,000 × 3.791)	758,200
Principal (2,500,000 × 0.621)	1,552,500
	2,310,700

8   The provision for reorganisation costs cannot be recognised because it relates to post-acquisition events.

Goodwill on the acquisition of Target Ltd

	£
Purchase consideration at fair value	4,287,360
Less: group share of fair value of net assets acquired	
(80% × 4,814,000)	(3,851,200)
	436,160

D2 Preparation question: Consolidated profit and loss account

ORSINO GROUP PLC
CONSOLIDATED PROFIT AND LOSS ACCOUNT
FOR THE YEAR ENDED 31 DECEMBER 20X6

	£m
Turnover (290 + 110)	400.0
Cost of sales (162 + 51 + 10 (W1))	223.0
Gross profit	177.0
Distribution costs (48.8 + 12.4)	61.2
Administration expenses (16.2 + 8.6 + 2 (W3))	26.8
	89.0
Share of operating profit in associated undertaking (W4)	(4.5)
Profit before taxation	84.5
Taxation (25 + 12 + 3)	40.0
Profit after taxation	44.5
Minority interests (W5)	3.2
Profit for the year	41.3

Workings

1   *Inter-company trading Viola to Orsino*

Increase in profit in stock at 31 December 20X6 = £(20 − 10)m = £10m to cost of sales

2   *Minority interest in stock profit*

20% × £10m (W1) = £2m

3   *Goodwill amortisation*

	Viola		Sebastian	
	£m	£m	£m	£m
Cost		34		10
Net assets acquired				
Share capital	20		10	
Reserves	10		5	
	30		15	
	80%	(24)	$^1/_3$	(5)
		10		5
Amortisation	$^1/_5$	2	$^1/_5$	1
		↓		↓
		Charged to expenses		Included with share of associate's profit

4   *Share of operating profit in associate*

	£m
Share of profit before tax ($^1/_3 \times$ £19.5m)	6.5
Share of intra group stock profit ($1/3 \times$ £30m)	(10.0)
	(3.5)
Less amortisation of goodwill	(1.0)
	(4.5)

5   *Minority interests*

	£m
Share of profit after tax (£26m × 20%)	5.2
MI in stock profit (W2)	(2.0)
	3.2

D3 Preparation question: Status of investment

(a)   The *Statement of Principles for financial reporting* sets out three alternative ways in which investments can be treated.

    (i)   Where the **investor controls the investee**, the controlling entity (the parent) and the controlled entity (the subsidiary) form a group. **Consolidated financial statements** are prepared for the group. The gains, losses, assets, liabilities and cash flows of the parent and the subsidiary are aggregated in order to present the financial performance and position of the **group as a single economic entity**. This treatment is required by FRS 2 *Accounting for subsidiary undertakings*.

    (ii)   Where the investor:

        (1)   **Shares control** over the investee with others, or

        (2)   Has neither control or joint control but **exerts significant influence** over the investee's operating and financial policies

    the investee is a **joint venture or an associate** and the **equity method** is used, as required by FRS 9 *Associates and joint ventures*. The investor's share of the results and net assets of the investee are not combined with the investor's own activities and resources, but are brought into its financial statements on a **single line in the profit and loss account and balance sheet respectively**. This treatment recognises the investor's share of the results and net assets, but does not misrepresent the extent of its influence over the investee.

    (iii)   Where the investor does **not exercise control, joint control or significant influence**, the only amounts recognised in the consolidated financial statements are the **investment** (at cost or current value) and **any investment income**.

(b) *Harbour Ltd*

Port plc owns 80% of the equity share capital of Harbour Ltd. Therefore Port plc clearly **controls** Harbour Ltd and Harbour Ltd is a **subsidiary undertaking**.

Inlet Ltd

Port plc owns 40% of the equity share capital of Inlet Ltd. This is **not sufficient to control** Inlet Ltd, but the fact that there are **no other major shareholdings** indicates that Port plc can exercise **significant influence** over the policies adopted by Inlet Ltd. Therefore Inlet Ltd is an associated undertaking of Port plc.

Bay Ltd

Port plc owns 31.25% of the equity share capital of Bay Ltd. A holding of 20% or more of the voting rights normally suggests that the investor can exercise significant influence (and therefore has an associated undertaking). However, **another investor** holds 62.5% of the equity share capital and clearly **exercises control** in practice (by making Bay Ltd adopt policies that do not meet with the approval of Port plc). FRS 9 specifically states that if an investee persistently implements policies that are inconsistent with the investor's strategy, the investor does not exercise significant influence. Therefore Bay Ltd is a **simple fixed asset investment**.

(c)

	Port plc £'000	Harbour Ltd £'000	Adjustments £'000	Consolidated £'000
Turnover (W1)	65,000	45,000	(8,000)	102,000
Cost of sales (W1)	(35,000)	(25,000)	8,000	
(W2)			(120)	(52,120)
Gross profit	30,000	20,000	(120)	49,880

Workings

1   *Intra-group sales*

			£'000	£'000
DEBIT	Turnover		8,000	
CREDIT	Cost of sales			8,000

Elimination of the sales made by Port plc to Harbour Ltd

2   *Provision for unrealised profit*

Stocks relating to intra-group sales have increased by £600,000 (3,000 − 2,400)

Provision for unrealised profit is £120,000 (600 × 25/125).

(d) **Adjustments to the consolidated balance sheet**

(i)

		£'000	£'000
DEBIT	Consolidated reserves	600	
CREDIT	Stocks		600

Unrealised profit eliminated from the stocks of Harbour Ltd (3,000 × 25/125).

This adjustment is needed because the consolidated financial statements must present the activities of the group as a **single economic entity**. Port plc has made a profit of 25% of cost on its sales to Harbour Ltd. Harbour Ltd has not yet sold all these goods to third parties and so part of the profit made by Port plc has **not yet been realised by the group** and must be eliminated from the consolidated financial statements.

(ii)

		£'000	£'000
DEBIT	Consolidated reserves	200	
CREDIT	Share of net assets of associate		200

Group share of unrealised profit eliminated from the net assets of Inlet Ltd (40% × 2,500 × 25/125).

The rationale behind this adjustment is similar to the rationale behind adjustment (i). Some of the goods sold by Port plc to Inlet Ltd remain in stock and therefore the stocks of Inlet Ltd must be **adjusted to eliminate the unrealised profit**. Because Inlet Ltd is an associate rather than a subsidiary, the consolidated balance sheet does not include the individual assets and liabilities of Inlet Ltd. Instead the group share (40%) of the net assets of Inlet Ltd are reported in a single line within fixed assets. **Therefore only the group share of the unrealised profit is eliminated**.

D4 Preparation question: Associate

Top tips. You must work through questions of this type in a very methodical way: keep your schedules and workings neat and cross referenced. Take time to establish the group structure and think through the adjustments. To produce your answer an effective technique for Part (a) would be:

Step 1   Set up a proforma (including captions relating to the associate).

Step 2   Bring in the figures relating to the holding company and subsidiary only.

Step 3   Bring in the associate using equity accounting as a separate stage. This technique helps avoid confusion between the accounting treatment of the subsidiary and the associate.

J GROUP CONSOLIDATED BALANCE SHEET AS AT 31 DECEMBER 20X5

	£'000	£'000
Fixed assets		
Tangible assets		
Freehold property (W2)	3,570.00	
Plant and machinery (795 + 375)	1,170.00	
		4,740.00
Investment in associate (W8)		475.20
		5,215.20
Current assets		
Stock (W3)	855	
Debtors (W4)	620	
Cash at bank and in hand (50 + 120)	170	
	1,645	
Creditors: amounts falling due within one year (W5)	1,590	
Net current assets		55.00
Total assets less current liabilities		5,270.20
Creditors: amounts falling due after more than one year		
(500 + 100)		600.00
		4,670.20
Capital and reserves		
Called up share capital		2,000.00
Profit and loss account (W9)		1,778.10
Shareholders' funds		3,778.10
Minority interests (W6)		892.10
		4,670.20

Workings

1. *Group structure*

2. *Freehold property*

	£'000
J plc	1,950
P Ltd	1,250
Fair value adjustment	400
Additional depreciation $(400 \times 50\% \div 40) \times 6$ years (20X0-20X5)	(30)
	3,570

3. *Stock*

	£'000
J plc	575
P Ltd	300
PUP $(100 \times {}^{25}/_{125})$	(20)
	855

4. *Debtors*

	£'000
J plc	330
P Ltd	290
	620

5. *Creditors due < 1 year*

	£'000
J plc: bank overdraft	560
trade creditors	680
P Ltd: trade creditors	350
	1,590

6. *Minority interest*

	£'000
Net assets of P Ltd	1,885.0
Fair value adjustment (W11)	370.0
Less PUP: sales to J plc	(20.0)
sales to S Ltd $(80 \times {}^{25}/_{125} \times 30\%)$	(4.8)
	2,230.2
Minority interest (40%)	892.10

7. *Goodwill*

	£'000	£'000
P Ltd		
Cost of investment		1,000
Share of net assets acquired		
Share capital	1,000	
Reserves	200	
Fair value adjustment	400	
	1,600	
Group share	60%	(960)
Fully amortised		40

	£'000	£'000
S Ltd		
Cost of investment		500
Share of net assets acquired		
Share capital	750	
Reserves	150	
	900	
Group share	30%	(270)
		230

Amortisation $= \dfrac{230}{5} \times 2 =$ 92

8   *Investment in associate*

	£'000
Share of net assets (30% × 1,140)	342.0
Less PUP	(4.8)
Add unamortised goodwill (230 – 92)	138.0
	475.2

9   *Profit and loss account*

	J £'000	P £'000	S £'000
Reserves per question	1,460.0	885.0	390.0
Adjustments			
Unrealised profit (W10)		(24.8)	
Fair value adjustments (W11)		(30.0)	
		830.2	390.0
Less pre-acquisition reserves		(200.0)	(150.0)
	1,460.0	630.2	240.0
P: 60% × 630.2	378.1		
S: 30% × 240	72.0		
Less amortisation of goodwill: P	(40.0)		
S	(92.0)		
	1,778.1		

10   *Unrealised profit*

	£'000
On sales to J (parent co) 100 × 25/125	20.0
On sales to S (associate) 80 × 25/125 × 30%	4.8
	24.8

11   *Fair value adjustments*

	Difference at acquisition £'000	Difference now £'000
Property	400	400
Additional depreciation: 200 × 6/40	–	(30)
	400	370

∴ Charge £30,000 to P&L

D5 Baden

> **Top tips.** Part (a) of this question is quite straightforward, requiring you to distinguish between an associate and an ordinary investment. Part (b) required you to apply FRS 9. This question is a real test of your knowledge of FRS 9.
>
> Attempt the question under timed conditions making sure that you address all parts of the requirements.
>
> For part (b) you need to adopt a logical approach and should not get put off by any points where you are unsure but continue to deal with the rest of the question to get the marks where you are more confident.
>
> **Examiner's comment.** Part (a) was well answered. Many candidates had learnt the various classifications in great detail and scored well. Part (b) was not well answered, however, with difficulties found in dealing with goodwill, post acquisition profits and elimination of inter-company profits.

Marking scheme

				Marks	
(a)	(i)	Passive role		1	
		Accounting policies		1	
		Significant influence		2	
		Dividend policy		2	
		Board representation		1	
			Available	7	
			Maximum		6
	(ii)	Entity		1	
		Not carry on trade		1	
		Indicators		2	
		Accounting		2	
			Available	6	
			Maximum		4
(b)	(i)	Fair value		1	
		Cost of investment/investment		4	
		Goodwill		1	
		Profit/loss account		4	
			Available	10	
			Maximum		9
	(ii)	Profit and loss account		3	
		Balance sheet		3	
		Available/maximum			6
					25

(a) (i) An investor exercises **significant influence** over an associate, so the associate will often use **similar accounting policies**. In addition, the investor must retain a **participating interest** in the investee company. Under FRS 9, a holding of **20%** or more of voting rights **suggests but does not ensure**, significant influence. The investee's dividend policy is also a significant indicator of the status of the investment.

Where the investment is purely retained for the cash flow effect of dividend receipts and with no exercise of significant influence then an ordinary investment is suggested.

(ii) A **joint venture** must be a **separate entity** (body corporate, partnership or unincorporated body carrying out a trade). All significant operational and financial decisions must be taken **jointly** by the participants. The **gross equity method** is used for accounting purposes.

A **joint arrangement** is in force where the participants derive benefits from products/services taken **in kind** rather than a share of financial results. Alternatively, a participant's share of output/results is determined by its supply of inputs to the arrangements.

Joint arrangements are accounted for by **participants** accounting for their **share of assets, liabilities and cash** flows. (*Note.* This will produce similar results to proportional consolidation.)

(b) (i) CALCULATION OF GOODWILL AT 1 JANUARY 20X7

	£m	£m
Tangible fixed assets	30	
Current assets	31	
Creditors (short term)	(20)	
Creditors (long term)	(8)	
Fair value of net assets	33	
30% thereof		9.9
Cost		14.0
Goodwill		4.1

Note. Goodwill in the balance sheet of investee is excluded by FRS 9.

CARRYING VALUE 31.12.20X8 IN THE BALANCE SHEET

	£m
Investment cost	14.0
30% post acquisition profit	
$(32 - 9 - 10)$	3.9
Amortised goodwill $4.1 \times 2/4$	(2.0)
Fair value adjustment for depreciation	
$2 \times 20\% \times (30 - 20) \times 30\%$	(1.2)
	14.7

Alternative calculation

	£m	£m
Net assets		
Per question	46	
Less PUP	(10)	
	36	
Group share: 30%		10.8
Fair value increase		
Net assets at 31.12.X8	46	
Less profit for 20X7 and 20X8 $(32 - 9)$	23	
Net assets at acquisition	23	
Fair value	33	
Increase in fair value	10	
Group share: 30%		3.0
		13.8
Goodwill		4.1
		17.9
Less goodwill amortisation		(2.0)
Depreciation		(1.2)
Investment in associate		14.7

BADEN
CONSOLIDATED PROFIT AND LOSS ACCOUNT (EXTRACTS)
FOR THE YEAR ENDED 31 DECEMBER 20X8

	£m	£m
Share of associate profit (30% × 29)	8.7	
Less goodwill	(1.0)	
Intercompany profit	(3.0)	
Depreciation adjustment	(0.6)	
		4.1
Exceptional item		
Associate (30% × 10)		3.0
Interest payable		
Associate (30% × 4)		1.2
Taxation on profit on ordinary		
Activities (30% × 3)		0.9

(ii) Under gross equity accounting for joint ventures, the above is expanded.

BADEN
CONSOLIDATED PROFIT AND LOSS ACCOUNT

		£m
Turnover group and share of joint venture	Y +	53.1
[(212 – 35) × 30% = 53.1]		
Less share of joint venture turnover		(53.1)
Group turnover		Y

In the consolidated balance sheet the investment calculated above (£14.7m) is split between gross assets and liabilities.

BADEN
CONSOLIDATED BALANCE SHEET (EXTRACT)

		£m
Share of gross assets		
Fixed assets	37	
Current assets (31 – 10)	21	
	$\overline{58}$ × 30%	17.4
Fair value		3.0
Goodwill		4.1
Less written off		(2.0)
Depreciation adjustment		(1.2)
		21.3
Share of gross liabilities: 30% × (12 + 10)		(6.6)
		14.7

D6 Preparation question: 'D' shaped group

(a) 'D' SHAPED GROUP
CONSOLIDATED BALANCE SHEET AS AT 31 DECEMBER 20X9

	£'000
Intangible assets (W2)	126
Tangible fixed assets (720 + 60 + 70)	850
Current assets (175 + 95 + 90)	360
Creditors : amounts falling due within one year	
Trade creditors (120 + 65 + 45)	(230)
	1,106
Share capital and reserves	
£1 ordinary shares	400
Profit and loss account (W4)	600
	1,000
Minority interest (W3)	106
	1,106

Workings

1   *Group Structure*

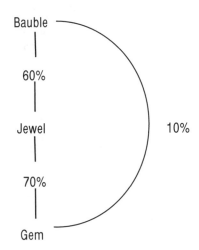

Bauble interest in Gem

	– direct	10%
	– indirect (60% × 70%)	42%
		52%
Minority interest in Gem		48%

ANSWERS

2   Goodwill

	£'000	B in J £'000	£'000	B in G £'000	£'000	J in G £'000
Cost of investment		142		43		100
Share of net assets acquired as represented by:						
Share capital	100		50		50	
Reserves	45		40		40	
	145		90		90	
Group share	60%		10%			70%
		87		9		63
Goodwill		55		34		37

Total goodwill = £126,000

3   Minority interests

	Jewel £'000	Gem £'000
Net assets per question	190.0	115
Adjustments		
Unimpaired goodwill re Gem (W2)	37.0	
Less: COI in Gem	(100.0)	–
	127.0	115
	× 40%	× 48%
	= 50.8	= 55.2
		106

4   Consolidated reserves

	B £'000	J £'000	G £'000
Per Q	560	90	65
Less: pre acquisition reserves of subsidiaries		(45)	(40)
		45	25
Share of J post acquisition (60% × 45)	27		
Share of G post acquisition (52% × 25)	13.0		
	600		

(b) **Goodwill**

Bauble in Jewel Ltd group

	£'000
Cost of investment	142
Net assets acquired	
Jewel 60% (100 + 60 − 100)	(36)
Gem 42% (50 + 40)	(37.8)
	68.2
Bauble in Gem (as per part (a))	34.0
	102.2

D7 Question with analysis: X Group

> **Top tips.** This question covers various aspects of complex groups, including sub-subsidiaries, associates, intra-group profit elimination, contingencies, fair value adjustments and the write off of goodwill. It is important with this type of question to spend time clarifying the group structure and relationships before launching into it. Note that here we are dealing with two subsidiaries and an associate. The equity accounting of W uses 30% (this is what the group controls) and a minority interest is shown.
>
> **Examiner's comment.** Many candidates produced poor quality workings which were difficult to follow. Candidates had difficulty with the fair value and accounting policy adjustments and often calculated the relative shareholdings of the group and minority interest incorrectly.

X GROUP
BALANCE SHEET AS AT 31 MARCH 20X9

	Workings	£m
Tangible fixed assets	2	1,058
Investment in associate	7	47
Goodwill	4	40
Net current assets (640 + 360 + 75 − 15)		1,060
Long term creditors		(365)
		1,840
Share capital		360
Share premium		250
Reserves	6	1,071
		1,681
Minority interests	5	159
		1,840

Workings

1   *Group structure*

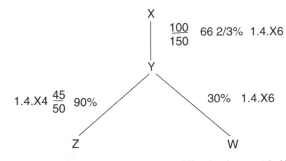

Effective interest in Z	Effective interest in W
Group 66 2/3% x 90% = 60%	Group 66 2/3% x 30% = 20%
Minority interest = 40%	

2   *Fair values*

Y	At acquisition		At balance sheet date
	£m		£m
Tangible fixed assets	30	(9)*	21
Intangible fixed assets	(30)		(30)
Stock	(6)		–
Provision b/d	(9)		–
Contingent asset	36		–
	21 ← Difference (30) →		(9)

* Additional depreciation [30 × 10% × 3]

Z	At acquisition		At balance sheet date
	£m		£m
Tangible Fixed Assets	10	(3)**	7
Stock	(5)		—
	5 ←	Difference +2 →	7

** Additional depreciation $[10 \times 10\% \times 3]$

3   *Provision for unrealised profit*

	£m
Sales to X	44
Sales to Y	16
	$\underline{60} \times 25\% = £15m$

4   *Goodwill: X in Y Group*

	£m	£m
Cost of investment		320
Share of consolidated separable net assets		
Y		
Share capital	150	
Share premium	120	
Reserves	120	
Less cost of investment in Z	(90)	
Fair value adjustment (W2)	21	
	321	
Group share : $66^2/_3\%$		(214)
Z		
Share capital	50	
Share premium	10	
Reserves	20	
Fair value adjustment (W2)	5	
	85	
Group share: 60%		(51)
		55
Amortisation to date (3/11)		(15)
		40

5   *Minority interest*

		£m	£m
Y	Net assets per question	480	
	Less: cost of investment in Z	(90)	
	cost of investment in W	(50)	
	Investment in associate	47	
	Fair value adjustment (W2)	(9)	
		378	
	$\times 33^1/_3\%$		126
Z	Net assets per question	90	
	Fair value adjustment (W2)	7	
	Provision for unrealised profit (W3)	(15)	
		82	
	$\times 40\%$		32.8
			158.8

6   *Consolidated reserves*

	X £m	Y £m	Z £m	W £m
Per question	1,050.0	210	30	17
Provision for unrealised profit (W3)			(15)	
Fair value adjustment (W2)		(30)	2	
	1,050.0	180	17	17
Less: pre-acquisition		(120)	(20)	(7)
		60	(3)	10
Y ($66^2/_3\% \times 60$)	40.0			
Z ($60\% \times (3)$)	(1.8)			
W ($20\% \times 10$)	2.0			
Amortisation of goodwill				
X in Y group (W4)	(15.0)			
W ($66^2/_3\% \times 6$) (W8)	(4.0)			
	1,071.2			

7   *Investment in associate*

	£m
Share of net assets ($30\% \times 103$)	30.9
Goodwill (W8)	16.1
	47.0

8   *Goodwill in W*

	£m	£m
Cost of investment		50.0
Net assets acquired		
Share capital	80	
Share premium	6	
Reserves	7	
	93	
Group share: 30%		(27.9)
		22.1
Amortised (3/11)		(6.0)
		16.1

D8 Largo

Top tips. In this question you had to prepare a consolidated balance sheet of a group where there were multiple shareholdings. You had to determine the date at which control was gained for the purpose of the group accounts. You were also required to deal with deferred tax arising on the fair value of the tangible fixed assets and the impairment of a brand name.

Easy marks. As always, there are easy marks for basic consolidation techniques and for determining the group structure. If you did not correctly value the consideration given, this would not result in a significant loss of marks as it was only one element of the goodwill calculation.

Examiner's comment. This question was well answered in most cases. However, many candidates did not charge the additional depreciation on the fair value increase on the property of the subsidiaries, and failed to treat the brand name correctly on acquisition.

	Marks
Discussion of method of accounting for shareholdings	3
Equity of Fusion	6
Equity of Spine	5
Fair value calculation – assets	3
Fair value of consideration	3
Brand name	2
Property, plant and equipment	3
Group reserves	2
Micro	3
Available	30
Maximum	25

LARGO GROUP
CONSOLIDATED BALANCE SHEET AT 30 NOVEMBER 20X4

	£m
Fixed assets	
Tangible assets (329 + 185 + (W2) 46.5 + 64 (W2) 27.5 – 9 brand)	643.0
Intangible assets (53.6 (W2) + 7)	60.6
Investment in associate (W4)	11.6
	715.2
Net current assets	199.0
Total assets less current liabilities	914.2
Provision for liabilities	(45.0)
	869.2
Capital and reserves	
Share capital	460.0
Share premium [30 + (150 × 1.30) + (30 × 1.30)]	264.0
Retained earnings (W6)	94.4
	818.4
Minority interests (W4)	50.8
	869.2

Workings

1   *Group structure*

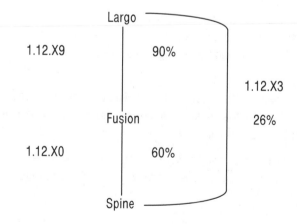

Effective interest (90% × 60% + 26% =   80%
∴ Minority interest   20%
                                        100%

2 *Fair Value Differences*

	Fusion	Spine
	£m	£m
Net assets (carrying value)		
Share capital	110	50
Share premium	20	10
Profit and loss account	136	30
	266	90
Fair value (per question – net of deferred tax)	300	110
	34	20
Add back deferred tax (see note (b) in question)		
[(150 – 100) × 30%] [(70 – 40) × 30%]	15	9
	49	29

Note. There is a flaw in the question as it is set. This answer (in line with the one published by the examiner) bases the fair value differences on the information given in note (a) of the question then uses note (b) to calculate the deferred tax. It would be equally valid to base the fair value differences on the information in note (b), which would have given differences of £50m and £30m.

Fair value adjustments

	At acq'n 1.12.X3	Movement (5%)	At B/S date 30.11.X4
Fusion	£m	£m	£m
Property (W3)	49	(2.5)	46.5
Spine			
Property (W3)	29	(1.5)	27.5

3 *Goodwill*

	Largo in Fusion Group		Largo in Spine	
	£m	£m	£m	£m
Cost of combination (150 × £2.30*)/(30 × £2.30*)		345		69
Fair value of net assets acquired:				
Fusion				
Share capital	110		50	
Share premium	20		10	
Retained earnings (1.12.X3)	136		30	
Fair value adjustments: (W2)	49		29	
Cost of investment in Spine	(50)			
	265		119	
Group share	90%	(238.5)	26%	(30.94)
Spine				
Share capital	50			
Share premium	10			
Retained earnings (1.12.X3)	30			
Fair value adjustments: (W2)	29			
	119			
Group share	54%	(64.26)		
		42.24		38.06
Amortisation (1/3)		(14.08)		(12.69)
		28.16		25.37
			53.57	

*The market price of the shares is calculated by reference to the market capitalisation of Largo: £644 million ÷ 280 million shares (460 – 150 – 30) = £2.30 per share. Therefore the premium on each share is £1.30.

4 Investment in associate

	£m
Share of fair value of assets of associates (40% × 24)	9.6
Goodwill not yet amortised (see below)	2.0
	11.6

Goodwill:	
Cost of investment	11
Net assets acquired (40% × 20)	(8)
	3
Less amortisation (1/3)	(1)
	2

5 Minority interest

	Fusion £m	Spine £m
Net assets at balance sheet date per question	268	95
Fair value adjustments (W2)	46.5	27.5
Cost of investment in Spine	(50)	
Impairment of brand (9 – 7)	(2)	–
	262.5	122.5
MI share (10%/20% effective interest (W1))	26.3	24.5

50.8

6 Retained earnings

	Largo £m	Fusion £m	Spine £m
Per question	120.0	138.0	35.0
Fair value change (W2)		(2.5)	(1.5)
Impairment loss		(2.0)	
		133.55	33.55
At acquisition		(136.0)	(30.0)
		(2.5)	3.5
Group share of Fusion ((2.5) × 90%)	(2.3)		
Group share of Spine (3.5 × 80%)	2.8		
Income from associate ((24 – 20) × 40%)	1.6		
Amortisation (W3) (14.08 + 12.69)	(26.7)		
Amortisation – associate (W4)	(1.0)		
	94.4		

D9 Case study question: Rod

Top tips. This question required candidates to prepare a consolidated balance sheet of a complex group. Candidates were given a basic set of data – information concerning current accounting practices – which required adjustment in the financial statements, and information about the implementation of 'new' accounting standards. This type of question will appear regularly on this paper (obviously with different group scenarios and different accounting adjustments). Candidates had to deal with adjustments relating to tangible fixed assets, stock and defined benefit pension schemes. Part (c) is a practical question on key issues. In part (d) do not be tempted to waffle. Part (e) concerns ethics, a topic new to this syllabus.

Examiner's comment. Generally speaking, candidates performed quite well on this question but often struggled with the accounting for the defined benefit pension scheme. Many candidates treated one of the subsidiaries as an associate. In this situation, where the relationship between the companies has been incorrectly determined, marks are awarded for the methodology used in the question.

		Marks
(a)	Defined benefit pension scheme	5
(b)	Shareholding	3
	Capital and reserves – Line	6
	Fixed assets – Line	4
	Capital and reserves – Reel	8
	Fair value adjustment	3
	Tangible group fixed assets	2
(c)	(i) Provision: current practise	4
	acceptability	2
	(ii) Fine: intangible asset	3
	acceptability	2
(d)	I mark per valid point	10
(e)	For	2
	Against	2
	Conclusion	1
	Available	55
	Maximum	50

(a) **Defined benefit pension scheme**

The defined benefit pension scheme is treated in accordance with FRS 17 *Retirement benefits*.

The pension scheme has a deficit of liabilities over assets:

	£m
Fair value of scheme assets	125
Less: present value of obligation	(130)
	(5)

The deficit is reported as a liability in the balance sheet.

The profit and loss account for the year includes:

	£m	£m
Current service cost (in operating profit)		110
Net finance cost (shown adjacent to interest):		
Interest cost	20	
Expected return on plan assets	(10)	
		10
		120

The statement of total recognised gains and losses for the year includes:

	£m
Actuarial gain on defined benefit pension scheme assets	15

Adjustment to the group accounts:

DEBIT Profit and loss account reserve	£105m	
CREDIT Debtors		£100m
CREDIT Defined benefit pension scheme		£5m

Working

	Asset £m	Liability £m
B\fwd	–	–
Cash	100	
Current service cost		110
Expected return on plan assets	10	
Interest cost	–	20
∴ Actuarial gain	15	–
	125	130

(b) ROD GROUP
CONSOLIDATED BALANCE SHEET AT 30 NOVEMBER 20X3

	£m	£m
Fixed assets		
Intangible assets (18 + 20 + 12.5) (W2)		50.5
Tangible assets (W3)		1,930.0
		1,980.5
Current assets		
Stocks (300 + 135 + 65 – 20)	480	
Debtors (240 + 105 + 49 – 100)	294	
Cash at bank and in hand	220	
	994	
Creditors: amounts falling due within one year	(220)	
Net current assets		774.0
Total assets less current liabilities		2,754.5
Provision for liabilities and charges		(180.0)
Pension scheme liability		(5.0)
		2,569.5
Capital and reserves:		
Called up share capital		1,500.0
Share premium		300.0
Profit and loss account (W4)		502.4
		2,302.4
Minority interest (W5)		267.1
		2,569.5

Workings

1   *Group structure*

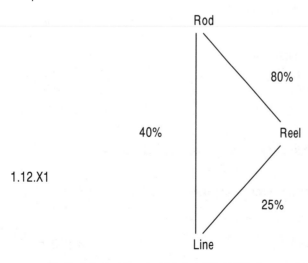

1.12.X1

Rod's total holding in Line is 60% (40% direct + 80% × 25% indirect).

2   *Goodwill*

	£m	£m
Reel		
Cost of investment		640
Net assets acquired		
Share capital	500	
Share premium	100	
Profit and loss account	100	
Fair value adjustment	10	
	710	
Group share (80%)		(568)
		72
Less amortisation (3/4)		(54)
		18

	Rod in Line		*Reel in Line*	
	£m	£m	£m	£m
Cost		160		100
Net assets acq'd				
Share capital	200		200	
Share premium	50		50	
P&L	50		50	
	300		300	
Share	40%	(120)	25%	75
		40		25
Amortisation (2/4)		(20)		(12.5)
		20		12.5 *

* The £12.5m is what is **controlled** by the group so is included on the top part of the balance sheet but must deal with the fact that only 80% of Reel's investment is **owned** by the group so a MI must be reflected (see W5) and only the group share of the amortisation charge will hit group P&L reserves.

3   *Tangible assets*

	£m
Rod	1,230
Reel	505
Line	256
	1,991
Less adjustment to tangible assets of Line (W6)	(56)
Reel trade discount net of depreciation (6 × 5/6)	(5)
	1,930

Note. FRS 15 states that the cost of a tangible fixed asset should be measured net of trade discounts. The trade discount must be deducted from Reel's tangible assets.

4   *Profit and loss account*

	Rod	Reel	Line
	£m	£m	£m
Per question	625.0	200	60
Fair value adjustment realised		(10)	
Development costs written off		(20)	
Trade discount on tangible assets less depreciation		(5)	
Adjustment for excess depreciation (W6)			14
At acquisition		(100)	(50)
	625.0	65	24
Group share of Reel (80% × 65)	52.0		
Group share of Line (60% × 24)	14.4		
Less defined benefit pension scheme (part (a))	(105.0)		
Less amortisation of goodwill (W2)			
Reel	(54.0)		
Line (20 + (80% × 12.5))	(30.0)		
	502.4		

5   *Minority interests*

	£m	£m
Reel		
Net assets at balance sheet date	800	
Investment in Line	(100)	
Development stocks written off	(20)	
Trade discount on fixed assets less depreciation	(5)	
Goodwill in Line (W2)	12.5	
	687.5	
MI share (20%)		137.5
Line		
Net assets at balance sheet date:	380	
Elimination of revaluation reserve (W6)	(70)	
Adjustment for excess depreciation (W6)	14	
	324	
MI share (40%)		129.6
		267.1

6   *Adjustment to tangible assets of Line*

An adjustment must be made to re-state the tangible fixed assets of Line from their revalued amount to depreciated historic cost, in line with group accounting policies.

The revaluation took place after acquisition, so the adjustment does not affect goodwill.

		Depreciated
	Valuation	historic cost
	£m	£m
Cost at 1 December 20X1 (date of acquisition by Rod)	300	300
Depreciation (300/6)	(50)	(50)
NBV at 30 November 20X2	250	250
Revaluation	70	–
Revalued amount	320	
Depreciation (320/5)	(64)	(50)
NBV at 30 November 20X3	256	200

Adjustment required to the group accounts:

DEBIT Revaluation reserve	£70m	
CREDIT Profit and loss account reserve (64 – 50)		£14m
CREDIT Tangible assets (256 – 200)		£56m

(c) (i) **Restructuring of the group**

FRS 12 *Provisions, contingent liabilities and contingent assets* **contains specific requirements** relating to **restructuring provisions**. The general recognition criteria apply and FRS 12 also states that **a provision should be recognised** if an entity has a **constructive obligation** to carry out a restructuring. A constructive obligation exists where **management has a detailed formal plan** for the restructuring and has also raised a **valid expectation** in those affected that it will carry out the restructuring. In this case, the company made a **public announcement** of the restructuring **after the year end**, but it had actually **drawn up the formal plan and started to implement it before the year end**, by communicating the plan to trade union representatives. Although the plan is **expected to take two years to complete**, it appears that the company **had a constructive obligation to** restructure at the year end. Therefore **a provision should be recognised**.

FRS 12 states that a restructuring provision should include **only the direct expenditure** arising from the restructuring. Costs that relate to the **future conduct of the business**, such as training and relocation costs, **should not be included**. Measuring the provision is likely to be difficult in practice, given that the restructuring will take place over two years. FRS 12 requires the provision to be the **best estimate** of the expenditure required to settle the present obligation at the balance sheet date, **taking all known risks and uncertainties into account**. There **may be a case for providing £50 million** (total costs of £60 million less relocation costs of £10 million) and the company **should certainly provide at least £15 million** (£20 million incurred by the time the financial statements are approved less £5 million relocation expenses). FRS 12 requires **extensive disclosures** and these **should include an indication of the uncertainties** about the amount or timing of the cash outflows.

(ii) **Fine for illegal receipt of a state subsidy**

FRS 10 *Goodwill and intangible assets* defines an **intangible asset** as a **non financial fixed asset** that **does not have physical substance** but is **identifiable** and is **controlled by the entity** through custody or legal rights. The fine **does not meet this definition**. The subsidy was used to offset trading losses, not to generate future income. The fine should be charged as an expense in the profit and loss account for the year ended 30 November 20X4. As it is material it should be separately disclosed either on the face of the profit and loss account or in the notes as required by FRS 3 *Reporting financial performance*.

(d) **Problems of reporting financial performance**

Rod spends considerable amounts of money on research that ultimately creates economic benefits and enhances shareholder value. However, this research does not meet the criteria for deferral under SSAP 13 *Accounting for research and development* because of the time lag between the expenditure and the revenue that it generates. Therefore the company's activities appear to reduce profits, rather than increase them. The company's expertise is part of its inherent goodwill and cannot be valued reliably at a monetary amount. Therefore it is not recognised on the balance sheet.

There is a strong argument that traditional financial reporting is inadequate to deal with 'knowledge led' companies such as Rod. It is possible that the capital markets will undervalue the company because the financial statements do not reflect the 'true' effect of the company's research activities. The economy is becoming more 'knowledge based' and many companies find themselves in this situation.

The market value of a company is based on the market's assessment of its future prospects, based on available information. Analysts have developed alternative measures of performance such as Economic Value Added (EVA). These take factors such as expenditure on research and development expenditure into account, so that they attempt to assess estimated future cash flows. There is a growing interest in ways of measuring shareholder value as opposed to earnings.

Analysts and other users of the financial statements now recognise the importance of non-financial information about a company. The ASB *Statement: Operating and Financial Review* recommended that companies present a description of the business, its objectives and its strategy. The OFR should analyse the main factors and influences that may have an effect on future performance and should comment on how the directors have sought to maintain and improve future performance. The directors of Rod can use the OFR to make the markets aware of its research activities and the way in which they give rise to future income streams and enhance shareholder value.

(e)   **Internal auditor bonus**

For

The chief internal auditor is an employee of Rod, which pays a salary to him or her. As part of the internal control function, he or she is helping to **keep down costs and increase profitability**. It could therefore be argued that the chief internal auditor should have a reward for adding to the profit of the business.

Against

Conversely, the problem remains that, if the chief internal auditor receives a bonus based on results, he or she may be **tempted to allow certain actions, practices or transactions which should be stopped**, but which are increasing the profit of the business, and therefore the bonus.

Conclusion

On balance, it is **not advisable** for the chief internal auditor to receive a bonus based on the company's profit.

D10 Case study: Exotic

Top tips. The consolidation section of this question is quite straightforward as long as you remember how to calculate the MI of a sub-subsidiary. In part (b) you should be looking at the FRS 3 conditions for an operation to be disclosed as discontinued. Points to watch in this question are the treatment of intercompany transactions, the calculation of minority interest, presentation and supporting workings and the correct treatment for part (b). Part (c) required candidates to advise a client about the acceptability of certain accounting practices used by that client. These related to joint ventures and intangibles. Part (d) required candidates to discuss the issues surrounding environmental reporting.

Easy marks. With complex groups, remember to sort out the group structure first. There are enough straightforward marks available here if you remember your basic rules for consolidations. The consolidation is quite straightforward as long as you remember how to calculate the MI of a sub-subsidiary.

(a)   (i)   EXOTIC GROUP
                CONSOLIDATED PROFIT AND LOSS ACCOUNT
                FOR THE YEAR ENDED 31 DECEMBER 20X9

	£'000
Turnover (W2)	92,120
Cost of sales (W3)	27,915
Gross profit	64,205
Distribution costs (3,325 + 2,137 + 1,900)	7,362
Administrative expenses (3,475 + 950 + 1,900)	6,325
Operating profit	50,518
Interest paid	325
Profit before tax	50,193
Taxation (8,300 + 5,390 + 4,241)	17,931
Profit after tax	32,262
Minority interest (W4)	3,713
Retained profit for the year	28,549
Retained profit b/f (W5)	37,560
Retained profit c/f	66,109

(ii)   EXOTIC GROUP
        CONSOLIDATED BALANCE SHEET
        AS AT 31 DECEMBER 20X9

	£'000
Intangible fixed asset: goodwill (W6)	4,107
Tangible fixed assets (W7)	72,787
Current assets (W8)	19,446
Current liabilities (3,563 + 10,023 + 48)	(13,634)
	82,706
Share capital	8,000
Profit and loss account (see note)	66,109
Shareholders' funds	74,109
Minority interest (W9)	8,597
	82,706

Workings

1   *Group structure*

        Exotic
   1.1.20X5 | 90%
        Melon
   1.1.20X7 | 80%
        Kiwi

   Minority interest
   In Melon = 10%
   In Kiwi = 100% − (90% × 80%) = 28%

2   *Turnover*

	£'000	£'000
Exotic		45,600
Melon		24,700
Kiwi		22,800
		93,100
Less intercompany sales		
Melon	260	
Kiwi	480	
		(740)
Less intercompany sale of fixed assets		(240)
		92,120

3   *Cost of sales*

	£'000
Exotic	18,050
Melon	5,463
Kiwi	5,320
	28,833
Less intercompany sales (as above)	(740)
Less cost of intercompany fixed asset to Exotic	(200)
Less excess depreciation (240 − 200) × 20%	(8)
Add unrealised profit on stock	
Melon ($60 \times 33^{1}/_{3}/133^{1}/_{3}$)	15
Kiwi (75 × 25/125)	15
	27,915

4   Minority interest

	£'000
Melon plc: 10% × (10,760 − 15)	1,074
Kiwi plc: 28% × (9,439 − 15)	2,639
	3,713

5   Reserves b/f

	Exotic plc £'000	Melon plc £'000	Kiwi plc £'000
Per question	20,013	13,315	10,459
Less: pre-acquisition		(1,425)	(950)
		11,890	9,509
Melon: 90% × 11,890	10,701		
Kiwi plc: 90% × 80% × 9,509	6,846		
	37,560		

6   Goodwill on acquisition

	£'000	£'000
Melon investment in Kiwi		
Investment cost		3,800
Assets acquired		
Shares	2,000	
Pre-acquisition reserves	950	
	2,950	
Group share (80%)		2,360
		1,440
Exotic investment in Melon		
Investment cost		6,650
Assets acquired		
Shares	3,000	
Pre-acquisition reserves	1,425	
	4,425	
Group share (90%)		3,983
Goodwill		2,667
Total goodwill		4,107

7   Tangible fixed assets

	£'000
Exotic	35,483
Melon	24,273
Kiwi	13,063
	72,819
Less profit on sale of intercompany fixed asset: (240 − 200)	(40)
Add back excess depreciation: (240 − 200) × 20%	8
	72,787

8   Current assets

	£'000
Exotic	1,568
Melon	9,025
Kiwi	8,883
	19,476
Less unrealised profit on stock (W3)	
Melon	(15)
Kiwi	(15)
	19,446

9   *Minority interest*

		£'000	£'000
Melon:	Net assets per question	27,075	
	PUP	(15)	
	Investment in Kiwi	(3,800)	
	Goodwill	1,440	
		24,700	
	× 10%		2,470
Kiwi:	Per question	21,898	
	PUP	(15)	
		21,883	
	× 28%		6,127
			8,597

Note. In this question you can insert the figure for consolidated reserves from the consolidated profit and loss account. However, for completeness, a reserve working may be shown as follows.

	Exotic	*Melon*	*Kiwi*
	£'000	£'000	£'000
Reserves per question	32,138	24,075	19,898
Provision for unrealised profit		(15)	(15)
Disposal of fixed assets: profit	(40)		
depreciation	8	–	–
	32,106	24,060	19,883
Melon: pre-acquisition		(1,425)	
Kiwi: pre-acquisition		–	(950)
		22,635	18,933
Share of Melon: 22,635 × 90%	20,372		
Share of Kiwi: 18,933 × 72%	13,631		
	66,109		

(b)   **Effect of Madiera plc on consolidated P&L a/c**

	Discontinued operations	
	£'000	£'000
Turnover		2,000
Cost of sales	(2,682)	
Less provision at 31.12.X8	500	
		(2,182)
Gross loss		(182)
Distribution costs		(18)
Administrative expenses		(100)
Operating loss		(300)
Loss on termination of discontinued operations		
(427 – 115 + 36)		(348)
Loss on ordinary activities before tax		(648)

FRS 3 (format 1)

	£'000
Turnover	
Discontinued operations	2,000
Operating loss	
Discontinued operations	(800)
Less provision at 31.12.X8	500
	(300)
Loss on termination of discontinued activities	(348)
Loss before tax	(648)

(c)   **Goodwill arising on acquisition of Zest Software**

The company believes that this goodwill has an **indefinite economic life** and therefore it **will not be amortised**. FRS 10 *Goodwill and intangible assets* states that this treatment is **acceptable provided that:**

(i)   The **durability** of the acquired business **can be demonstrated**.

(ii)   It justifies estimating the useful economic life to be indefinite.

(iii)   The **goodwill is capable of continued measurement** so that **annual impairment reviews are feasible.**

Durability depends on factors such as the nature of the business; the stability of the business in which the acquired business operates; and the typical life spans of the products to which goodwill relates. **Software products generally have short lives and the sector is not noted for stability.** In these circumstances **it may be difficult to demonstrate that the goodwill is durable.**

In addition, goodwill is **unlikely to be capable of continued measurement** because the business of Zest Software **has been merged with the existing business** of Exotic. Therefore the goodwill will be subsumed within the existing business and will be difficult to track and measure.

These factors suggest that the goodwill should be amortised. By amortising goodwill the company will avoid having to carry out annual impairment tests as required by FRS 10 and FRS 11 *Impairment of fixed assets and goodwill.*

Interest in joint venture

FRS 9 *Associates and joint ventures* states that **joint ventures should be included in the consolidated financial statements using the gross equity method**. This means that the investors share of gross assets, gross liabilities and any unamortised goodwill arising on the acquisition should be shown together in the balance sheet, normally under fixed asset investments. Therefore **the net liability in the joint venture cannot be offset against the loan.** (Both the Companies Act 1985 and FRS 5 *Reporting the substance of transactions* also prohibit offsetting.)

This leaves a **net liability of £3 million** (the company's share of the net assets of the joint venture of £3 million less negative goodwill of £6 million). FRS 9 states that **where a group holds an interest in the net liabilities of a joint venture this should be shown as a provision or a liability**, rather than as a fixed asset. However, in this case the **net liability arises from negative goodwill**, rather than net liabilities in the joint venture itself. FRS 10 states that **negative goodwill should be reported as a negative asset below positive goodwill.**

Therefore **there is an argument for reporting the net liability of £3 million as a fixed asset investment** (with adequate disclosure in the notes to the financial statements).

FRS 10 states that negative goodwill should be recognised in the profit and loss account in the periods in which it is recovered.

(d)   **Environmental reporting**

At present, UK companies are not specifically required to report any information about the way in which their activities affect the environment.

Some accounting standards require disclosure of specific environmental information:

(i)   **FRS 3** *Reporting financial performance* requires details of **large and unusual items** recognised in the profit and loss account; these may include environmental costs.

(ii)   **FRS 12** *Provisions, contingent liabilities and contingent assets* requires **disclosure of information about provisions and contingent liabilities relating to environmental matters.**

(iii)   The Reporting Statement (RS1*)* on the ***Operating and Financial Review*** recommends that companies describe **business risks related to environmental issues**, and that they disclose **details**

of potential environmental liabilities and environmental protection costs. The Companies Act 2006 introduced a requirement for companies (except those with the scope of small companies exemptions) to prepare a Business Review. Amongst its contents (which are very similar to those of RS1) is a requirement to show analysis using other key performance indicators (including information relating to environmental and employee matters).

Apart from this, companies can disclose as much or as little information as they wish in whatever way that they wish.

In practice companies often present information **selectively or in such a general way that it is meaningless.** This means that it is difficult to compare the performance of different companies. However, many large companies publish extensive and extremely informative 'environmental reports' that are completely separate from the financial statements themselves. Because most environmental disclosures **do not have to be audited**, users cannot yet rely on the environmental information included in the financial statements.

Progas's operations clearly do have an impact on the environment and the company **should seriously consider disclosing environmental information** in its financial statements. By acknowledging its responsibility for the environment, a company **can enhance its reputation and distinguish itself from competitors**. Information that would be useful to users of the financial statements might include:

(i)   Details of emissions, including reductions/increases from the previous year;

(ii)   The **impact of gas emissions** on the environment and **action taken** to minimise this impact;

(iii)   **Expenditure on restoring the countryside** after pipelines have been laid;

(iv)   Details of any **infringement of environmental laws/guidelines** including details of any **fines**.

There are a number of **codes of practice** which companies may follow, for example, the *Sustainability Reporting Guidelines* published by the Global Reporting Initiative (GRI). The company may also consider signing up to the Eco Management and Audit Scheme (EMAS). This would involve agreeing to a specific code of practice with the environmental report being validated by an accredited independent verifier.

D11 Preparation question: Part disposal

ANGEL AND SHANE

BALANCE SHEET AS AT 31 DECEMBER 20X8

	£'000
Fixed assets	200
Investment in Shane [(190 × 35%) + 21.5]	88
Net current assets (580 + 160)	740
	1,028
Share capital	500
Profit and loss account (W1)	528
	1,028

PROFIT AND LOSS ACCOUNT FOR THE YEAR ENDED 31 DECEMEBER 20X8

		£'000
Operating profit (110 + 6/12 × 30)		125.00
Share of operating profit of associate (30 × 35% × 6/12)		5.25
		130.25
Profit on sale of subsidiary (W3)		75.15
Profit before tax		205.40
Tax − 40 + (12 × 6/12)	46.0	
− Share of associate (12 × 6/12 × 35%)	2.1	(48.1)
Profit after tax		157.3
Minority interest (18 × 6/12 × 30%)		(2.7)
Profit for the year		154.6

ANSWERS

STATEMENT OF RESERVES

	£'000
As at 1 January 20X8	373.4
Profit for the year	154.6
As at 31 December 20X8	528.0

Workings

1   *Reserves c/f*

	Angel £'000	Shane £'000
Per Q	400	90
Add: profit on disposal (160 − (120 × ½))	100	
Less: pre acquisition reserves of Shane		(10)
	500	80
Share of Shane post acquisition (35% × 80)	28	
	528	

2   *Reserve b/f*

Angel	330.0
Shane (72 − 10) × 70%	43.4
	373.4

3   *Exceptional item*

	£'000
Holding Co Profit	
Sale proceeds	160
Cost (120 × ½)	(60)
	100

		£'000
Group profit		
H Co Profit		100
Less: post-acq reserves now sold on		
at disposal date (72 + 18 × 6/12) =	81	
at acquisition	(10)	
	71	
	× 35%	= (24.85)
		75.15

Alternative

	£'000
Sale proceeds	160.00
Less: net assets disposed of (190 − 6/12 × 18) × 35%	(63.35)
Less: goodwill 43 (W4) × ½	(21.50)
	75.15

4   *Goodwill*

	£'000	£'000
Cost		120
Acquired		
Share capital	100	
P&L	10	
	110 × 70%	(77)
		43

D12 Plans

Marking scheme

			Marks
Plan 1	Share premium		2
	Shares at discount		1
	Gain or loss		1
	Distribution		1
	Calculations:	share	5
		cash	3
			13
Available			
Plan 2	Share premium		2
	Merger accounting discussion		2
	X financial statements		2
	W group		3
			9
Available			
Plan 3	Cash consideration		1
	Impairment		2
	Calculations		3
	Intercompany items		2
			8
		Available	30
		Available	30
		Maximum	25

There are a number of reasons why a group may re-organise.

- To reduce gearing by floating a business
- Companies may be transferred to another business during a divisionalisation process
- To create efficiencies of group structure for tax purposes

The impact of each of the proposed structures is discussed below.

Plan 1

The implications of this plan will be different, depending on the choice of purchase consideration.

Share for share exchange

If the purchase consideration is in the form of shares, then a share premium account will need to be set up in the books of Y. This share premium account must comprise the minimum premium value, which is the excess of the book value of the investment over the nominal value of the shares issued: £70m – £50m = £20m.

The impact on the individual company accounts and on the group accounts is as follows.

	Note	X £m	Y £m	Z £m	Group £m
Tangible fixed assets		600	200	45	845
Cost of investment in Y	1	130			
Cost of investment in Z	2		70		
Net current assets		160	100	20	280
		890	370	65	1,125
Share capital	3	120	110	40	120
Share premium	4		20		
Profit and loss account	5	770	240	25	1,005
		890	370	65	1,125

Notes

1   *Cost of investment in Y*

This is increased by the total value of the shares issued: £50m + £20m = £70m.

2   *Cost of investment in Z*

Transferred to Y. The book value of the investment is preserved.

3   *Share capital*

Y's share capital is increased by the nominal value of the shares issued, £50m.

4   *Share premium*

This is as discussed above.

5   *Profit and loss account*

Goodwill arising on the purchase of Z is £10m (£70m – (£40m + £20m)). This will have been written off to reserves. The group profit and loss account is calculated as follows.

	£m
X	770
Y	240
Z's PARR (25 – 20)	5
Goodwill (post-acquisition)	(10)
	1,005

Cash purchase

If the purchase consideration is in the form of cash, a gain or loss on the sale of Z will arise in the books of X. This does not count as a distribution as the cash price of £75m is not in excess of the fair value of the net assets of Z, £80m. The effect on the accounts would be as follows.

	Note	X £m	Y £m	Z £m	Group £m
Tangible fixed assets		600	200	45	845
Cost of investment in Y		60			
Cost of investment in Z	1		75		
Net current assets	2	235	25	20	280
		895	300	65	1,125
Share capital		120	60	40	120
Profit and loss account	3	775	240	25	1,005
		895	300	65	1,125

Notes

1   *Cost of investment in Z*

This is the cash consideration of £75m.

2   *Net current assets*

X's cash increases by £75m and Y's cash decreases by £75m.

3   *Profit and loss account*

X's profit and loss account has been increased by £5m, being the profit on the sale of the investment in Z. This is eliminated on consolidation as it is an intra-group transaction. The consolidated profit and loss account is calculated in exactly the same way as in the share for share exchange.

Plan 2

This restructuring plan involves a demerger of Y and Z from the X group and the formation of a separate W group. The transaction may be viewed as a distribution by X to its shareholders in the form of shares in W.

It is likely that this group reconstruction will qualify as a merger under FRS 6 *Acquisitions and mergers*. This will get round the necessity of creating a share premium account. Assuming that the FRS 6 criteria are met, and that no other inter-company transactions involving transfers of shares and cash had taken place, the effect on the accounts will be as follows.

	Note	X £m	W £m
Tangible fixed assets		600	245
Net current assets		160	120
		760	365
Share capital	1	120	130
Profit and loss account	2	640	235
		760	365

Notes

1   *Share capital*

W issued 130m £1 shares.

2   *Profit and loss account*

	£m
X	
Per question	770
Less distribution	(130)
	640

	£m	£m
W		
Y's profit and loss		240
Z's profit and loss		25
		265
Share capital balance on merger account		
W shares issued	130	
Y share capital	(60)	
Z share capital	(40)	
		(30)
		235

Plan 3

This restructuring plan is a rationalisation, aimed at simplifying the group structure. An important point to take into account is that the investment in Z in the books of X may be impaired. Z was originally purchased for £70m, with goodwill of £10m arising, but the assets have been transferred to Y at book value of £60m. Z will be a shell company with a net asset value of £60m and this will be shown as an intercompany account with Y. The cost of X's investment in Z should be reduced to £60m, with a corresponding charge to the profit and loss account. The accounts would appear as follows.

	Note	X £m	Y £m	Z £m	Group £m
Tangible fixed assets		600	245		845
Cost of investment in Y		60			
Cost of investment in Z	1	60			
Net current assets	2	160	60	60	280
		880	305	60	1,125
Share capital		120	60	40	120
Revaluation reserve	3		5		
Profit and loss account	4	760	240	20	1,005
		880	305	60	1,125

Notes

1   *Cost of investment in Z*

	£m
Per question	70
Less impairment	(10)
	60

2   *Net current assets*

Y's net current assets are £100m + £20m less intercompany creditor £60m.

Note that this calculation is based on the assumption that the £10m loss in X's books, the revaluation gain in Y's books and the loss on the transfer of assets to Y in Z's books are intercompany items and can be ignored. The calculation of group profit and loss account is then the same as for Plan 1.

3   *Revaluation reserve*

This is the gain on the purchase of the assets from Z: £65m – £60m.

4   *Profit and loss account*

X's individual profit and loss account is £770m less the impairment of £10m, which gives £760m.

The group profit and loss account is calculated as follows.

	£m
X	770
Y	240
Z (post acquisition)	5
	1,015
Less goodwill	(10)
	1,005

Z's profit and loss account is £20m, ie £25m less £5m loss on transfer of assets.

Summary and conclusion

There are advantages and disadvantages to each of the three plans. Before we could make a recommendation we would need more information about why the group wishes to restructure.

Plan 1 does not change the group financial statements. From an internal point of view it results in a **closer relationship** between Y and Z. This may be advantageous if Y and Z are close geographically or in terms of similarity of business activities. Alternatively, it might be advantageous for tax reasons.

Plan 2 does have a **dramatic effect on the group financial statements**. Total **distributable profits fall** from £1,005 to £875m (X £640m, W group £235m). However, the W group may benefit from being more closely knit, and this may enhance overall growth.

Plan 3 is an example of **divisionalisation**: the assets and trade of Z are transferred to Y and Z becomes a shell company. This could result in cost savings overall. Furthermore, Z becomes a non-trading company and this could be used for some other purpose. It should be noted that, with Plan 3, there is no effect on the group financial statements.

D13 Ejoy

Top tips. This question required the production of a consolidated profit and loss account of a group. Candidates were expected to calculate and impairment test the investment in two subsidiaries, to account for a joint venture, to deal with impairment and hedging of financial assets, and account for a pre-acquisition dividend and a discontinued operation.

Easy marks. Do not spend too long on the discontinued operation. You would not be penalised too heavily if you got this wrong.

Examiner's comment. Overall the question was quite well answered, with the majority of candidates achieving a pass mark. However, candidates answered the financial instruments part of the question quite poorly. The main problem seemed to be the application of knowledge; candidates could recite the principles of accounting for financial instruments but could not deal with the practical application thereof. The calculation of the goodwill was done well, as was the accounting for the pre-acquisition dividend. However, the impairment testing of the investment in the subsidiary was poorly answered. Candidates need to understand this procedure as it will be a regular feature of future papers.

Marking scheme

	Marks
Goodwill	7
Joint venture	2
Financial assets	7
Dividend	2
Income statement	7
Tbay	4
Minority interest	2
Available	31
Maximum	25

EJOY
CONSOLIDATED PROFIT AND LOSS ACCOUNT FOR THE YEAR ENDED 31 MAY 20X6

	£m
Turnover (including share of joint venture)(2,500 + 1,500 + 10)	4,010
Less share of joint venture's turnover (50% × 20)	(10)
Group turnover	4,000
Cost of sales (1,800 + 1,200 + 4 (W2))	(3,004)
Gross profit	996
Other income (70 + 10 – 3 (W5) – 16 (W6) + 7 (W7))	68
Distribution costs (130 + 120)	(250)
Administrative expenses (100 + 90)	(190)
Group operating profit	624
Share of operating profit in joint venture (50% × 4)	2
	626
Interest payable (W8)	(133)
Profit on ordinary activities before tax	493
Tax on profit on ordinary activities:	
Group (200 + 26)	(226)
Joint venture (50% × 2)	(1)
Profit for period from continuing operations	266
Minority interest (W10)	1
Group profit for the period	267

Workings

1   *Group structure*

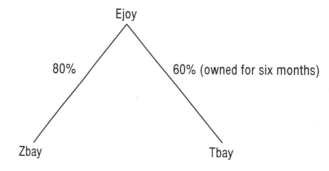

Ejoy

80%   60% (owned for six months)

Zbay   Tbay

Tbay is not consolidated because it was acquired with a view to resale and has not previously been consolidated. Therefore it is exempt from consolidation under FRS 2. Instead it is treated as a financial asset at fair value through profit or loss (see W7).

2   *Impairment of goodwill (Zbay)*

	£m
Goodwill (W3)	35.0
Carrying amount of net assets (80% × 612.9 (W4))	490.3
	525.3
Recoverable amount	521.0
Impairment loss: all allocated to goodwill	4.3

Note. £4.3m is rounded to £4m.

3   *Goodwill (Zbay)*

	£m
Cost of investment	520
Less fair value of identifiable assets and liabilities acquired (80% × 600)	(480)
	40
Less amortisation (40 ÷ 8)	(5)
	35

4 *Carrying amount of net assets at 31 May 20X6 (Zbay)*

	£m
Fair value of identifiable assets and liabilities acquired (1 June 20X4)	600.0
Profit for year to 31 May 20X5	20.0
Profit for year to 31 May 20X6 per draft profit and loss account	34.0
Less impairment loss (loan asset) (W8)	(41.1)
	612.9

5 *Joint venture*

Elimination of group share of gain on disposal (50% × 6) = £3 million

6 *Dividend income (Tbay)*

Minority share eliminated (40% × 40) = £16 million

7 *Gain on investment (Tbay)*

	£m
Fair value of investment at 31 May 20X6 (72 × £3.10)	223.2
Less carrying amount (221 − 5)	(216.0)
Gain (to profit and loss account)	7.2

Note. The £7.2m is rounded to £7m. The investment in Tbay is at fair value through profit or loss, so the transaction costs are not included in the cost of the investment but instead are treated as a finance cost (FRS 26).

8 *Interest payable*

	£m
Per draft profit and loss account (50 + 40)	90.0
Impairment loss (loan asset held by Zbay) (W9)	41.1
Interest receivable on bond held by Ejoy (50 × 5%)	(2.5)
Interest received on interest rate swap held by Ejoy	(0.5)
Transaction costs on purchase of Tbay (see (W7))	5.0
	133.1

Note. £133.1m is rounded to £133m. Because the interest rate swap is 100% effective as a fair value hedge, it exactly offsets the loss in value of £1.7 million (50 − 48.3) on the bond. The bond is an 'available for sale' item (per FRS 26) and therefore the loss would normally be taken to equity, but because hedge accounting is adopted both the gain on the swap and the loss on the bond are recognised in profit and loss. The net effect on profit and loss is nil.

9 *Impairment loss (loan asset held by Zbay)*

	£m
Carrying value of loan (a financial asset)	60.0
Less present value of expected future cash flows (20 × 0.9433)	(18.9)
Impairment loss	41.1

Note. The £20 million is expected to be received on 31 May 20X7, ie in one year's time.

10 *Minority interest*

	£m
Profit for period per question	34.00
Less impairment loss on loan asset (W9)	(41.10)
Impairment loss	(7.1)
	× 20%
	1.4

D14 Case study: Base group

Top tips. Part (a) required a consolidated profit and loss account. This included the calculation of the profit/loss on a disposal of shares/deemed disposal, adjustments for inter company profit, retirement benefits, convertible debt instruments and share options as well as dealing with accounting for associates, minority interests and goodwill. The question included a deemed disposal. However, if you missed this, you would only be penalised once for this mistake. Part (b) deals with intangibles and revenue recognition. In part (c) there are always easy marks to be had for backing up your arguments.

Easy marks. There are a lot of easy marks here for basic consolidation technique, which, even if you missed complications like the deemed disposal, you could still gain.

Examiner's comment. In general this question was well answered. However, some candidates used proportional consolidation for the subsidiary, and few treated the share options correctly.

Marking scheme

			Marks
(a)		Turnover	1
		Cost of sales	4
		Distribution/administration	1
		Interest expense	2
		Investment income	1
		Taxation	1
		Goodwill	5
		Inter-company profit	2
		Retirement benefit – explanation	2
		Debt – explanation	1
		Share options – explanation	1
		Associate	4
		Minority interest	2
		Deemed disposal	3
		Disposal of shares	2
(b)		Revenue recognition	6
(c)	(i)	Strategic issue	1
		Sustainable performance	1
		Transparency	1
		Best practice	1
		Responsible ownership	1
		Performance	1
		Reduction of risks	1
		Reputation	1
		Exploitation	1
		Governments	1
		External awards	1
		Cultural/social pressures	1
	(ii)	1 mark per point up to a maximum	7
		Available	55
		Maximum	50

(a)   BASE GROUP
      CONSOLIDATED PROFIT AND LOSS ACCOUNT FOR THE YEAR ENDED 31 MAY 20X3

	£m	£m
Turnover (3,000 + 2,300 + 450)		5,750
Cost of sales (W2)		(3,839)
Gross profit		1,911
Distribution costs (240 + 230 + 90)		(560)
Administrative expenses (200 + 220 + 60)		(480)
Operating profit		871
Profit on disposal of shares in subsidiaries (W3)		9
Share of operating loss of associate (W4)		(2)
Interest payable:		
Group (W5)	(40)	
Associate (12 × 3/12 × 40%)	(1)	
		(41)
Investment income receivable (100 − 200/350 × 70)		60
Other finance income (W7)		3
Profit on ordinary activities before taxation		900
Tax on profit on ordinary activities:		
Group (130 + 80 + 27)	(237)	
Associate (36 × 3/12 × 40%)	(4)	
		(241)
Profit on ordinary activities after taxation		659
Minority interests (W8)		(73)
Profit for the year		586

Workings

1   *Group structure*

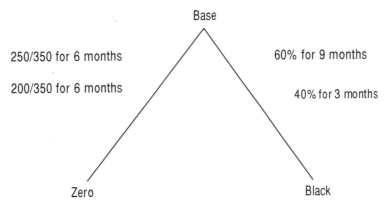

Base

250/350 for 6 months   60% for 9 months

200/350 for 6 months   40% for 3 months

Zero   Black

Zero was a subsidiary throughout the year.

Black became an associate on 1 March 20X3; the share issue reduced Base's shareholding, resulting in a deemed disposal.

2   *Cost of sales*

	£m
Base	2,000.0
Zero	1,600.0
Black (300 × 9/12)	225.0
	3,825.0
Amortisation of goodwill (9 + 4.5) (W6)	13.5
Retirement benefit (W7)	(2.0)
Share options (3 − 1)	2.0
	3,838.5

Note. The loss in the value of the share options is included in cost of sales because the options were received in exchange for trade debtors.

3   *Profit on disposal of shares in subsidiaries*

Zero

	£m	£m
Sale proceeds		155
Less net assets disposed of		
Share capital	350	
Profit and loss account at start of year	400	
Profit for current year (160 × 6/12)	80	
Fair value adjustment (770 – 350 – 250)	170	
	1,000	
Share disposed of (50/350)		(143)
Goodwill not yet amortised (50/250 × 35) (W6)		(7)
		5

Black

	£m	£m
Carrying value of net assets after the new issue:		
At date of issue	480	
Proceeds of issue (100 × 2.65)	265	
	745	
Group share (40%)		298.0
Less: group share of net assets before issue (60% × 480)		(288.0)
Gain		10.0
Goodwill not yet amortised (20/60 × 19.5) (W6)		6.5
		3.5

Total profit on disposal is £8.5 million (rounded to £9 million).

4   *Share of operating loss of associate*

	£m
Operating profit for the period (100 × 3/12)	25.0
Provision for unrealised profit (90 × 30%)	(27.0)
	(2.0)
Group share (40%)	(0.8)
Goodwill written off (W6)	1.0
	(1.8)

5   *Interest payable: Group*

	£m
Base	20
Zero	10
Black (12 × 9/12)	9
	39
Convertible debt ((20 – 16) ÷ 4)	1
	40

6   *Goodwill*

	Zero	*Black*
	£m	£m
Cost of investment	600	270
Less: fair value of net assets acquired:		
(250/350 × 770)	(550)	
(60% × 400)		(240)
	50	30
Amortisation to 31 May 20X2	(10)	(6)
	40	24
Amounts amortised for year to 31 May 20X3:		
6 months to 1 December 20X2 (10 × 6/12) (5)	(5)	
9 months to 1 March 20X3 (6 × 9/12)	–	(4.5)
As at disposal/deemed disposal date	35	19.5

	sold	remaining	'disposed	remaining
	(50/250)	(20/250)	(20/60)	(40/60)
	7	28	6.5	13

6 months to 31 May 20X3 (28 × 6/42))	(4)	
3 months to 31 May 20X3 (ass.) (13 × 3/39)		(1)
	24	12

7   *Retirement benefits*

	£m
Amount originally included in cost of sales	6
Amount that should be included (current service cost only)	(4)
Adjustment (reduction)	2

The actuarial

I loss of £5 million is recognised in the statement of total recognised gains and losses. The net amount of interest cost and expected return on assets (£3 million) is shown as 'other finance income'.

8   *Minority interests*

	£m
Zero to 1 December 20X2 (100/350 × 160 × 6/12)	23
Zero to 31 May 20X3 (150/350 × 160 × 6/12)	34
Black to 1 March 20X3 (40% × 52 × 9/12)	16
	73

(b)   **Revenue from the sale of software under licences**

At present there is **no UK accounting standard covering revenue recognition**. This means that for the time being in theory **the company can adopt any policy that it wishes**. However, there have recently been several high profile cases in which companies have been criticised for adopting questionable revenue recognition policies. The ASB has recently issued an amendment to FRS 5 which gives guidance on applying the general principles in FRS 5 to revenue recognition. The ASB's *Statement of Principles for Financial Reporting* should also be applied.

There are **two main problems** with the company's existing policies. One is that **revenue may be recognised before services are performed**. The Amendment to FRS 5 states that **revenue should only be recognised to the extent that an entity has performed its contractual obligations.**

The other problem concerns **deferred income**. Under the *Statement of Principles*, deferred income is not a 'true' liability, because there is no obligation to repay the amounts paid in advance. However, the Amendment to FRS 5 states that **the seller should recognise a liability where it receives payment in advance of performance.** The liability represents its obligation to provide goods or services under the contract. This suggests that it is **acceptable to recognise software rentals over the term of the agreement.**

(c) (i) There are a number of factors which encourage companies to disclose social and environmental information in their financial statements.

Public interest in corporate social responsibility is steadily increasing. Although financial statements are primarily intended for investors and their advisers, there is growing recognition that companies actually have **a number of different stakeholders**. These include **customers, employees and the general public,** all of whom are **potentially interested** in the way in which a company's operations affect the natural environment and the wider community. These stakeholders can have a **considerable effect on a company's performance**. As a result many companies now deliberately attempt to build a **reputation for social and environmental responsibility**. Therefore the disclosure of environmental and social information is essential. There is also growing recognition that **corporate social responsibility is actually an important part of an entity's overall performance.** Responsible practice in areas such as reduction of damage to the environment and recruitment **increases shareholder value**. Companies that act responsibly and make social and environmental disclosures are **perceived as better investments** than those that do not.

Another factor is **growing interest by governments and professional bodies**. Although there are **no IFRSs** that specifically require environmental and social reporting, it may be required by **company legislation**. In the UK, the **ASB recommends** (in a reporting statement on best practice issued in January 2006) that **listed companies should prepare an Operating and Financial Review** in which they are required to disclose information about the key environmental risks that the business faces and about its policies towards employees. There are now a number of **awards for environmental and social reports** and high quality disclosure in financial statements. These provide further encouragement to disclose information. This information must also be disclosed in the Business Review required by CA 2006.

At present companies are normally able to disclose **as much or as little information as they wish in whatever manner that they wish**. This causes a number of **problems**. Companies tend to disclose information **selectively** and it difficult for users of the financial statements to **compare the performance of different companies**. However, there are **good arguments** for continuing to allow companies a certain amount of freedom to determine the information that they disclose. If detailed rules are imposed, **companies are likely to adopt a 'checklist' approach** and will **present information in a very general and standardised way**, so that it is of very little use to stakeholders.

(ii) The Base Group could improve its disclosure of 'Corporate Environmental Governance' by including the following information in its financial statements:

(1) A general description of its **policies** relating to the environment

(2) Descriptions of the **ways in which the company seeks to manage and minimise environmental risks**

(3) **Details** of any **serious pollution incidents** that have occurred during the year and details of any **fines** imposed for environmental offences

(4) A report on the company's **environmental performance** including **details of acid gas and other emissions** and details of how the company's activities affect the natural environment in other ways. The report should include **narrative information** (descriptions of how the risks are reduced) and **numerical information** if this is verifiable

(6) Details of the company's **targets (key performance indicators)** for reducing emissions and other forms of pollution and whether these have been met; **historical data** should be included here if this is practicable

There exist a number of **guidelines** that set out the information that should be disclosed in an environmental report (for example, the Global Reporting Initiative (GRI) framework of performance indicators). The guidance is **non-mandatory, but represents best practice**. Ideally, the environmental information should be **audited.**

D15 Hyperinflation

> **Top tips**. FRS 24 is a fairly recent standard, so you may get a question on it.

(a)   A foreign operation normally has the same functional currency of its parent when:

   (i)   The foreign company is merely an **extension** of the **investing company** operations overseas.
   (ii)   The foreign company is **dependent** upon the investing company for financing.
   (iii)   The foreign company **cash flows** have a **material impact** on those of the investing company.
   (iv)   The majority of the **transactions** are denominated in the **investing company currency**.

A foreign operation normally has a different functional currency from is parent when:

   (i)   The foreign operation is **separate** or **independent**.

   (ii)   The normal operations are denominated in the **local currency**.

   (iii)   The normal operations are (at least partially) **financed locally**.

   (iv)   The foreign operation has a management team committed to maximisation of the **local currency profits**.

   (v)   The **financial statements** of the **foreign operation** are be **expressed** in the **local currency** as the **best indicator** of the **performance locally**.

Factors which may be taken into account in determining the **functional currency** include the following.

   (i)   **Pricing** and **market conditions**. Are they determined locally or by the investing company?
   (ii)   Does the foreign operation buy **goods and services locally** or rely on imports?
   (iii)   How is the foreign operation **financed**? Locally or by the investing company?
   (iv)   What is the extent of **inter company trading**?

(b)   **The effects of hyper-inflation on the financial statements**

The effects of hyper-inflation can **reduce the usefulness** of financial statements in the following ways:

- The amounts at which assets are stated in the balance sheet are **unlikely to reflect their current values**.

- The **level of profit** for the year may be **misleading**. Income appears to increase rapidly, while expenses such as depreciation may be based on out of date costs and are artificially low.

- It is therefore difficult to make any **meaningful assessment** of an entity's performance as **assets are understated** and **profits are overstated**.

These are well known disadvantages of basing financial statements on historic cost and they affect most entities. However, where there is hyper-inflation these problems are exacerbated. In addition, where an entity's financial statements are translated into pounds, hyper-inflation often gives rise to **significant exchange differences** which may **absorb reserves**.

How hyper-inflation should be dealt with in the financial statements

FRS 24 **does not provide a definition** of hyper-inflation. However, it does include guidance as to characteristics of an economic environment of a country in which hyper-inflation may be present. These include, but are not limited to, the following.

- The general population prefers to keep its wealth in **non-monetary assets** or in a relatively **stable foreign currency**

- Interest rates, wages and prices are **linked to a price index**

- The cumulative **inflation rate** over three years is **approaching, or exceeds, 100%**

FRS 24 states that the financial statements of an entity that reports in the currency of a hyper-inflationary economy should be **restated in terms of the measuring unit current at the balance sheet date.** This involves remeasuring assets and liabilities by **applying a general price index**. The **gain or loss on the net monetary position is included in net income** and **separately disclosed.** The fact that the financial statements have been restated should also be disclosed, together with details of the index used.

FRS 23 *The effects of changes in foreign exchange rates* states that where there is hyper-inflation, the financial statements of a foreign operation **should be restated** in accordance with the requirements of FRS 24 **before they are translated into the currency of the reporting entity**. In this way users are made aware of the effect of hyper-inflation on the results and net assets of the entity.

(c) (i)

(1)

	Value (E million)	Exchange rate	£m
30 November 20X3	20	1.34	14.93
30 November 20X7	20	17.87	1.12

(A material reduction in value)

(2)

	Value (E million)	Index	Exchange rate	£m
30 November 20X7	20 ×	3254/100	17.87	36.42

(ii) In example (1) the tremendous reduction is due to **severe exchange rate movements** and has nothing at all to do with trading performance from the assets.

In example (2) a paper gain emerges simply as **a result of revaluation locally**, again this has little to do with trading performance and reflects an unrealised holding gain measured locally. However, this method does eliminate the 'disappearing assets' problem and FRS 24 requires restatement using this method where there is hyperinflation.

D16 Question with helping hands: Zetec

Top tips. This question required candidates to produce a consolidated profit and loss account and balance sheet for a parent company and its foreign subsidiary. Adjustments had to be made before consolidation to bring the subsidiary's financial statements into line with 'local' accounting standards.

Examiner's comment. Candidates generally made good attempts at the translation of the foreign subsidiary and the calculation of goodwill, inter company profit in stock, and the gain in translation. At the same time, there were problems with the 'extraordinary' items and surprisingly with the rates of exchange to be used in translating the P&L and balance sheet of the subsidiary. However, generally the performance on this question was good.

Marking scheme

	Marks
Consolidated P&L	13
Consolidated balance sheet	12
	25

ZETEC GROUP
CONSOLIDATED BALANCE SHEET AS AT 31 OCTOBER 20X2

	£m
Goodwill (W3)	18
Intangible asset (W1)	3
Tangible fixed assets (180 + 95 (W1) + 19.2 (W2))	294
Net current assets (146 + 329 – 3) (W5)	172
Creditors due after one year (74 + 80)	(154)
	333

Capital and reserves	
Ordinary shares of £1	65
Share premium	70
Retained earnings (W7)	162
Translation reserve (W12)	23
	320
Minority interests (W4)	13
	333

ZETEC GROUP PLC
CONSOLIDATED PROFIT AND LOSS ACCOUNT
FOR THE YEAR ENDED 31 OCTOBER 20X2

	£m
Turnover (revenue) (325 + 50 (W10) – 15 (W5))	360
Cost of sales (189 + 25.8 – 15 (W5) + 3 (W5))	(203)
Gross profit	157
Distribution and administrative expenses	
84 + 9 (W8)	(93)
Interest: 2 + 4 (W8)	(6)
Profit before tax	58
Taxation 15 + 6 (W8)	(21)
Profit after tax	37
Minority interest	(1)
	36

Workings

1   *Translation of subsidiary's balance sheet/adjustment to FRS*

	Per qu Krm	Adjustments	Note	Total	Rate (Note 1)	£m
Tangible fixed assets	380			380	4	95.0
Intangible assets	12		2	12	4	3.0
Net current assets	116			116	4	29.0
Long-term creditors	(320)			(320)	4	(80.0)
Net assets	188			188		47.0
Ordinary shares: 1 kr	48			48	6	8.0
Share premium	18			18	6	3.0
Revaluation reserve	12		3	12	6	2.0
Retained earnings						
Pre acqn	98	(13)	3	85	6	14.2
				163		27.2
Post acqn	12					
(110 – 98)		13	4	25	5	5.0
Translation reserve					balance	14.8
	188					47.0

Notes

1   Translate assets and liabilities at the rate ruling at the balance sheet date, and share capital and pre-acquisition reserves at the historic rate. Post-acquisition reserves are as calculated above. The translation reserve is the balancing figure.

2   Aztec has allocated the excess of the price paid for its acquisition of a company over the fair value of the company's net assets to 'market share'. However, this should be re-classified as goodwill.

3   As the fixed asset has been physically damaged, this constitutes an impairment (a loss caused by a consumption of economic benefits) rather than a decrease in market value. Such revaluation losses must be written off to the profit and loss account as per FRS 11, which has happened in the case of the whole deficit of Kr 9m. No adjustment need be made in respect of this amount.

4   Aztec has written the prior year adjustment of Kr 13m off to the current period's profit and loss account. Under FRS 3, it should be treated as a prior year adjustment and charged against opening reserves, ie deducted from pre-acquisition profits and added back to post-acquisition profits. This part of the extraordinary item should be eliminated from the consolidated P&L (see below).

2   *Fair value adjustment*

	Acquisition Krm	B/S date Krm
Book values (W1)		
Share capital	48	48
Share premium	18	18
Revaluation reserve	12	12
Pre-acquisition reserves	85	85
	163	163
Fair value adjustment (balancing figure)	77	77
Post acquisition reserves (as above)		25
	240	265

Fair value adjustment in £ = 77/4 = £19.25

3   *Goodwill arising on acquisition of Aztec*

	Krm	Krm	Rate	£m
Cost of investment		264		
Less fair value of				
net assets acquired	240			
Group share: 80%		192		
		72	6	12
FX gain		–	β	6
		72	4	18

4   *Minority interests*

	£m
Net assets at balance sheet date (265 ÷ 4) (W2)	66.2
Minority share	× 20%
Minority interests	13.2

5   *Unrealised profit in stock*

Although the goods sold by Zetec to Aztec have been consumed in the manufacturing process, they have not been sold and are included in closing finished goods stock. Hence, the unrealised profit must be eliminated on consolidation. The profit sits in Zetec's (the parent) books and must therefore be adjusted in full against its profits.

Goods transferred from Zetec at selling price	£ 15m
Percentage profit on selling price	× 20%
Unrealised profit sitting in Zetec	£3m

6   *Settlement of debt from stock transfer*

A gain would be made by Aztec, calculated as follows:

	Krm
Liability arising on transfer of the goods at 31 May 20X2: 15m × 5.2	78
Settlement on 31 July 20X2: 15m × 4.2	63
Gain	15

This would have already been included in Aztec's profit and loss account (in cost of sales) and is therefore recorded in Aztec's P&L in the amount of Kr 15 million in cost of sales and included in the group accounts accordingly.

7   *Group retained earnings*

	Zetec	Aztec
Zetec per question	161	
Aztec post acquisition (W8)		5
Adjustment for unrealised profit (W5)	(3)	
Share of Aztec: 80% × 5	4	
	162	

8   *Translation of Aztec profit and loss account*

	Krm	Rate	£m
Turnover	250	5	50.0
Cost of sales *	(129)	5	25.8
Gross profit	121		24.2
Distribution and administrative expenses	(46)	5	(9.2)
Interest payable	(20)	5	(4.0)
Profit before tax	55		11.0
Tax	(30)	5	(6.0)
Profit after tax	25		5.0

* Cost of sales	Krm
Per question	120
Impairment	9
	129

9   *Elimination of extraordinary item*

The extraordinary items figure of Kr 22m in the accounts of Aztec has been eliminated as follows.

	Krm
Write off of fixed asset charged to cost of sales (W8)	9
Accounting policy adjustment to opening reserves*	13
	22

*This will effectively result in a debit balance on post acquisition revaluation reserves. On consolidation this will have to be offset against group reserves and minority interests. (see W10 below).

10 *Movement on retained earnings*

	£m
Retained earnings at 1 November 20X1 [161 − (35 − 4)]	130
Profit for period	36
Dividends paid	(4)
Retained earnings as at 31 October 20X2	162

11   *Analysis of exchange gain*

	£m
Closing net assets at closing rate (188 ÷ 4)	47.0
Opening net assets at opening rate (163 ÷ 6)	(27.2)
Increase in net assets	19.8
Less profit for year (W1)	(5.0)
Translation reserve c/f (W1)	14.8
Included in translation reserve (80%)	11.8
Included in minority interest (20%)	3.0
	14.8

12   *Total exchange differences recognised in translation reserve*

	£m
On translation of financial statements (W11)	11.8
On goodwill (W3)	6.0
On fair value adjustments [80% × (77 ÷ 4 − 77 ÷ 6)]	5.1
	22.9

D17 Memo

Top tips. In this question, you had to produce a consolidated profit and loss account and balance sheet for a parent company and its foreign subsidiary. Adjustments had to be made for intercompany items such as loans and stock, and candidates had to deal with the treatment of goodwill as a foreign currency asset. Exchange gains and losses had to be recognised in the financial statements.

Easy marks. Just setting out the proforma and doing the mechanics of translation will earn you easy marks, even if you struggle with more difficult aspects.

Examiner's comment. This question was well answered. Candidates generally made good attempts at the translation of the foreign subsidiary, the calculation of goodwill, intragroup profit in stock, and the gain on translation. At the same time, there were problems with the treatment of goodwill as a foreign currency asset, and the exchange gain on the intercompany loan.

Marking scheme

		Marks
(a)	Consolidated balance sheet	6
	Translation of sub-balance sheet	4
	Goodwill	1
	Minority interest	1
	Post acquisition reserves	5
	Consolidated profit and loss account	5
	Unrealised profit	4
	Loan	3
	Available	29
	Maximum	25

(Movement on reserves and exchange gain analysis not asked for)

MEMO GROUP
CONSOLIDATED BALANCE SHEET AT 30 APRIL 20X4

	£m	£m
Fixed assets		
Intangible assets: Goodwill (W4)	8	
Tangible assets	367	
		375
Current assets (355 + 48.6 − 0.6) (W8)	403	
Creditors: amounts falling due within one year	(234)	
Net current assets		169
Total assets less current liabilities		544
Creditors: amounts falling due after more than one year (30 + 18.6 − 5)		(44)
		500
Capital and reserves		
Share capital		60
Share premium		50
Profit and loss account (W5)		363
Translation reserve (W9)		9
		482
Minority interests (W6)		18
		500

MEMO GROUP
CONSOLIDATED PROFIT AND LOSS ACCOUNT FOR THE YEAR ENDED 30 APRIL 20X4

	£m
Turnover (200 + 71 − 6)	265
Cost of sales (120 + 48 − 6 + 0.6) (W8)	(163)
Gross profit	102
Distribution costs and administrative expenses (30 + 10)	(40)
Amortisation of goodwill (W4)	(2)
Interest payable	(1)
Interest receivable	4
Exchange gains (W7)	1
Profit before taxation	64
Tax (20 + 4)	(24)
Profit after taxation	40
Minority interests (25% × 7.9) (W3)	(2)
Group profit for the year	38

Workings

1   *Group structure*

Memo

1 May 20X3   75%

Random

Cost = 120m crowns
PAR = 80m crowns

2   *Translation of balance sheet*

	CRm	Rate	£m
Tangible fixed assets	146.0	2.1	69.5
Current assets	102.0	2.1	48.6
Creditors within one year (60 + 1.2 (W7))	(61.2)	2.1	(29.1)
Creditors after more than one year (41 – 2 (W7))	(39.0)	2.1	(18.6)
	147.8		70.4
Share capital	32	2.5	12.8
Share premium	20.0	2.5	8.0
Profit and loss account:			
Pre-acquisition	80.0	2.5	32.0
	132.0		52.8
Post– acquisition (15 + 0.8) (W7)	15.8	2.0	7.9
Translation reserve	___	Bal fig	9.7
	147.8		70.4

3   *Translation of profit and loss account*

	CRm	Rate	£m
Turnover	142	2	71
Cost of sales	(96)	2	(48)
Gross profit	46	2	23
Distribution and administrative expenses	(20)	2	(10)
Interest payable	(2)	2	(1)
Exchange gain (W7)	0.8	2	0.4
Profit before tax	24.8	2	12.4
Tax	(9.0)	2	(4.5)
Profit for the year	15.8	2	7.9

4   *Goodwill*

	CRm	CRm	Rate	£m
Cost of investment		120.0		
Less fair value of net assets acquired				
Share capital	32			
Share premium	20			
Profit and loss account	80			
	132			
Group share (75%)		(99.0)		
		21.0	2.5	8.4
Amortisation (21 ÷ 5)		(4.2)	2.1	(2.0)
FX gain		–	β	1.6
At 30.4.X4		16.8		8.0

	£m
Net book value (16.8 ÷ 2.1)	8
Amortisation (4.2 ÷ 2.1)	2

5   *Profit and loss account*

	£m
Memo	360.0
Random (75% × 7.9 (W2))	5.9
Provision for unrealised profit (W8)	(0.6)
Amortisation of goodwill (W4)	(2.0)
	363.3

6 *Minority interest*

	£m
Minority interest share of net assets (25% × 70.4)	17.6

7 *Exchange gains and losses in the accounts of Random*

Loan to Random (creditors falling due after more than one year)

	CRm
At 1 May 20X3 (£5 million × 2.5)	12.5
At 30 April 20X4 (£5 million × 2.1)	(10.5)
Gain	2.0

Inter-company purchases (creditors falling due within one year)

	CRm
Purchase of goods from Memo (£6 million × 2)	12.0
Payment made (£6 million × 2.2)	(13.2)
Loss	(1.2)

Exchange differences in profit and loss account (retranslated to sterling)

	£m
Gain on loan (2 ÷ 2)	1.0
Loss on creditors/purchases (1.2 ÷ 2)	(0.6)
	0.4

8 *Provision for unrealised profit*

	£m
Sale by parent to subsidiary (6 million × 20% × ½)	0.6

9 *Translation reserve*

	£m	£m
Closing net assets at closing rate (147.8 ÷ 2.1)	70.4	
Less opening net assets at opening rate (132 ÷ 2.5)	(52.8)	
		17.6
Less reported profit (15.8 ÷ 2)		(7.9)
		9.7
Group (75%)		7.3
Exchange gain on retranslation of goodwill (21 ÷ 2.5 − 21 ÷ 2.1)		1.6
		8.9

10 *Consolidated profit and loss account (proof)(not needed to complete the question)*

	£m
Balance at 1 May 20X3 (360 − 34 + 8)	334.0
Profit for the period (34 + 7.9 − 2 − 0.6 − 2)	37.3
Less dividend paid (Memo)	(8.0)
Balance at 30 April 20X4	363.3

D18 Preparation question: Cash flow statement

LORNA PLC
CASH FLOW STATEMENT FOR THE YEAR ENDED 30 SEPTEMBER 20X9

	£'000	£'000
Operating activities		
Receipts from customers (W1)		3,170
Payments to suppliers (W2)		(928)
Payments to employees (W3)		(718)
Other cash operating expenses (W4)		(786)
Cash flow from operating activities		738
Returns on investments and servicing of finance		
Interest paid W5	(67)	
Investment income (60 × 15%)	9	
		(58)
Taxation (210 + 204 − 251 + 141 − 252)		(52)
Capital expenditure (W6)		(1,338)
Dividends paid (350 + 180 − 200)		(330)
Financing (W7)		1,090
Cash inflow		50

Workings

1   *Receipts*

	£'000
Turnover	3,536
Opening debtors	194
Closing debtors	(260)
Non-cash payment from Doon	(300)
	3,170

2   *Payments to suppliers*

	£'000
Materials	1,079
Opening creditors	253
Closing creditors	(234)
Opening stocks	(628)
Closing stocks	758
Non-cash supplies from Doon	(300)
	928

3   *Payments to employees*

	£'000
Labour	758
Share issue [10,000 @ (5 − 1)]	(40)
	718

4   *Other cash operating expenses*

	£'000
Production overheads	453
Selling and distribution	221
Administration	252
Government grant amortisation	80
Depreciation (750 + 525 − 745 − 310)	(220)
	786

Note. Remember that the government grant amortisation is a *credit*.

5   *Interest paid*

	£'000
Interest payable	85
Amortisation and debenture:	
Discount (5% of 1m) ÷ 5 years	(10)
Premium (4% of 1m) ÷ 5 years	(8)
	67

6   *Capital expenditure*

	£'000
Fixed assets: opening	(2,640)
closing	3,368
Investment	800
Government grants: opening (75 + 160)	235
closing (125 + 220)	(345)
amortisation	(80)
	1,338

7   *Financing*

	£'000
Debenture issue: 1m @ 5% discount	950
New share issue	100
Share premium: (80 less 40 related to employee share scheme)	40
	1,090

D19 Preparation question: Consolidated cash flow statement

SWING PLC CASHFLOW STATEMENT FOR THE YEAR ENDED 31 DECEMBER 20X5

	£
Net cash inflow from operating activities	20,100
Taxation	(4,000)
Capital expenditure	
Purchase of fixed assets (W1)	(13,000)
Acquisition and disposals	
Purchase of subsidiary	(1,000)
Cash acquired with subsidiary	200
	(800)
	2,300

Notes to the cashflow statement

Note 1 – Reconciliation of operating profit to operating cashflows

	£
Operating profit	20,000
Depreciation	5,000
Increase in stocks	(4,400)
Increase in debtors	(1,700)
Increase in creditors	1,200
Net cash inflow from operating activities	20,100

Working: Fixed assets

FIXED ASSETS

	£		£
B/f	25,000	c/f	35,000
On acquisition	2,000	Depreciation	5,000
Additions	13,000		
	40,000		40,000

D20 Portal

Top tips. The examiner for the current syllabus paper has stated that the emphasis is on advising management and on realistic scenarios. Part (b) could come under the heading of advice and Part (a), which involves using your knowledge to correct the accountant's work, could come under both headings. This is a slightly different slant on cash flow statements, requiring adjustments to be made to an incorrectly prepared statement. The best approach would be to use the same workings as for a normal preparation question, piece together the details from the question, then recalculate the correct cash effects. Leave sufficient time for Part (b).

Marking scheme

			Marks
(a)	Net cash inflow	8	
	Taxation	3	
	Sale of tangible fixed assets	4	
	Minority interest	2	
	Joint venture	2	
	Disposal of subsidiary and cash disposed of	2	
	Available	21	
	Maximum		18
(b)	Subjective		7
	Available	28	
	Maximum		25

(a) PORTAL GROUP
     CASH FLOW STATEMENT FOR THE YEAR ENDED 31 DECEMBER 20X0

	Working	£m	£m
Net cash inflow from operating activities	1		692
Dividend received from joint venture			10
			702
Returns on investments and servicing of finance			
Interest received		26	
Interest paid		(9)	
Dividend paid to minority interest	2	(31)	
			(14)
Taxation	3		(115)
Capital expenditure			
Purchase of tangible fixed assets		(380)	
Sale of tangible fixed assets	4	195	
			(185)
Acquisitions and disposals			
Disposal of subsidiary		75	
Cash of subsidiary disposed of		(130)	
Purchase of interest in joint venture		(25)	
			(80)
Net cash inflow before use of liquid resources and financing			308
Increase in short term deposits			(143)
Net cash inflow			165

Workings

1   *Net cash inflow from operating activities*

	£m
Per question	875
Add back loss on disposal	25
Adjustments for current assets/liabilities of subsidiary*	
Stock	(60)
Debtors	(50)
Creditors (130 – 25)	105
Deduct pre-tax profit on joint venture (55 + 20)	(75)
Interest receivable	(27)
Interest payable	19
Deduct profit on sale of fixed assets	(120)
	692

Note. The movements in current assets used by the accountant to calculate net cash inflow from operating activities incorrectly include amounts relating to the subsidiary disposed of.

2   *Dividend paid to minority interest*

	£m
Difference per question (balance sheet movement)	40
Profit for year	75
Sale of subsidiary (20% × 420)	(84)
	31

3   *Taxation*

	£m
Per question (balance sheet movement)	31
Tax on joint venture	20
Tax on subsidiary disposed of	25
Tax on profit	(191)
Cash outflow	(115)

4   *Sale of tangible fixed assets*

	£m
Per question (carrying value)	1,585
Transferred to joint venture	(200)
Subsidiary disposed of	(310)
Sale and leaseback	(1,000)
Profit on sale	120
Cash inflow	195

(b)   *Cash flow statements: presentation to directors of Portal plc*

General purpose

The purpose of cash flow statements is to provide information which is not shown in the other financial statements. This information is important because the success and survival of every reporting entity depends on its ability to generate or obtain cash. For example, the tax authorities require an actual cash payment, which will differ for a number of reasons from the tax charge shown in the profit and loss account. Some of the information, such as the purchase or sale of tangible fixed assets, is apparent or can easily be computed from the balance sheet or profit and loss account, but the complexity of the financial statements may make this hard to see in respect of some items.

Group cash flow statements

Consolidated profit and loss accounts and balance sheets can hide the amount of cash actually paid to acquire a subsidiary, or received on disposal, in situations where part of the consideration is in the form of shares. FRS 1 requires cash flows relating to the consideration to be reported under acquisitions and disposals in the consolidated cash flow statement. Similarly, the dividend paid to minority interest is shown, as is the dividend received from associates or joint ventures.

However, a possible limitation of consolidated cash flow statements is that they can obscure the cash profile of companies within the group. For example, if there were two subsidiaries, one with a high cash flow from operations and one with high returns on investments, consolidation would obscure this. This is a limitation of consolidated accounts generally.

Accounting ratios

Useful information derived from the cash flow statement can be used in accounting ratios for analysis purposes. In the case of Portal plc, it might be useful to show the proportion of net cash inflow from operating activities which has been spent on purchasing fixed assets:

$$\frac{\text{Purchase of tangible fixed assets}}{\text{Net cash inflow from operating activities}} = \frac{380}{692} = 54.9\%$$

It would be useful to know how much of this relates to maintenance of existing operating capacity and how much relates to increasing capacity with a view to enhancing future earnings. However, this information cannot be derived from the cash flow statement.

It would also be useful to know how the cash flow after investment has been utilised. This can be done by comparing the net cash inflow before use of liquid resources and financing with the net cash increase in the period. In the case of Portal this works out as (308 − 165)/308 = 46.4%. In other words 46.4% of this net cash inflow has been used to take out short term deposits.

Another useful ratio is interest cover, based not on profit before interest and tax as in conventional ratio analysis, but on operating cash flow:

$$\frac{\text{Net cash flow from operating activities}}{\text{Interest paid}} = \frac{692}{9} = 76.8 \text{ times}$$

Further limitations

- The cash flow statement does not provide information about future cash flows.

- The reconciliation can be misinterpreted. Naïve investors may perceive the adding back of depreciation/amortisation as sources of funds.

- Some regard the cash flow statement as derivative.

D21 Case study question: Andash

Top tips. In tackling part (a), remember that time management is the key to cash flow questions. Set out your proforma and workings and do not spend too long on the fiddly bits. In the absence of complete information about profit earned by the associate in the period, our answer assumes that no dividend was paid by Joma. Part (b) asked you to explain the importance of the ASB's *Statement of Principles* to corporate reporting and whether this document takes into account the business and legal constraints placed on companies. The question also required candidates to explain the treatment of accounting for the decommissioning of a piece of equipment, a provision for deferred taxation and a discussion of whether the treatment of the above is consistent with the respective statement.

Easy marks. In Part (a) these are available for basic cash flow aspects – working capital calculations, minority interest, tax and interest. Follow our order for the workings – the easy ones come first. In Part (b), though deferred tax is a difficult area generally, this particular question was fairly straightforward. Credit would be given for wide-ranging answers, so easy marks could be picked up for sensible, valid points.

Marking scheme

		Marks
(a)	Cash flows from operating activities	2
	Adjustments	4
	Net cash generated from operations	3
	Interest	2
	Tax	2
	Associate	3
	Plant and machinery	3
	Sale of subsidiary	2
	Minority interest	3
	Long term borrowings	1
	Dividend paid	1
	Goodwill	3

(b)	(i)	Importance	4
		Business and legal constraints	3
	(ii)	Reasons	5
		Damage due to extraction	2
		Accounting	4
		Computation	5
		Reasons	2
	(iii)	Treatment consistent	5
		Available	59
		Maximum	50

(a) ANDASH
CASH FLOW STATEMENT
FOR THE YEAR ENDED 31 OCTOBER 20X6

	£m	£m
Net cash flow from operating activities (W1)		1,444
Returns on investment and servicing of finance		
Interest paid (W4)	118	
Dividend to minority interest (W6)	20	
		(138)
Tax paid (W5)		(523)
Capital expenditure and financial investment (W2)		(1,320)
Acquisitions and disposals		
Purchase of associate	(10)	
Sale of subsidiary (32 – 5)	27	
		17
Equity dividends paid		(50)
Cash outflow before management of liquid resources and financing		(570)
Financing		
Issue of ordinary shares (60 – 50)	10	
Issue of debt (3,100 – 2,700)	400	
		410
Decrease in cash in the period (300 – 140)		(160)

Workings

1   *Net cash flow from operating activities*

	£m
Operating profit per question (2,900 – 1,870 – 499)	531
Impairment loss (W9)	(78)
Corrected operating profit	453
Depreciation	260
Impairment and amortisation: 78 (W8) + 9 (W2)	87
	800
Increase in stocks (2,650 – 2,300 + 8)	(358)
Increase in debtors (2,400 – 1,500 + 4)	(904)
Increase in creditors (4,700 – 2,800 + 6)	1,906
	1,444

2   *Plant and machinery*

PLANT AND MACHINERY (NBV)

	£m		£m
Balance b/d	4,110	Depreciation	260
		Impairment (W9)	6
Share options (10 – 1)	9	Disposal of subsidiary	10
∴ Additions	1,320	Balance c/d (5,170 – 1 (W7) – 6 (W9))	5,163
	5,439		5,439

3   *Goodwill*

GOODWILL

	£		£
Balance b/d	130	Amortisation: 90/10	9
		Impairment	72
		Disposal of subsidiary	10
		Balance c/d (111 – 72 (W9))	39
	130		130

4   *Interest paid*

INTEREST PAYABLE

	£m		£m
		Balance cd	40
Interest paid	118		
		Profit and loss a/c	148
Balance c/d	70		
	188		188

5   *Tax paid*

TAX PAYABLE

	£m		£m
Disposal of subsidiary	7	Current tax b/d	770
		Deferred tax b/d	300
∴ Tax paid	523		
Current tax c/d	300	Profit and loss account	160
Deferred tax c/d	400		
	1,230		1,230

6   *Dividend paid to minority interest*

MINORITY INTEREST

	£m		£m
		Balance b/d	180
∴ Dividend paid	20		
		Profit and loss account	40
Balance c/d	200		
	220		200

7

ASSOCIATE

	£m		£m
b/f	–		
Acquisition	60		
Profit and loss account*	1		
		c/f (adjusted)	61
	61		61

		£m
*Share of profits 25% × (£32m − £20m)		3
Less: unrealised profits 25% × (£16 − £8m)		(2)
		1

As no information is given about profit for the period, it is assumed no dividend was received from the associate. No information is given about tax, so it is not possible to show this separately.

8   *Share options*

The basic rule in FRS 20 *Share-based payment* is that when equity instruments are issued to acquire goods or services, they should be measured at the fair value of those goods and services. An adjustment is required to reduce the options and the plant by £1m to £9m.

9   *Impairment loss in Broiler*

	£
Net assets	266
Goodwill (90 × 8/10)	72
Total value	338
Recoverable amount	(260)
Impairment loss	78

Adjustments required:	
Written off against goodwill	72
Remainder (presumed) written off against tangible fixed assets	6
	78

(b)   (i)   The ASB's *Statement of Principles for Financial Reporting* sets out the **principles that underpin the preparation of general purpose financial statements**. The purpose of the *Statement of Principles* is to assist the ASB in the preparation of future standards and to **assist preparers of financial statements in applying standards** and in **dealing with topics that are not yet covered** by accounting standards. This means that in theory, UK accounting standards are based on the *Statement of Principles*, which covers:

- The objective of financial statements
- The reporting entity
- The qualities that make the information in financial statements useful
- The elements of financial statements
- When elements should be recognised in financial statements
- Measurement in financial statements
- Presentation of financial information
- Accounting for interests in other entities.

The *Statement of Principles* adopts a **balance sheet based approach**. It **defines assets and liabilities** and explains the conditions that must be met before they are recognised. **Gains and losses are defined in relation to assets and liabilities**; a gain is recognised when assets increase or liabilities decrease; a loss is recognised where liabilities increase or assets decrease. There are advantages of this approach, not least that it **helps to prevent 'creative accounting'** where the economic substance of a transaction is different from its legal form. However, it is **very different from the way in which most preparers of accounts view the basis of accounting**: the allocation of transactions to accounting periods.

There are other problems. The *Statement of Principles* is a **theoretical document** and financial statements are used for **practical purposes** including determining dividend payments, tax payments and directors' remuneration. Standards based on the *Statement of Principles* are sometimes **difficult to apply**, particularly for smaller entities. In theory, preparers of financial statements can use the

Statement as a **source of guidance** in situations where a transaction is not covered by a specific standard, but probably few do in practice.

A further issue is that the ASB's work is now largely being driven by the **need to converge with IFRSs.** The IASB is making increasing use of **fair value accounting**, which is **incompatible** with the *Statement of Principles* (as this favours current or deprival value as an alternative to historic cost). IFRSs also require **'recycling'** of gains and losses from equity to the profit and loss account in some situations. This is **also inconsistent** with the *Statement*.

(ii)   **Situation 1**

FRS 12 *Provisions, contingent liabilities and contingent assets* states that a provision should be recognised if all of the following apply.

- There is a present obligation as a result of a past transaction or event.
- It is **probable** that a **transfer of economic benefits** will be required to settle the obligation.
- A **reliable estimate** can be made of the **amount** of the obligation.

In this case, the obligating event is the **installation of the facility** and it occurred before the year end. The operating licence has created a **legal obligation** to incur the cost of decommissioning the facility, the expenditure is **probable** and the **amount can be measured reliably.**

Because the entity cannot operate the facility without incurring an obligation to pay for decommissioning, **the expenditure also enables it to acquire economic benefits** (income from operating the facility). Therefore Nette **recognises an asset** as well as a provision and **depreciates the asset over its useful life of 20 years**.

Nette **recognises a provision for the cost of removing the facility**, but **does not include the cost of rectifying the damage** caused by the extraction of natural gas until it is incurred. This means that a provision for rectifying the damage caused by extraction is **recognised over the life of the facility**. The provision is **discounted** to its net present value as the time value of money is material.

The accounting treatment is as follows:

BALANCE SHEET AT 31 OCTOBER 20X7 (EXTRACTS)

	£m
Tangible fixed assets	
Extraction facility	200
Decommissioning costs (W)	40
	240
Depreciation (240 ÷ 20)	(12)
	228
Provisions	
Provision for decommissioning at 1 November 20X6	40
Plus unwinding of discount (40 × 5%)	2
	42
Provision for damage caused by extraction (W)	1.33
	43.33

PROFIT AND LOSS ACCOUNT FOR THE YEAR ENDED 31 OCTOBER 20X7 (EXTRACTS)

	£m
Depreciation	12
Provision for damage caused by extraction	1.33
Unwinding of discount	2

Working

	£m
Provision for decommissioning costs at 1 November 20X6 (80% × 50)	40
Provision for damage caused by extraction at 31 October 20X7	
(20% × 50 × 2.66 ÷ 20)	1.33

Situation 2

The company should **recognise a provision for deferred tax relating to the building** and there is a **deferred tax asset relating to the warranty**. Per FRS 19 *Deferred tax* the calculation is as follows:

	£m	£m
Building		
Tax written down value (75% × 8)	6	
Net book value (9 – 1.8)	(7.2)	
		1.2
Other timing differences		40.0
Total timing differences (liabilities)		41.2
Warranty provision		4
Tax losses		70
Total timing differences (assets)		74

Therefore the company **recognises a deferred tax liability of £12.4 million** (41.2 × 30%) and **can also recognise a deferred tax asset for the same amount**. It will only be able to recognise the full amount of the deferred tax asset if it can prove that **suitable taxable profits are available to offset the loss** in future.

(iii) **Treatment of the items and the *Statement of Principles***

It can be argued that some of the assets and liabilities involved are **not 'true' assets and liabilities** and therefore that they **should not be recognised**.

Under the *Statement of Principles*, the company would have to **recognise the full discounted liability** for the decommissioning costs and a corresponding asset. **Assets** are defined **as rights or other access to future economic benefits controlled by an entity as a result of past transactions or events**. Many would argue that the decommissioning is a **future cost** and that therefore it **does not meet this definition**. In addition, the treatment required by the *Statement of Principles* (and FRS 12) means that **depreciation** on the asset is treated as an **operating cost** and the **unwinding of the discount** is treated as a **finance cost**; this is **inconsistent**.

The *Statement of Principles* defines **liabilities** as **obligations of an entity to transfer economic benefits as a result of past transactions or events**. Strictly speaking, the deferred tax provision **does not meet this definition**; only an **actual liability** to the tax authorities can be an obligation at the balance sheet date. A deferred tax liability **can be avoided**, for example, with tax planning, or if a company makes future losses. Still less does the deferred tax asset meet the definition of an asset, because it depends on the availability of future profits.

In addition, the **grant** towards the building has been treated as a **deferred credit** and is therefore a liability. It **does not meet the definition of a liability** unless it has to be repaid.

D22 Case study question: Squire

Top tips. Part (a) of his question required candidates to prepare a group cash flow statement. There were adjustments to be made for impairment, interest on a deferred consideration, retirement benefits and the purchase of a subsidiary in the year.

You need to use a bit of imagination in (b). Try to use your own experience to think of what you can find out about resource usage, also what you would like to know and how you can obtain evidence of what you would like to know.

In (c) observation is likely to be the most useful audit technique, although if staff are being observed, they may behave differently. You may have come up with other means for informing staff.

Part (d) focuses on the impact of stakeholder views and voluntary principles-based disclosure versus compulsory rules-based disclosure.

Examiner's comment (Part (a) only. The question was quite straightforward and candidates performed very well. There are several quite easy marks to be earned in a cash flow question and many candidates gained these marks. The only major criticism of candidates' answers was that the workings were sometimes difficult to follow or were not presented at all. This latter point is critical. Many candidates simply showed a line of numbers without any narrative. This is acceptable but if these numbers are wrong or not easily recognisable then marks are difficult to award.

(a)　SQUIRE GROUP
GROUP CASH FLOW STATEMENT FOR THE YEAR ENDED 31 MAY 20X2

	£m	£m
Net cash flow from operating activities		717
Dividends received from associate (W1)		50
Returns on investments and servicing of finance		
Interest paid (W2)	51	
Dividends paid to minority interests (W3)	5	
		(56)
Taxation (W4)		(134)
Capital expenditure		
Purchase of tangible fixed assets (W5)		(477)
Acquisitions and disposals		
Purchase of subsidiary undertaking	200	
Compensation paid in respect of subsidiary's onerous contract	30	
		(230)
Equity dividends paid (W6)		(70)
Cash outflow before management of liquid resources and financing		(200)
Financing		
Issue of shares (260 – 200)	60	
Repayment of loans (1,320 – 1,270)	(50)	
		10
Decrease in cash for the period		(190)

Note: Reconciliation of operating profit to net cash inflow from operating activities

	£m	£m
Operating profit (1,464 – 1,030)		434
Depreciation		129
Amortisation of goodwill (W7)		25
Decrease in stocks (1,300 – 1,160 – 180)		40
Increase in debtors (1,220 – 1,060)		(160)
Increase in creditors (2,310 – 2,075)		235
Pension asset		
Current and past service costs	20	
Contributions paid	(6)	
		14
Net cash flow from operating activities		717

Workings

1 *Dividends received from associate*

DIVIDENDS RECEIVED FROM ASSOCIATE

	£m		£m
Balance b/d	550	Share of corporation tax	20
Share of operating profit	65	Dividends received (balancing figure)	50
		Balance c/d	545
			615
	615		

2 *Interest*

INTEREST

	£m		£m
Unwinding of discount (54 – 50)	4	Balance b/d	45
Cash paid (balancing figure)	51	Profit and loss account	75
Balance c/d	65		
	120		120

3 *Minority interests*

MINORITY INTERESTS

	£m		£m
Dividend paid (balancing figure)	5	Balance b/d	345
Balance c/d	525	Acquisition (30% × 300)	90
		Profit for year	95
	530		530

4 *Taxation*

TAXATION

	£m		£m
Cash paid (balancing figure)	134	Balance b/d	
Balance c/d		Current	160
Current	200	Deferred	175
Deferred	200	Deferred (pension)	7
Deferred (pension)	13	Profit and loss account (225 – 20)	205
	547		547

5   *Tangible fixed assets*

TANGIBLE FIXED ASSETS

	£m		£m
Balance b/d	2,010	Depreciation	129
Acquisition	150	Impairment losses	220
Additions (balancing figure)	828	Balance c/d	2,639
	2,988		2,988

	£m
Cash flow	
Fixed asset additions	828
Less: creditor balance c/d	(351)
	477

6   *Equity dividends*

EQUITY DIVIDENDS

	£m		£m
Cash paid (balancing figure)	70	Balance b/d	30
Balance c/d	45	Paid and payable for the year	85
	115		115

7   *Intangible assets: goodwill*

INTANGIBLE ASSETS: GOODWILL

	£m		£m
Balance b/d	65	Amortisation (balancing figure)	25
Acquisition (note)	40	Balance c/d	80
	105		105

Note: goodwill on acquisition

	£m
Purchase consideration:	
Cash	200
Deferred consideration	50
	250
Less group share of net assets acquired (70% × 300)	(210)
	40

(b)   **The planning process**

The planning process for any investigative activity revolves around a consideration of **what information is needed,** where it **may be found** and **how to obtain it.**

Available information

In the case of an environmental audit, much information is probably already available in the form of accounting records; **heating and lighting costs**, for instance can be related to factors such as numbers employed, floor space and building volumes.

There are some fairly **standard aspects of good practice** in terms of energy conservation such as provision of wall and roof insulation; and thermostatic and time clock control of space and water heating systems. The existence and maintenance of such factors can be established from the appropriate records. In the UK, the energy utilities offer free advice on energy conservation and this should be considered. **Use of renewable resources** should be a matter of policy and the purchasing department should be able to comment on the extent to which it is achieved.

Expert advice

Other aspects of energy consumption require expert advice. For instance, the **compressed air circuits** used in many factories to power hand and machine tools can be extremely wasteful of energy if they are leaky, since this causes the compressor to be run for excessive periods to maintain pressure. However, it is a specialised engineering task to measure the actual efficiency of a pneumatic system.

If the organisation is a manufacturer, it would be appropriate to consider the extent to which the **products themselves** were **energy efficient** in use and made use of renewable resources both in use and in their construction. These are largely matters of design and it would be necessary to take technical advice.

(c) **Testing for employee awareness**

Employee awareness could be measured by **observation, questionnaire and interview.** In a large organisation a sampling approach could be taken. Observation could be largely unobtrusive and might provide a useful control on the results of interview, since some staff might make exaggerated claims about their environmental awareness.

Involvement of employees

The techniques of **internal marketing** could be used to involve employees. Internal marketing is the use of marketing techniques that are normally associated with communications flowing out from the organisation, for internal purposes. It is a concept associated with change management and therefore may be appropriate here.

A concerted campaign could be created. This could include messages in salary advices, posters, presentations, the **formation of discussion groups**, and the creation of a **suggestion scheme** specifically aimed at environmental issues. If there are any existing empowerment schemes such as quality circles, it may be possible to introduce an environmental dimension into them.

(d) **Stakeholder interest**

Public interest in corporate social responsibility is steadily increasing. Although financial statements are primarily intended for investors and their advisers, there is growing recognition that companies actually have **a number of different stakeholders**. These include **customers, employees and the general public,** all of whom are **potentially interested** in the way in which a company's operations affect the natural environment and the wider community. These stakeholders can have a **considerable effect on a company's performance**. As a result many companies now deliberately attempt to build a **reputation for social and environmental responsibility**. Therefore the disclosure of environmental and social information is essential.

Regulatory and professional interest

Another factor is **growing interest by governments and professional bodies**. Although there are **no IFRSs** that specifically require environmental and social reporting, it may be required by **company legislation**. There are now a number of **awards for environmental and social reports** and high quality disclosure in financial statements. These provide further encouragement to disclose information.

Performance impact

There is also growing recognition that **corporate social responsibility is actually an important part of an entity's overall performance.** Responsible practice in areas such as reduction of damage to the environment and recruitment **increases shareholder value**. Companies that act responsibly and make social and environmental disclosures are **perceived as better investments** than those that do not.

Compulsory or voluntary disclosure

At present companies are normally able to disclose **as much or as little information as they wish in whatever manner that they wish**. This causes a number of **problems**. Companies tend to disclose information **selectively** and it is difficult for users of the financial statements to **compare the performance of different companies**. However, there are **good arguments** for continuing to allow companies a certain amount of freedom to determine the information that they disclose. If detailed rules are imposed, **companies are likely to adopt a 'checklist' approach** and will **present information in a very general and standardised way**, so that it is of very little use to stakeholders.

D23 Baron

Top tips. If you got the analysis into continuing and discontinuing operations completely right – well done. You could, however, easily pass the question without doing so. There are a lot of basic calculations in this question, eg movement on provisions, dividends paid and so on. Don't let the length of the question put you off.

Marking scheme

		Marks
Cash flow from operating activities		10
Returns on investments and servicing of finance		3
Taxation		2
Capital expenditure		3
Acquisitions and disposals		3
Equity dividends		2
Management of liquid resources		3
Exceptional cash outflows		2
Presentation		5
	Available	33
	Maximum	25

BARON GROUP
CASH FLOW STATEMENT FOR THE YEAR ENDED 30 NOVEMBER 20X7

	£m
Cash inflow from operating activities (note 1)	875
Returns on investments and servicing of finance (note 2)	(214)
Taxation (W7)	(115)
Capital expenditure (note 2)	(312)
Acquisitions and disposals (note 2)	(80)
Equity dividends paid (W6)	(120)
Cash inflow before use of liquid resources and financing	34
Management of liquid resources (note 2)	(143)
Decrease in cash	(109)

Notes

1   *Reconciliation of operating profit to operating cash flows*

	Continu-ing £m		Discon-tinued £m		Total £m
Operating profit (W1)	458		184		642
Depreciation	141	(150 – 9)	9	(note (a))	150
Goodwill amortisation	20	(note (a))			20
Share of joint venture profit	(75)				(75)
Increase in stocks (incl Piece)	(40)		(60)		(100)
Increase in debtors (incl Piece)	(119)	(W2)	(50)	(Piece)	(169)
Increase in creditors (incl Piece)	327	(note (g))	105	(Piece)	432
Operating activities continuing operations	712		188		900
Bid defence	(5)	(W3)			(5)
Pension prepayment	(20)				(20)
	687		188		875

2   *Gross cash flows*

Returns on investments and servicing of finance

	£m
Interest received (4 + 27 – 5)	26
Interest paid (30 + 19 – 40)	(9)
Minority interest dividend (W4)	(231)
	(214)

Capital expenditure

Purchase of tangible fixed assets (note (d))	(380)
Sale of tangible fixed assets (W5)	68
	(312)

Acquisitions and disposals

Cash paid to acquire interest in joint venture (note (b))	(25)
Cash disposed on sale of subsidiary (note (a))	(130)
Cash element of disposal proceeds (note (a))	75
	(80)

Management of liquid resources

Purchase of corporate bonds (see note (e))	(35)
Purchase of government securities (increase) (see note (e)) (51 – 23)	(28)
Cash on seven day deposit (increase) (see note (e)) (101 – 21)	(80)
	(143)

Note. None of the above are deemed to be 'cash' under the terms of FRS 1 revised.

Workings

1   *Operating profit*

	£m
Operating profit per P&L (continuing operations)	438
Add back bid defence costs	20
	458
Operating profit on discontinued operations	184
	642

2   *Debtors*

	£m
At 30.11.X7	680
Pension prepayment (note (f) in question)	(20)
Interest receivable (note (f) in question)	(5)
	655
At 30.11.X6	540
Interest receivable (note (f) in question)	(4)
	536
Increase (before allowing for disposal)	119

3   *Bid defence*

	£m
20X6 Provision b/f	15
20X7 P&L charge	20
	35
20X7 Provision c/f	30
Paid	5

4   *Dividend paid to minority interest*

MINORITY INTEREST MEMORANDUM WORKING ACCOUNT

	£m		£m
Disposal of MI in Piece			
(420 × 20%)	84	Balance b/f 1.12.X6	570
Balancing figure = cash paid	231	P&L: minority interest share	75
Balance c/f 30.11.X7	330		
	645		645

5   *Disposal of fixed assets*

	£m
Net book value of all disposals (note (d)) (680 – 95)	585
Assets of Piece sold (at NBV)	(310)
Assets transferred to joint venture (note (b))	(200)
NBV of fixed assets sold	75
Loss on disposal (per P&L account)	(7)
Sale proceeds	68

6   *Equity dividends paid*

	£m
Balance b/f 1.12.X6 (note (g))	70
Appropriation	130
Balance c/f 30.11.X7 (note (g))	(80)
Paid	120

7   *Taxation*

	£m
Balance b/f 1.12.X6	150
Taxation balance disposed on sale of subsidiary	(25)
Taxation attributable to joint venture	(20)
P&L tax charge for year	191
Balance c/f 30.11.X7	(181)
Tax paid	115

D24 George

> **Top tips**. Slightly simpler than an exam question, this is nevertheless useful practice for calculations of goodwill.

(a)   **Goodwill on consolidation of Bungle Ltd**

	£'000
Purchase consideration	
Shares 8m × ¾ × £4	24,000
Deferred cash 8m × 0.873 × £1	6,984
	30,984
Fair value of net assets	
Balance sheet value	23,300
Tangible fixed assets (Note 1)	8,750
Stock (Note 2)	600
Debtors	(400)
Loan (Note 30	(314)
Provision (Note 4)	800
Fair value of net assets	32,736
Goodwill	
Purchase consideration	30,984
Fair value of net assets (80% × 32,736)	26,189
Goodwill	4,795

Notes

1   *Tangible fixed assets*

	£'000
Land and buildings	15,000
Depreciated replacement cost: £22m × 5/8	13,750
	28,750
Balance sheet value	20,000
Fair value adjustment	8,750

2   *Stock*

	£'000
Replacement cost	12,000
Write down net realisable value (500 – 100)	(400)
	11,600
Balance sheet value	11,000
Fair value adjustment	600

3   *Long term loan*

	£'000
Discounted repayment amount (4,000 × 0.816) + (400 × 2.624)	4,314
Balance sheet value	4,000
Fair value adjustment	(314)

4   Provisions

The £400,000 for **closure costs** is a committed amount and therefore should be **provided** for.

The £800,000 of **integration costs** however have **not been committed** to and indeed there are no detailed plans yet formulated therefore this **should not be provided for**.

(b)   GEORGE PLC
CONSOLIDATED BALANCE SHEET AT 30 JUNE 20X3

	£'000	£'000
Fixed assets		
Intangible fixed assets: goodwill (W1)		4,795
Tangible assets (45,000 + 25,000 + 20,000 + 8,750)		98,750
		103,545
Current assets		
Stocks (W2)	41,850	
Debtors (15,000 + 10,000 + 9,000 – 1,200 – 4,00)	32,400	
	74,250	
Creditors: amounts falling due within one year		
Trade creditors (10,000 + 6,500 + 6,000 – 600)	21,900	
Tax payable (2,000 + 1,500 + 1,000)	4,500	
Dividend payable to minority(1,000 × 50%)	500	
Bank overdraft (5,000 + 4,000 + 3,000)	12,000	
	38,900	
Net current assets		35,350
Total assets less current liabilities		138,895
Creditors: amounts falling due after more than one year		
Long term loan (20,000 + 4,314)		(24,314)
		114,581
Provisions for liabilities and charges		
Deferred tax (2,000 + 1,000 + 1,500)	4,500	
Contingent payment (Part (a))	6,984	
Other (closure provision only)	400	
		(11,884)
		102,697
Capital and reserves		
Ordinary share capital (W3)		31,000
Share premium		28,000
Profit and loss (W4)		32,150
		91,150
Minority interest (W5)		11,547
		102,697

Workings

1 · *Goodwill*

Zippy Ltd: no goodwill – shares all purchased at par value at date of incorporation.

Bungle Ltd: £4,795,000 (Part a)

2   *Stocks*

	£'000
George	18,000
Zippy	12,000
Bungle	11,000
Fair value adjustment	600
Unrealised profit (1,500 × 20/1,200)	(250)
Stock in transit	600
Unrealised profit (600 × 20/120)	(100)
	41,850

3   *Ordinary share capital and share premium*

When George plc purchased Bungle Ltd 6,000,000 George plc shares were issued for £24,000,000.

Ordinary share capital:

	£'000
George plc (per question)	25,000
Issue (6,000 × £1)	6,000
	31,000

Share premium:

	£'000
George	10,000
Issue (6,000 × £3)	18,000
	28,000

4   *Consolidated profit and loss account*

	George £'000	Zippy £'000	Bungle £'000
Per question	24,000	8,000	9,300
Pre-acquisition	–	–	(9,300)
	24,000	8,000	–
Preference dividend receivable (10,000 × 10% × 50%)	500		
Unrealised profit on stock (1,500 × 20/120)	(250)		
Unrealised profit on stock in transit (600 × 20/120)	(100)		
Zippy (100%)	8,000		
	32,150		

5   *Minority interest*

	£'000
Zippy: preference shares	5,000
Bungle (20% × £32,736,000)	6,547
	11,547

D25 A Group

> **Top tips.** As usual in this kind of question, it is important to establish the group structure before you launch into it. Be careful to distinguish between control and ownership.

(a)   See the group structure working (W1).

(b)   A, B, C AND D
       CONSOLIDATED BALANCE SHEET AS AT 31 DECEMBER 20X8

	£'000	£'000
Intangible fixed assets (W4)		6,916
Tangible fixed assets		
(56,000 + 50,000 + 45,000 + 3,600 (W3) + 1,300 (W3))		155,900
Investment in associate (W7)		30,480
		193,296
Current assets		
Stocks (25,000 + 26,000 + 22,000 – 2,600 (W2))	70,400	
Trade debtors (20,000 + 20,000 + 19,000 – 4,000 – 2,000)	53,000	
Bank balances (6,000 + 5,000)	11,000	
	134,400	
Creditors: amounts falling due within one year		
Trade creditors (12,000 + 13,000 + 12,000 – 4,000 – 2,000)	31,000	
Taxation (6,000 + 6,500 + 6,000)	18,500	
Bank overdrafts	2,000	
	51,500	
Net current assets		82,900
		276,196
Creditors: amounts falling due after more than one year		
Long-term loans (25,000 + 20,000)		(45,000)
		231,196
Capital and reserves		
Called up share capital		80,000
Share premium account		15,000
Profit and loss account (W8)		80,364
		175,364
Minority interest (W6)		55,832
		231,196

Workings

1   *Group structure*

       B and C both came into A plc's control on 1.1.X2.

Effective interests in C (controlled through B so indirect subsidiary of A):

A (80% × 60%)	48%
Minority	52%

Effective interest in D (B has significant influence so indirect associate of A):

(80% × 40%)	32%

Note. The investment in associate will include 40% of D's net assets, as this is what the group controls. The minority interest in B will be allocated 8% (20% × 40%).

2 *Provision for unrealised profit*

On sales by B to A and C (adjusting B's P&L and group stock):

$^{20}/_{120}$ × (8,400 + 7,200) = £2,600,000

On sales by B to D (adjusting B's P&L and investment in associate, as stock is held by D):

$^{20}/_{120}$ × £7,800 × 40% = £520,000

3 *Fair value adjustments*

B Ltd

	At acquisition £'000	Change £'000	At b/s date £'000
Freehold land	3,000		3,000
Plant and machinery	2,000		2,000
Additional depreciation			
(2,000 × 7/10)		(1,400)	(1,400)
Stocks	1,000	(1,000)	
Contingent asset	1,500	(1,500)	–
	7,500	(3,900)	3,600

C Ltd

	At acquisition £'000	Change £'000	At b/s date £'000
Freehold land	1,000		1,000
Plant and machinery	1,000		1,000
Additional depreciation			
(1,000 × 7/10)		(700)	(700)
Stock	500	(500)	–
	2,500	(1,200)	1,300

4 *Goodwill*

On acquisition of B group:

	£'000
Cost of investment	90,000
Share of consolidated separable net assets acquired	
B: 80% (75,000 + 5,000 + 15,000 + 7,500 (W3) – 43,200 (W5))	(47,440)
C: 48% (45,000 + 6,000 + 13,000 + 2,500 (W3))	(31,920)
	10,640
Less amortisation to date (7/20)	(3,724)
	6,916

On acquisition of D

	£'000	£'000
Cost of investment (16m × £1.75)		28,000
Share of net assets acquired		
Share capital	40,000	
Share premium	8,000	
P&L account	12,000	
40%	60,000	24,000
		4,000
Less amortisation to date (6/20)		(1,200)
		2,800

5   *B's cost of investment in C*

(27m × £1.60) = £43,200,000

6   *Minority interest*

B:

	£'000	£'000
Net assets per question	125,700	
Less provision for unrealised profit (W2)		
(2,600 + 520)	(3,120)	
Add fair value adjustment (W3)	3,600	
Less cost of investments	(71,200)	
Add goodwill re D (W4)	2,800	
	57,780	
	× 20%	11,556

D:

	£'000	£'000
Net assets per question	70,500	
	× 8%	5,640

C:

	£'000	£'000
Net assets per question	73,000	
Add fair value adjustment (W3)	1,300	
	74,300	
	× 52%	38,636
		55,832

7   *Investment in associate*

	£'000
Share of net assets (40% × 70,500)	28,200
Less PUP (W2)	(520)
	27,680
Unamortised goodwill (W4)	2,800
	30,480

8   *Profit and loss account*

	A £'000	B £'000	C £'000	D £'000
Per question	59,000	45,700	22,000	22,500
Less: PUP (W2)		(2,600)		
PUP (W2)		(520)		
FV adjs (W3)		(3,900)	(1,200)	
	59,000	38,680	20,800	22,500
Less pre-acquisition		(15,000)	(13,000)	(12,000)
		23,680	7,800	10,500
B (80% × 23,680)	18,944			
C (48% × 7,800)	3,744			
D (32% × 10,500)	3,360			
Less: amortisation of goodwill (W4) C	(3,724)			
D (80% × 1,200)	(960)			
	80,364			

D26 A, B, C and D

> **Top tips.** In this question you had to explain the impact of a group reconstruction on a group of companies and prepare the balance sheets of individual group companies and the group balance sheet including a break down of the group retained earnings.. The question was similar to a previous question on group reconstructions and to a question in the pilot paper. It is likely that where a cash flow question is asked in an examination, then a reconstruction question will be asked in Section B in order to allow candidates to demonstrate their knowledge of group accounting.
>
> **Easy marks.** There are no easy marks in this question, other than for setting out your computations logically.
>
> **Examiner's comment.** This question was surprisingly poorly answered. Candidates did not seem to be able to deal with the basic principles of the reconstruction nor could they deal with the accounting for the purchased goodwill. The implications of the movement in the investments within the group companies were not apparently understood by most candidates.

(a)   (i)   **Impact on A's accounts**

A's investment in B is **increased by the value of the shares issued by B** as consideration for the sale of D. The book value of the shares in D is the cost of A's **investment in D less the cash consideration of £50 million**. The **Companies Act does not allow shares to be issued at a discount**, but this has **not occurred** because:

(1)   the market value of the shares in D is £420 million (200 million × £2.10)

(2)   the nominal value of the purchase consideration is £160 million (£110 million in shares plus £50 million cash).

The investments in C and in D are **no longer recognised**.

The **reserves of A are reduced by £800 million** due to the **sale of the investment in C.**

A's accounts are **not affected** by the issue of the shares in E as these are **issued to the shareholders of A,** not to A itself.

Impact on B's accounts

The investment in D is recognised in B's accounts at its **book value of £450 million**.

Share capital increases by £110 million (the **nominal value** of the shares issued to A) and the **share premium** account **increases by £290 million:**

	£m
Book value of investment in D	450
Less nominal value of shares issued	(110)
Less cash consideration	(50)
	290

Impact on C's accounts

C has been **demerged** from the A group and has **become a subsidiary of E**, a new parent company. E has issued shares to the **individual shareholders of A** in exchange for A's investment in C. The effect of this is that A has made a **distribution of the cost of the investment in C** to its shareholders and A's **reserves are reduced by £800 million** (see above).

The **individual accounts** of C are **not affected**.

Impact on D's accounts

The **individual accounts** of D are **not affected**.

(ii)   BALANCE SHEETS AT 30 NOVEMBER 20X4 (AFTER GROUP RECONSTRUCTION)

	A	B	D	Group
	£m	£m	£m	£m
Tangible fixed assets (W1)	1,700	1,000	300	3,095
Investment in B (1,250 + 450 – 50)	1,650			
Investment in D		450		
Goodwill (30 + 15) (W2, W4)				45
Net current assets (1,400 + 50)	1,450	750	100	2,300
	4,800	2,200	400	5,440
Share capital	1,000	610	200	1,000
Share premium (see part (i))	1,950	490	125	1,950
Profit and loss account (2,650 – 800)	1,850	1,100	75	2,490
	4,800	2,200	400	5,440

(b)   GROUP RESERVES AT 30 NOVEMBER 20X4

	A	B	D
	£m	£m	£m
Per individual accounts after reconstruction	1,850	1,100	75
At acquisition		(450)	(50)
	1,850	650	25
B	650		
D	25		
Less goodwill amortisation			
(20 + 6) (W2,4)	(26)		
Impairment (W4)	(9)		
	2,490		

Alternative calculation: proof

	A £m	B £m	C £m	D £m
Per individual accounts				
before reconstruction	2,650	1,100	400	75
At acquisition		(450)	(250)	(50)
	2,650	650	150	25
B	650			
C	150			
D	25			
Less goodwill amortisation				
(20 + 40 + 6) (W2,3,4)	(66)			
Impairment (40 + 9) (W3,4)	(49)			
Demerger of C (800 + 150 – 40 – 40)	(870)			
	2,490			

Workings

1 *Tangible fixed assets*

	£m	£m
A		1,700
B		1,000
D		300
Fair value adjustments on consolidation:		
A (W2)	50	
D (W4)	45	
		95
		3,095

2 *Goodwill: B*

	£m	£m
Cost of investment		1,250
Less: fair value of net assets acquired:		
Share capital	500	
Share premium	200	
Profit and loss account	450	
Fair value adjustment (balancing figure)	50	
		(1,200)
		50
Amortisation (2/5)		(20)
		30
Carrying value after impairment test		30

Therefore no impairment.

3 *Goodwill: C*

	£m	£m
Cost of investment		800
Less fair value of net assets acquired:		
Share capital	300	
Share premium	150	
Profit and loss account	250	
		(700)
		100
Amortisation (2/5)		(40)
		60
Carrying value after impairment test		20
Impairment loss		40

4   *Goodwill: D*

	£m	£m
Cost of investment		450
Less: fair value of net assets acquired:		
Share capital	200	
Share premium	125	
Profit and loss account	50	
Fair value adjustment (balancing figure)	45	
		(420)
		30
Amortisation (1/5)		(6)
		24
Carrying value after impairment test		15
Impairment loss		9

E1 Accounting framework for SMEs

Top tips. This question required candidates to discuss the need to develop a set of IFRSs especially for small to medium-sized entities (SMEs). Do not be tempted to waffle or repeat yourself.

Easy marks. This is a knowledge-based question, so all marks are easy if you know it.

Examiner's comment. This question was generally well answered and the topic will feature in future exams.

Marking scheme

		Marks
(a)	Subjective	7
(b)	Purpose	3
	Definition	4
	How to modify	6
	Items not dealt with	3
	Full FRS	3
	Available	26
	Maximum	25

(a)   **Issues in developing an accounting framework for SMEs**

(i)   **The purpose of a framework and the type of entity to which it should apply**

The main objective of an accounting framework for small and medium entities (SMEs) is that it should provide the users of SME financial statements with **relevant, reliable and understandable information**. The standards should be **suitable for SMEs** and should **reduce the financial reporting burden** on SMEs. It is generally accepted that SME standards should be built on the **same conceptual framework** as full FRSs.

It could also be argued that SME standards should **allow for easy transition** to full FRS as some SMEs will become listed entities or need to change for other reasons. This would mean that SME standards **can never be separately developed from first principles** (as some would prefer) but instead would be a **modified version of full UK GAAP**. Some argue that ease of transition is not important as relatively few SMEs need to change to 'big GAAP' in practice.

There is a strong case for developing 'little GAAP' from first principles ('think small first'). The information **needs of users** of the accounts of SMEs are **often quite different** from those of the users of public company financial statements.

In theory, the **definition** of an SME could be based on **size** or on **public accountability** or on a combination of the two. In practice, the definition is mainly based on size. The Financial Reporting Standard for Smaller Entities (FRSSE) may be adopted by 'small' companies and the definition is **based on the size limits** laid down in the **Companies Act 1985**. **To qualify as small**, an entity must not exceed two or more of the following thresholds in a year: **turnover £5.6 million; balance sheet total £2.8 million; average number of employees 50.** However, there are several disadvantages of basing the definition on size limits alone. Size limits are **arbitrary.** Most people believe that SMEs are **not simply smaller versions of listed entities**, but differ from them in more fundamental ways.

The most important way in which SMEs differ from other entities is that they are **not usually publicly accountable**. Using this as the basis of a definition raises other issues: which types of company are publicly accountable? At present, companies which have **issued shares to the public and banking, insurance and financial services companies must follow full FRS (or IFRS)**. The definition of 'publicly accountable' could be extended to include companies that provide **essential public services** (utility companies) and any entity with **economic significance** (which in turn would have to be defined). This would mean that SME standards could potentially be used by a very large number of entities covering a very large range in terms of size. Alternatively the definition could be based on the way in which the entity is owned and managed, for example, on the number of shareholders, or on the degree of separation between the owners and the managers.

(ii) **How existing standards could be modified to meet the needs of SMEs**

The starting point for modifying existing standards should be the most likely **users** of SME financial statements and their **information needs**. SME financial statements are mainly used by **lenders** and **potential lenders, the tax authorities** and **suppliers**. In addition, the **owners and management** (who are often the same people) may be dependent on the information in the financial statements. SME financial statements must **meet the needs** of their users, but the **costs** of providing the information **should not outweigh the benefits.**

There is considerable scope for **simplifying disclosure and presentation requirements**. Many of the existing requirements, for example those related to financial instruments, segmental reporting and earnings per share, are **not really relevant** to the users of SME financial statements. In any case, lenders and potential lenders are normally able to ask for additional information (including forecasts) if they need it.

Clearly the SME standards have to be sufficiently rigorous to produce information that is relevant and reliable. However, it is difficult to reduce the financial reporting burden on SMEs without **simplifying** at least some of the more **complicated measurement requirements**.

(iii) **How items not dealt with by the FRSSE should be treated**

Because the FRSSE does not **cover all possible transactions** and events, there will be occasions where an SME has to **account for an item that it does not deal with**. For example, the FRSSE does not cover group situations. Where a transaction or event is not dealt with in the FRSSE, an entity should have regard to full FRS and UITF Abstracts, but these are not mandatory. Therefore in practice:

(1) the entity could **apply the relevant full FRS**, while still following the FRSSE otherwise

(2) management could **use its judgement** to develop an accounting policy based on the relevant full FRS, or the *Statement of Principles* or other sources, as long as this resulted in relevant, reliable, comparable and understandable information and in a true and fair view

(3)   the entity could continue to follow its **existing practice**.

In theory, the **first alternative is the most appropriate**. The argument against it is that SMEs may then effectively have to comply with **two sets of standards**.

(b)   Originally, International Accounting Standards (IASs) were **designed to be suitable for all types of entity**, including SMEs and entities in developing countries. Large listed entities based their financial statements on national GAAP which normally **automatically complied** with IASs. In recent years, IASs and IFRSs have become **increasingly complex and prescriptive**. They are now designed **primarily** to meet the information needs of **institutional investors in large listed entities** and their advisers. In many countries, IFRSs are **used mainly by listed companies**.

There is a case for continued use of full IFRSs by SMEs. It can be argued that the **main objectives** of general purpose financial statements **are the same for all types of company**, of whatever size. Compliance with full IFRSs ensures that the financial statements of SMEs **present their financial performance fairly** and gives them greater **credibility**. It also ensures their **comparability** with those of other entities.

There are also many arguments for developing a separate set of standards for SMEs. Full IFRSs have become very **detailed and onerous** to follow. The **cost** of complying may **exceed the benefits** to the entity and the users of its financial statements. At present, an entity cannot describe their financial statements as IFRS financial statements unless they have complied with every single requirement.

SME financial statements are normally **used by a relatively small number of people**. Often, the **investors** are also **involved in day to day management**. The **main external users** of SME financial statements tend to be **lenders and the tax authorities**, rather than institutional investors and their advisers. These users have **different information needs** from those of investors. For these users, the accounting treatments and the detailed disclosures required may sometimes **obscure the picture** given by the financial statements. In some cases, **different, or more detailed information may be needed.** For example, related party transactions are often very significant in the context of SME activities and expanded disclosure may be appropriate.

Most interested parties favour separate international standards for SMEs.

E2 Seejoy

Top tips. Do not be put off by the fact that this is a football club. These are normal accounting transactions. Sale and leaseback, in particular, should be familiar to you and player registrations follow the normal rules for the intangibles.

Easy marks. The sale and leaseback is actually quite straightforward if you have practised questions on this topic. The player registration is quite straightforward too, once you have identified the issues.

Marking scheme

	Marks
Sale and leaseback	10
Player registrations	5
Bond	7
Player trading	5
Available	27
Maximum	25

(a)   **Sale and leaseback of football stadium**

The proposal is for a sale and leaseback which be treated as a **finance lease**. The accounting treatment for such a transaction is dealt with by SSAP 21 *Accounting for leases and hire purchase contracts.* As the **substance of the transaction is a financing transaction** this would not be dealt with as a sale so the **stadium would remain on the balance sheet** as a fixed asset and be depreciated but will now be valued at the sales value of £15 million. The **excess of the sales value over the carrying value** will be recognised as **deferred income** and credited to the profit and loss account over the period of the finance lease.

When the sale takes place on 1 January 20X7 the double entry will be:

DEBIT CASH	£15m	
CREDIT Fixed assets		£12m
CREDIT Deferred income		£3m

On this same date the finance lease will also be recognised:

DEBIT Fixed assets	£15m	
CREDIT Obligations under finance leases		£15m

In the financial statements for the year ending 31 December 20X7 the effects will be as follows:

PROFIT AND LOSS ACCOUNT

	£'000
Depreciation of stadium (£15m/20 years)	(750)
Finance charge ((£15m – £1.2m) × 5.6%)	(773)
Deferred income (£3m/20 years)	150

BALANCE SHEET

Fixed assets

Stadium (£15m – £0.75m)	14,250

Current liabilities

Rental payment	1,200

Long term liabilities

Obligations under finance leases (£15m – (£1.2m × 2) + £0.773m)	13,373
Deferred income (£3m – £0.15m)	2,850

There is little doubt that this form of sale and leaseback will improve the cash flow of the club as £15 million will be received on 1 January 20X7. However, the required accounting treatment by SSAP 21 will mean that the sale and leaseback has **significant and detrimental effects** on the financial statements. The **profit** shown in the profit and loss account is likely to **decrease** as the finance charge on the lease significantly outweighs the deferred income credit to the profit and loss account. If the £15 million receipt is not used to pay off existing long term creditors then the overall **gearing** of the club will **increase** as the finance lease obligation is included on the balance sheet.

It might be worth investigating the possibility of a **sale and leaseback** agreement which **results in an operating lease** rather than a finance lease. In such a leaseback, as the sale is at fair value, the **profit can be recognised immediately** in the profit and loss account and the stadium will be deemed to have been sold and removed from the balance sheet. There will also be no obligation for leases in liabilities on the balance sheet. The downside however is that any increase in the residual value of the stadium would be lost.

(b)   **Player registrations**

The player registrations are **capitalised** by the club as intangible fixed assets under FRS 10 *Goodwill and intangible assets.* This is an **acceptable** accounting treatment as the transfer fees classify as assets as it is probable that expected future benefits will flow to the club as a result of the contracts and the cost can be measured reliably at the amount of the transfer fees actually paid.

According to FRS 10 intangible fixed assets which are capitalised should be **amortised over their useful** life. There is a rebuttable presumption that this useful life does not exceed 20 years. Therefore on the face of it claiming a useful life of 10 years might be acceptable. However FRS 10 recommends that amortisation reflects the useful life of the assets and the pattern of economic benefits. Therefore the proposal to amortise the transfer fees over a period of 10 **years is not acceptable as the contracts are only for 5 years and 3 years**.

In terms of **cash flow** this proposal regarding the amortisation would have **no effect** at all. It would simply be a bookkeeping entry which would reduce the amortisation charge to the profit and loss account.

The potential payment to the two players' former clubs of £5 million would not appear to be probable due to the current form of the club. Therefore under FRS 12 *Provisions, contingent liabilities and contingent assets* no provision would be recognised for this amount. However the possible payment does fall within the FRS 12 definition of a contingent liability which is a possible obligation arising out of past events whose existence will be confirmed only by the occurrence or non-occurrence of one or more uncertain future events not wholly within the control of the entity. Therefore as a contingent liability the amount and details would be disclosed in the notes to the financial statements.

(c)   **Issue of bond**

What the club is proposing here is known as **securitisation**. This particular type of securitisation is often called 'future flow' securitisation. In some forms of securitisation a special purpose vehicle is set up to administer the income stream or assets involved in which case there is potentially an off balance sheet effect. However, in this case there is no special purpose vehicle and therefore the only accounting issue is how the bond is to be treated under FRS 26 *Financial instruments: measurement*.

The bond will be recorded as a financial liability and will either be classified as a financial liability at fair value through profit or loss or as a financial liability measured at amortised cost. To be a financial liability at fair value through profit or loss the bond must either be held for trading or be part of a group of financial assets, financial liabilities, or both, that are managed on a fair basis. It is unlikely that this is the case therefore the bond will be classified as measured at **amortised cost**.

The bond will be **initially recognised at its fair value** which is the amount for which the liability can be settled between knowledgeable and willing parties in an arm's length transaction. Fair value at inception will normally be the amount of the consideration received for the instrument. Subsequent to initial recognition the instrument will be measured using amortised cost.

When the bond is issued on 1 January 20X7 it will be measured at the value of the consideration received of £47.5 million (£50m × 95%).

At 31 December 20X7 the valuation will be:

	£m
Initial value	47.5
Interest at 7.7%	3.7
Cash paid	(6.0)
Balance sheet value	45.2

In terms of cash flow the issue of the bond will bring **£47.5 million** into the club. The bond is effectively secured on the income stream of the future corporate hospitality sales and season tickets receipts, and due to this security the coupon rate of interest is lower than the market rates. The money is to be used to improve the grounds which is an appropriate use of long-term funds. However, the proposal to pay the short term costs of the players' wages out of these long term funds is a **misuse of long term capital** which is likely to lead to future liquidity problems.

(d)   **Player trading**

In accounting terms there is **no issue** to deal with at 31 December 20X6 as the potential sale of the players will **not fall to be classified as 'held for sale'** fixed assets under FRED 32 *Disposal of non-current assets* *and presentation of discontinued operations.* In order for these players to classify as held for sale they would need to be available for immediate sale which they are not.

However the club must consider carrying out an **impairment review** of the fixed assets at 31 December 20X6. If the players are sold for the anticipated figure of £16 million then the following loss will be incurred:

	£m
Carrying value at 1 May 20X7	
A Steel (£20m − (£4m + 4/12 × £4m)	14.7
R Aldo (£15m − (£10m + 4/12 × £5m)	3.3
	18.0
Potential sales value	16.0
Potential loss	2.0

This potential loss of £2 million on the sale of these players may be evidence of impairment and a **review** should be carried out at 31 December 20X6 and the **players' value written down to recoverable amount**.

In terms of cash flow, the sale of the players would **provide much needed cash**. However as the club is performing poorly currently the sale of the two best players **may lead to even worse performance** which is likely to have a detrimental affect on ticket sales and the liquidity of the club in future.

F1 Handrew

Top tips. This question dealt with the implications of a move to IFRS by a company. It is likely to become less frequent, though topical at the moment. Additionally, the impact of the changes of accounting policy on three key performance ratios had to be calculated and discussed. The question dealt with leases, plant and equipment, and investment properties, and the ratios to be adjusted were ROCE, gearing, and the PE ratio.

Easy marks. Marks were allocated for general principles, which candidates can easily score highly on. Additionally, marks were allocated for a report format. Marks are only given for the report if candidates set out the report in a formal way, with appendices for detailed calculations, but this is easy to do.

Examiner's comment. The question was quite well-answered although frequently the adjustments to the profit for the year and balance sheet were inaccurate, and candidates could not deal with the deferred tax implications.

Marking scheme

		Marks
Report		4
(a)	Discussion	18
(b)	Discussion and calculation	7
	Available	29
	Maximum	25

REPORT

To: Directors of Handrew
From:
Subject: Impact of the move to International Financial Reporting Standards (IFRS)
Date: June 2005

This report discusses the impact of the change to IFRS on the financial statements for the year ended 31 May 2005, including the effect of the change on three key performance ratios. Calculations are included in an Appendix.

Leases

Like UK GAAP, IFRS classifies leases into finance leases and operating leases. A finance lease **transfers substantially all the risks and benefits of ownership** to the lessee while an operating lease does not. Unlike UK GAAP, IFRS requires leases to be **separated** into **land and buildings components**. A lease of **land** is **normally classified as an operating lease**; a lease of **buildings** may be **either a finance lease or an operating lease.**

There are several indications that the company's **leases of land** *are* **operating leases. Title does not pass** at the end of the lease term. In addition, at 1 June 2004 the **present value of the lease commitments was only 73% of the fair value of the land** (for a lease to be a finance lease the present value of the lease commitments must normally be 'substantially all' of the fair value of the leased asset). The **lessor intends to redevelop the land**, which also suggests that Handrew does not enjoy the benefits of ownership. In contrast, **title to the buildings does pass** to the company at the end of the lease term; the **present value of the lease commitments is 96% (**substantially all) **of the fair value of the buildings**; and the buildings are **leased for a period equal to their economic life.** The substance of the agreement appears to be that Handrew **has purchased the buildings** and the leases are financing arrangements, rather than rental agreements. The **leases of the buildings are finance leases.**

The buildings must be treated as assets of the company and **recognised on the balance sheet. Fixed assets will increase by £86 million at 1 June 2004** (the inception of the lease). The buildings should be **depreciated** over 20 years and therefore there will be an **expense of £4.3 million** and the **carrying value of the buildings will be £81.7 million** at 31 May 2005. The company should also **recognise a corresponding liability for the lease rentals.** At 31 May 2005 this is **£81.2 million** (see Appendix**). Current liabilities will increase by £5.1 million** (the amount due on 31 May 2006) and **non-current liabilities will increase by £76.1 million. Interest of £5.2 million will be recognised** in the profit and loss account. The **tax charge for the year will also be affected**, as lease rentals on the buildings will no longer be included in the profit and loss account as a taxable expense.

Leases of land **will continue to be treated as operating leases** and lease rentals of £10 million will be recognised in the profit and loss account.

Plant and equipment

Both UK GAAP and IFRS require **residual values** of fixed assets **to be reviewed at each year end**. Under UK GAAP, residual value is based on prices prevailing at the date of acquisition. Under IFRS, residual value is **based on current prices.** Any **changes in residual value** are **reflected in the depreciation charge** and are accounted for **prospectively,** as a change in estimation technique.

Therefore under IFRS the residual value of the asset would be **£8 million** rather than £4 million. This means that the **depreciation charge** for the year ended 31 May 20X5 will be **£1 million**, rather than £2 million as at present (see Appendix).

Investment properties

Under IFRS, investment properties may be measured **either at cost or at fair value.** If a property is **measured at fair value, gains and losses** on remeasurement **must be recognised in the profit and loss account.** As **the company wishes to do this**, it will **adopt the fair value model.** Under IFRS, fair value is normally taken to be **market value, rather than existing use value**. Therefore the hotel should be valued at **£50 million**. Because **the market price is obtainable** if the land is sold for redevelopment, the land **should be valued at £50 million** and the **building at nil.**

Profit for the year is increased by the **revaluation gain of £15 million.** Of this amount, **£5 million has been previously recognised in equity** (and in the statement of total recognised gains and losses) and would be **transferred to the profit and loss account.** IFRS **requires deferred tax to be provided on revaluation gains,** regardless of whether there is an actual intention to sell the property.

Impact on performance ratios

Three key performance ratios have been calculated as follows:

	UK GAAP	IFRS
Return on capital employed	$\dfrac{130}{520} \times 100\% = 25\%$	$\dfrac{151.7}{606.2} \times 100\% = 25\%$
Gearing ratio	$\dfrac{40}{480} \times 100\% = 8.3\%$	$\dfrac{120.9}{485.3} \times 100\% = 24.9\%$
Price earnings ratio	$\dfrac{£6}{£0.5} = 12$	$\dfrac{£6}{£0.552} = 10.9$

There is very **little effect on return on capital employed**. **Profit has increased** by £21.7 million, mainly because the operating lease rentals have been excluded and the gain on revaluation has been included. However, **capital employed has also increased**, due to the recognition of the finance lease liability.

Gearing has increased significantly, mainly because of the recognition of the finance lease liability.

As a consequence of the increase in profits, **earnings per share has risen** and therefore the **price earnings ratio has fallen**.

Appendix: impact of the change to IFRS on profit, taxation and the balance sheet

1   *Effect on profit*

	£m	£m
Profit before interest and tax under UK GAAP		130
Add back operating lease rentals		10
Less depreciation on building (86 ÷ 20)		(4.3)
Effect of increase in residual value: add back excess depreciation (W2)		1
Investment property: revaluation gain (5 + 10)		15.0
Profit before interest and tax under IFRS		151.7
Interest		
Under UK GAAP	5	
Add interest on finance leases (W1)	5.2	
		(10.2)
Taxation		
Under UK GAAP	25	
Add increase in charge under IFRS (Appendix 2)	6.2	
		(31.2)
Profit after interest and tax under IFRS		110.3
Earnings per share under IFRS:	$\dfrac{110.3}{200} = 55.2\text{p}$	

2   *Effect on taxation*

	Current tax £m	Deferred tax £m	Total £m
Operating lease rentals (increase in profit)	10.0		
Interest expense on finance lease (decrease in profit)	(5.2)		
Reduction of depreciation on plant (increase in profit)		1	
Gain on investment property (increase in profit)		15	
	4.8	16	20.8

3   *Effect on balance sheet amounts*

	Share capital and reserves £m	Non-current liabilities £m	Net assets £m
At 31 May 2005 under UK GAAP	480.0	40.0	520.0
Lease (W1)			
Liability		86.0	86.0
Operating lease rentals	10.0	(10.0)	
Depreciation	(4.3)		(4.3)
Interest	(5.2)	5.2	
Current liability		(5.1)	(5.1)
Plant: depreciation (W2)	1.0		1.0
Investment property: gain	10.0		10.0
Tax (Appendix 2)	(6.2)	4.8	(1.4)
	485.3	120.9	606.2

Workings

1   *Finance lease*

	£m
Net present value of future lease commitments	86.0
Interest at 6%	5.2
Repayment	(10.0)
Total liability at 31 May 20X5	81.2
Interest at 6%	4.9
Repayment	(10.0)
Total liability at 31 May 20X6	76.1

Therefore £5.1 million (10 − 4.9) is included in current liabilities.

2   *Excess depreciation*

	£m
Cost	20
Depreciation for year ended 31 May 2004 (20 − 4 ÷ 8)	(2)
Carrying value at 1 June 20X4	18
Residual value at 1 June 20X4	(11)
Depreciable amount	7
Annual depreciation charge (7 ÷ 7)	1

F2 Guide

Top tips. This is a topical question, which required you to draft a report on the impact of a move to International Financial Reporting Standards in terms of the practical factors that a company should consider and the effects on debt covenants, performance related pay, and the views of financial analysts.

Easy marks. Part (a) gives ten easy marks for common sense. Learn our answer carefully, in case this question comes up again.

Examiner's comment. The question was generally well-answered, although some candidates wrote about the reasons why differences in national accounting practices had arisen. This type of answer obviously did not score many marks. The discussion of the practical implications of a move to IFRS was quite good, but candidates failed to see the problems relating to the recognition of debt covenants and the impact on performance related pay.

			Marks
(i)	Factors	10	
(ii)	Debt covenants	5	
(iii)	Performance related pay	5	
(iv)	Views of analysts	5	
Report		4	
	Available	29	
	Maximum		25

REPORT

To: Directors of Guide
From:
Subject: Potential impact of the move to International Financial Reporting Standards (IFRS)
Date: December 20X3

As requested, I have set out my views on the potential impact of the move from reporting under UK GAAP to reporting under IFRS.

Practical factors to consider in implementing the change to IFRS

The change to IFRS should be **planned in detail** well before the first IFRS accounts are due to be prepared. The company should consider the following matters:

(a)   Do the staff have the **relevant technical knowledge** and **experience** of IFRS? Almost certainly the company will need to **recruit IFRS experts** and to **arrange appropriate training** for everybody likely to be affected. This should include managers of subsidiaries as well as Head Office staff, because they too will need to understand the effects of the change, for example, when preparing budgets.

(b)   **Which IFRSs** will particularly affect the company? Staff need to understand the **main differences** between UK GAAP and IFRS as they affect the financial statements. Because the company provides insurance and banking services, it is likely that **financial instruments** and **foreign currency translation** will be major issues; the standards on financial instruments are **particularly complex.** UK GAAP has only recently adopted versions of these standards, which **differ considerably** from the previous UK accounting standards.

(c)   Are the **accounting systems adequate** to produce IFRS information? The finance staff will need to be clear about the nature of the **information required**, not only for the actual **accounting**, but for **disclosure.** It should be noted that IFRS **will almost certainly require more information about fair values** than UK GAAP.

(d)   Are there any **agreements** of which the terms are **defined by reference to UK GAAP**? These will probably include **debt covenants** and schemes relating to **performance related pay** (discussed below) and there may be other agreements that depend on the **future financial performance** of the company.

The company will need to **keep all stakeholders in the business informed** about the **impact** that the change to IFRS could have on reported performance. Key stakeholders include **analysts** (discussed in more detail below), **employees** and **loan creditors**. The company should **quantify the effect** of the transition to IFRS on the financial statements **as soon as possible**.

It is also worth noting that the IASB currently has **several major projects in progress**, including projects on business combinations, revenue recognition and reporting financial performance. These will all result in **new IFRSs within the next few years**. In addition, the IASB is carrying out a short term **convergence project** with the US Financial Accounting Standards Board (FASB) which will also result in **several changes to existing IFRSs** in the near future. It is important that those responsible for the IFRS financial statements are made aware of new developments as they occur.

Debt covenants

As noted above, debt covenants and other legal contracts **will be affected by the change** to IFRS. Because IFRS requires **extensive use of fair values** to measure assets and liabilities, **key measures** such as **interest cover** and **gearing** are likely to be **significantly affected. Earnings** may also change significantly. Debt covenants based on these measures may need to be **renegotiated**, otherwise the company will have to **continue to keep accounting records in UK GAAP** as well as in IFRS, which would be time consuming and possibly costly.

Performance related pay

Where a company makes share based payments, it is required to **recognise both the additional equity (in reserves) and the related expense**. The relevant IFRS **will apply** to any scheme for paying directors or employees in shares or share options. This means that employee share schemes directly affect reported earnings. (FRS 20 *Share based payment*, which is virtually identical to IFRS 2, has now been adopted in the UK.)

Performance criteria are normally based on measures such as **earnings per share** or **earnings before interest, tax, depreciation and amortisation (EBITDA)**. These **may no longer be appropriate**. Greater use of **fair values** and **'recycling' of gains and losses** mean that these measures **may become volatile**. This volatility may not be a direct consequence of staff performance and therefore it would be **undesirable** for it to trigger pay awards or executive bonuses. The company will **need to look for alternative measures** and will probably need to **redesign its incentive schemes** and methods of determining staff bonuses.

Finally, schemes are probably **based on earnings prepared under UK GAAP**. Even where existing performance measures are still appropriate, the company will **need to take account of the effect of the change** to IFRS upon reported earnings and to **adjust the criteria** if necessary.

Views of financial analysts

The company should **communicate the effects of the change** from UK GAAP to IFRS to the markets and to investment analysts **as soon as these are quantified**. This is necessary in order to give the analysts confidence in the finance team's ability to deal with IFRS (and therefore in the accuracy of the financial statements) and more importantly, in order **to manage the expectations of the market. Share prices may be adversely affected** if there are **unexpected changes in earnings** and other key performance measures.

Communication about the potential impact of IFRS is normally in the form of **presentations,** but may be in other forms, such as press releases. Analysts will be particularly interested in **the effect of earnings volatility** because they need to discount future profits in order to arrive at a fair value for the business. Analysts will also need **information that is transparent** and will be assisted if **formats, disclosures and measurement bases** are, as far as possible, **comparable.**

I hope that you find this report helpful. Please do not hesitate to contact me should you require any further information or assistance.

Mock Exams

BPP
LEARNING MEDIA

ACCA

Paper P2

Corporate Reporting (United Kingdom)

Mock Examination 1

Question Paper	
Time allowed	
Reading and planning	**15 minutes**
Writing	**3 hours**
This paper is divided into two sections	
Section A	**ONE compulsory question to be attempted**
Section B	**TWO questions ONLY to be attempted**

DO NOT OPEN THIS PAPER UNTIL YOU ARE READY TO START UNDER EXAMINATION CONDITIONS

SECTION A – This ONE question is compulsory and MUST be attempted

Question 1

(a) Jay, a public limited company, has acquired the following shareholdings in Gee and Hem, both public limited companies.

Date of acquisition	Holding acquired	Fair value of net assets	Consideration
Gee		£m	£m
1 June 20X3	30%	40	15
1 June 20X4	50%	50	30
Hem			
1 June 20X4	25%	32	12

The following balance sheets relate to Jay, Gee and Hem at 31 May 20X5.

	Jay	Gee	Hem
	£m	£m	£m
Tangible fixed assets	300	40	30
Investment in Gee	48	–	–
Investment in Hem	22	–	–
Current assets	100	20	15
Current liabilities	(110)	(10)	(12)
Long term liabilities	(60)	(4)	(3)
	300	46	30
Called up share capital of £1	100	10	6
Share premium account	50	20	14
Revaluation reserve	15	–	–
Reserves	135	16	10
	300	46	30

The following information is relevant to the preparation of the group financial statements of the Jay Group.

(i) Gee and Hem have not issued any new share capital since the acquisition of the shareholdings by Jay. The excess of the fair value of the net assets of Gee and Hem over their carrying amounts at the dates of acquisition is due to an increase in the value of Gee's non-depreciable land of £10 million at 1 June 20X3 and a further increase of £4 million at 1 June 20X4, and Hem's non-depreciable land of £6 million at 1 June 20X4. There has been no change in the value of non-depreciable land since 1 June 20X4. Before obtaining control of Gee, Jay did not have significant influence over Gee but has significant influence over Hem. Jay has accounted for the investment in Gee at market value with changes in value being recorded in the revaluation reserve. The market price of the shares of Gee at 31 May 20X5 had risen to £6 per share as there was speculation regarding a takeover bid.

(ii) On 1 June 20X4, Jay sold goods costing £13 million to Gee for £19 million. Gee has used the goods in constructing a machine which began service on 1 December 20X4. Additionally on 31 May 20X5, Jay purchased a portfolio of investments from Hem at a cost of £10 million on which Hem made a profit of £2 million. These investments have been incorrectly included in Jay's balance sheet under the heading 'Investment in Hem'.

(iii) Jay sold some machinery with a carrying value of £5 million on 28 February 20X5 for £8 million. The terms of the contract, which was legally binding from 28 February 20X5, was that the purchaser would pay an initial deposit of £2 million followed by two instalments of £3·5 million (including total interest of £1 million) payable on 31 May 20X5 and 20X6. The purchaser was in financial difficulties at the year end and subsequently went into liquidation on 10 June 20X5. No payment is expected from the liquidator. The deposit had been received on 28 February 20X5 but the first instalment was not received. The terms of the agreement were such that Jay maintained title to the machinery until the first instalment was paid. The machinery was still physically held by Jay and the machinery had been treated as sold in the financial statements. The amount outstanding of £6 million is included in current assets and no interest has been accrued in the financial statements.

(iv)   Gee is considered to be an income generating unit in its own right. At 31 May 20X5, Jay has determined that the recoverable amount of Gee is £62 million and that of Hem is £68 million.

(v)   Group policy is to depreciate plant and equipment on a reducing balance basis over ten years. Depreciation is calculated on a time-apportionment basis. Goodwill arising on acquisition is capitalised in the balance sheet and not amortised as the useful life of goodwill was believed to be indefinite.

(vi)   There are no inter-company amounts outstanding at 31 May 20X5.

Required

Prepare the consolidated balance sheet of the Jay Group as at 31 May 20X5 in accordance with UK Generally Accepted Accounting Practice.

(Candidates should calculate figures to one decimal place in £ million)   **(29 marks)**

(b)   In the year ended 31 May 20X6, Jay purchased goods from a foreign supplier for $8 million on 28 February 20X6. At 31 May 20X6, the creditor was still outstanding and the goods were still held by Jay. Similarly Jay has sold goods to a foreign customer for $4 million on 28 February 20X6 and it received payment for the goods in dollars on 31 May 20X6. Additionally Jay had purchased an investment property on 1 June 20X5 for $28 million. At 31 May 20X6, the investment property had a fair value of $24 million.

Jay would like advice on how to treat these transactions in the financial statements for the year ended 31 May 20X6. Its functional and presentation currency is the pound sterling.   **(10 marks)**

	Dollar:£	Average rate ($:£) for year to
Exchange rates		
1 June 20X5	1.4	
28 February 20X6	1.6	
31 May 20X6	1.3	1.5

(c)   Jay has a reputation for responsible corporate behaviour and sees the workforce as the key factor in the profitable growth of the business. During the year, the company made progress towards the aim of linking environmental performance with financial performance by reporting the relationship between the eco-productivity index for basic production and water and energy costs used in basic production. A feature of this index is that it can be segregated at site and divisional level, and can be used in the internal management decision-making process.

Discuss what matters should be disclosed in Jay's annual report in relation to the nature of corporate citizenship, in order that there might be a better assessment of the performance of the company.

(11 marks)

(Total marks = 50)

SECTION B – TWO questions ONLY to be attempted

Question 2

The consolidated financial statements of Dietronic, a public limited company, for the year ended 30 November 20X3 are as follows.

PROFIT AND LOSS ACCOUNT		BALANCE SHEET	
	£'000		£'000
Group operating profit	13,000	Fixed assets	18,500
Interest income	940	Goodwill	1,500
Profit on sale of subsidiary	100	Current assets	8,000
Profit before tax	14,040	Current liabilities	(4,000)
Taxation	(5,000)	Long term debt	(3,000)
Minority interests	(3,000)		21,000
Profit attributable to shareholders	6,040		
		Share capital: £1 ordinary shares	5,000
		Reserves	10,000
		Minority interest	6,000
			21,000

There have been a number of changes in the composition of the group during the year. The changes in the group and the accounting practices are set out below.

(i)   Dietronic had created on 1 July 20X3 a new management company in which it holds 80% of the ordinary share capital with the remainder being held by an employee share ownership trust. Dietronic had invested £160,000 in the company at the balance sheet date, and Dietronic had incurred £400,000 in administrative set-up costs. These costs have been treated as goodwill on consolidation as the setting up the new company constitutes a 'notional' acquisition with the set up cost being included in the cost of acquisition. The shares held by the employee share ownership trust were issued at a price of £2 per share and are included in the consolidated balance sheet of Dietronic at this amount within current assets. The share capital of the management company is 100,000 ordinary shares of £1.

(ii)   Dietronic acquired 70% of the ordinary share capital of Dairy, a public limited company, on 31 October 20X2. On acquisition of Dairy, the financial assets of the company were reduced from the book value of £1.2 million to £600,000. This reduction came about as a result of the directors' assessment of the fair value of the investments after taking into account the 'marketability' of the portfolio. On 31 December 20X2, all the investments were sold for £1 million net of costs and the profit on disposal reported in 'interest income' in the consolidated profit and loss account. The financial assets sold were wholly unquoted investments.

(iii)   Dietronic had a 100% owned German subsidiary which was set up in 20X0 by Dietronic. The subsidiary was sold on 1 December 20X2 for 600,000 euros (£400,000). The subsidiary is included in the holding company's accounts at a cost of £300,000 at 30 November 20X2 and the net assets at the same date included in the consolidated financial statements were 540,000 euros (£360,000). All exchange differences arising on the translation of the subsidiary's financial statements have been taken to a separate exchange reserve and the cumulative total on this reserve is £40,000 debit as at 1 December 20X2 before the receipt of the dividend. Dietronic has calculated the gain on the sale of the subsidiary as follows.

	£'000
Sale proceeds	400
Cost of investment	(300)
Gain on sale	100

The closing rate/net investment method was used to consolidate the financial statements of the subsidiary (the functional currency of the subsidiary is the euro). During the year to 30 November 20X2, the German subsidiary had declared and accounted for a proposed dividend of 48,000 euros. This had been included in the holding company's financial statements at the exchange rate ruling when the dividend was declared (£1 = 1.6 euros). This dividend was received on 1 December 20X2 by Dietronic and recorded in the cash book and dividends receivable account. The exchange rate at 1 December 20X2 was (£1 = 1.5 euros).

(iv)   On 1 June 20X3 Dietronic acquired a 25% share in a newly formed company, Diet, a public limited company. Diet has been classified as an associated company in the financial statements but no details have been shown on the face of the balance sheet or profit and loss account as Dietronic feels that the results and net assets of the associate are immaterial. The only amount included in the financial statements as regards the associate is the purchase consideration of £2.1 million which has been added to tangible fixed assets. The fair value of the net assets of Diet at the date of acquisition was £6.8 million. The directors are confident that Diet will be successful in future years with profits in the next financial year and dividends of 10p per share forecast for five years. If the investment in Diet were to be sold at 30 November 20X3, it is anticipated that it would realise £1.8 million.

DIET PLC
SUMMARISED BALANCE SHEET
AT 30 NOVEMBER 20X3

	£'000	£'000
Fixed assets at cost		5,000
Net current assets		2,000
		7,000
Ordinary share capital of £1		7,600
Reserves at 30 November 20X2	80	
Loss for year to 30 November 20X3	(680)	
		(600)
		7,000

The directors are seeking advice as to the acceptability of the accounting practices used for the above changes in the composition of the group. A discount rate of 5% should be used in any calculations and goodwill is amortised over four years with a full year's charge in the year of acquisition.

Required

(a)   Discuss the nature of any amendments required to the consolidated financial statements of Dietronic plc in order to bring the accounting practices used for the changes in the composition of the group into line with UK GAAP.
(17 marks)

(b)   Redraft the consolidated financial statements of Dietronic plc in accordance with these amendments.

(8 marks)

(Total = 25 marks)

Question 3

Gear Software, a public limited company, develops and sells computer games software. The turnover of Gear Software for the year ended 31 May 20X3 is £7 million, the balance sheet total is £4 million and it has 40 employees. There are several elements in the financial statements for the year ended 31 May 20X3 on which the directors of Gear require advice.

(a)   Gear has two cost centres relating to the development and sale of the computer games. The indirect overhead costs attributable to the two cost centres were allocated in the year to 31 May 20X2 in the ratio 60:40 respectively. Also in that financial year, the direct labour costs and attributable overhead costs incurred on the development of original games software were carried forward as work-in-progress and included with the balance sheet total for stock of computer games. Stock of computer games includes directly attributable overheads. In the year to 31 May 20X3, Gear has allocated indirect overhead costs in the ratio 50:50 to the two cost centres and has written the direct labour and overhead costs incurred on the development of the games off to the profit and loss account. Gear has stated that it cannot quantify the effect of this write off on the current year's profit and loss account. Further it proposes to show the overhead costs relating to the sale of computer games within distribution costs. In prior years these costs were shown in cost of sales. **(9 marks)**

(b)   In prior years, Gear has charged interest incurred on the construction of computer hardware as part of cost of sales. It now proposes to capitalise such interest and to change the method of depreciation from the straight-line method over four years to the reducing balance method at 30% per year. Depreciation will now be charged as cost of sales rather than administrative expenses as in previous years. Gear currently recognises revenue on contracts in proportion to the progression and activity on the contract. The normal accounting practice within the industrial sector is to recognise revenue when the product is shipped to customers. The effect of any change in accounting policy to bring the company in line with accounting practice in the industrial sector would be to increase turnover for the year by £500,000. **(6 marks)**

The directors have requested advice on the changes in accounting practice that they have proposed for stock and work-in-progress and fixed assets in the light of the introduction of FRS 18 *Accounting policies.*

(c)   In relation to a failed acquisition, a firm of accountants has invoiced Gear for the sum of £300,000. Gear has paid £20,000 in full settlement of the debt and states that this was a reasonable sum for the advice given and is not prepared to pay any further sum. The accountants are pressing for payment of the full amount but on the advice of its solicitors. Gear is not going to settle the balance outstanding. Additionally Gear is involved in a court case concerning the plagiarism of software. Another games company has accused Gear of copying their games software and currently legal opinion seems to indicate that Gear will lose the case. Management estimates that the most likely outcome will be a payment of costs and royalties to the third party of £1 million in two years' time (approximately). The best case scenario is deemed to be a payment of £500,000 in one year's time and the worst case scenario that of a payment of £2 million in three years' time. These scenarios are based on the amount of the royalty payment and the potential duration and costs of the court case. Management has estimated that the relative likelihood of the above payments are best case = 30% chance, most likely outcome = 60% chance, and worst case = 10% chance of occurrence. The directors are unsure as to whether any provision for the above amount should be made in the financial statements. **(7 marks)**

(d)   In the event of the worst case scenario occurring the directors of Gear are worried about the viability of their business as the likelihood would be that current liabilities would exceed current assets and it is unlikely that in the interim period there will be sufficient funds generated from operational cash flows. **(3 marks)**

Required

Write a report to the directors of Gear Software plc explaining the implications of the above information contained in paragraphs (a)-(d) for the financial statements.

(Total = 25 marks)

Question 4

Autol, a public limited company, is based in the UK and currently prepares its financial statements under UK GAAP (Generally Accepted Accounting Practice). The company currently operates in the telecommunications industry and has numerous national and international subsidiaries. It is also quoted on the London Stock Exchange. The company invests heavily in research and development which it writes off immediately, and uses merger accounting for its subsidiaries wherever possible. Additionally it has recently adopted FRS 17 *Retirement benefits* and FRS 19 *Deferred tax.* It wishes to expand its business activities and raise capital on international stock exchanges. The directors are somewhat confused over the financial reporting requirements of multi-national companies as they see a variety of local GAAPs and reporting practices being used by these companies including the preparation of reconciliations to alternative local GAAPs, and the use of accounting standards of the International Accounting Standards Board (IASB).

The directors have themselves considered the use of US GAAP in the financial statements but are unclear as to whether US GAAP can be utilised in UK financial statements. Further, the directors are aware of the fact that all European Union (EU) listed companies are required to prepare their consolidated financial statements in accordance with the accounting standards of the IASB from 1 January 2005 and require advice on the potential impact on reported profit of a move to these standards given their current accounting practice in the areas of deferred tax, research and development, retirement benefits and merger accounting.

Required

Write a report suitable for presentation to the directors of Autol plc that sets out the following information.

(a)   The variety of local GAAPs and reporting practices currently being used by multi-national companies setting out brief possible reasons why such companies might prepare financial statements utilising a particular set of generally accepted accounting practices **(6 marks)**

(b)   Advice as to whether a UK based company such as Autol could prepare a single set of consolidated financial statements that comply only with US GAAP **(3 marks)**

(c)   The problems relating to the current use of GAAP reconciliations by companies and whether the use of such reconciliations is likely to continue into the future **(5 marks)**

(d)   The potential impact on the reported profit of Autol if it prepared its consolidated financial statements in accordance with the accounting standards of the IASB in relation to accounting for deferred tax, research and development expenditure, retirement benefits and mergers **(11 marks)**

(Total = 25 marks)

Answers

DO NOT TURN THIS PAGE UNTIL YOU HAVE
COMPLETED THE MOCK EXAM

A PLAN OF ATTACK

If this were the real Corporate Reporting exam and you had been told to turn over and begin, what would be going through your mind?

The answer may be 'I can't do this to save my life'! You've spent most of your study time on groups and current issues (because that's what your tutor/BPP Study Text told you to do), plus a selection of other topics, and you're really not sure that you know enough. The good news is that this may get you through. The first question, in Section A, is very likely to be on groups. In Section B you have to choose three out of four questions, and at least one of those is likely to be on current issues – a new IFRS, ED or discussion paper. So there's no need to panic. First spend **five minutes or so looking at the paper**, and develop a **plan of attack**.

Looking through the paper

The compulsory question in Section A is, as a case study on groups, in this case a complex group. You also have a fairly easy bit on corporate citizenship. In **Section B** you have **four questions on a variety of topics:**

- Question 2 requires you to adjust and redraft financial statements.
- Question 3 requires a discussion about issues concerning a change in a accounting policy.
- Question 4 is about the implications of a move to IFRS.

You **only have to answer three out of these four questions.** You don't have to pick your optional questions right now, but this brief overview should have convinced you that you have enough **choice** and variety to have a respectable go at Section B. So let's go back to the compulsory question in Section A.

Compulsory question

Question 1 requires you to **prepare a consolidated balance sheet for a complex group**. This question looks daunting, partly because of the piecemeal acquisition aspects. However, there are easy marks to be gained for basic consolidation techniques such as intragroup trading. Part (c) is a good source of easy marks too.

Optional questions

Deciding between the optional questions is obviously a personal matter – it depends how you have spent your study time. However, here are a few pointers.

Question 2 requires adjustment and re-drafting. It is time-pressured and complex. Best avoided.

Question 3 has easy marks for knowledge of IAS 8, and looks worse than it is.

Question 4 is fairly straight forward if you know the topic. In our opinion, everyone should do this question.

Allocating your time

BPP's advice is always allocate your time **according to the marks for the question** in total and for the parts of the question. But **use common sense.** If you're doing Question 1 but have no idea about fair value, jot down something (anything!) and move onto Part (b), where most of the easy marks are to be gained.

Forget about it!

And don't worry if you found the paper difficult. More than likely other candidates will too. The paper is marked fairly leniently and always has a good pass rate. If this were the real thing, you would need to **forget** the exam the minute you left the exam hall and **think about the next one**. Or, if it's the last one, **celebrate**!

Question 1

Top tips. Part (a) of this question examined business combinations acquired in stages. The examiner has said that this and future questions will be structured around a core question which examines group accounting principles. Bolted on to this core will be adjustments for aspects such as accounting for financial instruments, assets 'held for sale', pensions, or maybe incorrect accounting entries. In this question, candidates had to account for the acquisition, inter-company sales, an associate, and an impairment test. Additionally, there were some revenue recognition issues to be dealt with. Part (b) deals with foreign currency transactions. Part (c) on corporate citizenship is the kind of question you can expect to find regularly as part of Question 1.

Easy marks. There are marks for basic consolidation techniques, including setting out the proforma, adding items, and working out the group structure. Part (c) has easy marks available for any sensible points.

Examiner's comment. The step-by-step acquisition was not well-answered, with candidates unsure how to calculate the goodwill arising on the acquisitions. Similarly, the nature of the impairment testing of goodwill did not seem to be understood. Many candidates could not account for the associate, and actually used acquisition techniques instead of equity accounting to consolidate it, giving a minority interest of 75%. The elimination of the inter-company profit was quite well done but some candidates did not allocate part of the revaluation surplus arising on the fair value of the net assets at acquisition to the minority interest. Overall, the question was not particularly well-answered, mainly because of a lack of understanding of the basic technique of step-by-step acquisitions.

Marking scheme

		Marks
(a)	Property, plant and equipment	4
	Goodwill	4
	Associate	4
	Investment	1
	Current assets	1
	Current liabilities	3
	Creditors due after one year	3
	Share capital	1
	Revaluation reserve	1
	Profit and loss account	6
	Minority interest	
	Current liabilities	
	Impairment	3
(b)	Stock, goods sold	10
(c)	Corporate citizenship:	
	Corporate government	3
	Ethics	3
	Employee reports	3
	Environment	3
	Available	54
	Maximum	50

(a) JAY GROUP
     CONSOLIDATED BALANCE SHEET AT 30 MAY 20X5

	£m	£m
Fixed assets		
Intangible assets: goodwill (W2)		2.0
Tangible assets		353.2
Investment in associate (W3)		13.0
Investment (10 – 0.5) (W8)		9.5
		377.7
Current assets (120 – 6) (W10)	114	
Creditors: amounts falling due within one year	(120)	
Net current liabilities		(6.0)
Total assets less current liabilities		371.7
Creditors: amounts falling due after more than one year		(64.0)
		307.7
Capital and reserves		
Share capital		100.0
Share premium		50.0
Revaluation reserve (W5)		12.0
Profit and loss account (W4)		133.7
		295.7
Minority interest (W6)		12.0
		307.7

Workings

1   *Group structure*

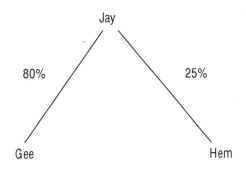

	Jay	
80%		25%
Gee		Hem

2   *Goodwill: Gee*

	£m
Cost of combination	45
Less fair value of net assets acquired	
80% × 50	(40)
	5
Impairment (W9)	(3)
	2

Note: Although the original stake in Gee was 30%, Jay did not exercise significant influence over Gee and therefore Gee was not an associate. Therefore goodwill has been calculated using fair values on the date that control was gained (1 June 20X4).

3   *Investment in associate*

Cost of investment	12
Profit for year ended 31 May 20X5 (25% × 36 – 32)	1
	13

Alternative calculation:

	£m	£m
Net assets at balance sheet date		
Per balance sheet	30	
Fair value adjustment	6	
	36	
Group share (25%)		9
Goodwill:		
Cost of investment	12	
Fair value of net assets acquired (25% × 32)	(8)	
		4
		13

Note: The recoverable amount of the investment in the associate is £17 million (25% × 68). This is higher than the carrying amount and therefore the associate is not impaired.

4   *Profit and loss account*
Retained earnings

	Jay £m	Gee £m	Hem £m
Per question	135.00	16.0	10
Adjustments			
PUP on machinery (W8)	(5.70)		
PUP on associate share of investments (W8)	(0.50)		
Impairment of debtor (W10)	(1.10)		
Pre-acquisition retained earnings (Note)		(6.0)	(6)
		10	4
Group share			
Gee (80% × 10)	8.00		
Hem (25% × 4)	1.00		
Impairment of goodwill	(3.00)		
	133.70		

Note. Pre acquisition earnings calculated as:

	Gee £m	Hem £m
Fair value of net assets	50	32
Less: FV increase	(14)	(6)
Share capital	(10)	(6)
Share premium	(20)	(14)
	6	6

5   *Revaluation reserve*

	£m
Jay	15
Increase in value of investment in Gee: after first acquisition	(3)
	12

6   *Minority interest*

	£m
Net assets at balance sheet date	46
Plus fair value adjustment	14
	60
MI share (20%)	12

7   *Tangible fixed assets*

	£m	£m
Jay		300
Gee		40
Fair value adjustment (land)		14
Machine		
Cost	5	
Less depreciation $(3/12 \times 10\% \times 5)$	(0.1)	
		4.9
Provision for unrealised profit (W8)		(5.7)
		353.2

Note that Jay has retained title to the machinery because the first instalment has not been paid.

8   *Provision for unrealised profit*

Sales from Jay to Gee

	£m
Profit $(19 - 13)$	6.0
Less depreciation on machine constructed with goods: $(6 \times 10\% \times 6/12)$	(0.3)
	5.7

Sale of investments from Hem to Jay

	£m
Group share of profit $(25\% \times 2)$	0.5

9   *Impairment of goodwill: Gee*

	Goodwill £m	Net assets £m	Total £m
Carrying value at 31 May 20X5	5	46	51
Fair value adjustment		14	14
	5	60	65
Recoverable amount			62
Impairment			3

10   *Impairment of debtor*

	£m
Cost of machinery	8.0
Less deposit received	(2.0)
Bad debt written off	6.0
Less net book value of machine (included in tangible assets)	(4.9)
Impairment loss deducted from profit and loss account	1.1

(b)   The initial transaction of the purchase of goods from the foreign supplier would be **recorded in the ledger accounts at £5 million ($8/1.6)**. Therefore both the purchase and the creditor would be recorded at this amount. At the year end the creditor is **restated to the closing rate** but the **stock remains at £5 million**. Therefore the creditor is restated to £6.2 million ($8m/1.3) and an **exchange loss** is taken to the profit and loss account of £1.2 million (£6.2 – 5m).

On the **sales** the original transaction is recorded at £2.5 million ($4m/1.6) as both a sale and a debtor. When payment is made the amount actually received in sterling is £3.1 million ($4m/1.3) and an **exchange gain** is recorded in the profit and loss account of £0.6 million (£3.1 – 2.5m).

When the **investment property** was first purchased it should have been recognised in the balance sheet at £20 million ($28m/1.4). At the year end the investment property has fallen in value to $24 million and the exchange rate has changed to 1.3. Therefore at 31 May 20X6 the property would be **valued at £18.5 million ($24m/1.3)**.

The fall in value of £1.5 million (£20 – 18.5m) is recognised in the **statement of total recognised gains and losses** (STRGL) as a **loss on an investment property** according to SSAP 19 *Accounting for investment properties*. The loss is a mixture of a fall in value of the property and an gain due to the exchange rate movement. However, as the investment property is a non-monetary asset there is no requirement under FRS 23 to recognise the **foreign currency element separately.**

(c)   **Nature of corporate citizenship**

Increasingly businesses are expected to be **socially responsible as well as profitable**. Strategic decisions by businesses, particularly global businesses nearly always have wider social consequences. It could be argued, as Henry Mintzburg does, that a company produces two outputs: goods and services, and the social consequences of its activities, such as pollution.

One major development in the area of corporate citizenship is the **environmental report.** While this is not a legal requirement, a large number of UK FTSE 100 companies produce them. Worldwide there are around 20 award schemes for environmental reporting, notably the ACCA's.

Mineral plc shows that it is responsible with regard to the environment by disclosing the following information.

(i)   The use of the **eco-productivity index** in the financial performance of sites and divisions. This links environmental and financial performance

(ii)   The **regeneration of old plants**

(ii)   The development of **eco-friendly cars**. Particularly impressive, if successful, is the project to develop a new aluminium alloy car body. Aluminium is rust-free, and it is also lighter, which would reduce fuel consumption.

Another environmental issue which the company could consider is **emission levels** from factories. Many companies now include details of this in their environmental report.

The other main aspect of corporate citizenship where Mineral plc scores highly is in its **treatment of its workforce.** The company sees the workforce as the key factor in the growth of its business. The car industry had a reputation in the past for **restrictive practices,** and the annual report could usefully discuss the extent to which these have been eliminated.

Employees of a businesses are **stakeholders** in that business, along with shareholders and customers. A company wishing to demonstrate good corporate citizenship will therefore be concerned with **employee welfare.** Accordingly, the annual report might usefully contain information on details of working hours, industrial accidents and sickness of employees.

In conclusion, it can be seen that the annual report can, and should go **far beyond the financial statements** and traditional ratio analysis.

Question 2

Marking scheme

				Marks
(a)	Start-up costs		5	
	Financial assets		4	
	Overseas subsidiary		5	
	Associate		5	
		Available	19	
		Maximum		17
(b)	Start-up costs		2	
	Financial assets		3	
	Overseas subsidiary		2	
	Associate		3	
		Available	10	
		Maximum		8
		Available	29	
		Maximum		25

(a) (i) **New management company**

Dietronic has recognised **start up costs** of £400,000 as goodwill, despite the fact that **only a 'notional acquisition'** has taken place. In effect, the company has **recognised internally generated goodwill**, which is **prohibited** by FRS 10 *Goodwill and intangible assets*. It is difficult to justify this treatment, which will **increase reported profits**. This is because the costs will be **amortised** through the profit and loss account over four years, **rather than written off immediately**. UITF Abstract 24 *Accounting for start up costs* states that start up costs should be accounted for on a **basis consistent with similar costs incurred as part of the entity's ongoing activities** or on a basis consistent with other costs that do not meet the criteria for recognition as assets. The start up costs are **administrative** and this suggests that they must be treated as an **expense**. Therefore there is an **additional expense of £300,000** (£400,000 less the £100,000 already included in the profit and loss account as amortisation).

The employee share ownership trust (ESOP trust) holds assets on behalf of employees and these should be treated as **assets of the property management company** (as the sponsoring company), but they **cannot be included in the consolidated balance sheet** because the shares are **not assets of the group**. Therefore the shares must be removed from the balance sheet. This **reduces current assets by £40,000** (20,000 × £2) and **minority interest is also reduced by £40,000**.

(ii)   **Dairy**

The directors have carried out a **fair value exercise** that **reduced the carrying value** of the financial assets **shortly before selling them at a profit**. This appears to be a **deliberate attempt to enhance profits on disposal**. The fair value exercise took place when Dairy was acquired, so **FRS 7 *Fair values in acquisition accounting* should have been applied**. As the shares were unquoted, they should have been valued at the amount that they could have been sold at in an arm's length transaction between informed and willing parties. The **subsequent sale proceeds** two months after the valuation probably **provide the most reliable evidence** of the fair value of the shares at the date of acquisition. Therefore the investments should be **valued at this amount** rather than at the directors' valuation.

Therefore in the balance sheet:

- **Goodwill is reduced by £280,000** (1,000,000 – 600,000 × 70%).
- **Goodwill amortisation is reduced by £140,000** (280,000 × 2/4)
- **The profit and loss account reserve is reduced by £140,000**

In the profit and loss account:

- **Interest income is reduced by £400,000**
- **Minority interest is reduced by £120,000** (400,000 × 30%)
- **Amortisation expense is reduced by £70,000** (280,000 × ¼)

(iii) **Sale of German subsidiary**

FRS 23 *The effects of changes in foreign exchange rates* states that when the financial statements of a foreign operation are translated to a presentation currency the **resulting exchange differences are recognised in equity** (in reserves and in the statement of total recognised gains and losses for the year). On **disposal** of the subsidiary, these **exchange differences should be 'recycled'** and **recognised in the profit and loss account**. This means that the calculation of the gain on sale should be as follows:

	£'000
Sale proceeds	400
Net assets sold	(360)
Exchange reserve	(40)
Dividend receivable (48,000 ÷ 1.6)	30
	30

Note: because the subsidiary was set up by Dietronic, rather than acquired, there is **no goodwill.**

There is also an **exchange gain on retranslation of the dividend:**

	£'000
Dividend receivable (48,000 ÷ 1.6)	30
Dividend received (48,000 ÷ 1.5)	32
	2

(iv)   **Associate (Diet)**

The results and net assets of the associate are **not immaterial** and **should be included** in the consolidated financial statements.

The carrying value of the investment at 30 November 20X3 is:

	£'000	£'000
Cost of investment		2,100
Loss for year (25% × 680 × 6/12)		(85)
Less goodwill amortised:		
Cost of investment	2,100	
Fair value of net assets acquired (25% × 6.8)	(1,700)	
	400	
Amortisation charge (400 × ¼)		(100)
		1,915

FRS 9 *Associates and joint ventures* states that investors should account for their share of a loss making associate even though there is no obligation to make good the deficit.

The fact that the company has **incurred losses** suggests that an **impairment review** is necessary. This involves comparing the **carrying amount with the recoverable amount**, which is the **higher of net realisable value** and **value in use**. **Net realisable value** is the **anticipated selling price** of £1.8 million. **Value in use** could be calculated as the **cash flows expected from the dividends over the next five years**: £822,510 (7.6 million × 25% × 10p × 4.329). To this would need to be **added** the **net realisable value in five years time**, which is unknown. Therefore **net realisable value should be taken as the recoverable amount** and the **impairment loss is £115,000**. The investment in the associate is **written down to £1.8 million**.

(b)   DIETRONIC GROUP
        PROFIT AND LOSS ACCOUNT FOR THE YEAR ENDED 30 NOVEMBER 20X3

	Original £'000	(i) £'000	(ii) £'000	(iii) £'000	(iv) £'000	Amended £'000
Group operating profit	13,000	(300)				12,700
Share of losses in associate					(85)	(85)
Amortisation of goodwill			70		(100)	(30)
Interest income	940		(400)			540
Profit on sale of subsidiary	100			(70)		30
Impairment loss					(115)	(115)
Exchange gain				2		2
Profit before tax	14,040					13,042
Income tax expense	(5,000)					(5,000)
Profit for the year	9,040					8,042
Minority interests	(3,000)		120			(2,880)
	6,040					5,162

BALANCE SHEET AT 30 NOVEMBER 20X3

	Original £'000	(i) £'000	(ii) £'000	(iii) £'000	(iv) £'000	Amended £'000
Tangible fixed assets	18,500				(2,100)	16,400
Investment in associate					2,015	
					(100)	
					(115)	1,800
Goodwill	1,500	(300)	(280)			
			140			1,060
Current assets	8,000	(40)		2		7,962
Current liabilities	(4,000)					(4,000)
Long-term debt	(3,000)					(3,000)
	21,000					20,222
Share capital	5,000					5,000
Reserves	10,000	(300)	(280)	2	(85)	
			140		(100)	
					(115)	9,262
Minority interest	6,000	(40)				5,960
	21,000					20,222

Question 3

Top tips. In this question you were required to discuss the issues and implications of changes in accounting practice, and accounting for provisions for a company. Make sure that you are able to distinguish between a change in an accounting policy and a change in an accounting estimate. Remember that the provision for the costs of the court case needs to be discounted.

Easy marks. In Part (a) there are easy marks for rote knowledge of FRS 18, which you should know as it has fairly recently been examined.

Examiner's comment. The question was relatively straightforward but candidates seemed to struggle to identify the fundamental issues in the case presented to them.

Marking scheme

				Marks
(a)	FRS 18 explanation		4	
	Cost centres		6	
		Available	10	
		Maximum		9
(b)	Hardware		3	
	Revenue recognition		3	
		Available/maximum		6
(c)	Provisions	Available	8	
		Maximum		7
(d)	Going concern	Available/maximum		3
	Report		2	
		Available		29
		Maximum		25

REPORT

To: Directors of Gear Software
From:
Subject: Implications of various transactions for the financial statements for the year ended 31 May 20X3
Date: June 20X3

As requested, I explain below the implications of several transactions for the financial statements.

One general point worth noting is that the company cannot apply the Financial Reporting Standard for Smaller Entities (FRSSE), as it does not qualify as a 'small company' as defined by the Companies Act. Although the number of employees is less than 50, both turnover and balance sheet total exceed the limits. Companies must satisfy two or more of the size criteria in order to be eligible to adopt the FRSSE. In addition, the company is a plc.

(a)   **Cost centres**

FRS 18 *Accounting policies* distinguishes between changes in accounting policy and changes in estimation techniques. A change to an accounting policy involves a change in the way in which an item is recognised, measured or presented.

The indirect overhead costs are directly attributable to the two cost centres and are included in the stock valuation in the balance sheet. The only change has been a change to the way in which the costs are allocated. There have been **no changes to the way in which they are recognised, measured or presented**. This change is **not a change in accounting policy**, but a **change in an estimation technique**.

Direct labour and overhead costs were previously carried forward as work in progress and included in the balance sheet as part of stocks. They are now written off to profit and loss as they are incurred. There has been a change in the way in which these costs are recognised and presented and therefore there is a **change in accounting policy**.

Overhead costs relating to the sale of computer games were previously included in cost of sales and are now included in distribution costs. There has been a **change in the way in which these costs are presented** and again, there has been a **change in accounting policy**.

FRS 18 states that an entity's accounting policies should be **reviewed regularly** to ensure that they remain the **most appropriate to its particular circumstances** for the purpose of giving a true and fair view. However, accounting policies **should not be changed unless the benefit to users outweighs the disadvantages**. Changes to accounting policies make it more difficult for users to compare an entity's financial statements with those for earlier periods.

FRS 3 *Reporting financial performance* requires a change in accounting policy to be recognised **retrospectively**, by making a **prior period adjustment**. The opening balance of reserves is adjusted and comparative figures are restated. FRS 18 requires **details** of changes to accounting policies, including the **reason** why the new accounting policy is thought more appropriate and the **effect** of a prior period adjustment on the financial statements for the **current and prior period**. Therefore the company would normally be required to **disclose** the **effect of the write off** of the development costs on the current year's profit and loss account. Where it is **not practicable** to disclose the effect of a change, **that fact, together with the reasons**, should be stated.

FRS 18 states that a change in estimation technique should not normally be accounted for as a prior period adjustment. The effect of the change in allocating overheads should be **included in the profit and loss account for the current period.**

(b)   **Computer hardware and revenue on contracts**

FRS 15 *Tangible fixed assets* **allows the capitalisation of finance costs** where these are **directly attributable** to the construction of tangible fixed assets. There is a change to the way in which the interest is recognised and presented and therefore there is a **further change in accounting policy.**

The change in the method of depreciation is a **change in an estimation technique**, rather than a change in accounting policy. However, there has also been a **change in the way in which depreciation is presented** in the financial statements and this *is* **a change in accounting policy**.

The requirements of FRS 3 and FRS 18 will again apply. The accounting policy changes must be **applied retrospectively** by means of a prior period adjustment and details of the changes **must be disclosed**.

It is proposed to change the way in which contract revenue is recognised. FRS 18 states that an entity should **judge the appropriateness of its accounting policies** to its particular circumstances **against the objectives of relevance, reliability, comparability and understandability**. Accounting policies **should be consistent with the requirements of applicable accounting standards and UITF Abstracts**. Depending on the exact circumstances, both the company's current accounting policy (recognising revenue as a contract progresses) and the proposed accounting policy (recognising revenue when the product is shipped to customers) may be appropriate. There is no conflict with the general principle in FRS 5 *Reporting the substance of transactions*, which is that an entity recognises revenue when it has performed under the contract. Because the proposed new policy is standard practice in the industry, the **comparability of the company's financial statements would be improved** and therefore the company **should change to the new policy**. Another advantage of adopting this policy is that turnover would increase and this is particularly important given that significant provisions may have to be recognised (see below). Again, the **accounting and disclosure requirements of FRS 18 apply** when accounting for and disclosing the change.

(c) **Provisions**

FRS 12 *Provisions, contingent liabilities and contingent assets* states that a provision should only be recognised if:

(a)   there is a **present obligation** as a result of a **past event**; and

(b)   it is **probable** (more likely than not) that a **transfer of economic benefits** will be required to settle the obligation; and

(c)   a **reliable estimate** can be made of the **amount** of the obligation.

In the case of the disputed invoice, the company's solicitors apparently do not believe that any further sums will be payable. On this basis, **no provision should be recognised**, but the company has a **contingent liability**. Information about the contingent liability should be **disclosed** in the financial statements, including the estimated financial effects and any uncertainties relating to the amount or timing of any outflow.

In contrast, it does appear that the company has a present obligation as a result of the plagiarism case and that payment is probable. A **provision should be recognised**. FRS 12 states that the amount recognised should be the **best estimate of the expenditure required to settle the obligation at the balance sheet date**. The estimate should **take the various possible outcomes into account** and the amount should be **discounted to present value** if the time value of money is material.

The **most likely outcome** is a **payment of £1 million in two years time**, which suggests a discounted amount of **£907,000** (£1 million × 0.907). It is also possible to calculate an amount **based on expected outcomes**:

	£
Best case (500,000 × 0.952 × 30%)	142,800
Most likely (1,000,000 × 0.907 × 60%)	544,200
Worst case (2,000,000 × 0.864 × 10%)	172,800
	859,800

The difference between this amount and the most likely outcome is not material in the context of the financial statements (considering that the amounts are based on estimates) and therefore a **provision of £860,000 should be recognised**.

(d) **Going concern**

FRS 18 states that an entity **should prepare its financial statements on a going concern basis** unless the directors either intend to liquidate the entity or to cease trading or have no realistic alternative but to do so. FRS 18 also states that management **should assess whether there are significant doubts about the entity's ability to continue as a going concern** and should **disclose any uncertainties** that cast significant doubt on this ability.

Therefore it **may be necessary to disclose** the fact that there are **concerns about the viability of the business**, should the worst outcome of the plagiarism case occur.

Question 4

Top tips. This question dealt with current corporate reporting practices of multinational companies and the potential impact on financial statements of a move from local GAAP to International Accounting Standards. Candidates were also expected to discuss the potential impact of the move from local GAAP to IAS in respect of certain accounting standards. An in depth knowledge of IAS was not required but simply a general knowledge of the impact of a move to IAS on financial statements.

Examiner's comment. Candidates answered the question quite well, seemingly being well prepared for this type of question. The question asked for a report to be written but many candidates did not take into account that this was a report suitable for presentation to the directors of the company and included irrelevant technical information which was not suitable for 'presentation to the directors'. Knowledge of the use of GAAP reconciliations by companies was generally quite poor. On the move from local GAAP to IAS/IFRS, the answers seemed to indicate that candidates needed to spend more time studying the implications of the move to IAS for UK companies. Candidates again seemed to find this element of the question quite difficult. The problem seemed to be centred around the ability to compare and synthesise information about alternate GAAPs.

Marking scheme

		Marks
(a)	Introduction	2
	Dual financial statements and reconciliation	3
	Mixed GAAP	1
	Local GAAP	1
	Reconciliation with IFRS	1
	Conclusions – variety	1
(b)	US GAAP accounts	3
(c)	Reconciliations	4
	Disclosure	2
(d)	Potential impact	11
	Style etc	3
	Available	32
	Maximum	25

Note: One of the purposes of this question was to assess candidates' ability to write a report to directors in language which is easily interpreted by the directors.

REPORT

To: Directors of Autol plc

From:

Subject: International convergence and financial reporting practice

Date: December 20X2

I set out below the information and advice that you have requested.

(a)   **Current reporting practices used by multi-national companies**

International convergence has become important largely because **business has become multi-national**. Users of financial statements (including stock exchanges and regulatory authorities) need to be able to **compare financial statements prepared in different countries**. However, a variety of different GAAPs are still in use.

In some countries, such as the UK, companies are required to **prepare and file financial statements under local GAAP**, but may then provide a **second set of financial statements in another GAAP** or a reconciliation to another GAAP. This may be required if the company has a foreign parent or if it is listed on a foreign stock exchange. In other countries, companies may be able to **choose between one or more GAAPs**, for example between local GAAP and IAS/IFRS.

Many multi-national companies adopt US GAAP. This is often seen as the **most rigorous system** and therefore companies believe that it will give their financial statements greater credibility than other GAAPs. **US GAAP gives access to the US capital markets, which still require a reconciliation from local GAAP to US GAAP.**

IAS/IFRS is rapidly gaining credibility and is now adopted by many European companies following the issue of the EU Regulation. It has the advantage for preparers that **many international standards allow a choice between 'benchmark treatment' and 'allowed alternative treatment'**. This means that **IAS/IFRS can still produce differing results** depending on which of the permitted treatments is adopted. This is a disadvantage for users, but **future international standards will not allow alternative treatments**. IAS/IFRS is expected to become much more rigorous in future.

The choice of GAAP normally reflects a company's operating environment or the capital markets in which it is listed (or is seeking a listing). For example, a UK company with operations in Hong Kong may reconcile UK GAAP to US GAAP and disclose the effect of different accounting treatments under UK GAAP and Hong Kong GAAP. It is also possible for companies to mix different GAAPs. For example, a company which operates in both the UK and the Netherlands might adopt accounting policies that comply with applicable UK and Dutch GAAP.

A variety of practices are in use, but in practice US GAAP remains the most popular choice with companies seeking access to international capital markets.

(b)   **Preparation of US GAAP financial statements**

It would be difficult for a UK based company to prepare a single set of consolidated financial statements under US GAAP. **UK companies are required to file financial statements with the Registrar of Companies; these must comply with UK GAAP, including the Companies Act 1985.** It is unlikely that US GAAP financial statements would be acceptable for this purpose. The shareholders are also entitled to receive a full set of financial statements prepared under UK GAAP.

The best course of action would be to prepare a statement reconciling UK GAAP to US GAAP. It would also be possible to prepare dual financial statements, but the cost of this might outweigh the benefits.

(c)   **Problems relating to the use of GAAP reconciliations**

Because full international convergence is unlikely in the short term, GAAP reconciliations will probably be used for many years to come. The UK and the IASB are committed to convergence, and **from 2005 onwards**

IAS/IFRS will be used throughout the EU. However, convergence of US GAAP and IAS/IFRS will be much more difficult to achieve.

The use of GAAP reconciliations is **not controlled by regulation**. For example, in many cases the auditors do not have to report on their truth and fairness. This may **reduce the credibility of the information provided.**

This also means that **companies may disclose the information in different ways**. Most companies show the reconciliation as a single note or in an Appendix, but in some cases the information appears in several different places in the financial statements and can be difficult to follow.

Some companies provide detailed information which may include summary performance statements, balance sheets, cash flow information and even non-financial disclosures and narrative discussion of the differences. Others only provide a reconciliation of profit or a reconciliation of shareholders' funds.

(d)   **Potential impact of compliance with IAS/IFRS**

The change from UK GAAP to international standards may have a significant effect on the company's reported profits. The four areas are discussed in turn below.

(i)   *Deferred tax*

FRS 19 *Deferred tax* and the equivalent IAS both require full provision for deferred tax. However, the IAS requires the calculation of the liability to be based on temporary differences, rather than timing differences (as required by FRS 19). This means that the deferred tax provision is likely to be higher under the IAS and reported profit will be reduced.

(ii)   *Development expenditure*

Under SSAP 13 *Accounting for research and development* companies may either write off development expenditure as it is incurred or recognise it as an intangible asset and amortise it over the period in which the new product or service is sold. Autol currently writes off development expenditure immediately. **The relevant IAS requires capitalisation and amortisation,** provided certain criteria are met. The change will affect the timing of the charge to the profit and loss account, rather than the amount. Expenditure will be matched with the revenue that it produces and **reported results may be less volatile.**

(iii)   *Retirement benefits*

FRS 17 *Retirement benefits* requires actuarial gains and losses to be recognised immediately in the statement of total recognised gains and losses, so there is no effect on reported results. **The IAS requires actuarial gains and losses to be recognised in the profit and loss account**. However, they need not be recognised immediately, but **may be deferred and recognised over the average remaining working lives of the employees. The change to IAS will reduce reported profit, but the degree to which results are affected will depend on the accounting policy adopted.**

(iv)   *Merger accounting*

FRS 6 *Acquisitions and mergers* **limits the use of merger accounting to situations in which there is a genuine merger**. However, IFRS 3 *Business combinations* outlaws 'uniting of interests' accounting, ie merger accounting altogether, so the combination will have to be accounted for as an acquisition.

I hope that this answers your queries. Please do not hesitate to contact me should you require any further information or assistance.

ACCA

Paper P2

Corporate Reporting (United Kingdom)

Mock Examination 2

Question Paper	
Time allowed	
Reading and planning	**15 minutes**
Writing	**3 hours**
This paper is divided into two sections	
Section A	**ONE compulsory question to be attempted**
Section B	**TWO questions ONLY to be attempted**

DO NOT OPEN THIS PAPER UNTIL YOU ARE READY TO START UNDER EXAMINATION CONDITIONS

SECTION A – This ONE question is compulsory and MUST be attempted

Question 1

Lateral, a public limited company acquired two subsidiary companies. Think and Plank, both public limited companies. The details of the acquisitions are as follows.

Subsidiary	Date of acquisition	Profit and loss reserve at acquisition £m	Ordinary share capital acquired £1 shares	Fair value of net assets at acquisition £m
Think	1 November 20X3	150	200	400
Plank	1 November 20X3	210	300	800

The draft balance sheets as at 31 October 20X5 are:

	Lateral £m	Think £m	Plank £m
Assets			
Fixed assets			
Land and buildings	200	190	300
Plant and machinery	500	200	480
Investments in subsidiaries			
Think	380		
Plank	340		
Held to maturity investments	30	–	–
	1,450	390	780
Current assets			
Stock	200	185	90
Debtors	170	80	100
Cash	40	30	50
	410	295	240
Fixed assets classified as held for sale		15	
		310	
Current liabilities	(360)	(110)	(150)
Net current assets	50	200	90
Creditors falling due after more than one year	(250)	(60)	(80)
Net assets	1,250	530	790
Equity and liabilities			
Share capital – ordinary shares of £1	400	250	500
Profit and loss account	850	280	290
Capital employed	1,250	530	790

The following information is relevant to the preparation of the group financial statements.

(i)   There have been no new issues of shares in the group since 1 November 20X3 and the fair value adjustments have not been included in the subsidiaries' financial records.

(ii)   Any increase in the fair values of the net assets over their carrying values at acquisition is attributable to plant and machinery. Plant and machinery is depreciated at 20% per annum on the reducing balance basis.

(iii)   Think sold plant and machinery to Lateral on 12 November 20X5. The transaction was completed at an agreed price of £15 million after selling costs. The transaction complies with the conditions in FRED 32 *Disposal of non-current assets and presentation of discontinued operations* for disclosure as assets 'held for sale'. The fixed assets had been valued at 'fair value less costs to sell' in the individual accounts of Think. At 1 November 20X4, this plant and machinery had a carrying value of £10 million and no depreciation on these assets has been charged to the year ended 31 October 20X5.

(iv) Lateral had purchased a debt instrument with five years remaining to maturity on 1 November 20X3. The purchase price and fair value was £30 million on that date. The instrument will be repaid in five years time at an amount of £37.5 million. The instrument carried fixed interest of 4.7% per annum on the principal of £37.5 million and has an effective interest rate of 10% per annum. The fixed interest has been received and accounted for but no accounting entry has been made other than the recognition of the original purchase price of the instrument. The group wishes to use FRS 26 *Financial instruments: measurement* to account for this instrument.

(v) Goodwill arising on the acquisition of Plank was impairment tested on 31 October 20X4 and no amortisation for the year was charged. On 31 October 20X4 an impairment loss of £28 million was recognised for Plank but no indication of impairment has arisen to date for Think. Plank is an income generating unit in its own right. At 31 October 20X5, the impairment loss of £28 million had partially reversed, and the company proposed to write back to goodwill the reversal of £12 million. The event which caused the impairment was government legislation relating to the markets in which Plank operates. This law was still in place at 31 October 20X5. Goodwill is amortised over four years.

(vi) On 31 October 20X5, after the accounting entries for goodwill had occurred, Lateral sold 100 million shares in Plank for £180 million. Lateral still maintains significant influence over Plank after the disposal of the shares. The receipt of the sale proceeds has been recorded in the cash book and as a reduction in the carrying value of the cost of the investment in the subsidiary.

Required

(a) Calculate the gain or loss that would be recorded in the group profit and loss account on the sale of the shares in Plank.
(6 marks)

(b) Prepare a consolidated balance sheet as at 31 October 20X5 for the Lateral Group in accordance with UK accounting standards.
(22 marks)

(c) In the year ended 31 October 20X6, Lateral entered into a contract to purchase plant and machinery from a foreign supplier on 30 June 20X7. The purchase price is $4 million. A non-refundable deposit of $1 million was paid on signing the contract on 31 July 20X6 with the balance of $3 million payable on 30 June 20X7. Lateral was uncertain as to whether to purchase a $3 million bond on 31 July 20X6 which will not mature until 30 June 20Y0, or to enter into a forward contract on the same date to purchase $3 million for a fixed price of £2 million on 30 June 20X7 and to designate the forward contract as a cash flow hedge of the purchase commitment. The bond carries interest at 4% per annum payable on 30 June 20X7. Current market rates are 4% per annum. The company chose to purchase the bond with a view to selling it on 30 June 20X7 in order to purchase the plant and machinery. The bond is not to be classified as a cash flow hedge but at fair value through profit or loss.

Lateral would like advice as to whether it made the correct decision and as to the accounting treatment of the items for 20X6 and 20X7. The company's functional and presentational currency is the pound sterling.
(12 marks)

	Dollar:£	Average rate ($:£) for year to
31 July 20X6	1.6	
31 October 20X6	1.3	1.5

(d) Lateral discloses the following information relating to employees in its financial statements.

(i) Its full commitment to equal opportunities
(ii) Its investment in the training of staff
(iii) The number of employees injured at work each year.

The company wishes to enhance disclosure in these areas, but is unsure as to what the benefits would be. The directors are particularly concerned that the disclosures on management of the workforce (human capital management) has no current value to the stakeholders of the company.

Discuss the general nature of the current information disclosed by companies concerning 'human capital management' and how the link between the company performance and its employees could be made more visible.
(10 marks)
(Total marks = 50)

Section B – TWO questions ONLY to be attempted

Question 2

Barking, an unlisted company, operates in the house building and commercial property investment development sector. The sector has seen an upturn in activity during recent years and the directors have been considering future plans with a view to determining their impact on the financial statements for the financial year to 30 November 20X4.

(a)   Barking wishes to obtain a stock exchange listing in the year to 30 November 20X4. It is to be acquired by Ash, a significantly smaller listed company in a share for share exchange whereby Barking will receive sufficient voting shares of Ash to control the new group. Due to the relative values of the company, Barking will become the majority shareholder with 80% of the enlarged capital of Ash. The executive management of the new group will be that of Barking.

As part of the purchase consideration, Ash will issue zero dividend preference shares of £1 to the shareholders of Barking on 30 June 20X4. These will be redeemed on 1 January 20X5 at £1.10 per share. Additionally Ash will issue convertible interest free loan notes. The loan notes are unlikely to be repaid on 30 November 20X5 (the redemption date) as the conversion terms are very favourable. The management of Ash have excluded the redemption of the loan notes from their cash flow projections. The loan notes are to be included in long term liabilities in the balance sheet of Ash. As part of the business combination Ash will change its name to Barking plc.   **(9 marks)**

(b)   The acquisition will also have other planned effects on the company. Barking operates a defined benefit pension scheme. On acquisition the scheme will be frozen and replaced by a group defined contribution scheme, and as a result no additional benefits in the old scheme will accrue to the employees. Ash's employees are also in a defined benefit scheme but it has been impossible in the past on a consistent and reasonable basis to identify the underlying assets and liabilities in the scheme. After acquisition, Ash's employees will be transferred to the group's defined contribution scheme, with the previous scheme being frozen.   **(5 marks)**

(c)   As a result of the acquisition the company will change the way in which it recognises sales of residential properties. It used to treat such properties as sold when the building work was substantially complete, defined as being when the roof and internal walls had been completed. The new policy will be to recognise a sale when a refundable deposit for the sale of the property has been received and the building work is physically complete. Legal costs incurred on the sale of the property are currently capitalised and shown as current assets until the sale of the property has occurred. Further it has been decided by the directors that as at 30 November 20X4, the financial year end, some properties held as trading properties of both companies would be moved from the trading portfolio to the investment portfolio of the holding company.   **(7 marks)**

(d)   The directors intend to carry out an impairment review as at 30 November 20X4 in order to ascertain whether the carrying amount of goodwill and other fixed assets can be supported by their value in use. The plan is to produce cash flow projections up to 20Y4 with an average discount rate of 15% being used in the calculations. The ten year period is to be used as it reflects fairly the long term nature of the assets being assessed. Any subsequent impairment loss is to be charged against the profit and loss account.   **(4 marks)**

Required

Draft a report to the directors of Barking, setting out the financial reporting implications of the above plans for the financial statements for the year to 30 November 20X4.

(Total = 25 marks)

Question 3

The Gow Group, a public limited company, and Glass, a public limited company, have agreed to create a new entity, York, a limited liability company on 31 October 20X6. The companies' line of business is the generation, distribution, and supply of energy. Gow supplies electricity and Glass supplies gas to customers. Each company has agreed to subscribe net assets for a 50% share in the equity capital of York. York is to issue 30 million ordinary shares of £1. There was no written agreement signed by Gow and Glass but the minutes of the meeting where the creation of the new company was discussed have been approved formally by both companies. Each company provides equal numbers of directors to the Board of Directors. The net assets of York were initially shown at amounts agreed between Gow and Glass, but their values are to be adjusted so that the carrying amounts at 31 October 20X6 are based on UK accounting standards.

Gow had contributed the following assets to the new company in exchange for its share of the equity:

	£m
Cash	1
Debtors – Race	7
Intangible assets – contract with Race	3
Land and buildings	6
Plant and machinery	3
	20

The above assets form an income generating unit (an electricity power station) in its own right. The unit provided power to a single customer, Race. On 31 October 20X6 Race went into receivership and the contract to provide power to Race was cancelled. On 1 December 20X6, the receivers of the customer provisionally agreed to pay a final settlement figure of £5 million on 31 October 20X7, including any compensation for the loss of the contract. Gow expects York will receive 80% of the provisional amount. On hearing of the cancelled contract, an offer was received for the power station of £16 million. York would be required to pay the disposal costs estimated at £1 million.

The power station has an estimated remaining useful life of four years at 31 October 20X6. It has been agreed with the government that it will be dismantled on 31 October 20Y0. The cost at 31 October 20Y0 of dismantling the power station is estimated at £5 million.

The directors of Gow and York are currently in the final stages of negotiating a contract to supply electricity to another customer. As a result the future net cash inflows (undiscounted) expected to arise from the income generating unit (power station) are as follows:

	£m
31 October 20X7	6
31 October 20X8	7
31 October 20X9	8
31 October 20Y0	8
	29

The dismantling cost has not been provided for, and future cash flows are discounted at 6% by the companies.

Glass had agreed to contribute the following net assets to the new company in exchange for its share of the equity:

	£m
Cash	10
Intangible asset	2
Stock at cost	6
Buildings – carrying value	4
Lease receivable	1
Lease payable	(3)
	20

The buildings contributed by Glass are held on a 10 year finance lease which was entered into on 31 October 20X0. The buildings are being depreciated over the life of the lease on the straight line basis. As from 31 October 20X6, the terms of the lease have been changed and the lease will be terminated early on 31 October 20X8 in exchange for a payment of £1 million on 31 October 20X6 and a further two annual payments of £600,000. The first annual payment under the revised terms will be on 31 October 20X7. York will vacate the buildings on 31 October 20X8 and the revised lease qualifies as a finance lease. The cash paid on 31 October 20X6 is shown as a lease receivable and the change in the lease terms is not reflected in the values placed on the net assets above. The effective interest rate of the lease is 7%.

Glass had entered into a contract with an agency whereby for every new domestic customer that the agency gained, the agency received a fixed fee. On the formation of York, the contract was terminated and the agency received £500,000 as compensation for the termination of the contract. This cost is shown as an intangible asset above as the directors feel that it represents the economic benefits related to the future reduced cost of gaining retail customers. Additionally, on 31 October 20X6, a contract was signed whereby York was to supply gas at fair value to a major retailer situated overseas over a four year period. On signing the contract, the retailer paid a non refundable cash deposit of £1.5 million which was included in the cash contributed by Glass. The retailer is under no obligation to buy gas from York but York cannot supply gas to any other company in that country. The directors intend to show this deposit in the profit and loss account when the first financial statements of York are produced. At present, the deposit is shown as a deduction from intangible assets in the above statement of net assets contributed by Glass.

(All calculations should be made to 1 decimal place and assume the cash flows relating to the income generating unit (electricity power station) arise at the year end.)

Required

(a) Discuss the nature and accounting treatment of the relationship between Gow, Glass and York. **(5 marks)**

(b) Prepare the balance sheet of York at 31 October 20X6, using UK accounting standards, discussing the nature of the accounting treatments selected, the adjustments made and the values placed on the items in the balance sheet. **(20 marks)**

(Total = 25 marks)

Question 4

Jones and Cousin, a public quoted company, operate in twenty-seven different countries and earn revenue and incur costs in several currencies. The group develops, manufactures and markets products in the medical sector. The growth of the group has been achieved by investment and acquisition. It is organised into three global business units which manage their sales in international markets, and take full responsibility for strategy and business performance. Only five per cent of the business is in the country of incorporation (UK). Competition in the sector is quite fierce.

The group competes across a wide range of geographic and product markets and encourages its subsidiaries to enhance local communities by reinvestment of profits in local educational projects. The group's share of revenue in a market sector is often determined by government policy. The markets contain a number of different competitors including specialised and large international corporations. At present the group is awaiting regulatory approval for a range of new products to grow its market share. The group lodges its patents for products and enters into legal proceedings where necessary to protect patents. The products are sourced from a wide range of suppliers, who, once approved both from a qualitative and ethical perspective, are generally given a long term contract for the supply of goods. Obsolete products are disposed of with concern for the environment and the health of its customers, with reusable materials normally being used. The industry is highly regulated in terms of medical and environmental laws and regulations. The products normally carry a low health risk.

The Group has developed a set of corporate and social responsibility principles during the period which is the responsibility of the Board of Directors. The Managing Director manages the risks arising from corporate and social responsibility issues. The group wishes to retain and attract employees and follows policies which ensure equal opportunity for all the employees. Employees are informed of management policies, and regularly receive in-house training.

The Group enters into contracts for fixed rate currency swaps and uses floating to fixed rate interest rate swaps. The cash flow effects of these swaps match the cash flows on the underlying financial instruments. All financial instruments are accounted for as cash flow hedges. A significant amount of trading activity is denominated in the Dinar and the Euro. The pound sterling is its functional currency.

Required

(a)   Describe the principles behind the Operating and Financial Review discussing whether the review should be mandatory or whether directors should be free to use their judgement as to what should be included in such a statement.   **(13 marks)**

(b)   Draft a report suitable for inclusion in an Operating and Financial Review for Jones and Cousin which deals with:

   (i)   The principal risks and relationships of the business   **(9 marks)**
   (ii)   The position of the business regarding its treasury policies.   **(3 marks)**

(Marks will be awarded in part (b) for the identification and discussion of relevant points and for the style of the report.)

(Total = 25 marks)

Answers

DO NOT TURN THIS PAGE UNTIL YOU HAVE
COMPLETED THE MOCK EXAM

A PLAN OF ATTACK

Managing your nerves

As you turn the pages to start this exam a number of thoughts are likely to cross your mind. At best, examinations cause anxiety so it is important to stay focused on your task for the next three hours! Developing an awareness of what is going on emotionally within you may help you manage your nerves. Remember, you are unlikely to banish the flow of adrenaline, but the key is to harness it to help you work steadily and quickly through your answers.

Working through this mock exam will help you develop the exam stamina you will need to keep going for three hours.

Managing your time

Planning and time management are two of the key skills which complement the technical knowledge you need to succeed. To keep yourself on time, do not be afraid to jot down your target completion times for each question, perhaps next to the title of the question on the paper.

Focusing on scoring marks

When completing written answers, remember to communicate the critical points, which represent marks, and avoid padding and waffle. Sometimes it is possible to analyse a long sentence into more than one point. Always try to maximise the mark potential of what you write.

As you read through the questions, jot down on the question paper, any points you think you might forget. There is nothing more upsetting than coming out of an exam having forgotten to write a point you knew!

Also remember you can only score marks for what is on paper; you must write down enough to help the examiner to give you marks!

Structure and signpost your answers

To help you answer the examiner's requirements, highlight as you read through the paper the key words and phrases in the examiner's requirements.

Also, where possible try to use headings and subheadings, to give a logical and easy-to-follow structure to your response. A well structured and signposted answer is more likely to convince the examiner that you know your subject.

Your approach

This paper has two sections. The first section contains one question which is compulsory. The second has three questions and you must answer two of them.

You have a choice.

- Read through and answer the Section A question before moving on to Section B
- Go through Section B and select the two questions you will attempt. Then go back and answer the question in Section A first
- Select the two questions in Section B, answer them and then go back to Section A

You will have fifteen minutes before the start of the exam to go through the questions you are going to do.

Time spent at the start of each question confirming the requirements and producing a plan for the answers is time well spent.

Question selection

When selecting the two questions from Section B make sure that you read through all of the requirements. It is painful to answer part (a) of a question and then realise that parts (b) and (c) are beyond you, by then it is too late to change your mind and do another question.

When reviewing the requirements look at how many marks have been allocated to each part. This will give you an idea of how detailed your answer must be.

Generally, you need to be aware of your strengths and weaknesses and select accordingly.

Doing the exam

Actually doing the exam is a personal experience. There is not a single *right way*. As long as you submit complete answers to question 1 and any two from questions 2 to 4 after the three hours are up, then your approach obviously works.

Looking through the paper

The compulsory case study question is, as will always be the case, on groups, in this case, disposal of a subsidiary. You also have some foreign currency transactions and a ten marker on human capital management. In Section B you have three questions on a variety of topics:

- Question 2 a wide ranging question covering the accounting implications of various policies.
- Question 3 is a multi-standard question, covering leasing, financial instruments, impairment and revenue recognition.
- Question 4 is on the management commentary.

You only have to answer three out of these four questions. You don't have to pick your optional questions right now, but this brief overview should have convinced you that you have enough choice and variety to have a respectable go at Section B. So let's go back to the compulsory question in Section A.

Compulsory question

Question 1 requires you to prepare a consolidated balance sheet for a group in which there has been a disposal. Additional complications are presentation of non-current assets held for sale, a debt instrument and an impairment loss. The key with this question, which you cannot avoid doing, is not to panic. There is a lot of number crunching, and you might not be able to complete the question. The thing to do is to set out your proformas and then patiently, but briskly, work through the workings, doing as much as you can. By using a strategy of picking the low hanging 'fruit' you could get 80% of the group aspects right which enables you to put 22 marks in the bank!

Optional questions

Deciding between the optional questions is obviously a personal matter – it depends how you have spent your study time.

One thing is clear – the optional questions all contain a discursive element and are all based around a scenario. The Examiner has said that the emphasis in this paper is on giving advice in a practical situation.

The secret is to plan your answer; break it down into bite sized subsections, clearly labelled to help your examiner to quickly conclude you understand the problem and have a logical answer.

Allocating your time

The golden rule is always allocate your time according to the marks for the question in total and for the parts of the question. But be sensible. If (for example) you have committed yourself to answering Question 5, but can think of nothing to say about fair value, you may be better off trying to pick up some extra marks on the questions you can do.

Afterwards

Don't be tempted to do a post mortem on the paper with your colleagues. It will only worry you and them and it's unlikely you'll be able to remember exactly what you wrote anyway. If you really can't resist going over the topics covered in the paper, allow yourself a maximum of half an hour's 'worry time', then put it out of your head! Relax as it's all out of your hands now!

Question 1

Top tips. In order to do Part (a) you need to work out the net assets of the investment disposed of. It is probably best to do the two parts together with a separate sheet for workings. In Part (c) try to break the transaction down into its components. The non-refundable deposit is the easiest aspect to deal with.

Easy marks. There are standard consolidation aspects in the calculation of goodwill and retained earnings. The question is constructed so that the basic consolidation calculations are not affected by the adjustments to the financial statements.

Examiner's comment (Part (a) only). Generally speaking the performance on this question was quite good.

The main problem areas were:

- Not adding back the sale proceeds of the shares to the cost of the investment in Plank. Candidates lost very few marks for this minor error. The only problem was that this error created 'negative goodwill' instead of positive goodwill.

- Candidates thought that, because Lateral still had significant influence over Plank after the disposal of shares, that Plank was still a subsidiary. Plank was in fact an associate. This error caused candidates many problems, not least the fact that they spent time consolidating an additional subsidiary.

- Candidates dealt quite well with the debt instrument. However many calculated the interest received based on the fair value and not on the principal amount. Again candidates only lost one mark for this error.

- The calculation of the group reserves was quite poor. The main reason was that this figure was dependent upon other calculations. That is the debt instrument, the post acquisition profit of the associate, the profit on the sale of shares and other adjustments. Thus errors earlier in the question would be compounded in this figure. Credit was given for the correct methodology even if the figures were inaccurate.

- The minority interest was normally calculated incorrectly as the profit and the depreciation on 'held for sale' assets was often not taken into account. Again marks were given if the principle used was sound.

Marking scheme

			Marks
(a)	Gain/loss on sale of shares		4
(b)	Plant and equipment		4
	Associate		4
	Investment		4
	Goodwill		7
	Sundry NCA		2
	Retained earnings		5
	Minority interest		2
(c)	Plant and machinery		
	Deposit		3
	Cash flow ledge		3
	Bond		3
	Forward contract		3
(d)	Nature of contract		
	Information		5
	Visibility		5
Available			54
Maximum			50

(a)   **Gain on the sale of shares in Plank**

	£m
Sale proceeds	180.0
Less: net assets disposed of (20% × 847.6) (W2)	(169.5)
Less goodwill not yet written off (100/300 × 8) (W3)	(2.7)
Profit on disposal	7.8

(b)   LATERAL GROUP
       CONSOLIDATED BALANCE SHEET AT 31 OCTOBER 20X5

	£m	£m
Fixed assets		
Intangible assets: goodwill (W2)		30
Tangible assets	390	
Plant and machinery (W6)	708	
		1,098
Investment in associate (W3)		344
Held to maturity investments (W8)		33
		1,505
Current assets		
Stocks	385	
Debtors	250	
Cash at bank and in hand	70	
	705	
Creditors: Amounts falling due within one year	(470)	
Net current assets		235
Total assets less current liabilities		1,740
Creditors: amounts falling due after more than one year		(310)
		1,430
Capital and reserves		
Share capital		400
Profit and loss account (W4)		925
		1,325
Minority interest (W5)		105
		1,430

Workings

1   *Group structure*

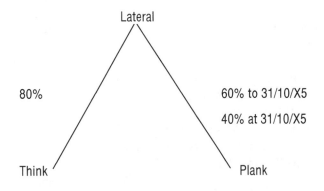

2   *Goodwill*

	Think		Plank	
	£m	£m	£m	£m
Cost of investment per individual balance sheets		380		340
Sale proceeds				180
Cost of combination		380		520
Less net assets acquired				
Share capital	250		500	
Profit and loss account	150		210	
Fair value adjustments	–		90	
	400		800	
Group share: 80%		(320)		
60%				(480)
		60		40
Impairment		–		(28)
		60		12
Amortisation (2/4)(1/3)		(30)		(4)
		30		8

Note. FRS 10 prohibits the reversal of impairment losses on goodwill unless the cause of the impairment has reversed. This is not the case here, because the government legislation is still in force.

3   *Investment in associate: Plank*

Net assets at balance sheet date:

	£m
Share capital	500.0
Profit and loss account	290.0
Fair value adjustments	90.0
Depreciation on fair value adjustment: (20% × 90) + (20% × 72)	(32.4)
	847.6

Investment in associate

	£m
Share of net assets at balance sheet date (40% × 847.6)	339.0
Add goodwill not yet written off (200/300 × 8)	5.3
	344.3

4   *Consolidated profit and loss account*

	Lateral	Think	Plank
	£m	£m	£m
At 31 October 20X5	850	280	290.0
At acquisition		(150)	(210.0)
		130	80.0
Additional depreciation on fair value adjustment (W3)			(32.4)
Profit on sale of shares in Plank to parent			
(180 – (100/300 × 520))	6.7		
Unrealised profit on 'held for sale' assets (15 – 10)		(5)	
Depreciation on 'held for sale' assets (10 × 20%)		(2)	
Gain on debt instrument (W7)	2.6		
	859.3	123	47.6
Share of Think (80% × 123)	98.4		
Share of Plank (40% × 47.6)	19.0		
Impairment of goodwill on Plank (200/300 × 28)	(18.7)		
Amortisation of goodwill: Think	(30.0)		
Plank: (200/300 × 4)	(2.7)		
	925.3		

5   *Minority interests*

Net assets at balance sheet date: Think

	31/10/X5
	£m
Share capital	250
Profit and loss account	280
Unrealised profit on 'held for sale' assets	(5)
Depreciation on 'held for sale' assets (W6)	(2)
	523

Minority share: 20% × 523 = £104.6m

6   *Plant and equipment*

The 'held for sale' assets reported in the balance sheet of Think are not 'held for sale' in the group as a whole and should therefore be included in the consolidated balance sheet at their carrying value less depreciation for the year ended 31 October 20X5.

	£m
Lateral	500
Think	200
Held for sale assets at carrying value	10
Less depreciation for year (20% × 10)	(2)
	708

7   *Held to maturity investment*

FRS 26 requires that this is measured at amortised cost at 31 October 20X5.

	At beginning of year	*Interest (10%)*	*Interest received(4.7%)*	*At end of year*
	£m	*£m*	*£m*	*£m*
2003/4	30	3	(1.76)	31.24
2004/5	31.24	3.12	(1.76)	32.6

Therefore the investment is carried at £32.6 million and there is a gain of £2.6 million in the profit and loss account.

(c)   The first part of this transaction is a **non-refundable deposit** of $1 million being paid on 31 July 20X6. As this is a non-refundable deposit it is **not a monetary item** and therefore should be **translated and included in** the balance sheet **as an asset as part of plant and machinery** at £625,000 ($1m/1.6). This will not be **retranslated** at the year end.

The company then had to make a decision about how to deal with the **risk** surrounding the fact that it would be required to pay $3 million on 30 June 20X7. The option that was chosen was to invest in the $3 million bond on 31 July 20X6 and to sell it on 30 June 20X7 in order to fund the purchase of the plant and machinery.

Initially the bond will be recognised on 31 July 20X6 at £1.9 million ($3m/1.6). The bond is being classified as at **fair value through profit** or **loss** but as the bond has a coupon rate of 4% which is the same as the market rate then its fair value at that date will be the same as its carrying value ie $3 million. However as a **monetary item** the bond must be **retranslated at the closing rate** of exchange at 31 October 20X6 to £2.3 million ($3 m/1.3) and the exchange gain of £0.4 million (£2.3m – 1.9m) must be taken to the profit and loss account. There will also be **accrued interest** on the bond of $30,000 ($3m × 4% × 3/12) which will be translated at the average rate in the profit and loss account at £20,000 and at the closing rate as accrued income in the balance sheet at £23,000, the exchange difference being recognised in the profit and loss account.

In the year to 31 October 20X7 the effect of the bond will depend upon the movement in interest rates. As the bond is a fixed interest rate investment its value will be **dependent upon the movement in interest rates**.

If interest rates increase then the bond will reduce in value. Therefore by purchasing the bond the company has exposed itself to **interest rate risk**. To **eliminate** this interest rate risk then the company could enter into a **interest rate swap agreement** to exchange its fixed rate interest receipts for floating rate interest receipts. If this were to happen then the interest rate swap would be designated as a **hedging instrument** of the bond.

If the company had alternatively entered into a **forward contract** to purchase the $3 million for £2 million then **initially** this contract would have a **fair value of zero**. At the year end (31 October 20X6) the forward contract should be revalued to its fair value:

On the open market $3m would cost
                          $3m/1.3 = £2.3

Under the forward contract, $3m costs = £2m

Gain on forward contract   £0.3m

Under FRS 26, for hedge accounting to be applied, the hedge must be between 80% and 120% effective. Therefore we need to calculate the gain/loss on the hedged item (the purchase of the fixed asset) to test the effectiveness.

Amount expected to pay as at 31 October 20X6: $3m/1.3 =	£2.3m
Amount expected to pay out at year end 31.10.X6: $3m/1.6 =	£1.9m
Loss	£0.4m

Therefore effectiveness is £0.3m/£0.4m = 75%.

This falls outside the required effectiveness, which must be between 80% and 120%. Therefore the contract cannot be treated as a cash flow hedge, and should be treated as a normal financial asset at fair value through profit and loss. The gain on the forward contract should be posted to the income statement.

DEBIT   Financial asset   £0.3m
CREDIT   Income statement   £0.3m

*BPP note: The fair value option has been restricted and the bond could only be treated this way if it met the definition of 'held for trading'.

By purchasing the bond the company has **eliminated its exchange rate risk but introduced an element of interest rate risk**. The much simpler and more effective option would have been to enter into the forward contract.

(d)   Although many large companies disclose information about 'Human Capital Management' the **type and level of disclosure varies**. In the UK, the **Companies Act** requires the disclosure of information such as **employee numbers, policies relating to equal opportunities, information on disabled employees** and **staff remuneration**. Companies often adopt a '**checklist' approach**, often disclosing only the **minimum amount** of information required. Other companies may be more proactive. In practice, publishing information about human capital management **can enhance the reputation of a company** and **help it to recruit and retain high quality staff**.

The company wishes to help stakeholders to **understand the link** between its **performance** and **the way that it manages its employees**. As well as **information on equal opportunities** and **health and safety** at work it could disclose the following:

(i)   A **description** of the company's **policies** relating to the **recruitment, retention and motivation of employees**

(ii)   Employee **numbers** and other appropriate information about the **composition of the workforce**

(iii)   Details of **staff remuneration**

(iv)   Details of **amounts invested** in **training** and **developing employees** and also **descriptions** of the company's **policies and practices** in this area

BPP
LEARNING MEDIA

(v)   A description of the way in which the company ensures **management succession**.

Information should be provided **consistently** from period to period and should be **comparable with previous periods**. This means that the company will need to develop **key performance indicators**.

The most obvious vehicle for these disclosures is the **Operating and Financial Review** as this is management's analysis of the key factors and risks affecting the company's performance. Many companies also publish **separate social or employee reports,** which can be targeted at particular stakeholder groups, such as investors or current and potential employees and the general public.

Question 2

> **Top tips.** This was a wide ranging question, requiring you to set out the financial reporting implications of certain future plans that a company was considering. The question required quite detailed knowledge of certain accounting standards although a good mark could be attained by outlining the main areas of concern. Retirement benefits, revenue recognition, investment properties, impairment and reverse acquisitions were examined.
>
> **Easy marks.** The advantage of this kind of question is that if you are on shaky ground on one area you can gain marks on another. To that extent it is easier than a question on a single topic. Easy marks were available for setting out the principles underlying the problem, for using the report format and for clarity of the report.
>
> **Examiner's comment.** This question was well answered, because candidates obtained the easy marks available.

Marking scheme

		Marks
Reverse acquisition	4	
Preference capital	2	
Loan notes	3	
Retirement benefits	5	
Revenue recognition	5	
Investment properties	3	
Impairment review	4	
Report	3	
Available	29	
Maximum		25

REPORT

To: Directors of Barking
From:
Subject: Financial reporting implications of plans for the financial statements for the year ended 30 November 20X4
Date: December 20X3

I set out below my comments on the financial reporting implications of your future plans.

(a)   **Acquisition of Ash**

    This type of acquisition is known as a **'reverse acquisition'**. Technically it is Ash which acquires Barking and the **legal form of the transaction is that Ash is the parent**. However, Ash will issue a large number of shares to the shareholders of Barking and the **directors of Barking will control the acquired entity**. The **substance** of the transaction is that **Barking is the acquirer.**

There is **very little adequate guidance** on accounting for reverse acquisitions under UK GAAP. FRS 6 *Acquisitions and mergers* deals only with the situation where an entity becomes a subsidiary of a parent undertaking. The **Companies Act regards Ash as the parent** and requires Ash to prepare consolidated accounts in which it treats Barking as an acquired subsidiary. However, the UITF has issued an information sheet in which it concluded that in some situations it would be **appropriate to invoke the 'true and fair view override'** and to account for a combination as a reverse acquisition. It would therefore be logical to report the **substance** of the arrangement and to **treat Barking as the acquirer** for the purpose of the consolidated financial statements. (Note: reverse acquisitions *are* addressed by the equivalent international standard, IFRS 3 *Business combinations*. Under IFRS 3 Barking would be treated as the acquirer.)

If reverse acquisition accounting is applied, the **assets and liabilities of Ash**, rather than the assets and liabilities of Barking are **remeasured to fair value**. The **equity shares issued by Ash are included in the cost of the purchase consideration** at their **fair value** at the date of exchange.

Part of the purchase consideration will be in the form of **zero rated preference shares** and **interest free loan notes**. The preference shares are redeemable and therefore must be treated as **liabilities, not equity**. FRS 26 *Financial instruments: measurement* (which applies to listed companies) requires them to be carried at **amortised cost**. Although there is no interest charge as such **there is a finance cost**, because the shares will be **redeemed at a premium** and a **finance cost must be recognised in the profit and loss account for the year ended 30 November 20X4**. This is **based on the effective interest rate**. The preference shares should be measured at their fair value if acquisition accounting is used. The discounted redemption proceeds could be taken as the fair value of the shares if there is no market price that can be used.

Although the **loan notes appear to be liabilities**, the fact that they are **convertible** and therefore are **unlikely to be redeemed** suggests that in substance **they are actually equity**. FRS 25 *Financial instruments: disclosure and presentation* states that where there is **no genuine commercial possibility** that an option to transfer economic benefits will be exercised, the instrument should be reported **within shareholders' funds**. **Fair value can be based on the value of the shares** into which the loan notes will eventually be converted.

(b) **Pension schemes**

The defined benefit pension scheme of Barking is to be frozen. Under FRS 17 *Retirement benefits*, an **estimate of the present value of the scheme** is made and **recognised in the balance sheet** of the company. Because there will be **no new entrants** to the scheme, the **current service cost will probably increase** as the present members grow older and get nearer to retirement age.

The **defined contribution scheme** will present few accounting problems. The **cost** of providing pensions is the **amount of the contributions payable in the current period**. The employer has no further obligations.

Ash's defined benefit pension scheme will also be frozen. There is an added complication here because the existing scheme is a **multi-employer plan**. FRS 17 states that where (as in this case) it is **not possible to identify the company's share of the underlying assets and liabilities** in the scheme, **a defined benefit scheme can be accounted for as if it were a defined contribution scheme**. The fact that this has been done must be **disclosed** in the notes to the financial statements; the company will also have to disclose any available information about the **existence of a surplus or deficit** in the scheme that may affect future contributions; and the **basis used** to determine that surplus or deficit and the **implications, if any, for the company**. Ash will need to **determine the net assets** of the scheme in order to establish the net asset or liability that will be recognised when the employees are transferred to the new scheme.

(c) **Revenue recognition and investment properties**

Although the new policy will mean that revenue is recognised at a **later stage than previously** it allows revenue from the sale of a property to be **recognised before there is a legal contract**. The deposit is **refundable** and this **suggests that there is not yet a legal contract**. A sale is normally completed when **legal title passes** to the buyer. It is necessary to look at the various acts which have to be performed under a sales contract. It may be possible to **recognise revenue when cash is received**, but **only if there are no**

substantial acts still to be performed. It is also necessary to **look at industry practice** as users of the financial statements will need to be able to **compare Barking's performance with that of other companies in the same sector**.

It is **not appropriate** to **recognise legal costs as an asset**. They **do not qualify** either as **development expenditure** or as **any other intangible asset**. They represent **expenses** of the company and should be treated as such.

The company intends to transfer some properties from the trading portfolio to the investment portfolio. UITF Abstract 5 states that when properties are reclassified as investment properties, they **cease to be valued at the lower of cost and net realisable value** and instead are **measured at open market value**. The **transfer is made at the lower of cost and net realisable value** and **any reduction in the carrying value** is charged in the **profit and loss account.**

(d)   **Impairment review**

An impairment review **compares the carrying value of assets with their recoverable amount. Recoverable amount** is the **higher of net realisable value and value in use.** Because there has been an upturn in the property market, **net realisable value is likely to be higher than recoverable amount** and there will be **no impairment** and no need to calculate value in use.

However, there will be potential **problems if it is necessary to calculate value in use**. FRS 11 *Impairment of fixed assets and goodwill* states that only in **exceptional circumstances** should the period covered by the cash flow projections extend to **more than five years before a steady growth rate is assumed**. The proposed discount rate of 15% appears **high**, particularly in view of the long time period to be used and it is **likely to produce inaccurate figures**. Therefore a **shorter period and a lower discount rate should be used.**

Impairment losses are normally **recognised in the profit and loss account**, but where properties have been **revalued upwards** any loss should **first be set against the revaluation surplus** in the revaluation reserve with **only the excess being taken to the profit and loss account**.

Question 3

> **Top tips**. As this is a multi-issue question, it is important to allocate your time sensibly between the different aspects. Do not spend too long on Gow's not assets at the expense of Glass's.
>
> **Easy marks**. Part (a) is straightforward. Marks can be gained for backing up your arguments even if you come to the wrong conclusion.

Marking scheme

			Marks
(a)	Nature of relationship and accounting treatment		5
(b)	Impairment and calculation		7
	FRS 26		3
	Lease		5
	Revenue		4
	Issues with values contributed		2
		Available	26
		Maximum	25

(a) FRS 9 *Associates and joint ventures* defines **a joint** venture as a contractual arrangement between two or more parties that undertake an economic activity that is subject to joint control on a long term basis. Control is defined as the power to direct the financial and operating policies of the entity with a view to gaining economic benefits from its activities. Joint control in turn is where none of the entities alone can control the joint venture but together they can do so and decisions on financial and operating policy, economic performance and financial position required each venturer's consent.

On the face of it, it would appear that York is a joint venture jointly controlled by Gow and Glass. Both venturers appear to have joint control and have contributed assets and other resources to the joint venture. The only issue however is that there is **no written contract** and the definition of a joint venture is that it is a contractual arrangement. However, the **substance of the arrangement** should be considered and with the minutes of the discussions about the setting up of the venture being formally approved by both companies this would certainly imply a contractual arrangement.

In terms of the accounting for such a joint venture the **gross equity method** should be used in the group accounts of both Gow and Glass.

(b) **Gow's net assets**

The loss of the only customer of the power station (an income generating unit) would be an **indicator of a possible impairment** of that income generating unit. Therefore according to FRS 11 *Impairment of fixed assets and goodwill* an **impairment test** must be carried out on the power station. The power station has a current carrying value of £20 million. This must be compared to the recoverable amount of the power station which is the higher of the power station's net realisable value and its value in use.

The net realisable value is the potential sale proceeds (offer of £16m) less the disposal costs (£1m). The value in use is the discounted value of the expected future cash flows from the power station. The future dismantling costs of £5 million must also be included in this calculation as it has been agreed with the government that this will take place therefore it is a liability.

Carrying value   =   £20 million
Net realisable value   =   £16 million – £1 million = £15 million
Value in use (W1)   =   £21 million

Therefore the recoverable amount is the higher of £21 million and £15 million. As this recoverable amount of £21 million is actually higher than the carrying value of the power station (£20m) then there is **no impairment**. The discounted present value of the dismantling costs must be shown as a long term provision and as part of the cost of land and buildings.

There is however a further issue with Gow's assets and that is the debt from Race. FRS 26 *Financial instruments: measurement* states that **financial assets must be assessed at each balance sheet date for impairment**. It is highly likely that the **debt from Race is impaired** as Race has gone into receivership. The value of the amount to be received is the anticipated cash from the final settlement. As the cash is not likely to be received for a year then it should be discounted.

Value of debtor (W2) = £3.8 million

A further factor here is that the **value of contract with Race** shown as an intangible asset will now be **zero**.

Glass's net assets

The **building remains an asset** of the joint venture and there is **no reason to alter its carrying value**. However its **remaining useful will change** and the future depreciation charges will be £2 million each year for the next two years. As this is a **change in estimate** it is accounted for **prospectively** not retrospectively.

The lease liability must be assessed under FRS 26 to determine whether it is to be derecognised. In this case there is a change to the lease term but it **will not be derecognised**. The lease liability, however, will change and will be measured at the **present value of the future cash payments**.

Value of lease liability (W3) = £1.1 million

The **lease receivable is also extinguished** as this is the payment of £1 million on 31 October 20X6.

FRS 10 states that if intangible fixed assets are to be recognised in the balance sheet they must give a right to future economic benefits, be capable of being disposed of separately from the business and have a readily ascertainable market value. The **payment to the agency** of £0.5 does not meet any of these criteria and **cannot be recognised as an intangible asset** and must be removed from the balance sheet.

The terms of the contract with the overseas retailer can in fact be **split into two separate contracts** in accordance with the application notes to FRS 5 *Reporting the substance of transactions*. There is one contract to provide gas to the overseas retailer and the income from this will be accounted for in the normal way when gas is supplied. The other element of the contract is not to supply gas to any other company in that country over the four year period. Therefore the **£1.5 million deposit** received should not be taken to the profit and loss account immediately but spread over the four year period. The deposit should not have been deducted from intangible assets but instead should be shown as **deferred income**.

Intangible assets (W4) = £3 million

Deferred income (W5) = £1.5 million

BALANCE SHEET OF YORK AS AT 31 OCTOBER 20X6

	£m	£m
Land and buildings (6 + 4 + 4) (W1)		14.0
Plant and machinery		3.0
Intangible assets (W4)		3.0
		20.0
Current assets		
Stock	6.0	
Debtors (W2)	3.8	
Cash (1 + 10)	11.0	
		20.8
		40.8
Lease liability (W3)		(1.1)
Long term provision (W1)		(4.0)
Deferred income (W5)		(1.5)
		34.2
Share capital		30.0
Reserves (balance figure)		4.2
		34.2

Workings

1 *Value in use: power station*

	£m
Cash flow	
31 Oct 20X7 (6 × 0.943)	5.7
31 Oct 20X8 (7 × 0.890)	6.2
31 Oct 20X9 (8 × 0.840)	6.7
31 Oct 2010 ((8 − 5) × 0.792)	2.4
	21.0

The dismantling costs must also be discounted and added into the value of land and buildings: £5 million × 0.792 = £4 million

2   *Value of debtor: Race*

Discounted present value = £5 million × 80% × 1/1.06

                    = £3.8 million

3   *Value of lease liability*

£0.6 million × 1/1.07	=	£0.56 million
£0.6 million × 1/(1.07 × 1.07)	=	£0.52 million
		£1.08 rounded to £1.1 million

4   *Intangible assets in Glass*

	£m
Per balance sheet	2.0
Less agency fee	(0.5)
Add value of overseas deposit	1.5
	3.0

5   *Deferred income*

Deposit from overseas retailer = £1.5 million

Question 4

> **Top tips**. In part (b), make full use of the information in the question, but do not simply regurgitate it.
>
> **Easy marks**. Part (a) is very straightforward book work. Part (b) also has easy marks for style and layout.

Marking scheme

			Marks
(a)	Principle		6
	Mandatory discussion		7
		Available/maximum	13
(b)	Principal risks		9
	Treasury policies		3
		Available/maximum	12
	Style and presentation		2
		Available	27
		Maximum	25

(a)   In May 2005 the ASB issued Reporting Standard 1 *The Operating and Financial Review* (OFR). The standard was developed in response to the Government's **proposals for a statutory OFR**. However in November 2005 the Government changed its mind and announced that there would no **longer be a statutory requirement** for an OFR but instead the OFR would be at the choice of the directors of a company. The OFR guidance issued by the ASB remains as an indication of best practice and was renamed as Reporting Statement 1.

The **principles and objectives** of an OFR are as follows.

(i)   It is specifically prepared **for the shareholders of the company** not for investors in general, although it may be of interest to other parties.

(ii)   The OFR **reflects the directors' view** of the business.

(iii)   It should be a **clear and balanced analysis** of the strategic position and direction of the business which should help members to assess those strategies and their potential for success.

(iv)   The OFR should be **forward looking** and should identify those trends and factors that will help members to assess the current and future performance of the business.

(v)   Members should be **warned** that some information is not verifiable and of **any uncertainties** underpinning the information.

(vi)   The OFR should **complement the financial statements** by providing useful financial and non-financial information which is not to be found in the financial statements

(vii)   The OFR should provide **all information** that might reasonably be expected to **influence** the shareholders.

(viii)   The OFR should be **balanced and neutral** and deal equally with favourable and unfavourable information.

(ix)   The OFR and **key performance indicators** should be comparable over time.

The arguments for a mandatory OFR are largely to do with content and comparability. It is argued that a mandatory OFR will make it easier for companies themselves to judge what is required in such a report and the required standard of reporting, thereby making such reports more **robust**, **transparent and comparable**. If an OFR is not mandatory then there may be **uncertainty** as to content and the possibility of possible mis-information. There is also the risk that without a mandatory OFR directors may take a **minimalist approach** to disclosure which will make the OFR less useful and the information to be disclosed will be in hands of senior executives and directors.

However, the **arguments against** a mandatory OFR are that it could **stifle the development of the OFR** as a tool for communication and may lead to a **checklist approach** to producing it. It is argued that a mandatory OFR is not required as market forces and the needs of investors should lead to companies feeling the pressures to provide a useful and reliable report.

(b)

Jones and Cousin
Annual Report 20X6
Operating and Financial Review

Introduction

Jones and Cousin is a public quoted company and the group develops, manufactures and markets products in the medical sector. This report is designed to assist members of the group in understanding and assessing the strategies of the group and the potential success of these strategies.

Risks

The group faces a number of risks which will be considered under the headings of:

* Market risk
* Product risk
* Currency risk

Market risk

The market in which the group operates is quite fiercely competitive and contains a number of different competitors including specialised and large international corporations. There is the risk that any technical advances or product innovations by these competitors could adversely affect the group's profits. Also this element of competition also means that there is a risk of loss of market share or lower than expected sales growth which could affect the share price.

The sector in which the group operates is heavily monitored by governments and the group's share of revenue in a market sector is often determined by government policy. The group is therefore heavily dependent upon governments providing the funds for health care. Any reduction in funds by governments would almost certainly lead to a fall in revenue for the group.

Product risk

The products of the group are not inherently risky. However, there is always the possibility of a problem with products which may lead to legal action which would be costly and damage the group's reputation and goodwill. The industry is highly regulated in terms of both medical and environmental laws. Any such claims would have an adverse effect on sales, profit and share price.

There will always be innovations in this market sector and the group is careful to protect its products with patents and will enter into legal proceedings where necessary to protect those patents. There is also the problem of infringing the patents of others. If claims were brought for infringement of patents of other companies this would be costly and damaging and alternative products would have to be found.

There are constantly new products being developed by the group, which is costly in terms of research and development expenditure. Product innovation may not always be successful and this highly regulated market may not always gain the regulatory approval required.

Currency risk

The group operates in twenty-seven different countries and earns revenue and incurs costs in several different currencies. Although the pound sterling is the group's functional currency only 5% of its business is in the UK. Therefore exchange fluctuations in the main currencies in which it trades may have a material effect on the group's profits and cash flows.

Relationships

The group sources its products from a wide range of suppliers largely in the form of long-term contracts for the supply of goods. The group has a policy of ensuring that such suppliers are suitable from both qualitative and ethical perspectives.

The group has a set of corporate and social responsibility principles for which the Board of Directors is responsible. The risks that the group bears from these responsibilities are managed by the Managing Director. The group operates in many geographical areas and encourages its subsidiaries to help local communities to reinvest in local educational projects. Great care is taken by the group to ensure that obsolete products are disposed of responsibly and safely. Wherever possible reusable materials are used.

Group policy is to attract and retain employees and to maintain an equal opportunities policy for all employees. To this end employees regularly receive in-house training and are kept informed of management policies.

Treasury policies

The group uses derivative products to protect against both currency risk and interest rate risk. This is done by the used of fixed rate currency swaps and using floating to fixed rate interest rate swaps. All financial instruments are accounted for as cash flow hedges which means that gains and losses are recognised initially in reserves and are only released to the profit and loss account when the hedged item also affects the profit and loss account.

ACCA
Paper 2
Corporate Reporting (United Kingdom)

Mock Examination 3
Pilot Paper

Question Paper	
Time allowed	
Reading and planning	**15 minutes**
Writing	**3 hours**
This paper is divided into two sections	
Section A	This ONE question is compulsory and MUST be attempted
Section B	TWO questions ONLY to be answered

DO NOT OPEN THIS PAPER UNTIL YOU ARE READY TO START UNDER EXAMINATION CONDITIONS

Pilot paper

Paper P2

Corporate Reporting (UK)

Time allowed

Reading and planning:	15 minutes
Writing:	3 hours

This paper is divided into two sections:

Section A – This ONE question is compulsory and MUST be attempted

Section B – TWO questions ONLY to be attempted

Do NOT open this paper until instructed by the supervisor.

During reading and planning time only the question paper may be annotated. You must NOT write in your answer booklet until instructed by the supervisor.

This question paper must not be removed from the examination hall.

Warning

The pilot paper cannot cover all of the syllabus nor can it include examples of every type of question that will be included in the actual exam. You may see questions in the exam that you think are more difficult than any you see in the pilot paper.

SECTION A: This question is compulsory and MUST be attempted

Question 1

The following draft financial statements relate to Zambeze, a public limited company:

ZAMBEZE
DRAFT GROUP BALANCE SHEETS AT 30 JUNE

	20X6	20X5
	£m	£m
Fixed assets		
Goodwill	30	25
Tangible assets	1,315	1,005
Investment in associate	270	290
	1,615	1,320
Current assets		
Stock	650	580
Debtors	610	530
Cash at bank and in hand	50	140
	1,310	1,250
Creditors: amounts falling due within one year	(1,581)	(1,430)
Net current liabilities	(271)	(180)
Total assets less current liabilities	1,344	1,140
Creditors: amounts falling due after more than one year	(850)	(600)
Net assets	494	540
Capital and reserves		
Called up share capital	100	85
Share premium account	30	15
Revaluation reserve	50	145
Profit and loss account	254	250
Minority interest – equity	60	45
Capital employed	494	540

ZAMBEZE
DRAFT GROUP PROFIT AND LOSS FOR THE YEAR ENDED 30 JUNE 20X6

	£m
Turnover	4,700
Cost of sales	(3,400)
Gross profit	1,300
Distribution and administrative expenses	(600)
Finance costs (interest payable)	(40)
Share of profit in associate	30
Profit before tax	690
Taxation (including tax on income from associate £10 million)	(210)
Profit after taxation	480
Minority interest	(25)
Profit attributable to members of parent company	455

ZAMBEZE
DRAFT GROUP STATEMENT OF TOTAL RECOGNISED GAINS AND LOSSES
FOR THE YEAR ENDED 30 JUNE 20X6

	£m
Profit for the financial year	455
Foreign exchange difference of associate	(5)
Impairment losses on tangible assets offset against revaluation surplus	(95)
Total recognised gains and losses for the period	355

ZAMBEZE
DRAFT RECONCILIATION OF GROUP SHAREHOLDERS' FUNDS
FOR THE YEAR ENDED 30 JUNE 20X6

	£m
Total recognised gains and losses for the period	355
Dividends paid	(446)
New shares issued	30
Total movement during the year	(61)
Shareholders' funds at 1 July 20X5	495
Shareholders' funds at 30 June 20X6	434

The following relates to Zambeze.

(i)   Zambeze acquired a seventy per cent holding in Damp, a public limited company, on 1 July 20X5. The fair values of the net assets acquired were as follows:

	£m
Tangible fixed assets	70
Stock and work in progress	90
	160

The purchase consideration was £100 million in cash and £25 million (discounted value) deferred consideration which is payable on 1 July 20X6. The difference between the discounted value of the deferred consideration (£25 million) and the amount payable (£29 million) is included in 'interest payable'. Zambeze wants to set up a provision for reconstruction costs of £10 million retrospectively on the acquisition of Damp. This provision has not yet been set up.

(ii)   There had been no disposals of tangible fixed assets during the year. Depreciation for the period charged in cost of sales was £60 million.

(iii)   Creditors: amounts falling due within one year comprised the following items:

	20X6 £m	20X5 £m
Trade creditors	1,341	1,200
Interest payable	50	45
Taxation	190	185
	1,581	1,430

(iv)   Creditors: amounts falling due after more than one year comprised the following:

	20X6 £m	20X5 £m
Deferred consideration – purchase of Damp	29	–
Liability for the purchase of tangible fixed assets	144	–
Loans repayable	621	555
Provision for deferred tax	30	25
Retirement benefit liability	26	20
	850	600

(v)   The retirement benefit liability comprised the following:

	£m
Movement in year	
Liability at 1 July 20X5	20
Current and past service costs charged to profit and loss	13
Contributions paid to retirement benefit scheme	(7)
Liability 30 June 20X6	26

There was no actuarial gain or loss in the year.

(vi)   Goodwill was impairment tested on 30 June 20X6 and any impairment was included in the financial statements for the year ended 30 June 20X6. Group policy is to amortise goodwill over five years but because goodwill was impairment tested on 30 June 20X6, no amortisation was charged in the year.

(vii)   The Finance Director has set up a company, River, through which Zambeze conducts its investment activities. Zambeze has paid £400 million to River during the year and this has been included in dividends paid. The money was invested in a specified portfolio of investments. Ninety five per cent of the profits and one hundred per cent of the losses in the specified portfolio of investments are transferred to Zambeze. An investment manager has charge of the company's investments and owns all of the share capital of River. An agreement between the investment manager and Zambeze sets out the operating guidelines and prohibits the investment manager from obtaining access to the investments for the manager's benefit. An annual transfer of the profit/loss will occur on 30 June annually and the capital will be returned in four years time. The transfer of £400 million cash occurred on 1 January 20X6 but no transfer of profit/loss has yet occurred. The balance sheet of River at 30 June 20X6 is as follows:

RIVER: BALANCE SHEET AT 30 JUNE 20X6

	£m
Investment at fair value through profit or loss	390
	390
Share capital	400
Retained earnings	(10)
	390

Required

(a)   Prepare a group cash flow statement for the Zambeze Group for the year ended 30 June 20X6 using the indirect method.   **(35 marks)**

(b)   Discuss the issues which would determine whether River should be consolidated by Zambeze in the group financial statements.   **(9 marks)**

(c)   Discuss briefly the importance of ethical behaviour in the preparation of financial statements and whether the creation of River could constitute unethical practice by the finance director of Zambeze.   **(6 marks)**

(Total = 50 marks)

Two marks are available for the quality of the discussion of the issue regarding the consolidation of River and the importance of ethical behaviour.

Section B: TWO questions ONLY to be attempted

Question 2

Electron, a public limited company, operates in the energy sector. The company has grown significantly over the last few years and is currently preparing its financial statements for the year ended 30 June 20X6.

Electron buys and sells oil and currently has a number of oil trading contracts. The contracts to purchase oil are treated as fixed assets and amortised over the contracts' durations. On acceptance of a contract to sell oil, fifty per cent of the contract price is recognised immediately with the balance being recognised over the remaining life of the contract. The contracts always result in the delivery of the commodity. **(4 marks)**

Electron has recently constructed an ecologically efficient power station. A condition of being granted the operating licence by the government is that the power station be dismantled at the end of its life which is estimated to be 20 years. The power station cost £100 million and began production on 1 July 20X5. Depreciation is charged on the power station using the straight line method. Electron has estimated at 30 June 20X6 that it will cost £15 million (net present value) to restore the site to its original condition using a discount rate of five per cent. Ninety-five per cent of these costs relate to the removal of the power station and five per cent relates to the damage caused through generating energy. **(7 marks)**

Electron has leased another power station, which was relatively inefficient, to a rival company on 30 June 20X6. The beneficial and legal ownership remains with Electron and in the event of one of Electron's power stations being unable to produce energy, Electron can terminate the agreement. The leased power station is being treated as an operating lease with the net present value of the income of £40 million being recognised in the profit and loss account. The fair value of the power station is £70 million at 30 June 20X6. A deposit of £10 million was received on 30 June 20X6 and it is included in the net present value calculation. **(5 marks)**

The company has a good relationship with its shareholders and employees. It has adopted a strategy of gradually increasing its dividend payments over the years. On 1 August 20X6, the board proposed a dividend of 5p per share for the year ended 30 June 20X6. The shareholders will approve the dividend along with the financial statements at the general meeting on 1 September 20X6 and the dividend will be paid on 14 September 20X6. The directors feel that the dividend should be accrued in the financial statements for the year ended 30 June 20X6 as a 'valid expectation' has been created. **(3 marks)**

The company granted share options to its employees on 1 July 20X5. The fair value of the options at that date was £3 million. The options vest on 30 June 20X8. The employees have to be employed at the end of the three year period for the options to vest and the following estimates have been made:

Estimated percentage of employees leaving during vesting period at:

Grant date 1 July 20X5	5%
30 June 20X6	6%
Effective communication to the directors	

(4 marks)
(2 marks)

Required

Draft a report suitable for presentation to the director of Electron which discusses the accounting treatment of the above transactions in the financial statements for the year ended 30 June 20X6, including relevant calculations.

(Total = 25 marks)

Question 3

The following balance sheet relates to Kesare Group, a public limited company at 30 June 20X6:

	£'000
Assets	
Fixed assets	
Tangible assets	10,000
Goodwill	6,000
Other intangible assets	5,000
Financial assets (cost)	9,000
	30,000
Debtors	7,000
Other receivables	4,600
Cash	6,700
Current assets	18,300
Trade creditors	(5,000)
Current tax liability	(3,070)
Creditors: amounts falling due within one year	(8,070)
Net current assets	10,230
Creditors: amounts falling due after more than one year	
Long term borrowings	(10,000)
Deferred tax liability	(3,600)
Employee benefit liability	(4,000)
	(17,600)
Net assets	22,630
Capital and reserves	
Share capital	9,000
Profit and loss account	9,130
Other reserves	4,500
Capital employed	22,630

The following information is relevant to the above balance sheet.

(i)   The financial assets are valued at fair value through profit or loss but are shown in the above balance sheet at their cost on 1 July 20X5. The market value of the assets is £10.5 million on 30 June 20X6. Taxation is payable on the sale of the assets.

(ii) Other tangible assets comprise an asset which was purchased on 1 July 20X5 for £5 million and which qualifies for a government capital grant of £1 million. The asset has a useful life of five years. The grant has been credited to the profit and loss account and capital allowances are restricted by the amount of the grant. Assume a tax writing down allowance of 25% per annum.

(iii) The defined benefit plan had a rule change on 1 July 20X5. Kesare estimate that of the past service costs of £1 million, 40 per cent relates to vested benefits and 60 per cent relates to benefits that will vest over the next five years from that date. The past service costs have not been accounted for and the actuarial gain before accounting for the past service costs was £600,000.

(iv) The company had purchased an investment property on 1 July 20X5 at a cost of £3 million. This was included in tangible assets at this amount at 30 June 20X6. The value of the property at 30 June 20X6 was £5 million and the gain was included in the profit and loss account. The company had no intention of selling the property in the near future. The property qualifies for capital allowances at 4% per annum. No deferred taxation had been provided for on the investment property.

(v)   Assume taxation is payable at 30%.

Required

(a)   Discuss the main objectives of the recognition of deferred taxation and the conceptual principles upon which the timing difference approach to deferred taxation is based.   **(7 marks)**

(b)   Show, with suitable explanations, any adjustments that would be required to the deferred tax liabilities and balance sheet amounts as a result of items (i) – (iv) above.   **(18 marks)**

(Total = 25 marks)

Two marks will be awarded for the quality of the discussion of the objectives and conceptual principles in (a).

Question 4

A significant number of entities and countries around the world have adopted International Financial Reporting Standards (IFRS) as their basis for financial reporting, often regarding these as a means to improve the quality of information on corporate performance. However, while the advantages of a common set of global reporting standards are recognised, there are a number of implementation challenges at the international and national levels if the objective of an improved and harmonised reporting system is to be achieved.

Required

(a)   Discuss the implementation challenges faced by the International Accounting Standards Board (IASB) if there is to be a successful move to International Financial Reporting Standards.

(18 marks)

(b)   The Accounting Standards Board recently issued FRED 36 *Business combinations* (IFRS 3) and amendments to FRS 2 *Accounting for subsidiary undertakings*. The proposals radically change the basis of reporting business combinations and transactions with minority interests.

Discuss how the above exposure draft will fundamentally affect the existing accounting practices for business combinations   **(7 marks)**

(Total = 25 marks)

Two marks will be awarded for the quality of the discussion of the ideas and information.

Answers

DO NOT TURN THIS PAGE UNTIL YOU HAVE
COMPLETED THE MOCK EXAM

A PLAN OF ATTACK

Managing your nerves

As you turn the pages to start this exam a number of thoughts are likely to cross your mind. At best, examinations cause anxiety so it is important to stay focused on your task for the next three hours! Developing an awareness of what is going on emotionally within you may help you manage your nerves. Remember, you are unlikely to banish the flow of adrenaline, but the key is to harness it to help you work steadily and quickly through your answers.

Working through this mock exam will help you develop the exam stamina you will need to keep going for three hours.

Managing your time

Planning and time management are two of the key skills which complement the technical knowledge you need to succeed. To keep yourself on time, do not be afraid to jot down your target completion times for each question, perhaps next to the title of the question on the paper.

Focusing on scoring marks

When completing written answers, remember to communicate the critical points, which represent marks, and avoid padding and waffle. Sometimes it is possible to analyse a long sentence into more than one point. Always try to maximise the mark potential of what you write.

As you read through the questions, jot down on the question paper, any points you think you might forget. There is nothing more upsetting than coming out of an exam having forgotten to write a point you knew!

Also remember you can only score marks for what is on paper; you must write down enough to help the examiner to give you marks!

Structure and signpost your answers

To help you answer the examiner's requirements, highlight as you read through the paper the key words and phrases in the examiner's requirements.

Also, where possible try to use headings and subheadings, to give a logical and easy-to-follow structure to your response. A well structured and signposted answer is more likely to convince the examiner that you know your subject.

Your approach

This paper has two sections. The first section contains one long case study question which is compulsory. The second has three questions and you must answer two of them.

You have a choice.

- Read through and answer the Section A question before moving on to Section B

- Go through Section B and select the three questions you will attempt. Then go back and answer the question in Section A first

- Select the three questions in Section B, answer them and then go back to Section A

You are allowed 15 minutes before the start of the exam to go through the questions you are going to do.

Time spent at the start of each question confirming the requirements and producing a plan for the answers is time well spent.

Question selection

When selecting the two questions from Section B make sure that you read through all of the requirements. It is painful to answer part (a) of a question and then realise that parts (b) and (c) are beyond you, by then it is too late to change your mind and do another question.

When reviewing the requirements look at how many marks have been allocated to each part. This will give you an idea of how detailed your answer must be.

Generally, you need to be aware of your strengths and weaknesses and select accordingly.

Doing the exam

Actually doing the exam is a personal experience. There is not a single *right way*. As long as you submit complete answers to question 1 and any two from questions 2 to 4 after the three hours are up, then your approach obviously works.

Looking through the paper

The compulsory question is a case study. It starts with a group cash flow statement, then draws on your knowledge of criteria for consolidation, and finally goes into ethical matters. In Section B you have three questions on a variety of topics:

- Question 2 is a multi-standard question dealing with environmental provisions, leasing, EABSD and share-based payment.
- Question 3 is all about deferred tax. Nasty.
- Question 4 is a nice practical question on implementing IFRS with a current issues aspect thrown in.

You only have to answer two out of these three questions. You don't have to pick your optional questions right now, but this brief overview should have convinced you that you have enough choice and variety to have a respectable go at Section B. So let's go back to the compulsory question in Section A.

Compulsory question

Part (a) requires you to prepare a consolidated cash flow statement for a group in which there as been an acquisition. Additional complications include a few misclassifications. Work through Part (a) systematically, but leave plenty of time for parts (b) and (c), where easy marks may be gained.

Optional questions

Deciding between the optional questions is obviously a personal matter – it depends how you have spent your study time.

In our opinion, unless you love deferred tax, avoid question 3. It is easier to pick up marks when the question is on a variety of topics.

One thing is clear – the optional questions all contain a discursive element and are all based around a scenario. The Examiner has said that the emphasis in this paper is on giving advice in a practical situation.

The secret is to plan your answer; break it down into bite sized subsections, clearly labelled to help your examiner to quickly conclude you understand the problem and have a logical answer.

Allocating your time

The golden rule is always allocate your time according to the marks for the question in total and for the parts of the question. But be sensible. If (for example) you have committed yourself to answering Question 5, but can think of nothing to say about fair value, you may be better off trying to pick up some extra marks on the questions you can do.

Afterwards

Don't be tempted to do a post mortem on the paper with your colleagues. It will only worry you and them and it's unlikely you'll be able to remember exactly what you wrote anyway. If you really can't resist going over the topics covered in the paper, allow yourself a maximum of half an hour's 'worry time', then put it out of your head! Relax as it's all out of your hands now!

SECTION A
Question 1

Top tips. Some students don't like group cash flow statements, but they really are a gift. You can simply ignore any complications – at least to start off with – and concentrate on getting the easy marks (see below). Set out your proforma, and, if you can, try to set out your workings in the order shown in our answer. This order has been designed so that the easy workings come first. Part (b) requires straightforward bookwork knowledge of the criteria for consolidation, but also application of this knowledge to the matter of River. Part (c) requires a general discussion of ethical behaviour, but also, more specifically, how these general principles may be applied in the case of River.

Easy marks. Look at the marking scheme for Part (a). There are six marks for operating activities – most of which you know from your non-group cash flow studies at earlier levels. The property plant and equipment working has a few complications, but the same complications come up regularly, so if you learn our working you can't go too far wrong. Tax, interest and dividends are all straightforward. Turning to parts (b) and (c), as indicated above, there are easy marks for a more general discussion, as well as trickier marks for specific application. And write clearly, so you earn those extra two marks for communication.

Marking scheme

		Marks
(a)	Operating activities	6
	Retirement benefit	3
	Associate	3
	Subsidiary treatment	4
	Property, plant and equipment	3
	Goodwill	2
	Minority interest	3
	Taxation	3
	Dividend paid	3
	Interest	2
	River	2
	Issue of shares	1
		35
(b)	Issues	9
(c)	Ethical discussion	3
	River	3
		50

BPP
LEARNING MEDIA

(a)   ZAMBEZE GROUP
        CASH FLOW STATEMENT FOR THE YEAR ENDED 30 JUNE 20X6

	£m	£m
Net cash flow from operating activities (note)		855
Dividends received from associate (W2)		35
Returns on investments and servicing of finance		
Interest paid (W3)	31	
Dividend paid to minority interest (W5)	58	
		(89)
Taxation (W4)		(190)
Capital expenditure and financial investment		
Purchase of tangible fixed assets (W1)	251	
Investment in River	400	
		(651)
Acquisitions and disposals		
Purchase of Damp		(100)
Equity dividends paid (W6)		(46)
Cash outflow before management of liquid resources and financing		(186)
Financing		
Issue of shares	30	
Increase in debt (621-555)	66	
		96
Decrease in cash in the period		(90)

Note: Reconciliation of operating profit to net cash in flow from operating activities

	£m	£m
Operating profit (690 + 40 - 30)		700
Depreciation		60
Impairment of goodwill (W7)		8
Decrease in stocks (650 – 580 – 90)		20
Increase in debtors (610 – 530)		(80)
Increase in trade payables (1,341 – 1,200)		141
Pension asset		
Current and past service costs	13	
Contributions paid	(7)	
		6
		855

Workings

1   *Purchase of tangible fixed assets*

TANGIBLE FIXED ASSETS

	£m		£m
Balance b/d	1,005	Depreciation	60
Creditor c/d	144	Impairment losses	95
Acquisitions	70	Balance c/d	1,315
Additions (bal. fig.)	251		
	1,470		1,470

2   *Dividend received from associate*

INVESTMENT IN ASSOCIATE

	£m		£m
Balance b/d	290	Foreign exchange loss	5
Share of operating profit	30	Share at corporation tax	10
		Dividend received (bal. fig.)	35
		Balance c/d	270
	320		320

3   *Interest paid*

INTEREST PAYABLE

	£m		£m
Unwinding of discount on purchase (29 – 25)	4	Balance b/d	45
Cash paid (bal. fig.)	31	Profit and loss a/c	40
Balance c/d	50		
	85		85

4   *Taxation*

TAX PAYABLE

	£m		£m
Cash paid	190	Balance b/d	
Balance c/d		Current	185
Current	190	Deferred	25
Deferred	30	Profit and loss account (210 – 10)	200
	410		410

5   *Dividend paid to minority interests*

MINORITY INTERESTS

	£m		£m
Dividend paid (bal. fig.)	58	Balance b/d	45
Balance c/d	60	Acquisition: 30% x 160	48
		Profit for year	25
	118		118

6   *Equity dividends paid*

		£m
Per reconciliation of shareholders' funds		446
Less investment in River		(400)
Equity dividends paid		46

7   *Impairment of goodwill*

INTANGIBLE ASSET: GOODWILL

	£m		£m
Balance b/d	25	Impairment (bal. fig.)	8
Acquisition (note)	13	Balance c/d	30
	38		38

Note: Goodwill on acquisition

	£m
Purchase consideration	
Cash	100
Deferred	25
	125
Less group share of identifiable	
net assets acquired: 70% × 160	(112)
	13

(b)   The circumstances under which companies are required to consolidate an investment are set out in the Companies Act1985 and in FRS 2 *Accounting for subsidiary undertakings*.

CA 1985 defines a subsidiary undertaking as one in which the parent:

- Has a majority of the **voting rights**
- Is a **member** and can appoint/remove a **majority of the board of directors** (entitled to the majority of voting rights)
- Is a member and controls alone a majority of the voting rights **by agreement** with other members
- Has the right to exercise a **dominant influence** through the Memorandum and Articles or a control contract
- It has the **power to exercise or actually exercises dominant influence**, as defined below

Further definition was required to stop the increasing practice of the use of the non-consolidated (quasi) subsidiary. The following extra definitions were added by FRS 2.

- **Control**: the ability of an undertaking to direct the financial and operating policies of another undertaking with a view to gaining economic benefits from its activities.
- **Dominant influence**: the ability to direct the financial and operating policies of another undertaking with a view to gaining benefits from its activities.
- **On a unified basis**: two or more undertakings are managed on a unified basis if the whole of the operations of the undertakings are integrated and managed as a single unit.
- **Held on a long-term basis**: any interest held other than exclusively with a view to subsequent resale.

FRS 2 essentially views control as being shareholder control, mainly through voting power. However, FRS 5 *Reporting the substance of transactions* sees control as deriving from other sources. It defines a quasi-subsidiary and gives circumstances where quasi-subsidiaries will need to be consolidated. Control of decision making is not enough: the reporting entity must control the decision making with a view to **obtaining benefits** from the entity over which it has control. It must be able to prevent others from exercising decision making powers and enjoying benefits. In addition, for control to apply, the "parent" must be exposed to the risks and rewards of ownership.

Applying the above criteria to Zambese's relationship with River.

(i) Zambese controls River, through its **operating guidelines.**

(ii) The control is exercised with a view to **obtaining financial benefits** from River. Zambese receives 95% of the profits and 100% of the losses of River.

(iii) Zambese has the risks and rewards of ownership.

Zambese therefore controls River, and River should be consolidated.

(c) **Ethical behaviour** in the preparation of financial statements, and in other areas, is of **paramount importance**. This applies equally to preparers of accounts, to auditors and to accountants giving advice to directors. Accountants act unethically if they use "creative" accounting in accounts preparation to make the figures look better, and they act unethically if, in the role of adviser, they fail to point this out.

The creation of River is **a device to keep activities off Zambese's balance sheet**. In hiding the true nature of Zambese's transactions with River, **the directors are acting unethically.** Showing the payment of £400 million to river as a dividend is **deliberately misleading,** and may, depending on the laws that apply, be illegal.

The creation of River, and the failure to disclose and account for the transactions properly, puts Zambese's directors **in breach of three important principles** which must apply to the preparation of financial statements:

(i) **Complianc**e with generally accepted accounting principles (GAAP). FRS 2 and FRS 5 are not complied with.

(ii) Fair presentation, sometimes called the principle of **substance** over form. River is an example of off balance sheet finance, where the form does not reflect the economic substance of the transaction.

(iii) **Transparency** of disclosure. Disclosure must be sufficient for the reader of financial statements to understand fully the nature of the transaction.

The directors must correct this unethical behaviour by consolidating River, and by disclosing the true nature of the payment to River.

Question 2

Top tips. This is a multi-standard question on environmental provisions, leases, proposed dividend and a share option scheme. The good thing about this kind of question is that, even if you don't know all the standards tested, you can get marks for the ones you do know. The question on the power station is similar to one you will have already met in this kit, and you have come across longer, more complicated questions on share-based payment, a favourite topic with this examiner.

Easy marks. The proposed dividend is straightforward, as is the explanation (if not the calculations) for the provision. The treatment of share options provides 4 easy marks for nothing much in the way of complications.

Marking scheme

		Marks
Oil contracts		4
Power station		7
Operating leases		5
Proposed dividend		3
Share options		4
Effective communication		2
	AVAILABLE/MAXIMUM	25

REPORT

To: The Directors, Electron
From: Accountant
Date: July 20X6

Accounting treatment of transactions

The purpose of this report is to explain the accounting treatment required for the following items.

- Oil trading contracts
- Power station
- Operating lease
- Proposed dividend
- Share options

Oil trading contracts

The first point to note is that the contracts always result in the delivery of the commodity. They are therefore correctly treated as normal sale and purchase contracts, **not financial instruments.**

The adoption of a policy of **deferring recognising revenue and costs is appropriate** in general terms because of the duration of the contracts. Over the life of the contracts, costs and revenues are equally matched. However, there is a mismatch between costs and revenues in the early stages of the contracts.

In the first year of the contract, 50% of revenues are recognised immediately. However, costs, in the form of amortisation, are recognised evenly over the duration of the contract. This means that **in the first year, a higher proportion of the revenue is matched against a smaller proportion of the costs.** It could also be argued that revenue is inflated in the first year.

While there is no detailed guidance on accounting for this kind of contract, FRS 18 *Accounting policies* may apply. Under FRS 18, the question of whether revenue has arisen is judged independently from the matching concept according to whether an asset has been created. Oil purchases result in a tangible fixed asset, while oil sales result in revenue. This approach of asset creation (and conversely recognising an expense when a liability is created) is consistent with, and indeed derives from, the *Statement of Principles*.

The current practice is also **out of line with** the principles of revenue recognition set out in the **Amendment to FRS 5** *Reporting the substance of transactions*. This says that revenue is generated when a seller performs obligations, and in exchange the seller obtains the rights to consideration. Thus, **revenue should be recognised as performance takes place,** when, as here, performance takes place over time.

It would be advisable, therefore, to match revenue and costs, and to **recognise revenue evenly** over the duration of the contract.

Power station

FRS 12 *Provisions, contingent liabilities and contingent assets* states that a provision should be recognised if:

- There is a present obligation as a result of a past transaction or event and
- It is probable that a transfer of economic benefits will be required to settle the obligation
- A reliable estimate can be made of the amount of the obligation

In this case, the obligating event is the installation of the power station. The operating licence has created a legal obligation to incur the cost of removal, the expenditure is probable, and a reasonable estimate of the amount can be made.

Because Electron cannot operate its power station without incurring an obligation to pay for removal, **the expenditure also enables it to acquire economic benefits** (income from the energy generated). Therefore Electron correctly **recognises an asset** as well as a provision, and **depreciates this asset over its useful life of 20 years.**

Electron should recognise a provision for the cost of removing the power station, but should not include the cost of rectifying the damage caused by the generation of electricity until the power is generated. In this case the cost of rectifying the damage would be 5% of the total discounted provision.

The accounting treatment is as follows:

BALANCE SHEET AT 30 JUNE 20X6 (EXTRACTS)

	£m
Tangible fixed assets	
Power station	100
Decommissioning costs (W)	13.6
	113.6
Depreciation (113.6 ÷ 20)	(5.7)
	107.9

	£m
Provisions	
Provision for decommissioning at 1 July 20X5	13.6
Plus unwinding of discount (13.6 × 5%)	0.7
	14.3
Provision for damage (0.7 (W) ÷ 20)	0.1
	14.4

PROFIT AND LOSS ACCOUNT FOR THE YEAR ENDED 30 JUNE 20X6 (EXTRACTS)

	£m
Depreciation	5.7
Provision for damage	0.1
Unwinding of discount (finance cost)	0.7

Working

	£m
Provision for removal costs at 1 July 20X5 (95% × (15 ÷ 1.05))	13.6
Provision for damage caused by extraction at 30 June 20X6	
(5% (15 ÷ 1.05))	0.7

Operating lease

One issue here is the substance of the lease agreement. SSAP 21 *Accounting for leases and hire purchase contracts* classifies leases as either finance leases or operating leases. A finance lease transfers substantially all the risks and rewards of ownership to the lessee, while an operating lease does not. The company retains legal ownership of the equipment and also retains the benefits of ownership (the equipment remains available for use in its operating activities). In addition, the present value of the minimum lease payments is only 57.1% of the fair value of the leased assets (£40 million ÷ £70 million). For a lease to be a finance lease, the present value of the minimum lease payments should be substantially all the fair value of the leased assets. (Substantially all generally means 90% or more.) Therefore the lease appears to be correctly classified as an operating lease.

A further issue is the treatment of the fee received. The company has recognised the whole of the net present value of the future income from the leases in the profit and loss account for 30 June 20X6, despite the fact that only a deposit of £10 million has been received. In addition, the date of inception of the lease is 30 June 20X6, so the term of the lease does not actually fall within the current period. SSAP 21 states that income from operating leases should be recognised on a straight line basis irrespective of when payments are due. An application note to FRS 5 is also relevant here. This does not allow revenue to be recognised before an entity has performed under the contract and therefore no revenue should be recognised in relation to the operating leases for the current period.

Proposed dividend

The dividend was proposed after the balance sheet date and therefore FRS 21 *Events after the balance sheet date* applies. This prohibits the recognition of proposed dividends unless these are declared before the balance sheet date. The directors did not have an obligation to pay the dividend at 30 June 20X6 and therefore there cannot be a liability. The directors seem to be arguing that their past record creates a constructive obligation as defined by FRS 12 *Provisions, contingent liabilities and contingent assets*. A constructive obligation may exist as a result of the proposal of the dividend, but this had not arisen at the balance sheet date.

Although the proposed dividend is not recognised it was approved before the financial statements were authorised for issue and should be disclosed in the notes to the financial statements.

Share options

The share options granted on 1 July 20X5 are equity-settled transactions, and are governed by FRS 20 *Share based payment*. The aim of this standard is to recognise the cost of share based payment to employees over the period in which the services are rendered. The options are generally charged to the profit and loss account on the basis of their fair value at the grant date. If the equity intruments are traded on an active market, market prices must be used. Otherwise an option pricing model would be used.

The conditions attached to the shares state that the share options will vest in three years' time provided that the employees remain in employment with the company. Often there are other conditions such as growth in share price, but here employment is the only condition.

The treatment is as follows:

(a) Determine the fair value of the options at grant date.

(b) Charge this fair value to the profit and loss account equally over the three year vesting period, making adjustments at each accounting date to reflect the best estimate of the number of options that will eventually vest. This will depend on the estimated percentage of employees leaving during the vesting period.

For the year ended 30 June 20X6, the charge to the profit and loss account is £3m × 94% × 1/3 = £940,000. Shareholders' equity will be increased by an amount equal to this profit and loss account charge.

Question 3

Top tips. To state the obvious, this is a question best avoided unless you like deferred tax. However, if you do, or if you dislike other topics more, the question may be broken down into components where you can get a foothold. Layout is important to avoid getting muddled.

In part (b) (iii) our answer has followed the examiner's. However, the matter is somewhat ambiguous. It assumes that the year end valuation has included the rule change. (If the £520,000 has not been accounted for, the entries would be Debit P & L, Credit liability with no effect on the actuarial gain. Furthermore deferred tax is provided on the net pension surplus or deficit, so even if the year end valuation did include the rule change, an extra £520,00 × 30% would be required.)

Easy marks. For those not fond of high speed number-crunching, there are some fairly easy marks in Part (a) available for a general discussion about concepts and the framework. In addition there are some easy marks for adjustments to the financial statements, most of which do not relate to the deferred tax aspects. In generally, however, this is not a question that lends itself to easy marks.

Marking scheme

			Marks
(a)	Quality of discussion		2
	Statement of Principles		1
	Timing differences		1
	Gains and losses		1
	Tax consequences		1
	Incremental liability		1
			7
(b)	Financial assets		4
	Grant		4
	Pension		4
	Investment property		4
	Adjustments		4
		AVAILABLE	20
		MAXIMUM	18
		AVAILABLE	27
		MAXIMUM	25

(a) FRS 19 *Deferred tax* is based on the idea that the future tax consequences of past transactions and events should be recognised as liabilities or assets in the financial statements. Differences arise between an entity's taxable profits and its results in its financial statements when gains and losses are included in tax assessments in periods different from those in which they are recognised in the financial statements. These differences are known as **timing differences.** For example, capital allowances for the cost of a fixed asset may be accelerated, ie received before the cost of the fixed asset is recognised in the profit and loss account.

FRS 19 requires a company to make **full provision** for the tax effects of timing differences. Both **deferred tax assets**, and **deferred tax liabilities** can arise in this way.

It may be argued that deferred tax assets and liabilities **do not meet the definition of assets and liabilities** in the ASB's *Statement of Principles*. According to the *Statement,* an asset is the right to receive economic benefits as a result of past events, and a liability is an obligation to transfer economic benefits, again as a result of past events. Under FRS 19, the tax effect of transactions are recognised in the same period as the transactions themselves, but in practice, tax is paid in accordance with tax legislation when it becomes a legal liability. There is a **conceptual weakness** or inconsistency, in that only one liability, that is tax, is being provided for in this way, and not other costs, such as overhead costs.

(b)   (i)   According to FRS 26, **financial assets** that are valued **at fair value through profit and loss** should, as the term suggests, be valued at fair value, not at cost. The increase in fair value should be taken to the profit and loss account. There will be an increase of £10,500,000 – £9,000,000 = £1,500,000 in the value of the asset, and the gain will be taken to the profit and loss account. For non-monetary assets, in the absence of a binding sale agreement, taxable profits are not affected and no future liability arises as a result of the revaluation, therefore there is no timing difference. However, FRS 19 states that, where an asset is continually revalued, with changes being recognised in the profit and loss account, deferred tax should be recognised on timing differences arising. Deferred tax should therefore be provided. The amount to be provided is £1,500,000 × 30% = £450,000.

(ii)   The **government grant** has been treated incorrectly. It has been credited to profit and loss account. SSAP 4 *Accounting for government grants* requires that grants should be credited to profit and loss account over the useful life of the asset. (SSAP 4 also permits a deduction from cost, but there is some doubt as to the legality of this.) The calculation of the timing difference and deferred tax is as follows:

	£'000
Cost of asset	5,000
Depreciation	(1,000)
Carrying value	4,000
Unamortised deferred income (1,000 – 200)	(800)
Net carrying value in financial statements	3,200
Cost of asset	5,000
Less grant	(1,000)
	4,000
Capital allowance (25%)	(1,000)
Tax written down value	3,000
Timing difference	200
Deferred tax (3,200 – 3,000) @ 30%	60

(iii)   The **defined benefit plan** needs to be adjusted to reflect the change. The vested benefits should be recognised immediately and the remainder spread over five years. The liability must be increased by 40% × £1m + (60% × £1m ÷ 5) = £520,000. The same amount is charged to retained earnings. This increase in the liability will reduce the actuarial gain to £600,000 – £520,000 = £80,000. Deferred tax of £80,000 × 30% = £24,000 will be recognised. Since the actuarial gain was recognised in the statement of total recognised gains and losses, the deferred tax will also be recognised there.

(iv)   The **investment property** is required by SSAP 19 to be included in the balance sheet at open market value. It should not be depreciated. The treatment of the gain is incorrect. These should not be taken to the profit and loss account, but to the investment revaluation reserve. Deferred tax is not provided on this gain, as there is no intention to sell the property and deferred tax is only recognised if there is a binding agreement to sell. However, deferred tax must be provided on the difference between depreciation, which is nil here, and the capital allowances of £3m × 4% = £120,000 per annum. The deferred tax, at 30%, will be £36,000.

The effect of these adjustments is shown below.

		Balance sheet	Profit and loss account	Other reserves
		£'000	£'000	£'000
Balance per balance sheet			9,130	4,500
(i)	Financial assets	9,000		
	Revaluation	1,500	1,500	
		10,500		
(ii)	Grant	(800)	200	
	Reversal of grant income		(1,000)	
	Depreciation of fixed asset	(1,000)	(1,000)	
(iii)	Pension costs – liability	(4,000)		
	Past service costs	(520)	(520)	
		(4,520)		
(iv)	Investment property		(2,000)	2,000
Increase in deferred tax (below)			(546)	(24)
			5,764	6,476
Deferred tax liability per balance sheet				3,600
Adjustment for				
Financial asset			450	
Government grant			60	
Pension costs (to STRGL)			24	
Investment property			36	
				570
Adjusted deferred tax liability				4,170

Question 4

Top tips. Part (a) of this question is topical and practical, and you should have been prepared for this topic to come up. If you weren't, learn our answer carefully – you may be able to apply it to some variant of the question in an exam. Part (b) is on current issues, specifically the changes proposed to accounting for business combinations in recent exposure drafts. The examiner has specifically stated that he will not set a whole question on an exposure draft, or test the detail. The focus will be on the main implications for the financial statements, as here.

Easy marks. As you can see from the marking scheme, much of the mark allocation is 'subjective'. Thus does not mean you can say anything you want or waffle, but it does mean that credit is given for any valid points, provided you can back them up with arguments. So keep writing and stay calm and logical. A quick answer plan will help.

Marking scheme

		Marks
(a)	Subjective	18
(b)	Subjective	7
		25

(a) **Practical matters**

Changing from local GAAP to IFRS is **likely to be a complex process** and should be **carefully planned**. Even if local GAAP and IAS/IFRS follow broadly the same principles there are still likely to be **many important differences** in the detailed requirements of individual standards.

BPP
LEARNING MEDIA

The company will also need to ensure that its overseas subsidiaries comply with any local reporting requirements. This **may mean that subsidiaries will have to prepare two sets of financial statements**: one using local GAAP; and one using IFRS (for the consolidation).

The process will be affected by the following.

(i)   The **differences between local GAAP and IFRS** as they affect the group financial statements in practice. The company will need to carry out a **detailed review of current accounting policies,** paying particular attention to areas where there are significant differences between local GAAP and IFRS. These will probably include deferred tax, business combinations, retirement benefits and foreign currency translation. It should be possible to estimate the effect of the change by preparing pro-forma financial statements using IFRS.

(ii) The **level of knowledge** of IFRS of current finance staff (including internal auditors). It will probably be necessary to **organise training** and the company may need to recruit additional personnel with experience of IFRS.

(iii) The group's **accounting systems**. Management will need to assess whether computerised accounting systems **can produce the information required** to report under IFRS. They will also need to produce new consolidation packages and accounting manuals.

There should be a **detailed plan** for the project, including timetables, management teams and resource requirements.

Lastly, the company **should consider the impact of the change** to IFRS on investors and their advisers. For this reason management should **try to quantify the effect** of IFRS **on results** and other key performance indicators as early as possible.

Problems of enforcement

The success of enforcement of IFRS depends on how rigorously they are enforced. In turn, this depends on the **robustness of the regulatory framework** of the country in which the standards are being implemented. In the EU, this is less of an issue, since endorsement is required as part of the implementation process. However, even here there are problems, since the **endorsement process** could **create standards** that are **different from those of the IFSB**.

Enforcement of IFRS requires an **international mechanism**. IOSCO has an infrastructure for listed companies and has put forward proposals for regulating interpretation and enforcement of IFRS. However, the situation is by no means uniform and is in a **state of flux**.

Other problems and challenges

(i)   The **legal framework** may present difficulties in adopting IFRS. In some countries, this will be more apparent than in others, such as the UK, where the legal framework and accounting standards – and UK FRS and IFRS – are a better fit.

(ii) **Small and medium entities** (SMEs) present particular problems. In recent years, IFRS have become **increasingly complex and prescriptive.** They are now designed **primarily** to meet the information needs of **institutional investors in large listed entities** and their advisers. In many countries, IFRS are **used mainly by listed companies.** There are arguments for the use of full IFRS and for the development of a separate IFRS for SMEs, as with the FRSSE in the UK.

(iii) **Translation** of IFRS could cause difficulty where it gives rise to ambiguity.

(iv) The **complexity and volume** of IFRS add to the difficulties of implementation, especially in countries where there is less expertise. There will be a tendency, where a choice is available, to choose the treatment most like existing local GAAP, rather than the best treatment.

All of the above have **cost and time implications**.

(b)   Under current accounting practice the objective of acquisition accounting is to reflect the **cost of the acquisition.** To the extent to which it is not represented by identifiable assets and liabilities (measured at their fair value), goodwill arises and is reported in the financial statements. **FRED 36** adopts a different perspective and requires the financial statements to reflect the **fair value of the acquired business.**

To date, accounting has been based on the 'parent entity concept'. Under the **parent entity concept** the extent of **non-controlling interests** and transactions with non-controlling interests are **separately identified** in the primary financial statements.

The proposals treat the group as a **single economic entity** ('entity concept') and any outside equity interest in a subsidiary is treated as part of the overall ownership interest in the group. As a consequence of this **changes in a parent's ownership interest, that do not result in a change of control, are to be recognised as changes in equity. No gain or loss will be recognised in profit or loss.**

Merger accounting will no longer be permitted. Under FRED 36, all business combinations are to be treated as acquisitions.

FRS 2 requires that goodwill arising on acquisition should only be recognised with respect to the part of the subsidiary undertaking that is attributable to the interest held by the parent entity. Under the proposals, **goodwill is to be recognised in full**; that is 100% of goodwill is recognised even if less than 100% is acquired. In other words, goodwill is to be shown **gross of non-controlling (minority) interest.**

After initial recognition, different rules will apply to goodwill. **Under FRED 36** goodwill, after initial recognition, is to be **measured at cost less impairment losses, and amortisation is not to be permitted.**

Under FRS 2, **costs incurred in connection with the acquisition** are accounted for as part of the investment. Under the proposals, they **will be charged in the profit and loss account.**

Business combinations must be measured and recognised as of the acquisition date **at the fair value of the acquiree, even if the business combination is achieved in stages or if less than 100 per cent of the equity interests in the acquiree are owned at the acquisition date**. Currently a business combination must be measured and recognised on the basis of the accumulated cost of the combination.

ACCA
Examiner's answers

Part 3 Examination – Paper 3.6(GBR)
Advanced Corporate Reporting (UK Stream)

December 2006 Answers

1   Cash flow statement Andash, a public limited company
                              For the year ended 31 October 2006

		£m
Net cash flow from operating activities		1,444
Returns on investment and servicing of finance (w(viii))		(138)
Taxation (w(vii))		(523)
Capital expenditure and financial investment (w(ii))		(1,320)
Acquisitions and disposals (w(ix))		17
Equity dividends paid		(50)
Cash outflow before management of liquid resources and financial		(570)
Financing – issues of ordinary shares (w(vii))	10	
Financing – increase in debt	400	410
Decrease in cash in the period		(160)

Workings

(i)   Cash flows from operating activities

		£m
Profit before taxation (below)		314
Adjustment for		
Profit on sale of subsidiary	(8)	
Depreciation	260	
Impairment and amortisation of goodwill (78 + 9)	87	
Associates profit	(1)	
Finance costs	148	486
		800
Increase in debtors (2400 – 1500 + 4)	(904)	
Increase in stock (2650 – 2300 + 8)	(358)	
Increase in creditors (4700 – 2800 + 6)	1,906	644
Net cash flow from operating activities		1,444

	£m
Profit before tax	391
Associates profit (iii)	1
Impairment of goodwill (iv)	(78)
Profit before tax	314

(ii)   **Plant and machinery**

FRS20 says that the fair value of the goods and services received should be used as the value of the share options issued. Therefore, the plant should be valued at £9 million and the share options at the same amount. There is no need to adjust depreciation because of the date of purchase, but 'other reserves' will fall by £1 million.

	£m
Plant and machinery balance 31 October 2005	4,110
Purchases – non-cash } above	9
Over valuation } above	1
Depreciation	(260)
Sale of subsidiary	(10)
Purchases in period (balancing figure)	1,320
Plant and machinery per balance sheet	5,170

The balance sheet figure for plant and machinery will be £5,169 million.

BPP
LEARNING MEDIA

(iii) Associate – Joma

The investment in the associate should be measured using the equity method

	£m	£m
Cost of investment		60
Share of post-acquisition reserves (25% × (£32 – £20)m)	3	
Inter company profit eliminated (25% × (£16 – £8)m)	(2)	
		1
		61

(iv) Impairment of Goodwill – Broiler

	Goodwill £m	Net Assets £m	Total £m
Carrying amount (90 – 2/10 of 90)	72	266	338
Recoverable amount			260
Impairment loss			(78)

Goodwill and the intangible/tangible assets of Broiler will be reduced by £78 million. The profit and loss account will be charged with this amount.

(v) Sale of subsidiary

The sale of the subsidiary should be taken into account in the cash flow statement as follows:

	DR	CR
Plant and machinery		10
Stock		8
Debtors		4
Cash at bank and in hand		5
Creditors	6	
Current tax payable	7	
Cash proceeds	32	
Goodwill disposed of		10
Profit on sale		8
	45	45

(vi) Tax paid

	£m	£m
Current tax payable 31 October 2005	770	
Deferred tax payable 31 October 2005	300	
		1,070
Profit and loss account		160
		1,230
Cash paid (balancing figure)		(523)
Sale of subsidiary		(7)
Current tax payable 31 October 2006	300	
Deferred tax payable 31 October 2006	400	
		700

(vii) Shares issued

Cash flow from the issue of shares is £(30 + 30 – 50)m i.e. £10 million. The shares issued for the purchase of Joma (from movements in shareholders funds) are taken from the issue proceeds set out in the reconciliation of changes in shareholders' funds.

(viii) Returns on investment and servicing of finance

Interest paid (40 + 148 – 70)	(118)
Dividends paid to minority interest (180 + 40 – 200)	(20)
	(138)

(ix) Acquisitions and disposals

Purchase of associate	(10)
Sale of subsidiary (32 – 5)	27
	17

2 (a) Foreign subsidiary, Chong

The following computation sets out the accounting treatment of the sale of foreign subsidiary, Chong.

	31 October 2005		31 October 2006
	$m		$m
Share capital	100		100
Profit and loss reserve	40		60
Shareholders' funds	140		160
Net assets	140		160
Translated into sterling:			
Net assets (140 ÷ 1·4)	100	(160 ÷ 1·3)	123
Share capital (100 ÷ 1·1)	91		91
Retained profits (40 ÷ 1·2)	33	33	
		(20 ÷ 1·5) 13	46
Exchange reserve	(24)	(24)	
		gain 10	(14)
	100		123

Gain/loss on sale	Misson	Group
	£m	£m
Sale proceeds (195 ÷ 1·3)	150	150
Cost of investment	(91)	
Net asset value		(123)
Exchange losses (24 – 10)		(14)
Gain on sale	59	13

FRS23, 'The Effects of Changes in Foreign Exchange Rates', requires the cumulative exchange losses of £14 million to be recognised in the profit and loss account for the year ended 31 October 2006. The exchange losses should be included as part of the gain on disposal. As a result the gain on sale is reduced to £13 million. The gain on sale is effectively the gain on sale in the parent company's financial statements (£59 million) less the cumulative profits already taken to the group profit and loss account of £46 million.

(b) Stock, Goods sold and Investment property

The stock and debtor initially would be recorded at 8 million dollars ÷ 1.6, i.e. £5 million. At the year end, the creditor is still outstanding and is retranslated at £1 = 1·3 dollars, i.e £6·2 million. An exchange loss of £(6·2 – 5) million, i.e. £1·2 million would be reported in the profit and loss account. The stock would be recorded at £5 million at the year end unless it is impaired in value.

The sale of goods would be recorded at $4 million ÷ 1.6, i.e. £2·5 million as a sale and as a debtor. Payment is received on 31 October 2006 in dollars and the actual value of dollars received will be $4 million ÷ 1·3, i.e. £3·1 million.

Thus a gain on exchange of £0·6 million will be reported in the profit and loss account.

The investment property should be recognised on 1 November 2005 at $28 million ÷ 1·4, i.e. £20 million. At 31 October 2006, the property should be recognised at $24 million ÷ 1·3, i.e. £18·5 million. The decrease in fair value should be recognised in STRGL as a loss on investment property. The property is a non-monetary asset and any foreign currency element is not recognised separately. When a gain or loss on a non-monetary item is recognised in STRGL, any exchange component of that gain or loss is also recognised in STRGL. If any gain or loss is recognised in equity on a non-monetary asset, any exchange gain/loss is also recognised in equity. SSAP 19 'Accounting for Investment Properties' requires all changes in market values including deficits to be taken to the STRGL unless a deficit or an individual investment property is expected to be permanent, in which case it is charged to the profit and loss account.

(c) Plant and machinery

Where a deposit is paid, the treatment depends upon whether the amount is refundable. If the deposit is refundable, then the amounts should be treated as monetary items and retranslated at the balance sheet date. In this case the deposit is not refundable and it should be recorded as plant and machinery debtors at a value of $1 million ÷ 1·6, i.e. £625,000.

FRS26 governs the accounting for the two instruments.

A cash flow hedge is a hedge of the exposure to variability in cash flows that:

(i) is attributable to a particular risk associated with a recognised asset or liability or a highly probable forecast transaction, and

(ii) could affect profit or loss

Cash flow hedge accounting involves the following accounting treatments:

(i) changes in the fair value of the hedging instrument attributable to the hedged risk are deferred as a separate component of equity to the extent the hedge is effective (rather than being recognised immediately in profit or loss)

(ii) the accounting for the hedged item is not adjusted

(iii) if a hedge of a forecast transaction subsequently results in the recognition of a non-financial asset or non-financial liability (or becomes a firm commitment for which fair value hedge accounting is applied), the entity has an accounting policy choice of whether to keep deferred gains and losses in equity or remove them from equity and include them in the initial carrying amount of the recognised asset, liability, or firm commitment (a so-called 'basis adjustment')

(iv) when the hedged item affects profit or loss (for instance through depreciation or amortisation), a corresponding amount previously deferred in equity is realised from equity ('recycled') and included in profit or loss.

(v) If the hedge is not 100% effective, the ineffectiveness is recognised in profit or loss.

Bond

The bond would be initially recognised on 31 July 2006 at $3 million ÷ 1.6 i.e. £1·9 million. As current market rates are 4%, the fair value and carrying value of the bond will be £1·9 million. On 31 October 2006, the value of the bond will have changed to £2·3 million ($3 million/1·3) and the exchange gain will be recognised in the profit and loss account (£0·4 million). The bond is classified as at fair value through profit or loss and therefore changes in fair value are recognised in profit or loss. At present interest rates are the same as the interest rates on the bond. However, because the interest rate on the bond is fixed, the company has exposed itself to the risk of decline in the market value of the bond. If interest rates rise then the value of the bond will fall because the bond will pay a lower interest rate than equivalent investments in the market. Thus this method of hedging risk would lead to a risk in the decline in the value of the bond itself. To eliminate such a risk, the company would need to enter into an interest rate swap agreement to exchange fixed interest payments for floating interest rate payments. Such an agreement would be designated as a hedging instrument of the bond. At 31 October 2006, the bond will have accrued interest which will be accrued in the balance sheet and be translated at average rate in the profit and loss account and closing rate in the balance sheet.

Forward contract

At inception, the forward contract has a fair value of zero. On 31 October 2006, the dollar has appreciated, such that $3 million for delivery on 30 June 2007 costs £2·3 million on the market. Therefore, the forward contract has increased in fair value by £0·3 million. Since the hedge is fully effective, the entire change in the fair value of the hedging instrument is recognised directly in equity. The following entry is made:

CR Equity	£300,000	
DR	Forward contract	£300,000

The deferred gain or loss remaining in equity on 30 June 2007 should either remain in equity and be released from equity as the machine is depreciated or otherwise affects profit or loss or be deducted from the initial carrying amount of the machine.

If the company purchases a bond then it will tie cash up in the bond until its maturity date, and will leave itself vulnerable to changes in the value of the bond unless a hedging instrument is created. The simplest and most effective way is to use a forward contract.

3 (a) Sale and leaseback

A sale and leaseback agreement releases capital for expansion, repayment of outstanding debt or repurchase of share capital. The transaction releases capital tied up in non liquid assets. There are important considerations. The price received for the asset and the related interest rate/rental charge should be at market rates. The interest rate will normally be dependent upon the financial strength of the 'tenant' and the risk/reward ratio which the lessor is prepared to accept. There are two types of sale and leaseback agreements. One utilising a finance lease and another an operating lease.

The accounting treatment is determined by SSAP21, 'Accounting for leases and hire purchase contracts'. The substance of the transaction is essentially one of financing as the title to the stadium is transferred back to the club. Thus a sale is not recognised. The excess of the sale proceeds over the carrying value of the assets is deferred and amortised to the profit and loss account over the lease term. The leaseback of the stadium is for the remainder of its economic and useful life and is therefore under SSAP21 treated as a finance lease. The stadium will remain as a fixed asset and will be depreciated.

The company does not wish to treat the transaction as a secured loan on an existing asset which has been the case with by some UK companies. The finance lease will come under the derecognition rules of FRS26, 'Financial Instruments: Measurement'.

The transaction will be recognised by the club as follows in the year to 31 December 2007:

	DR £m	CR £m
Receipt of cash 1 January 2007		
Cash received	15	
Stadium		12
Deferred income		3
	15	15
Assets held under finance lease	15	
Finance lease payable		15
Depreciation	0·75	
(15 ÷ 20 years)		
Assets held under finance lease		0·75

Year ended 31 December 2007 Profit and Loss Account	£ 000
Deferred income (£3m ÷ 20 years)	150
Depreciation	(750)
Finance charge (£15m − £1·2m) × 5·6%	(773)
Balance sheet	
Fixed assets	
Stadium (£15m − £750,000)	14,250
Current liabilities − rental payment	1,200
Long term liabilities	
Deferred income (£3m − £150,000)	2,850
Long term borrowings (15 − (1·2 × 2) + 0·773)	13,373

This form of sale and leaseback has several disadvantages. The profit for the period may decrease because of the increase in the finance charge over the deferred income. Similarly the gearing ratio of the club may increase significantly because of the increase in long term borrowings although the short term borrowings may be reduced by the inflow of cash. Unsecured creditors may have less security for their borrowings after the leasing transaction. It may be worth considering a sale and leaseback involving an operating lease as in this case the profit on disposal can be recognised immediately because the sale price is at fair value. The stadium will be deemed to be sold and will be removed from the balance sheet. Similarly a long term liability for the loan will not be recognised in the balance sheet, and the sale proceeds could be used to repay any outstanding debt. This form of sale and leaseback would seem to be preferable than the one utilising a finance lease although any increase in the residual value of the stadium would be lost.

(b)   Player Registrations

The players' transfer fees have been capitalised as intangible assets under FRS10, 'Goodwill and Intangible Assets' because it is probable that expected future benefits will flow to the club as a result of the contract signed by the player and the cost of the asset can be measured reliably, being the transfer fee. Intangible assets may not be revalued after their initial recognition. The exceptions are those intangible assets with a readily ascertainable market value but these assets are rarely found. FRS10 requires intangible assets such as the player contracts to be amortised over their useful life. Intangible assets with indefinite useful lives should not be amortised and should be impairment tested annually. There is a rebuttable presumption that the useful economic life does not exceed 20 years. Intangible assets amortised over 20 years or less should be reviewed for impairment at the end of the first full financial year and then if there is indication of impairment.

The amortisation method should reflect the pattern of the future economic benefits. The amortisation of the contracts over ten years does not fit. FRS10 recommends amortisation to be charged on the basis of useful life and the pattern of economic benefits. Therefore, the current method over ten years cannot be used as an accounting policy. The current amortisation level should be maintained. This proposal in any event would only mask the poor financial state of the club. It is a book entry which may help prevent negative equity but will not give a cash benefit. The fundamental strategy for the club should be to contract players which it can afford and to spend at levels appropriate to its income.

There does not appear to be any probability that the contingent liability will crystallise. Under FRS12, 'Provisions, Contingent Liabilities and Contingent Assets', a contingency is a possible obligation arising out of past events and whose existence will be confirmed only by the occurrence or non-occurrence of one or more uncertain future events not wholly within the control of the entity. At present the club is performing very poorly in the league and is unlikely to win the national league. Therefore, the contingent liability will not become a present obligation but will still be disclosed.

(c)   Issue of bond

This form of financing a football club's operations is known as 'securitisation'. Often in these cases a special purpose vehicle is set up to administer the income stream or assets involved. In this case, a special purpose vehicle has not been set up. The benefit of securitisation of the future corporate hospitality sales and season ticket receipts is that there will be a capital injection into the club and it is likely that the effective interest rate is lower because of the security provided by the income from the receipts. The main problem with the planned raising of capital is the way in which the money is to be used. The use of the bond for ground improvements can be commended as long term cash should be used for long term investment but using the bond for players' wages will cause liquidity problems for the club.

This type of securitisation is often called a 'future flow' securitisation. There is no existing asset transferred to a special purpose vehicle in this type of transaction and, therefore, there is no off balance sheet effect. The bond is shown as a long term liability and is accounted for under FRS26 'Financial Instruments: Measurement'. There are no issues of derecognition of assets as there can be in other securitisation transactions. In some jurisdictions there are legal issues in assigning future receivables as they constitute an unidentifiable debt which does not exist at present and because of this uncertainty often the bond holders will require additional security such as a charge on the football stadium.

The bond will be a financial liability and it will be classified in one of two ways:

(i)   Financial liabilities at fair value through profit or loss include financial liabilities that the entity either has incurred for trading purposes and, where permitted, has designated to the category at inception. Derivative liabilities are always treated as held for trading unless they are designated and effective as hedging instruments. An example of a liability held for trading is an issued debt instrument that the entity intends to repurchase in the near term to make a gain from short-term movements in interest rates. It is unlikely that the bond will be classified in this category.

(ii) The second category is financial liabilities measured at amortised cost. It is the default category for financial liabilities that do not meet the criteria for financial liabilities at fair value through profit or loss. In most entities, most financial liabilities will fall into this category. Examples of financial liabilities that generally would be classified in this category are trade creditors, note payables, issued debt instruments, and deposits from customers. Thus the bond is likely to be classified under this heading. When a financial liability is recognised initially in the balance sheet, the liability is measured at fair value. Fair value is the amount for which a liability can be settled between knowledgeable, willing parties in an arm's length transaction. Since fair value is a market transaction price, on initial recognition fair value will usually equal the amount of consideration received for the financial liability. Subsequent to initial recognition financial liabilities are measured using amortised cost or fair value. In this case the company does not wish to use valuation models nor is there an active market for the bond and, therefore, amortised cost will be used to measure the bond.

The bond will be shown initially at £50 million × 95%, i.e. £47·5 million as this is the consideration received. Subsequently at 31 December 2007, the bond will be shown as follows:

	£m
Initial recognition	47·5
Interest at 7·7%	3·7
Cash payment	(6)
Amount owing 31 December 2007	45·2

(d)   Player trading

The sale of the players will introduce cash into the club and help liquidity. The contingent liability will be extinguished as the players will no longer play for Seejoy. The club, however, is not performing well at present and the sale of the players will not help their performance. This may result in the reduction of ticket sales and, therefore, cause further liquidity problems. The proceeds from the sale of players may be difficult to estimate at present as the date of sale is significantly into the future. Also the sale of the players will not constitute 'held for sale' fixed assets under FRED32 'Disposal of non-current assets and presentation of discontinued operations' at 31 December 2006 as the players are not available for immediate sale.

If the sale proceeds are £16 million, then a loss on sale will be recorded of £2 million, if the players are sold on 1 May 2007.

	Transfer fee £m	Amortisation £m	Carrying amount £m
A. Steel	20	4 + 4/12 of 4	14·7
R. Aldo	15	10 + 4/12 of 5	3·3
			18
Sale proceeds (estimate)			16
Loss			2

As a loss on sale is anticipated on the players, an impairment review should be undertaken at 31 December 2006.

4 **(a)** FRS9, 'Associates and Joint Ventures' says that a joint venture is a contractual agreement between two or more parties that undertake an economic activity that is subject to joint control on a long term basis. Joint control occurs where none of the entities alone can control the joint venture but all together can do so and decisions or financial and operating policy, economic performance and financial position require each venturer's consent. Control is the power to direct the financial and operating policies of the entity with a view to gaining economic benefits from its activities. In this case York has been formed by two companies each with a fifty per cent share and having equal representation on the Board of Directors. Thus there is joint control. This type of joint venture normally involves the setting up of a company or partnership or other entity in which each of the joint venturers has an interest. The key thing about this type of entity is that there will be a contractual arrangement which establishes the joint control over it. Each venturer would normally contribute assets and other resources to the joint venture which would be included in the accounting records of the venturer and recognised as an investment in the joint venture. The gross equity method should be used for the joint venture in the group accounts. Proportional consolidation should not be used. The only issue is the fact that there is no written contract. The substance of the arrangement is important. The existence of a contractual arrangement can be shown in a number of ways, one of which is the minutes of discussions between the companies. In this case the minutes of the discussions have been formally approved, and this establishes the joint control over the venture.

(b)

York
Balance Sheet at 31 October 2006

	£m
Assets:	
Land and buildings	14
Plant and machinery	3
Intangible assets	3
	20
Current assets:	
Stocks	6
Debtors	3·8
Cash	11
	20·8
Lease payables	(1·1)
Long-term provision	(4)
	35·7
Equity and liabilities:	
Share capital	30
Reserves (capital)	4·2
Deferred income	1·5
Total equity	35·7

Gow's net assets

FRS11 'Impairment of Fixed Assets and Goodwill', sets out the events that might indicate that an asset is impaired. These circumstances include external events such as the decline in the market value of an asset and internal events such as a reduction in the cash flows to be generated from an asset or cash generating unit. The loss of the only customer of an income generating unit (power station) would be an indication of the possible impairment of the income generating unit. Therefore, the power station will have to be impairment tested.

The recoverable amount will have to be determined and compared to the value given to the asset on the setting up of the joint venture. The recoverable amount is the higher of the income generating unit's net realisable value (NRV), and its value-in-use. The NRV will be £15 million which is the offer for the purchase of the power station (£16 million) less the costs to sell (£1 million). The value-in-use is the discounted value of the future cash flows expected to arise from the cash generating unit. The future dismantling costs should be provided for as it has been agreed with the government that it will be dismantled. The cost should be included in the future cash flows for the purpose of calculating value-in-use and provided for in the financial statements and the cost added to the land and buildings (£4 million). The value-in-use based on a discount rate of 6% is £21 million. Therefore, the recoverable amount is £21 million which is higher than the carrying value of the income generating unit (£20 million) and, therefore, the value of the income generating unit is not impaired when compared to the present carrying value of £20 million.

Additionally FRS26, 'Financial Instruments: measurement', says that an entity must assess at each balance sheet date whether a financial asset is impaired. In this case the debtors of £7 million is likely to be impaired as Race has gone into receivership. The present value of the estimated future cash flows will be calculated. Normally cash receipts from debtors will not be discounted but because the amounts are not likely to be received for a year then the anticipated cash payment is 80% of (£5 million × 1/1·06), i.e. £3·8 million. Thus a provision for the impairment of the debtors of £3·2 million should be made. The intangible asset of £3 million would be valueless as the contract has been terminated.

Glass's Net Assets

The leased property continues to be accounted for as land and buildings and the carrying amount will not be adjusted. However, the remaining useful life of the buildings will be revised to reflect the shorter term. Thus the buildings will be depreciated at £2 million per annum over the next two years. The change to the depreciation period is applied prospectively not retrospectively. The lease liability must be assessed under FRS26 in order to determine whether it constitutes a de-recognition of a financial liability. As the change is a modification of the lease and not an extinguishment, the lease liability would not be derecognised. The lease liability will be adjusted for the one off payment of £1 million and re-measured to the present value of the revised future cash flows. That is £0·6 million/1·07 + £0·6 million/(1·07 × 1·07) i.e. £1·1 million. The adjustment to the lease liability would normally be recognised in the profit and loss account but in this case it will affect the net capital contributed by Glass. Thus the carrying value of the lease liability will be £(3 – 1 – 0·9) million i.e. £1·1 million.

The termination cost of the contract cannot be treated as an intangible asset. It is similar to redundancy costs paid to terminate a contract of employment. It represents compensation for the loss of future income for the agency. Therefore it must be removed from the balance sheet of York. FRS10 does not set out general recognition criteria for intangible assets but such assets have to be capable of being disposed of separately from the business and have a readily ascertainable market value. These criteria are not met. Also an intangible asset is a right to future economic benefits (FRS5 para 2) and this is not the case here as the cost of gaining future customers cannot be linked to this compensation.

Application note G para G22 to FRS5 'Reporting the Substance of Transactions' sets out the principles of the segregation of contracts into separable components. This is where a contract contains two or more elements which are in substance separate and are separately identifiable. In other words, the two elements can operate independently from each other. In this case, the contract with the overseas company has two distinct elements. There is a contract not to supply gas to any other customer in the country and there is a contract to sell gas at fair value to the overseas company. The contract has not been fulfilled as yet and therefore the payment of £1·5 million should not be taken to the profit and loss account in its entirety at the first opportunity. The non supply of gas to customers in that country occurs over the four year period of the contract and therefore the payment should be recognised over that period. Therefore the amount should be shown as deferred income and not as a deduction from intangible assets. The revenue on the sale of gas will be recognised as normal.

There may be an issue over the value of the net assets being contributed. The net assets contributed by Glass amount to £21·9 million whereas those contributed by Gow only totalled £13·7 million after taking into account any adjustments required by UKGAAP. The joint venturers have equal shareholdings in York but no formal written agreements, thus problems may arise if Glass feels that the contributions to the joint venture are unequal.

Workings

Value-in-use	£m 31 October 2007	£m 31 October 2008	£m 31 October 2009	£m 31 October 2010	£m Total
Net inflows	6	7	8	8	
Dismantling cost				(5)	
Discount factor	$1/1\cdot06$	$1/1\cdot06^2$	$1/1\cdot06^3$	$1/1\cdot06^4$	
	5·7	6·2	6·7	2·4	21

Provision for decommissioning is $£5m/1\cdot06^4$ i.e. **£4m**.

York
Balance Sheet at 31 October 2006

	Gow	Adjustment	Glass	Adjustment	Total
Cash	1	—	10		11
Debtors	7	(3·2)	—		3·8
Stock			6		6
Intangible assets	3	(3)	2	(0·5)	
				1·5	3
Land and buildings	6	4	4		14
Plant and machinery	3				3
Provision for decommissioning		(4)			(4)
Lease receivables			1	(1)	
Lease payables			(3)	1·9	(1·1)
	20	(6·2)	20	1·9	35·7
Share capital					30
Reserves – capital (difference)					4·2
Deferred income				1·5	1·5
					35·7

Contribution by Gow £(20 – 6·2)m i.e. **£13·8m.**
Contribution by Glass £(20 + 1·9)m i.e. **£21·9m.**

5 (a) The purpose of the Operating and Financial Review (OFR) is to present a balanced and comprehensive analysis of the development, position and performance of the entity in the year. Additionally, it deals with the main trends and factors behind the development, position and performance of the entity during the financial year and those factors which are likely to affect the entity in the future. The OFR should enable users to assess the strategies adopted by the entity and the potential success of those strategies. The key principles are as follows:

- The OFR should be seen through the eyes of the directors and should focus on those matters relevant to the members of the company.
- The review should look forward, identifying trends and factors relevant to the assessment of the current and future performance of the entity.
- The OFR should supplement and complement the financial statements so as to improve disclosure by providing additional financial and non-financial information.
- The review should be comprehensive, understandable, reliable, relevant and represent faithfully the underlying strategies and trends.
- Both good and bad aspects of the position of the entity should be discussed in a balanced and neutral way.
- The OFR should be comparable over time, and the information should be supportable.

The increase in transparency and accountability improves the links between strategy, performance and risk, and the evaluation of directors, and how they are paid. The principles are set out in a Reporting Statement 'The Operating and Financial Review'.

A mandatory OFR would make it easier for companies to judge the content of the reports and the necessary standard of reporting, and would mean that the reports may be more robust and comparable. If the OFR is not mandatory then this could lead to uncertainty, risks of non compliance and possible mis-information being shown in the Review. Directors may adopt a policy of stating the minimum amount of disclosure which will frustrate the significant benefits to be gained from using financial reporting as a strategic communication tool. 'Necessity to report' decisions will become subjective with possible legal outcomes. The minimalist approach may also prove problematic if directors' insurers reject claims because of 'non-disclosure' of information. Senior executives and the company board will play a more prominent role in deciding upon matters of OFR content than will be the case with mandatory reporting practice. Influential factors driving OFR disclosure practice may become those expected to have short-term financial impact, whether shareholder decisions may be influenced, and issues of risk management rather than the broader issues.

However, it can be argued that a mandatory OFR could produce stereo-typed reports which would be based on a checklist approach. Thus innovation in corporate reporting would be stifled. The power of market forces could be enough to ensure that entities produce relevant and reliable information. Every company is different as are their challenges and risks and in a non-mandatory environment, companies could produce individual OFR's to reflect those challenges and risks.

(b)

Jones and Cousin, a public quoted company
Annual Report 2006
Operating and Financial Review

(i) Introduction

Jones and Cousin is a global company engaged in the medical products sector. This review provides information to assist the assessment of strategies adopted by the company and the future potential of those strategies.

Principal risks and relationships

Trends:

Expenditure in the medical sector is often controlled by governments and is, therefore, affected by government policy. Thus the Group is largely dependent on governments providing funds for health care. Product innovation and the resultant increase in competition could lead to downward pressure on the price of goods and a decline in the Group's market share which could affect the operational results and hinder the growth of the Group.

Currency fluctuations:

The Group reports its results using the pound sterling as its functional currency. As there is only five per cent of the business in the country of incorporation (UK), fluctuations in exchange rates may have a material effect on the Group. If the exchange rate of sterling strengthens against the Dinar and Euro, then group turnover and operating profit would be lower on translation into sterling. As the manufacturing base is worldwide, the finished products when sold to the Group's selling operations could expose the Group to fluctuations in exchange rates.

Product liability claims and loss of reputation:

Although the products are not inherently high risk, there is a possibility of malfunction which could entail risk of product liability claims or recalls on the product. Both these events could be costly and harmful to the Group's reputation which is dependent upon product safety. Any product liability claims or product recalls would have a negative effect on cash flow and profit, and are likely to adversely affect sales of the product.

Highly Competitive markets:

The principal business units compete across many diverse geographic and product markets. Technical advances and product innovations by competitors could adversely affect the operating results. Some of the Group's competitors could have greater resources and may be able to sell products on more competitive terms. If the Group were to lose market share or lower than expected sales growth, there could be an adverse impact on the Group's share price and future strategies.

Patents and Products:

The Group protects its intellectual rights in its products and opposes third parties where there is a conflict with the group's patents. The Group may itself be subject to patent infringement claims. If the Group failed to protect its position, its competitive position could suffer and operating results be harmed. Similarly if any claims are successful then damages may have to be paid, or non patent infringing products developed, both of which would adversely affect results.

Product innovations will occur constantly in the sector and, therefore, the Group has to continually develop products to satisfy consumer needs and to provide cost and other advantages. Not all products will be brought to the market for several reasons, including failure to receive regulatory approval or infringement of patents. Thus there is a significant cost implication in the research and development of products. However, if new products do not remain competitive with competitors' products, then Group sales revenue could decline.

Relationships:

The Group has developed a set of corporate social responsibility principles which is the responsibility of the Board of Directors, and the Managing Director in particular. The Group contributes to the treatment and recovery of patients within its product range by providing solutions to health care needs. Although having a relatively minor impact on the environment compared to some companies, any obsolete products are disposed of in an environmentally friendly way so as not to potentially compromise the health of its customers. Reusable materials are used in the manufacture of products.

The Group fosters ethical relationships with its suppliers and encourages them to share the same social and environmental standards. In this way a long term relationship is expected to be developed with suppliers.

The Group's employment policies are based on equality of opportunity and the performance standards and goals are communicated to the employees. Jones and Cousin is committed to the provision of continuous training and development and open communication with its employees. Additionally the group encourages its subsidiaries to reinvest profits in local educational projects.

(ii)   **Position of the business**

Treasury policies:

Treasury policies are reviewed regularly by the Board. It is group policy to account for all financial instruments as cash flow hedges. As a result, changes in the fair values of financial instruments are deferred in reserves to the extent the hedge is effective and released to profit or loss in the time periods in which the hedged item impacts profit or loss.

The Group contracts fixed rate currency swaps and issues floating to fixed rate interest rate swaps to meet the objective of protecting borrowing costs. The cash flow effects of the interest rate swaps match the cash flows on the underlying instruments so that there is no net cash flow effect from movements in market interest rates. If the interest rate swaps had not been transacted there could have been an increase in the annual net interest payable by the Group.

P2 Pilot Paper (UK)
Corporate Reporting (United Kingdom)

1 (a) Zambeze Group
Group Statement of Cash Flows for the year ended 30 June 2006

	£m	£m
Net cash flows from operating activities (Note 1):		862
Cash contributions to pension scheme		(7)
Dividends received from associate (working 3)		35
Returns on investment and servicing of finance (Note 2)		(89)
Taxation (working 4)		(190)
Capital expenditure and financial investment (Note 2)		(651)
Acquisitions and disposals (Note 2)		(100)
Equity dividends paid (working 6)		(46)
Cash outflow before use of liquid resources and financing		(186)
Financing:		
issues of shares	30	
increase in debt	66	96
Decrease in cash in period		(90)

Note 1
Reconciliation of operating profit to net cash inflow from operating activities

		£m
Operating profit (690 + 40)		730
Depreciation		60
Impairment of goodwill (working 2)		8
Decrease in stock (650–580–90)	20	
Increase in debtors	(80)	
Increase in creditors	141	81
Associate's profit		(30)
Current and past service costs		13
		862

Note 2
Analysis of cash flows for headings netted in cash flow statement
Returns on investment and servicing of finance

	£m
Interest paid (working 5)	31
Minority interest – equity dividend	58
	89

Capital expenditure and financial investment

	£m
Purchase of tangible fixed assets (working 1)	(251)
Investment in River	(400)
	(651)

Acquisitions

	£m
Purchase of Damp	100
	100

Working 1

	£m
Tangible fixed assets	
Balance at 1 July 2005	1,005
Impairment losses	(95)
Depreciation	(60)
Purchases (by deduction)	395
Acquisition – Damp	70
Closing balance	1,315

Cash flow is £395 million minus the liability for tangible fixed assets of £144 million, ie £251 million.

BPP
LEARNING MEDIA

Working 2

	£m
Purchase of subsidiary:	
Net assets acquired	160
Group's share of net assets (70%)	112
Goodwill	13
Purchase consideration (100 + 25)	125

	£m
Goodwill:	
Balance at 30 June 2005	25
Goodwill on subsidiary	13
Impairment	(8)
Balance at 30 June 2006	30

	£m
Minority interest:	
Balance at 1 July 2005	45
Acquisition of Damp (160 x 30%)	48
Profit for year	25
Dividend	(58)
Balance at 30 June 2006	60

Working 3

	£m
Dividend from associate:	
Balance at 1 July 2005	290
Income (net of tax) (30–10)	20
Foreign exchange loss	(5)
Dividends received (difference)	(35)
Balance at 30 June 2006	270

Working 4

		£m	£m
Taxation:			
Balance at 1 July 2005	Income tax		185
	Deferred tax		25
Income statements (210–10)			200
Tax paid (difference)			(190)
Balance at 30 June 2006	Income tax	190	
	Deferred tax	30	
			220

Working 5

	£m
Interest paid:	
Balance at 1 July 2005	45
Profit and loss	40
Unwinding of discount on purchase	(4)
Cash paid (difference)	(31)
Closing balance at 30 June 2006	50

Working 6
The cash payment to River should be shown as "financial investment" of £400 million and the dividend paid will then be £(446–400) million, ie £46 million.

(b) FRS 2 *Accounting for subsidiary undertakings* essentially adopts the definitions of parent undertaking introduced by the Companies Act 1985. An undertaking is deemed to be a parent of another undertaking where:

(i) over more than one half of the voting rights are owned by the parent; or

(ii) the parent has the right to exercise dominant influence over the undertaking or

(iii) the parent is a member and has the right to appoint or remove members of the board of directors who hold the majority of the voting rights at board meetings; or

(iv) the parent has a participating interest in the undertaking and exercises dominant influence.

Dominant influence is that which is exercised to achieve the operating and financial policies desired by the holder of the influence. The influence has to be exercised and is identified by its effect in practice.

FRS 2 *The definition* is based on the power of one entity to "control" another through the exercise of share holder control. FRS 5 *Reporting the substance of transactions* takes the view that the definitions above are not conclusive in determining what entities are to be consolidated. FRS 5 defines a quasi subsidiary and envisages situations where the need to give a true and fair view will require the consolidation of quasi subsidiaries. The key feature is control which means the ability to direct the financial and operating policies to gain economic benefit from its activities. Control is also indicated by the ability to prevent others from exercising those policies or enjoying the benefits of the subsidiary's net assets. Control can be derived from a variety of sources and exercised in a number of ways. If the 'owner' has accepted real and severe constraints on the normal powers of ownership, then the real benefits of ownership must lie elsewhere. The ability to control decision making alone is not sufficient to establish control for accounting purposes but must be accompanied by the objective of obtaining benefits from the entity's activities. If a company obtains the benefits of ownership, is exposed to the risks of ownership, and can exercise decision making powers to obtain those benefits, then the company must control the third party. The overall substance of the arrangement must be considered.

Zambeze should consolidate River as Zambeze controls it through the operating guidelines. Zambeze also receives 95% of the profits and suffers all the losses of River. The guidelines were set up when River was formed and, therefore, the company was set up as a vehicle with the objective of keeping certain transactions off the balance sheet of Zambeze. The investment manager manages the investments of River within the guidelines and incurs no risk and receives 5% of the profits for the management services.

(c) Ethics in accounting is of utmost importance to accounting professionals and those who rely on their services. Accounting professionals know that people who use their services, especially decision makers using financial statements, expect them to be highly competent, reliable, and objective. Those who work in the field of accounting must not only be well qualified but must also possess a high degree of professional integrity. A professional's good reputation is one of his or her most important assets.

There is a very fine line between acceptable accounting practice and management's deliberate misrepresentation in the financial statements. The financial statements must meet the following criteria:

(i) Technical compliance: A transaction must be recorded in accordance with generally accepted accounting principles (GAAP).
(ii) Economic substance: The resulting financial statements must represent the economic substance of the event that has occurred.
(iii) Full disclosure and transparency: Sufficient disclosure must be made so that the effects of transactions are transparent to the reader of the financial statements.

In the case of River, it could be argued that the first criterion may be met because the transaction is apparently recorded in technical compliance with FRS, but technical compliance alone is not sufficient. The second criterion is not met because the transaction as recorded does not reflect the economic substance of the event that has occurred.

Accounting plays a critical function in society. Accounting numbers affect human behaviour especially when it affects compensation, and to deliberately mask the nature of accounting transactions could be deemed to be unethical behaviour.

River was set up with the express purpose of keeping its activities off the balance sheet. The Finance Director has an ethical responsibility to the shareholders of Zambeze and society not to mask the true nature of the transactions with this entity. Further, if the transaction has been authorised by the Finance Director without the authority or knowledge of the Board of Directors, then a further ethical issue arises. Showing the transfer of funds as a dividend paid is unethical and possibly illegal in the jurisdiction. The transfer should not be hidden and River should be consolidated.

2 Report to directors of Electron

Terms of reference
This report sets out the nature of the accounting treatment and concerns regarding the following matters:
- Oil contracts
- Power station
- Operating leases
- Proposed dividends
- Share options

Oil Contracts

The accounting policy adopted for the agreements relating to the oil contracts raises a number of concerns. The revenue recognition policy currently used is inflating revenue in the first year of the contract with 50% of the revenue being recognised, but a smaller proportion of the costs are recognised in the form of depreciation. Over the life of the contract, costs and revenues are equally matched but in the short term there is a bias towards a more immediate recognition of revenue against a straight line cost deferral policy. Additionally oil sales result in revenue whilst purchases of oil result in a tangible fixed asset. Under FRS18 *Accounting Policies*, the question of whether revenue has arisen is judged independently from the matching concept according to whether an asset has been created. If it has, revenue is recognised. Similarly, if a liability has been created in the period, a related expense may have occurred and is recognised. The Statement of Principles adopts this "asset" and "liability" approach also. Similarly the Amendment to FRS5 *Reporting the substance of transactions – Revenue Recognition*, is based on the principles that a seller generates revenue by performing contractual obligations and in exchange obtains the right to consideration. Thus when performance of a contract takes place over time the revenue should be recognised as performance takes place. The current accounting practice seems out of line with the basic principles of revenue recognition.

However, the election of the company to use some form of deferral policy for its agreements is to be commended as it attempts to bring its revenue recognition policy in line with the length of the agreements. The main problem is the lack of a detailed accounting standard on revenue recognition. The result is the current lack of consistency in accounting for long-term agreements. However, it may be advisable to adopt a deferral policy in terms of this type of revenue. The contracts always result in the delivery of the oil in the normal course of business and are not, therefore, accounted for as financial instruments as they qualify as normal sale and purchase contracts.

Power Station

Under FRS12 *Provisions, Contingent Liabilities and Contingent Assets*, a provision should be made at the balance sheet date for the discounted cost of the removal of the power station because of the following reasons:

(i)   the installation of the power station creates an obligating event
(ii) the operating licence creates a legal obligation which is likely to occur
(iii) the costs of removal will have to be incurred irrespective of the future operations of the company and cannot be avoided
(iv) a transfer of economic benefits (ie the costs of removal) will be required to settle the obligation
(v)   a reasonable estimate of the obligation can be made although it is difficult to estimate a cost which will be incurred in twenty years time (FRS12 says that only in exceptional circumstances will it not be possible to make some estimate of the obligation)

The costs to be incurred will be treated as part of the cost of the facility to be depreciated over its production life. However, the costs relating to the damage caused by the generation of energy should not be included in the provision, until the power is generated which in this case would be 5% of the total discounted provision. The accounting for the provision is shown in Appendix 1.

Operating Leases

Under SSAP21 *Accounting for leases and hire purchase contracts* a lease is classified as a finance lease if it transfers substantially all the risks and rewards "incident" to ownership. All other leases are classified as operating leases. In this case, the beneficial and legal ownership remains with Electron and Electron can make use of the power station if it so wishes. Also for a lease asset to be a finance lease the present value of the minimum lease payments should be substantially all of the fair value of the leased asset (normally 90 per cent or more). In this case this amounts to 57.1% (£40 million ÷ £70 million) which does not constitute "substantially all". Thus there does not seem to be any issue over the classification of the lease as an operating lease. The immediate recognition as income of the future benefit at net present value is a little more problematical. SSAP21 says that lease income from operating leases should be recognised on a straight line basis over the lease term unless another systematic and rational basis is more representative. This applies even if the payments are not made on such a basis. If a fee is received as an "up front" cash payment then FRS18 and FRS5 should be applied. If there is future involvement required to earn the fee, or there are retained risks or risk of the repayment of the fee, or any restrictions on the lessor's use of the asset, then immediate recognition is inappropriate. The present policy of recognising the total lease income as if it were immediate income which it is not, would be difficult to justify. Similarly, as regards the deposit received, revenue should only be recognised when there is performance of the contract. Thus as there has been no performance under the contract, no revenue should be accrued in the period.

Proposed dividend

The dividend was proposed after the balance sheet date and the company, therefore, did not have a liability at the balance sheet date. No provision for the dividend should be recognised. The approval by the directors and the shareholders are enough to create a valid expectation that the payment will be made and give rise to an obligation. However, this occurred after the current year end and, therefore, will be charged against the profits for the year ending 30 June 2007.

The existence of a good record of dividend payments and an established dividend policy does not create a valid expectation or an obligation. However, the proposed dividend will be disclosed in the notes to the financial statements as the directors approved it prior to the authorisation of the financial statements.

Share options

Equity-settled transactions with employees would normally be expensed on the basis of their fair value at the grant date. Fair value should be based on market prices wherever possible. Many shares and share options will not be traded on an active market. In this case, valuation techniques, such as the option pricing model, would be used. FRS20's objective for equity-based transactions with employees is to determine and recognise compensation costs over the period in which the services are rendered. In this case, the company has granted to employees share options that vest in three years' time on the condition that they remain in the entity's employ for that period. These steps will be taken:

(i) the fair value of the options will be determined at the date on which they were granted
(ii) this fair value will be charged to the profit and loss account equally over the three year vesting period with adjustments made at each accounting date to reflect the best estimate of the number of options that eventually will vest

Shareholders' equity will be increased by an amount equal to the profit and loss account charge. The charge in the profit and loss account reflects the number of options that are likely to vest, not the number of options granted or the number of options exercised. If employees decide not to exercise their options because the share price is lower than the exercise price, then no adjustment is made to the profit and loss account. Many employee share option schemes contain conditions that must be met before the employee becomes entitled to the shares or options. These are called vesting conditions and could require, for example, an increase in profit or growth in the entity's share price before the shares vest. In this case the vesting condition is the employment condition. £940,000 (£3 million x 94% x 1/3) will be charged in the profit and loss account and to equity at 30 June 2006.

Recommendations and conclusion

The above report sets out the recommendations regarding the accounting treatment of the items specified. It is imperative that the recommendations are followed as non-compliance with a single FRS constitutes a failure to follow UK GAAP for reporting purposes.

Appendix 1

	£m	£m
Present value of obligation at 1 July 2005 (15 ÷ 1.05)	14.3	
Provision for decommissioning (95% x 14.3)	13.6	
Provision for damage through extraction (5% x 14.3)		0.7

Balance Sheet at 30 June 2006

	£m	£m
Tangible fixed assets:		
Cost of power station	100	
Provision for decommissioning	13.6	
	113.6	
less depreciation (113.6 ÷ 20 years)	(5.7)	
Carrying value	107.9	
Other provisions:		
Provision for decommissioning 1 July 2005	13.6	
Unwinding of discount (13.6 x 5%)	0.7	
		14.3
Provision for damage (0.7 ÷ 20 years)		0.1
		14.4

Profit and Loss Account

	£m
Depreciation	5.7
Provision for damage	0.1
Unwinding of discount (finance cost)	0.7

A simple straight line basis has been used to calculate the required provision for damage. A more complex method could be used whereby the present value of the expected cost of the provision is provided for over 20 years and the discount thereon is unwound over its life.

3   (a)   The objective of accounting for deferred tax is to ensure that the future tax consequences of past transactions and events are recognised as assets or liabilities in financial statements. The objective is based on the definition of a liability set out in the *Statement of Principles*. A liability for deferred tax should be recognised only for past transactions or events that give rise to an obligation to pay more tax in the future. Timing differences arise out of differences between an entity's taxable profits and its results as stated in the financial statements. Gains and losses are included in tax assessments in periods different from those in which they are recognised in the financial statements. Past transactions and events will have future tax consequences if they are recognised as timing differences that have originated but not reversed at the balance sheet date. An entity will have an obligation to pay more tax or a right to pay less tax where it has no discretion to avoid the future reversal of a timing difference. (An entity may originate a new timing difference which may postpone tax payable or recoverable.) This approach has been called the "incremental liability approach" and the Accounting Standards Board believes it is consistent with the *Statement of Principles*.

(b) (i)   Financial assets that are valued at fair value through profit and loss should be valued at fair value with any increase in value going to the profit and loss account. Thus the gain of £1.5 million should be included in the profit and loss account and the balance sheet value increased. Revaluation of non-monetary assets does not give rise to a timing difference because taxable profits are not affected and no future tax liability arises as a result of the revaluation (unless there is a binding sale agreement). However, FRS19 states that deferred tax should be recognised on timing differences arising when an asset is continuously revalued to fair value with changes being recognised in the profit and loss account. Thus deferred tax should be provided of (£10.5 million – £9 million) @ 30%, ie £450,000.

(ii)   Government grant

Government grants are dealt with in SSAP4 *Accounting for government grants*. Grants should be credited to revenue over the useful life of the related asset and not credited fully in the year of receipt. Grants can be deducted from the cost of the asset or treated as a deferred credit of which a proportion would be credited to revenue annually. SSAP4 warns that Counsel's opinion is that a deduction from cost method is unlawful. The timing difference arising on this item would be:

	£000
Cost of asset	5,000
Depreciation	(1,000)
Carrying value	4,000
Unamortised deferred income (1,000 − 200)	(800)
Net carrying value in financial statements	3,200
Cost of asset	5,000
less grant	(1,000)
	4,000
Capital allowance (25%)	(1,000)
Tax written down value	3,000
Timing difference	200
Deferred tax (3200−3000) @ 30%	60

(iii) Pension costs

The defined benefit plan should recognise (40% of £1 million + 60% of £1 million/5) ie £520,000 of the past service costs as an increase in the liability. Retained earnings will be charged with the same amount. This increase in the liability will reduce the actuarial gain to (£600−£520)K, £80,000. Therefore, deferred tax of £80,000 x 30%, ie £24,000 will be recognised in the STRGL as the actuarial gain will have been recognised there.

(iv) Investment property

Investment properties should not be depreciated (SSAP19) but should be included in the balance sheet at their open market value. Changes in the value of the investment properties should not be taken to the profit and loss account but should be taken to the investment revaluation reserve. Thus the gain on the investment property (£2 million) should be taken out of the profit and loss account and credited to investment revaluation reserve. Deferred tax is only provided on the gain arising on the revaluation if there was an intention to sell the investment property. As the company has no intention to sell, then no deferred taxation is provided on the gain. However, the company will have to provide deferred taxation on the difference between nil depreciation and the capital allowances £120,000 claimed at the tax rate of 30%, ie £36,000.

		Balance Sheet £000	Profit and Loss Account £000	Other reserves £000
Balance per balance sheet			9,130	4,500
(i)	Financial assets	9,000		
	Revaluation	1,500	1,500	
		10,500		
(ii)	Grant	800	200	
	Reversal of grant income		(1,000)	
	Depreciation of fixed asset	(1,000)	(1,000)	
(iii)	Pension costs – liability	(4,000)		
	Past service costs	(520)	(520)	
		(4,520)		
(iv)	Investment property		(2,000)	2,000
Increase in deferred tax (below)			(546)	(24)
			5,764	6,476
Deferred tax liability per balance sheet				3,600
Adjustment for				
Financial asset			450	
Government grant			60	
Pension costs (to STRGL)			24	
Investment property			36	570
Adjusted deferred tax liability				4,170

4 **(a)** International Financial Reporting Standards (IFRS) were initially developed for the preparation of group accounts of listed companies. The use of IFRS is growing such that in some countries that are building or improving their accounting regulatory framework, IFRS based corporate reports are deemed to be more reliable and relevant than local GAAP reports. In many of these countries IFRSs are the statutory requirement for legal entities and, therefore, an implementation issue that has arisen is that the national law has to be reconciled with the requirements of IFRS.

Another implementation issue relates to small and medium-sized enterprises (SMEs) in terms of whether a separate set of standards should be developed and what should be the underlying conceptual and methodological basis for such standards. Effective implementation requires continuous interaction between the International Accounting Standards Board (IASB) and national regulators. The IASB has issued a draft Memorandum of Understanding on the role of Accounting Standard Setters and their relationship with the IASB. It identifies responsibilities that the IASB and other standard setters should adopt to facilitate the ongoing adoption of or convergence with IFRS.

With the increase in the number of entities applying IFRS, the demand for implementation guidance is growing. The International Financial Reporting Interpretations Committee (IFRIC) has been given the task of meeting this demand but there may be a need for additional coping mechanisms as a limited number of interpretations have been issued since the inception of IFRIC.

Variations in translation of IFRS could introduce inconsistency. In some countries the capacity for highly technical translation is low and there may be a conflict with existing national terminology and legislation. Additionally, time lags in the local "endorsement" process and in translating new IFRS could mean that financial reports may not be consistent with the latest body of standards. Additionally the successful implementation of IFRS will depend upon the robustness of the local regulatory framework. Effective corporate governance practices, high quality auditing standards and practices, and effective enforcement or oversight mechanisms will be required to underpin the IFRS. Often endorsement of the standards is required as part of the implementation process. For example, in the European Union, after IFRSs have been issued by the IASB, they must go through an endorsement process before companies listed in the European Union are required to apply them. This process could create standards that differ from those of the IASB.

Implementation of IFRS can have implications for a number of legislative areas. The more complex the regulatory framework, the more problems will arise. There can be tax, price control and company law implications, and certain sectors, such as banking and insurance, may be subject to additional regulation that may require special reporting requirements. Entities may find that they are in breach of existing covenants with lenders where the provision of funding is based on national GAAP ratios. Similarly corporate law may set out the requirements on distribution of dividends and unless the necessary corporate law amendments are made then dividend distributions would be based on national GAAP which might create confusion.

An international mechanism for the co-ordination of enforcement of IFRS is required. IOSCO provides an infrastructure for enforcement with respect to publicly listed companies. IOSCO has put forward proposals for the regulatory interpretation and enforcement of IFRS. On a more local level, the European Union has established the Committee of European Securities Regulators whose role is to improve co-ordination among securities regulators and ensure implementation of legislation in the European Union.

The complex nature of IFRS and the sheer volume of standards make the task of implementation difficult. The standards are deemed to be "principles based" and this may lead to inconsistencies of application, particularly in countries without a critical mass of experienced accountants. Most accountants will have been trained to apply domestic accounting standards, and where there are options in IFRS, then it is likely that the accounting practice closest to their National GAAP will be chosen. Similarly IFRSs utilise fair value measurement extensively and market information is required to more accurately reflect the value. The nature of this market information will vary around the world. If market information is not available, an alternative source can be obtained by simulating a hypothetical market or by using mathematical modelling. Experience of such techniques will vary worldwide, and this experience will be variable in such areas as actuarial estimation, impairment testing, and valuing share based payments. The concepts set out in IFRS may be new to some accounting professionals and may be difficult to grasp.

(b) Under current accounting practice the objective of acquisition accounting is to reflect the cost of the acquisition. To the extent to which it is not represented by identifiable assets and liabilities (measured at their fair value), goodwill arises and is reported in the financial statements. These exposure drafts adopt a different perspective and require the financial statements to reflect the fair value of the acquired business. The recognition of the acquired business at fair value will mean that any existing interest owned by the acquirer before it gained control will be remeasured at fair value at the date of acquisition with any gain or loss recognised in the profit and loss account.

The proposals treat the group as a single economic entity and any outside equity interest in a subsidiary is treated as part of the overall ownership interest in the group. As a consequence, transactions with minority shareholders are to be treated as equity transactions. No gain or loss will be recognised in the profit and loss account. Accounting for business combinations has to date been based on the "parent entity" concept where the extent of non-controlling interests and transactions with non-controlling interests are separately identified in the primary financial statements.

It is also proposed that goodwill is to be recognised in full even if control is less than 100%. FRS2 currently requires that goodwill arising on acquisition should only be recognised with respect to the part of the subsidiary undertaking that is attributable to the interest held by the parent entity.

Goodwill, after initial recognition, is to be measured at cost less impairment losses, and amortisation is not to be permitted. The ASB concluded that more useful information would be provided if goodwill was not amortised but subjected to a rigorous and operational impairment test. FRS10 "Goodwill and Intangible Assets" seeks to charge goodwill to the profit and loss account only to the extent that the carrying value of goodwill is not supported by the current value of goodwill within the acquired business.

Costs incurred in connection with an acquisition are not to be accounted for as part of the cost of the investment but will be charged in the profit and loss account. There will also be changes to the way in which some assets and liabilities acquired in a business combination are recognised and measured. The FRED requires assets and liabilities acquired to be measured and recognised at fair value at the acquisition date. Currently estimated fair values are used and guidance is given as to how to measure 'fair value' in the current standard. This guidance often results in the measurement of assets and liabilities in a manner which is inconsistent with fair value objectives.

P2 Pilot Paper (UK)
Corporate Reporting (United Kingdom)

1	(a)	Operating activities		6	
		Retirement benefit		3	
		Associate		3	
		Subsidiary treatment		4	
		Tangible fixed assets		3	
		Goodwill		2	
		Minority interest		3	
		Taxation		3	
		Dividend paid		3	
		Interest		2	
		River		2	
		Issue of shares		1	
				35	
	(b)	Issues		9	
	(c)	Ethical discussion		3	
		River		3	
			AVAILABLE/MAXIMUM	**50**	
2		Oil contracts		4	
		Power station		7	
		Operating leases		5	
		Proposed dividend		3	
		Share options		4	
		Effective communication		2	
			AVAILABLE/MAXIMUM	**25**	
3	(a)	Quality of discussion		2	
		Statement of Principles		1	
		Timing differences		1	
		Gains and losses		1	
		Tax consequences		1	
		Incremental liability		1	
				7	
	(b)	Financial assets		4	
		Grant		4	
		Pension		4	
		Investment property		4	
		Adjustments		4	
			AVAILABLE	**20**	
			MAXIMUM	**18**	
			AVAILABLE	**27**	
			MAXIMUM	**25**	
4	(a)	Subjective		18	
	(b)	Subjective		7	
			AVAILABLE/MAXIMUM	**25**	

Review Form & Free Prize Draw – Paper P2 Advanced Corporate Reporting (United Kingdom) (6/07)

All original review forms from the entire BPP range, completed with genuine comments, will be entered into one of two draws on 31 July 2007 and 31 January 2008. The names on the first four forms picked out on each occasion will be sent a cheque for £50.

Name: _____   Address: _____

_____

_____

How have you used this Kit?
(Tick one box only)

☐ Home study (book only)

☐ On a course: college _____

☐ With 'correspondence' package

☐ Other _____

Why did you decide to purchase this Kit?
(Tick one box only)

☐ Have used the complementary Study text

☐ Have used other BPP products in the past

☐ Recommendation by friend/colleague

☐ Recommendation by a lecturer at college

☐ Saw advertising

☐ Other _____

During the past six months do you recall seeing/receiving any of the following?
(Tick as many boxes as are relevant)

☐ Our advertisement in *Student Accountant*

☐ Our advertisement in *Pass*

☐ Our advertisement in *PQ*

☐ Our brochure with a letter through the post

☐ Our website www.bpp.com

Which (if any) aspects of our advertising do you find useful?
(Tick as many boxes as are relevant)

☐ Prices and publication dates of new editions

☐ Information on product content

☐ Facility to order books off-the-page

☐ None of the above

Which BPP products have you used?

Text	☐	Success CD	☐	Learn Online	☐
Kit	☑	i-Learn	☐	Home Study Package	☐
Passcard	☐	i-Pass	☐	Home Study PLUS	☐

Your ratings, comments and suggestions would be appreciated on the following areas.

	Very useful	Useful	Not useful
Passing ACCA exams	☐	☐	☐
Passing P2	☐	☐	☐
Planning your question practice	☐	☐	☐
Questions	☐	☐	☐
Top Tips etc in answers	☐	☐	☐
Content and structure of answers	☐	☐	☐
'Plan of attack' in mock exams	☐	☐	☐
Mock exam answers			

Overall opinion of this Kit	Excellent ☐	Good ☐	Adequate ☐	Poor ☐

Do you intend to continue using BPP products?   Yes ☐   No ☐

The BPP author of this edition can be e-mailed at: katyhibbert@bpp.com

Please return this form to: Nick Weller, ACCA Publishing Manager, BPP Learning Media Ltd, FREEPOST, London, W12 8BR

Review Form & Free Prize Draw (continued)

TELL US WHAT YOU THINK

Please note any further comments and suggestions/errors below.

Free Prize Draw Rules

1   Closing date for 31 July 2007 draw is 30 June 2007. Closing date for 31 January 2008 draw is 31 December 2007.

2   Restricted to entries with UK and Eire addresses only. BPP employees, their families and business associates are excluded.

3   No purchase necessary. Entry forms are available upon request from BPP Learning Media Ltd. No more than one entry per title, per person. Draw restricted to persons aged 16 and over.

4   Winners will be notified by post and receive their cheques not later than 6 weeks after the relevant draw date.

5   The decision of the promoter in all matters is final and binding. No correspondence will be entered into.